When the Rides Ends

The Autumn 2019
Owl Canyon Press
Hackathon Winners

When the Rides Ends

The Autumn 2019
Owl Canyon Press Hackathon Winners

featuring
the winning entries
from the
Owl Canyon Press
Short Story Hackathon No. 3

Chosen from 1100+ Entries
Received from 40 Countries

Edited by Gene Hayworth

With a foreword by
Rita Sommers-Flanagan

Owl Canyon Press
Boulder, Colorado

© 2020 by Owl Canyon Press
Cover photograph © 2020 by Gene Hayworth

First Edition, 2020
All Rights Reserved
Library of Congress Cataloging-in-Publication Data

When the Ride Ends —1st ed.
p. cm.
ISBN: 978-1-952085-99-4
2020931857

Owl Canyon Press
Boulder, Colorado

No part of this book may be reproduced in any form or by any electronic or mechanical means including information storage retrieval systems without permission in writing from the publisher, except by a reviewer, who may quote brief passages for review. Neither the authors, the publishers, nor its dealers or distributors shall be liable to the purchaser or any other person or entity with respect to any liability, loss, or damage caused or alleged to be caused directly or indirectly by this book.

"Among These Winters There Is One So Endlessly Winter" by Desirae Matherly. Copyright 2020 by Desirae Matherly. Used by permission of the author.

"So Many Infinitely Precious Things" by Michelle Denham. Copyright 2020 by Michelle Denham. Used by permission of the author.

"How We Watch What Is Burning" by Emily Polk. Copyright 2020 by Emily Polk. Used by permission of the author.

The Reign in Spain" by E. Michael Brehm. Copyright 2020 by E. Michael Brehm. Used by permission of the author.

"Made of Light" by India Choquette. Copyright 2020 by India Choquette. Used by permission of the author.

"Rainbow's End" by Curtis Clarke. Copyright 2020 by Curtis Clarke. Used by permission of the author.

"We Manifest How & When We Can" by Stu Croskell. Copyright 2020 by Stu Croskell. Used by permission of the author.

"Rejoice" by Elsa Cruz. Copyright 2020 by Elsa Cruz. Used by permission of the author.

"The New Adventures of Rainbow and Friends" by Phil Dyer. Copyright 2020 by Phil Dyer. Used by permission of the author.

"The best most excellent farm" by Carnegie Euclid. Copyright 2020 by Carnegie Euclid. Used by permission of the author.

"Pack" by M.J. Fahy. Copyright 2020 by M.J. Fahy. Used by permission of the author.

"A Girl Could Fall In Love With A Guy Like Jim" by Jilly Funnell. Copyright 2020 by Jilly Funnell. Used by permission of the author. "Everything Else" by Ella Kerr. Copyright 2020 by Ella Kerr. Used by permission of the author.

"922 Fessler Ln" by Alex Lee. Copyright 2020 by Alex Lee. Used by permission of the author.

"Alms for Jasmine" by Arthur Liu. Copyright 2020 by Arthur Liu. Used by permission of the author.

"Impossible Death" by Rebecca Loevy. Copyright 2020 by Rebecca Loevy. Used by permission of the author.

"Jasaun and the Apple Flooshe" by Jeffrey Montanye. Copyright 2020 by Jeffrey Montanye. Used by permission of the author.

"The Cat Girls" by Aaron Muller. Copyright 2020 by Aaron Muller. by Aaron Muller. Used by permission of the author.

"Letters from Bahati" by Tyler Nelson. Copyright 2020 by Tyler Nelson. Used by permission of the author.

"Time's Up" by Kate Osment. Copyright 2020 by Kate Osment. Used by permission of the author.

"The Trans-Europa" by Henry Silvia. Copyright 2020 by Henry Silvia. Used by permission of the author.

"A Plague of Angels" by Christian Smith. Copyright 2020 by Christian Smith. Used by permission of the author.

"The Pizza Boy" by Mary Spence. Copyright 2020 by Mary Spence. Used by permission of the author.

"How To Fake Your Own Death" by Emily Sperber. Copyright 2020 by Emily Sperber. Used by permission of the author.

"Some Time Had Passed Since The Animation" by Thos. West. Copyright 2020 by Thos. West. Used by permission of the author.

"SMILE!" by Elizabeth Wilder. Copyright 2020 by Elizabeth Wilder. Used by permission of the author.

CONTENTS

RITA SOMMERS-FLANAGAN
    Introduction 13

DESIRAE MATHERLY (First Place)
    "Among These Winters There Is One So Endlessly Winter" 17

MICHELLE DENHAM (Second Place)
    So Many Infinitely Precious Things 43

EMILY POLK (Third Place)
    How We Watch What Is Burning 57

FINALISTS

E. MICHAEL BREHM
    The Reign in Spain 75
INDIA CHOQUETTE
    Made of Light 95
CURTIS CLARKE
    Rainbow's End 114
STU CROSKELL
    We Manifest How & When We Can 141
ELSA CRUZ
    Rejoice 155
PHIL DYER
    The New Adventures of Rainbow and Friends 167
CARNEGIE EUCLID
    The Best Most Excellent Farm 184
M.J. FAHY
    Pack 205
JILLY FUNNELL
    A Girl Could Fall In Love With A Guy Like Jim 216
ELLA KERR
    Everything Else 238
ALEX LEE
    922 Fessler Ln 252
ARTHUR LIU
    Alms for Jasmine 271
REBECCA LOEVY
    Impossible Death 285

CONTENTS (CONT.)

JEFFREY MONTANYE
    Jasaun and the Apple Flooshe 295
AARON MULLER
    The Cat Girls 318
TYLER NELSON
    Letters from Bahati 331
KATE OSMENT
    Time's Up 343
HENRY SILVIA
    The Trans-Europa 351
CHRISTIAN SMITH
    A Plague of Angels 363
MARY SPENCE
    The Pizza Boy 375
EMILY SPERBER
    How To Fake Your Own Death 388
THOS. WEST
    Some Time Had Passed Since The Animation 408
ELIZABETH WILDER
    Smile! 421

ABOUT THE AUTHORS 437

Introduction

Long before I was notified that I'd won the 2018 Owl Canyon Hackathon, I'd joined the Owl Canyon Press fan club and become what I call an *Owly*. The folks that run Owl Canyon Press are exceptional—they've dared to crawl far further out on the contest limb than most, combining strict rules with generous rewards. The designers of this hackathon created a writing contest with a distinct twist. Some writers may experience such rules as a challenge to be overcome; other writers might find comfort in such a uniquely structured exercise; and still others may experience the whole thing as a way to rethink stalled plotlines or revive struggling but beloved characters. But whatever the motive, over a thousand more writers became *Owlies* this year.

You may be wondering about this twist—these interesting and quirky rules. Well, here they are: Write a story, using the opening paragraph provided. At paragraph 20, you must insert another provided paragraph. Sure, use dialogue, but make sure each of your paragraphs have at least 40 words. And wind things up at paragraph 50.

And the provided paragraphs? You'll become familiar with them as you read these wonderful stories, but it is worth noting that they aren't exactly easy paragraphs to wrestle with. Is Rainbow a dog, a jazz singer, a hedgehog, or an angel? Does the wall declare tragedy or hope? And what kind of chanting would a pizza boy do? In fact, why in the world would a pizza boy chant at all?

Who would guess that the exact same opening paragraph could launch stories so varied and vivid? Or that paragraph 20 could settle so nicely into plots ranging from an unlikely hike into scorched mountains where a meteor has landed to the mystical mind-melding of a young boy and a highly-evolved fox? The paragraphs provided seem to serve as curtains that pull back in the hands of these gifted writers to reveal heartbreak and hope, satire and silliness, adventure, and anarchy.

The winning story features the redemptive power of Rilke's poetry woven around a plot that moves from hopelessness to a future with real potential for the pizza kid. In this case, Rainbow is a genetically-enhanced creature akin to a fox. In second place, a blue-haired teen helps a loving old man take his dying wife, Rainbow, to see the meteor, and in third place, the shaman, Kimmie, speaks with ghosts and gods, sorting through her gifts and her history as the story develops. These first three stories are fascinating. You'll enjoy them, but don't stop there. All 27 have a strong kick, guaranteed to keep you reading and thinking. Enjoy! And maybe, consider becoming an *Owly* yourself next year.

Among These Winters There Is One So Endlessly Winter

By Desirae Matherly

Beyond the cracked sidewalk, and the telephone pole with layers of flyers in a rainbow of colors, and the patch of dry brown grass there stood a ten-foot high concrete block wall, caked with dozens of coats of paint. There was a small shrine at the foot of it, with burnt out candles and dead flowers and a few soggy teddy bears. One word of graffiti filled the wall, red letters on a gold background: Rejoice!

The kid wasn't the sort to notice the wall or the text, much less the flyers rippling in the warm October breeze, pinned to the poles that carried invisible transmissions from city to city. He typically ignored the aesthetic veneer of his surroundings in much the same way he was blind to the junk piles and the grubby-faced children or the broken porches of his deliveries. He had given up expecting pleasantries after his first few days as a pizza boy. Before long his identity and the job had melded, until he forgot his name and there was only, "You call this pizza, kid?" and "You're late, kid," or "Watch your step, kid." If anyone had used his name he wouldn't have responded, so used he had become to anonymity. The city itself had become anonymous in that long century and no one seemed to hold any significance beyond their labor.

The kid lived in the back half of a decades-old bungalow never meant to survive so long. His half of the house was essentially a creaky-floored room with a tub so small his knees pressed up in front of him uncomfortably. He washed quickly, weekly, and habitually in cold water, cleaned his face and mouth in the main room's sink, and captured the drinking water he would need for the day. The room was what he could afford and he didn't imagine anything better, especially since he had use of the garage and a bit of privacy between its storm-ready concrete walls to practice his one meaningful exercise: recitations of poetry which he offered up to no one, delivered in a monotone that he considered natural, in part because he could not hear the difference between a voice inclining up or cascading down, nor the pitches and pauses that would mark someone who understood the emotional register of what he was reading. His arbitrary study was toneless, but without anyone to tell him so, he practiced his orations without self-censure.

He had begun his recitals shortly after finding the book in a beaten box wedged behind a screen door at an abandoned house he had tried to deliver to, before he realized he was at the wrong address. The box had caught his eye because it seemed out of place. Why would anyone have left it in a door? After undoing the cord and unfolding the flaps, at first he merely thumbed through and wondered over the brevity of the lines and the yellowed curl of the pages. The book was old and falling apart, missing its first section and the last, consisting only of poems. He had never been a reader beyond the instruction that was forced on every child; poetry was not considered a useful skill for city youth, so he had never heard of Rainer Maria Rilke, whose name appeared again and again over lines of incomprehensible text. Once he arrived home, he sat on the floor cross-legged, holding the book in front of him as if in deep study. The posture suited him, one arm extended, the book held out so far he could barely see the lines. But the gesture of pretending to read made him hold his chin higher, and it was that feeling he wanted more of.

Another pose he soon found was grasping his chin with the left thumb and forefingers while drawing the right hand holding the book closer until his nose got in the way of seeing the words on the page. He could read the words, or most of them on one side of the page, and he found that sounding them out caused his chest to hum in a way that cheered him. Soon the emptiness and gloom of the garage drew him into it, and the first time he read the words aloud into its corners, he knew it was the right place to practice. For him, reciting Rilke was the closest thing to a spiritual undertaking he could know, not that he would have considered such a thing on his own. In fact, there is the question of whether he thought very much at all, given how much there had been to forget in his short life. Most things had been forgotten in that city, but this was not something he had realized just yet.

Even with these mysterious and awkward attributes and habits, the kid was fairly nondescript, not the sort to have a social life much less friends to admire him or chide him for being odd. The people who would have cared for him had never been caring, and he was very young when he began delivering pizzas for old man Gio. He had never returned home after taking on work. Why should he walk an hour east to be yelled at or cuffed in the head? The animal existence he had led in those days was not unusual, given how little joy there was left for anyone still on the coast. The brownouts were frequent, city services were unreliable, and the streets were dangerous, even at noon. No one had extra credits and even if they had, they would not have spent them on frivolities. The one staple was pizza, baked in brick ovens with great economy. Flour was cheap and though the sauce and cheese were partly-synthetic, no one asked too many questions about the meats in the pepperoni. The wealthy lived elsewhere, dined on delights unavailable to those who subsisted on pizza, and what jobs still remained were just enough to ensure a daily ration.

The kid didn't dwell on the past of the world, before the mass migrations toward the temperate North, partly because that history had been obscured for reasons poorly understood. He didn't imagine that his life would have been better a hundred years before because he wouldn't have known what better could have been. All to say, he didn't experience nostalgia or hopefulness, or any of the emotions those with a rich inner life have typically had available to them in the thick of dark times. Instead, he had the few threads of an existence: an employer, a landlord, and scant little left after they had settled his annual account. The city tax covered his use of water and provided enough electricity in the evening for him to read by in the garage which held no car. And that was the day-to-day workings of his life and the bleak surroundings held no interest for him as a result because the only pleasures left were sleep and sounding Rilke to the empty boxes in the dimly lit garage.

Every day was like any other, until one that began with a newness the kid found peculiar. He had readied himself for the daily deliveries and was walking to the bakery when lines of poetry began to form in his mind, not as ideas, but as syllables . . . *I think that the star glittering above me has been dead for a million years* . . . Puzzled, he reasoned that words could emerge from his mouth even without a book in his hands, and thus words could fill his mouth without being spoken. Unaccustomed to having realizations, he stopped there on the quiet street and pondered how unlike the garage it was, and yet, here were the words, ready to be spoken should he desire to say them. *I would like to step out of my heart and go walking beneath the enormous sky.*

Where had these words come from? He knew they were in the book that he recited from devotedly every night, but never had they intruded into his day. He turned onto the edge of the street that in another time had been lined with parked cars, but was made much narrower by the scrap and debris that choked the sidewalks. Most of the heaps were decades old, formed from the leavings of families who chose to evacuate the city then, while other mounds were fresher: the unmentionable refuse from buckets the people dumped in the evenings, created by those who did not pay the city tax and who squatted in the houses which had been beautiful in their own time. It was these people the kid feared the most because they had nothing to lose, and their house numbers did not appear on his circuit. He did not need to travel far down this street but it was the quickest way to the bakery, so he kept to the path through the high dry grasses lining what had once been a sidewalk. *You must be able to think back to streets in unknown neighborhoods, to unexpected encounters*, he thought. Stopping, he considered whether his nightly readings made him more vulnerable to stray thoughts. Was it dangerous to have so many intrusive words in his head? And what was an "unexpected encounter"? What could poetry do for him here, when meeting anyone at all could mean danger?

He sometimes wondered what kind of world Rilke had lived in, to have spent so much time describing things that did not exist. To have written so much about loneliness and sorrow, but to have been filled with voices. *More and more lonely, your path struggles on through incomprehensible mankind.* The kid found most people difficult to understand, and even more so because he was alone most of the time. He did not know what it would be like to have someone to talk to in the evenings, and he wasn't sure if he would like it. *All the more futile perhaps for keeping on toward the future, toward what has been lost.* He paused, turning the thought over in his mind. A future cannot be held like a pizza can, it cannot be eaten, it is not a warm blanket at night, and it is not a person that one meets and talks with. It is not a credit that buys a few hours of electricity every week and it is not a door which one can lock against the people who would otherwise hurt you if they thought you had something extra that they didn't. How does a "future" appear, what is it like to have a future, and then to lose it?

He continued on, puzzling through the distractions his mind churned through, the lines of poetry which billowed into his thoughts like clouds, at first connected but then wafting and reorganizing into other ideas, fresh perspectives which were sometimes disorienting but then also mesmerizing, ineluctable, compulsively pleasurable. Even when he picked up the first sack of pizzas for the day (the hard rolls filled with red paste and faux-fromage, the inscrutable "pepperoni" filling) his mind was elsewhere, and each house he visited on his route was a blur, every door that opened was forgotten and he didn't mind that no one smiled or acknowledged his role in bringing them their ration for the day.

He was pondering how quickly the deliveries had gone when walking past the wall he usually ignored, the red-lettered entreaty to "Rejoice!" that was by now so familiar he no longer saw it. *Only the won-back heart, can ever be satisfied: free through all it had given up, to rejoice in its mastery.* Could it be that there were lost things that could be retrieved, even if those things were futures? The thoughts that had come to him earlier in the day had led to this concept which now seemed original, glistening in its novelty. Slack-jawed, he studied the flyers which were silent, not fluttering as they sometimes were. The lack of rain allowed them to last for weeks, and the text was slightly blurry but distinct: "Rejoice for the Lost Child, the Nameless Pain of our Forgotten Futures, in which All will Return to Us as it once Was!" The words were the same on every flyer, a plea for hope in the middle of a barren life shared by most of the city's denizens. The wall had been painted many times before by city workers who tried to erase the message that reappeared every few months in the same blocky script. Someone apparently replaced the teddy bears and flowers, soaked them in libations, and lit the candles.

The kid knew there were people who sometimes met in secret places to talk over the world that had once existed. The "Lost Child" and the "Nameless Pain" described whatever it was that people felt when they thought about future times, or the return of old times, neither of which made any sense to him. He didn't know what the world had been like before his own life, and history had never been a subject the city schools considered important. Like poetry, study of the past was not a practical skill. What students learned instead was words—their singular and essential meanings—so that basic instructions could be conveyed and information recorded. Children learned numbers, so that calculations of credits and work debts could be explained by employers, tax agents, and landlords. Students learned basic hygiene, how to be punctual, conservative, obedient, and calm, even under chaotic circumstances. He recalled how they were taught to sit while teachers shouted nonsensical phrases at them, sirens blared and lights flashed; how the children protected their ears and eyes with their hands as they crouched, and lined up carefully behind the designated gonfalon as they followed the banner across an obstacle course lined with terrifying images without flinching. These were skills every child learned until their tenth year, at which point they were considered sufficiently prepared for adulthood. The kid was grateful that daily life had usually been uneventful, just as the city designers had hoped.

What was troubling could be seen in places like the wall; graffiti that colored the out-of-way corridors and backsides of buildings in colors that were rarely seen any more. Usually the word, "rejoice," but also the word "remember," and "return." Together, the three words meant something the city tried to suppress, but for whatever reason the kid could not fathom. He was thinking about this, and wondering where the people found paper in so many colors, along with the paint that gilded the letters he gently fingered: R, E, J, O, I, . . . when another thought came to him: *And the animals move patiently from one to the other—and everywhere around us, death is at home, and it watches us out of the cracks in Things, and a rusty nail that sticks out of a plank somewhere, does nothing day and night except rejoice over death* . . . It was this uncomfortable line of Rilke's that made him glance over his shoulder, and shiver, and look for a different way to go home than his usual path. This he did without questioning, as one other skill the city taught him was regarding gut instincts, and how one should always listen to messages that came without warning and did not connect to one's rational trajectory.

His alternate path took him behind the wall, through a corridor he usually avoided but was now a better way. Immediately he was reassured when the corridor opened to the side of a cliff, or what had once been the topside of an overpass before the original highway had become a brackish estuary, bringing the sea into the city's low places. He looked across to other streets now underwater and the ruined skeletal structures that had long since been salvaged for steel, and whatever else had once been valuable to a civilization in decline. That was when he heard the whimper tucked into the scrubby brush ahead of him. The pause he took was a long one, and he listened to the tension welling up inside his intestines, but not from alarm. What he felt instead was more like what he felt the day he had found the box inside the door of the abandoned house. Curious, he inched forward, stopping only when another line came to him, unbidden: *As if awakened, she turns her face to yours; and with a shock, you see yourself, tiny, inside the golden amber of her eyeballs suspended.* He slowly turned his head to the left and met the gaze of an animal unlike the ones he'd ever heard about, that had ever existed in the textbooks of his school: Not cat, not dog, not bird, but . . . *RAINBOW,* said the voice in his head.

The kid was very still and once again queried his instinct, finding only silence there. He spoke the word aloud, softly, to the creature that stared directly into his eyes, as he saw himself reflected in hers. *YES,* said the amber eyes. He did not have to ask whether the word was hers or Rilke's. He simply knew. *Help me,* she said, through a language that the kid had never heard before, but found exhilarating. He had never seen an animal, but only in pictures; even then, certainly not one so incredibly exotic. Her head was catlike and doglike at the same time, rimmed with a feathery softness that reflected so much light and iridescence, that he found her face impossible to contain in one moment. Ears stood out from her head in great triangles, tufted with shimmery threads of multiple colors. Her body was lithe, the feather-fur extending from her neck but becoming less full along her silvery torso and legs. Her feet terminated in toes with berry-brown pads and little claws a centimeter long; her tail bushed out into a furry oval with downy pastel tendrils, and while studying her, the word *FOX* came to him unbidden. Even so, she was not like the image of the mythical wild thing in his second grade letter book, but more wondrous, somehow kind in her expression, though the pain appeared there too, a pain that the kid understood even though he had never seen a being like her, even in a picture of fauna long forgotten by Earth, or as you and I would call it, extinct.

Carry me, the fox said, and he briefly looked down at his rough coveralls and tried to clean his palms in a gesture he had never explored before in a world where everything was soiled in some way and nothing was ever clean. He tried though, preparing his hands to touch the radiant fur that appeared luminous and pure. *Use the sack.* Of course, he thought. If he found her strange and magical, how would she appear to anyone else? As unlikely as meeting someone might be at this hour (it was beginning to grow late) he realized the sack would at least conceal her glimmering form, if not attract the hungry eyes of people who would suspect he carried a treasure hoard of pizza loaves, ripe for the plucking. He quickly untied the sack from his belt and transferred his own loaf to a netted bag he sometimes carried when picking through the rubbage heaps. Carefully he positioned the bag so that she could wriggle inside, with minimal help from his hand. She was on a small shelf of rock, so her angle assisted with her movement, though he could sense how weak she was. *I must rest now,* came to him in a soft rush of comprehension, and he studied his hand which carried a small amount of pearlescent dust from having touched her. Never had he felt something so soft, and never had his hand ached with such longing to remember how something felt against it. Without knowing why, he touched the glittering chitin to his brow and closed his eyes, knowing that his life would never be the same again.

Rainbow knew that the kid would not hurt her, even as she knew that staying where he had found her was risky. Having never been lost before, she did not know what to do. Nowhere in her banks of memory had she ever known the absence of human protection and controlled environments where her every whim was fulfilled. She was an expensive pet, and despite the many foolish transactions human beings made with each other over useless artifacts, she had never been such a transaction herself. *Gone.* She had no sense of what the word could mean, just as she did not know words like *alone*, or *frightened*, or *hungry*. Or, more precisely, she had not known the words until a few days ago, when the yacht she had been inhabiting as a passenger was overtaken by a storm. It was not an ordinary storm, even for this groaning planet that had suffered calamities for a hundred years or more. Rainbow knew these things because she had heard her master speak about the Earth with the other humans, though she did not pay much attention to the talk then, nestled as she was in her cozy window. What did a greater world mean to her, when she lived in the utmost of comfort, far away from the barren equatorial deserts, the depleted breadbaskets of the steppes, the swampy northern landscapes now considered developable real estate? These thoughts flickered through her as she tried to stay awake, coiled upside down in a bag slung over a human's shoulder.

The journey to wherever the kid lived was a hazy mishmash of memory to her, and she perceived it in dreamy packets of consciousness she couldn't make sense of. The sway of her weight in the sack, combined with the bounce she made against his side was hypnotizing. She felt like a swinging pendulum, and recalled the comfort of her hammock at home (spoiled fox that she was, she had such a luxury), and in some other moments she thought of the yacht's sickening motion during the first week they were on board. The cruise was still an adventure looming in the mind of her human keeper, and she was excited as well, eager to see the promised views of submerged cities that were now ruins, a testament to the melt of ice, the last glacier gone and mourned nearly a century before. Had she only known, she would not have wanted to see the coastal cities. They reminded her of carcasses through some deeper memory of wildness, inherited from some genetic strain of animal that had not been bred completely out of her. Floating in and out of time, she began to imagine the analogue of a ride she had once taken, a carnival wheel that went up and down again, and the lights she remembered from the botanical gardens at Winnipeg when she had sat close to Canto and he had held her, reassuring that she would be safe as she buried her shimmering face into the crook of his arm.

When the ride ended, she was lifted again. The kid slid her body onto a soft pile of clothing among the boxes in the garage. He pulled an old coat over the top, creating a cave that emanated the sweetness of old ladies who frequently powdered themselves—a light rose motif that played ironically well in the deep recesses of Rainbow's ancestral brain. The pizza kid lifted her head to help her lap water from a hubcap. He broke bits of pepperoni and crust into bite-sized pieces and left them where her tongue could reach them. Much later, she heard him practicing his orations like songs. Like monks chanting in the distance, they were a comfort.

As he read, she slept, and there were no more memories to trouble her with what had been or worries about what was to come. She heard through her dreams the sound of poetry, and it was that sound—monotonic as it was—that reassured her through the night. She would survive, and perhaps she would even make it back home. Perhaps Canto was safe too, and somewhere the kindness of a stranger was to be had, because it was the sort of world where people helped one another, and had always been; that she was sure of.

The fox was sleeping when the kid went to work and he hurried through his deliveries that day, eager to return to the garage. Gio raised his thick eyebrows when the kid had held open the bag, exposing the silvery dust inside. But the baker shoveled the pizzas in without a word, counting them by twos and he watched the kid disappear through the door faster than he'd ever seen him move. The kid's mind was free of poetry, but lingered instead on the strange being in his garage; had he known that she slept peacefully all day, he would not have hurried less. So quickly did he run home, he barely noticed the wall had been repainted again, the teddy bears had been removed along with the flowers and the candles, and the flyers had been cleaned from the telephone pole. He had seen it all cleared before, in a cyclical pattern of erase and repeat. And had it been that way when he ran by that morning? He couldn't be sure.

Rainbow was beginning to stir just as the kid came through the heavy door which opened into the garage from the house, book tucked under his arm. At first he started, as if he had forgotten she was in his garage, but then he proceeded slowly in, and seated himself a few feet away. She had not touched the pizza bits he had left her, but the water was nearly gone. He began to get up but she narrowed her eyes. *Not yet. I want to know who you are.* He hesitated, studying her face, her amber eyes somehow green in this light (had they changed?). She regarded him cautiously, and he almost heard her other questions, the ones she wouldn't allow to be projected. He could tell that she was unimpressed by the garage in the way she held herself partly off the floor, forepaws primly crossed. Perhaps she also didn't think very much of him, the way most people felt when they opened their doors for his deliveries. A shadow of contempt, along with all their withheld judgment, usually danced across their faces. With Rainbow, it was unclear what she meant by "know." No one ever wanted to know him, and without anything to exchange, he opened his book to read.

She was patient in her regard, realizing that this human lacked all the qualities of Canto—her heart panged as she thought of him, and she noticed the kid flinched a little as if in sympathy—and she allowed her feelings to flow from her until the kid could see all that she held back in saturated hues; he was a tall man, a gentle man, a man who was considerate of everyone. He dressed well, smelled nice, and had clean hands. He wore gloves when driving and liked to cook. He often gave Rainbow the choicest bits of *niupa* from the grill after cooling it in his hands. They traveled together, and she always had the finest views from the hotel windows, the airbus, the monorail . . . eyes welling, she glanced at the kid and saw he had looked down at his book and was shuffling through the pages. She did not intend to hurt him with her remembering.

The kid didn't know what to do with the images he now had in his mind of the life that Rainbow had lived. First, he wasn't accustomed to thinking of times and places separate from the ones he inhabited. It was disorienting to be sitting in the garage, and also be hurtling through a shining city on a streak of light with people finely dressed, drinking bubbly juices out of tall crystal cups with long stems. Then, there was also the matter of this man, and how handsome he looked through Rainbow's eyes. He seemed like the type of man who would politely decline a pizza, but pay for it anyway. He might even smile while doing so. The world that Rainbow came from was so unlike the one the kid had always known, there was no comparison. He wanted to forget that she had shared this world with him, even in flashing seconds, but he found it was impossible, and worse, he suddenly felt a desire to see all the things that she found familiar, and to taste them, to explore the city there, to travel on the edge of large windows and to look out at clean spaces with happy people and to smile. Yearning was a painful, new thing. For the kid, such a future hurt him nearly as much as the past that caused Rainbow to pine.

His feelings were overwhelming, so he decided to read. He chose a note that had been written on one of the blank pages by hand. It was in an old script, and he had often studied it, more distracted by its lettering than the words themselves. The handwritten words bore no name. It was an entire unbroken paragraph—a riddle—not a poem at all. But he had studied it many nights without reading it aloud, puzzling over what it could describe. His reading on this evening emerged from him with a new urgency, for the sake of his audience and the intensity of her listening. The sentences pierced the soft dark of the garage with a lightness bent by an illuminating quickness. The meanings shifted in his mind as he sounded the words aloud, not knowing the sum of them: *The land was clear as clear liquid; every dwelling began to celebrate itself as if greatest realization was strung secretly within humble ministry. And then we turned: look: Eclipses consumed by rainsparkles, with the rifts of heaven's weighed-down, gazing gates. Beneath, the left lands were clearer. Solemn, in anticipation of evening, a silent mouth, having drunk deeply, was overlooking bold flowers.*

Rainbow wasn't sure how to feel after he finished. No one had ever read words as a gift to her, directly to her. She usually watched the transactions of human beings with the same drowsy-eyed indifference, and only a mild curiosity for what they cared about, or what made them laugh, and in what way they admired her. She was sometimes the object of conversations, but rarely the listening subject. Canto sometimes spoke to her, when all of the other humans had left and they were alone. He told her stories about her ancestors, how they were hunted or lived brief lives, how they leapt high but then dove into the snow to catch mice which they crunched with their sharp teeth. She found this last part humorous, given that no one ate other living beings anymore, and she had never seen snow. She was aware that the Earth was very old and that humans were not. She knew herself to be unique. But never had she heard words that made her hunger for a world beyond her reach, and neither of them—the fox or the kid— had to ask what the subject of the poem had been.

Thank you, she offered. He nodded and looked down. As he had read the words to her, he had sensed her memories, which flashed along so quickly that he couldn't make meaning of them. He saw a field, stretching down across a land with hills in the distance and on either side. The sky was indigo, heavy with rain, but the grasses were also glistening with drops already fallen. He knew that he had never seen such a place, so it was a memory of hers, of green, sloping fields, and small houses dotting hillocks as far as the eye could see. He had no such images in his mind, but instead the city after a deluge, when the rain and wind would settle in for days, washing the dust into tiny rivers that closed off streets, making deliveries impossible. He stayed in during those times, when the sirens would wail outside to keep people indoors. More often weeks passed without rain and the only flowers were wild, dry, and brown.

Rainbow saw that the pizza boy was studying her thoughts and learning how to communicate with her. Her entry to his mind was closed in several places; there were fewer shared images between them, but enough to create the lacuna which could lead to friendship. She did not remember when she first knew Canto, now lost to her. He had been there from the beginning, and the imprints she had learned before him had been circumstantial: her nurse, her trainer, her handler. She knew how to communicate with humans once the emotional contract was struck between them; kindness continued would deepen the imprint. Any other treatment might have the reverse effect, though she had been fortunate to have endured few of those moments in her life.

"I want to see that place," the kid blurted. This went well beyond what Rainbow could have expected, and she questioned her own ability to perceive his thoughts, so sudden was his declaration. When she pressed, she could feel his surety, an unyielding premonition of adventure, much like what Canto had felt when he planned their sea journey. The thought reminded Rainbow of the excitement she had felt then too, before everything had gone terribly wrong, when they had been overtaken by the storm. She tucked her snout into her paws at the thought, and the kid regarded her, unsure. Carefully he extended his hand to her shoulder and he felt the thrill of her fur against his fingers. The powder lightly clung to his hand afterward, and fell onto the book in his hands. Unaccustomed to reassuring anyone but himself, he didn't know what to say.

But I am afraid. Her recognition was new, as was her hesitation. She had never turned away from a chance to travel, but then she knew it would not be the same with the kid, and there would be no window seats or full service sleeping cabins. She had already learned all that she needed to know about where they were, how meanly the people lived, and how meager their subsistence. She felt no desire to venture out into an unknown world without the protection that wealth provided, nor did she trust that the kid had any awareness of the journey she would need to undertake in order to make it home. Rainbow was careful to not let the kid into these thoughts, the ones that said "no" to his question which still hung in the air like a plucked string. Instead she reasoned, *It is a longer journey than you can imagine,* which also meant that she could not fathom the distance, nor the belief that she would ever see home again.

Unbidden, and without any act on his part but to breathe, the kid spoke words that he meant, but were not his own: "Leave one's own first name behind, forgetting it as easily as a child abandons a broken toy." Rainbow saw the language turn in his mind like jewels and the jewels opened like the petals of a flower. She had not seen this shift happen in a long time. Many of the humans she observed already had the meanings of words decided. The kid was receptive to images that arrived through her unbidden, unconscious. The words were keys made to fit their circuitry, as organic as they both were . . . her experiences formed impressions that she transmitted without intention, and in his charged and receptive consciousness, he received her memory. In ways neither could articulate, they formed a language between them that only they understood. And so it was that they formed a plan for leaving the city.

He knew right away she wouldn't want to ride in the bag. Her large angular ears flattened against her head and her lip curled. He didn't need to hear her thoughts about it. But when she paced forward and backward a few times and then sat back down, he knew that she recognized the dangers of travelling through the early morning streets exposed. They had discussed the trip multiple times and she knew that she must be carried in his pizza sack until they were alone. She also knew that she had been naive about the kindness people universally showed one another in the world. It was—unfortunately—based on recognition that she had lived her entire life in a protected comfort. In moments she permitted herself to think of her former life, and of the uncertainty that anyone else had survived the ordeal of the storm. But then she would shake the thoughts away, and concentrate on the task at hand.

I don't like the smell inside that sack. It's moldy. The kid smiled as much as he could and looked down at the coin in his hands. All his labor, the years spent delivering loaves of pizza and living in his little room were distilled in the heavy metal chip. His wages minus housing plus the paltry remnants of each month's excess did not leave him much, but with this amount he could board the train headed west through the tomato fields, perhaps even reach the other side of them. From there, he and Rainbow could set out on foot with a few days of concentrate foods and water. It wasn't a plan with any solid parts except the moment when Rainbow wouldn't have to lie still in the bag as he carried her.

The fox wasn't insensitive to the pains he was taking to keep her safe, but even inside the sack, she was vulnerable to the attention of others. She knew their best chance was to get out of the city unnoticed, and a little before dawn. She also recognized how limited the kid's resources were and what security he was leaving behind. She had watched him fold his few possessions into a tight square of cloth and slide it into a bag he slung across his body. The bag had been repaired many times, and was a gift from Gio, who, upon realizing the kid was serious about leaving, had offered it. Without asking questions, Gio had asked him to wait, and returned with the bag from the back room.

"You'll need this. Without a roof, you'll need it to keep your clothes dry." It was a simple gesture, but the kid had taken the waxcloth bag with thanks. Gio's normally stern face softened uncharacteristically and he rested his baker's hands on the counter. "When I was your age I traveled to Atlanta to see my sister. This bag was all I had. You'll be fine, kid." With that, he thumped the counter and walked back toward the ovens. The kid clutched the bag gratefully and walked out of the bakery for the last time. That had been a few hours before, and the reality was finally settling in that he was leaving—he was saying goodbye to the bungalow, the garage, and his life as a carrier of pizzas. His book of poetry fit neatly into the courier bag and he hadn't any other possessions to speak of, so there was nothing left to do but leave once Rainbow acquiesced to enter the sack.

"It's only until we are out of view. We may even have most of the boxcar to ourselves." Rainbow winced when he said "boxcar." She had accepted the repugnant idea that they would not have seats nor a window, but she still struggled to be excited about this train journey, so unlike all of the others she had taken. It would be as freight that they traveled, the way trains had continued on in the South long past the advancements made elsewhere in the country. When the migrations had first begun, people had driven their cars, until fuel became too expensive. The oil burners were scrapped for steel and other precious metals, which the railroad coveted. Electric cars had their day, along with other propulsion systems. But by that time the cost of road repair had made some municipalities close off many streets in favor of walking and bicycles. The trains in the North had advanced to elevated tracks, much more efficient for moving people over pedestrian areas, but in the South, most people continued in their old ways, experimenting with refits of old autos that hadn't been sold for junk, and tolerating the rough broken roads that still existed between larger towns. Rainbow knew all of this from Canto's discussions that took place on large screens. His office handled much of the transportation logistics for cross-continental travel, and so she often dozed in and out of long quarterly reports in the background, and arguments over the cost of mining operations and how much of this or that was required to power the city's infrastructure. It wasn't the sort of information she had ever cared to know, but she saw the value in it now when contemplating their trip overland. She glanced at the kid and knew that he had understood all of this, including her continuing distaste for travelling in a boxcar, in a moldy pizza sack, for an indefinite amount of time.

Once again, Rainbow endured the swing, the bump, the bounce, the rebounding method of travel by shouldered sack. Whereas before the sack had been a comfort after the terrifying hours spent huddled alone on the water bank, now it was a torment of repetition. It jogged another memory, one that she had already forgotten because of the now central trauma of her life: of floating in the raft on the ocean all night, and in the dark, alone. She did not remember how she had gotten there, only that she had trembled with the shock of it all, and had curled herself as small as she could make herself in order to fit in the area under the seat. There were no oars, meaningless to her, but had there been a human with her, they would have undoubtedly floated hours adrift. She could not remember the storm nor the moments before the water and wind came. She did not know if hours passed, or days. She did not know if Canto had placed her in the boat before leaving her to help others (something he would have done) or if she herself had run across the tilting decks to press the signals to deploy the raft. Though animal and not human, she had the DNA of several species in her, which created a combined survival instinct among them.

Humankind's fascination with domestic animals and artificial intelligence had led to her, an augmented lifeform, to be custom designed according to the preferences of the contract. And once the deal was struck, versions of her were awakened so that programming could begin. It was no secret, what she was. Her trainer had led her through the viewing hall so that she could see the different stages of her creation. Her role as a pet was explained, and she was told that she had been granted this knowledge as a means to understand her value and also her purpose: to comfort and encourage human beings to be the best version of themselves, just as she was the very best version of all her ancestors, who lived on in her chemistry and in the matter of her composition. The affectionate cats, the musical cockatiels, and countless obedient and loyal dogs—all formed a part of her heritage. And the fox? They were the most popular *phylo* in part because of their beauty and also because foxes had never been successfully domesticated as a single, unmodified species. Too hyperactive and curious, and with a short lifespan, the fox was not a desirable pet. But with the characteristics of a dog or cat—the steadiness of a Great Pyrenees or a Persian—the ideal balance was struck. The chitin? A bizarre add-on that Canto had requested because he'd always loved butterflies and the protein-laden powder they left on his fingertips.

The kid liked the silence when Rainbow wasn't talking, but instead remembering her life and reflecting on her existence. ("Silent friend of many distances, feel how your breath enlarges all of space . . .") He was fascinated by the way her mind turned objects—sometimes sense impressions and reasoned thoughts—many different ways before setting them down again. He knew that *she knew* that he listened; and it was that comfortable way they had of being together that helped him understand small things at first and then larger things. Understanding that there were people somewhere in the world who could create a being like Rainbow made him hopeful that they were wise. He enjoyed the images of Canto which she frequently returned to. And occasionally, he detected a kind of joy she felt whenever she allowed herself to imagine seeing him again. The kid smiled at this thought, glad that she was finally positive about the journey ahead of them, as daunting as it was. He trudged through the dark morning streets nurturing his first hopeful thought that there might be a place for him in this new world of the North.

Gio had told him to walk a short distance east until he came to the old railway, and to turn right, walking south along the tracks. The kid had thought to himself that walking east and then south in order to go north made no sense, but Rainbow had explained that sometimes a trip was twisty at the beginning before straightening out. He accepted this answer, but then there was the matter of the ancient rail bed itself, which offered him no confidence for what the tracks looked like on down the way. In one segment, the marsh on either side was almost level with his path, which had been raised as a part of the city's resilience program a hundred or more years before.

At the first track intersection he was to go right, walking north, until he arrived at the historic overpass and the train station would be nearby. He didn't expect to encounter anyone and he didn't, thankful that he lived on the side of the city that had already been given up. From what Rainbow knew he managed to learn that all of the people who could leave had left already, the remainder those too poor or ignorant of the truth that the world's coastlines were no longer places to settle. From her he had also learned that many parts of the sea were too warm for life, that southern Europe was a desert, that the Amazon was a grassland. It wasn't that Rainbow had a perfect understanding of geography, but that she had heard Canto say these things before in a way that was meaningful to other human beings. They looked sad whenever these places were mentioned, as if there had been a death among the circles they drew. When Rainbow's silence deepened, the kid recalled a line from his book of poetry: "Upon her beads, night after night, she counts the ancient curse."

The dawn was on his right as he walked and the kid realized that Rainbow had fallen asleep. He continued to think about the way ahead and all the things his city had forgotten to tell him about the world which he had learned from Rainbow. He had cried. He couldn't help it, and he didn't remember the last time he had felt this way, or if ever at all. It was a loss far greater than any he had known because he had never lost anything of value that he knew of. Even leaving his family had been a gain in his happiness, if one could call it that. He remembered the hard face of his ma for the first time in what felt like forever. He remembered all of the men as brothers, though they never stayed. He was not sure that anyone there knew him by name, or that he was seen any differently by them than anyone else who shared a plot in the stadium. When he had decided to leave, it was because he had heard that the next year of floods would cut them apart from the rest of the city. When he realized that no one seemed to care, he began walking north and west, lit by a dawn like this one, following 52nd across the last bridge to be built in the 90s. By the late morning on *that* day long ago, he had found Gio's bakery, where he bought a loaf with his last credit and was given a job almost immediately. The old man had seen the desperation and the fear on the face of the young boy, but more importantly, he was down one delivery kid and his buddy had a room to rent. In another time, people would have considered the similarity between both of these days as auspicious, but the kid trudged along allowing his thoughts to wander even further afield, in a timeless realm where all things past were also present and future.

According to Rainbow, there had once been a child of the gods, a wise and beautiful being who had come to walk the Earth of humans and determine whether another hundred years would bring sorrow or illumination. The child was born into a home where no one showed it love, and the blindness on the part of the adults developed into a canker of neglect. This neglect grew into a great wound, and all the pestilences of the world came to feed on it. First hunger came, and then illness came, and then the houses could not protect against water or serpents. The fish died. The forests became deserts and the rains moved North. The wound of the child swelled until the child was filled with infection and it died.

Many children died everywhere and generations after called it a miracle—the first miracle of the Forgotten Future. For without a future, why would any child choose to live?

It was midmorning when the kid arrived at the station and saw a train rumbling on the nearest track. The ramp had seen better days, perhaps when past generations were deciding to leave the city for good. Rainbow wriggled a little to show she was awake and yawned inside the stuffy sack. *Are we there yet?* "Nearly. I need to find the conductor." Gio had told him to find the blue door with the window and inquire about a ticket to Gainesville. From there he was to travel northwest for two days on foot to find the waterfall at Amicalola. The trail was the best way to travel north according to the baker, because walking through the mountains would be safer than the roads, and much cooler. The water might be uncontaminated and there would be the possibility of aid along the trail, for those who had begun the migration by foot had often begun living along the trail itself. Somehow they endured life without city services, without the shelter of concrete walls and pizza, and some of them helped travelers passing through.

The little man behind the blue door was helping a woman when the kid approached. She was thin and sharply dressed with a plumed hat, and she was accompanied by a large suitcase standing upright beside her. She smelled nicer than anyone the kid had ever encountered and yet she had the same expectant air about her that most people had everywhere. It was the anxiety of living in a city long abandoned, lacking the basic securities that had always defined civilization. He heard her curt remark to the conductor's question—"Richmond"—and in short order another gentleman emerged to help roll her bag to the train and load it. When the kid came to the window he placed his coin on the counter and looked at the short man with the blue cap and a wizened expression. The man's white moustache twitched once when the kid said "Gainesville." The old man studied the coin and then began to punch some numbers into a strange machine. It spat out a small chit of paper and he handed it to the kid. What happened next went far beyond what Gio had prepared him for.

"Son, you'll be riding on a different train than that lady that was here before. Some folks would say that she has the better seat, and therefore will enjoy her trip north more than most people. But you, my boy . . . you have in your hand the beginning of a new life." The man held the coin tilted in the light and showed the kid a number that had been buried in the detail of a mountain. "This coin was minted forty years ago when the city's evacuation included buses to and from the train, all with the hopes of offering people with no money the means to begin the Mountain Trail. I haven't seen one of these in a long time." Musing to himself, he placed the coin in a special box and took from under the box a small pamphlet. Glossy pictures of people walking into the trees beside a waterfall shone on the brochure. The conductor opened the panel and pointed to a name at the bottom of the page. "If this woman is still alive, ask someone at the station in Gainesville how to find her. Show her this ticket and she can help you." The kid followed the man as he stepped from his counter, opened the door, and pointed down the platform to Track C. "I'll be there momentarily to let you into your cabin." After the man returned to his counter, the kid felt Rainbow shift her body again, signaling her discomfort, but also her anticipation awakened by the word "cabin."

The cabin was surprisingly clean, and had at one time been used to transport whole families in each cell, offering them the privacy of a 9 x 9 room with a small square window that let in the air as the train rushed along. There was nothing resembling service of any kind, but there was privacy, which Rainbow took advantage of immediately, emerging from the grey morass that was the pizza sack. She stuck her nose out of the window and took in the warm air. For a moment, the kid decided that she looked happy, or as happy as a fox could appear without the reassurance she gave him that she was so. *But you know I am . . . what would make you think otherwise?* He marveled at her light, radiant form and the way her coat rippled in the wind. He sat across from her, looking through the open window back toward Savannah. He had not realized how much water was all around them. In the declining morning, as the sun mounted the sky, the tomato fields overtook everything in his view. He felt sorry for the people who spent their lives picking tomatoes, but he also wondered if they enjoyed a better life than the people who had lived in the stadium during the time he was a child there. Who's to say? Rainbow was now content, and she had lost everything that was important to her. (At this, the fox turned toward him and closed her eyes in agreement.) Perhaps it was those brief moments of joy that made up an entire life. Maybe, had he tried to leave the city years ago, he wouldn't have warranted Gio's generosity. After all, old man Gio had the coin all along and had never used it. But here they were, hurtling toward the stations that would gradually take them to Gainesville.

When they were boarding the train, the kid had looked back toward the eastern skyline, toward the sea, which had always been both prod and obstacle, punishment and also retribution for centuries of negligence. What had the city done to deserve this? What had the larger world done to bring about such a hard and fast fall? The conductor had looked at the kid expectantly, his moustache twitching once or twice when he asked the kid for his name. When the kid said "Rilke," the conductor wrote something on a small clipboard and punched his ticket. "Good luck, young Rilke," said the conductor, and the kid felt a surge of confidence from knowing finally who he was.

Rainbow had said nothing for a while, so happy she was to shake herself free of the awful sack and scent the air once the door was shut. After the train began to move she turned toward him and posited an arch question. *Rilke?* He grinned modestly and recited the first words of his new life, and the last of his old one: "And if the earthly no longer knows your name, whisper to the silent earth: I'm flowing. To the flashing water say: I am." She took in the sight of him, looking wistfully toward the city retreating further into the distance, and she knew finally what Canto had meant when he said he would always be with her.

So Many Infinitely Precious Things
By Michelle Denham

Beyond the cracked sidewalk, and the telephone pole with layers of flyers in a rainbow of colors, and the patch of dry brown grass there stood a ten-foot high concrete block wall, caked with dozens of coats of paint. There was a small shrine at the foot of it, with burnt out candles and dead flowers and a few soggy teddy bears. One word of graffiti filled the wall, red letters on a gold background: Rejoice!

 The lingering traces of the monsoon were already rapidly disappearing, the storm quick to depart as quickly as it came. Even the puddles were almost gone, and soon there would be nothing left but the faint scent of creosote and disturbed earth. The destruction of the shrine—Kimmie Jones hated to see it, because there was something distinctly pathetic about the loss of what once had so much splendor in grief. The people (undefined faces in undefined crowds expressing undefined mourning) had been maintaining the candles and other offerings with the kind of devotion found during Easter Mass for almost three weeks running, but the momentum was finally petering out and the monsoon had, without mercy, stripped away everything else.

 Never mix divinity and death, Kimmie's mentor told her. Let the dead be dead. Kimmie touched the now faded and weather-beaten photo of little Sarah Atherton and thought, *poor kid, they should have just let her stay dead.* Little golden Sarah Atherton with her little golden dog, both struck down by a drunk driver with the same random power of an ancient god striking down the unbelievers with lightning. So many people have met the same fate. So many dogs, too. But little Sarah, so golden, so bright, so photogenic, brought an outpouring of outrage that reached mythic levels.

Now here was Kimmie Jones. Standing on the street corner where a little girl and her dog were killed, looking at the remnants of worshipful grief, and thinking about how it was far too hot to deal with all this and she really needed more coffee. Out there, somewhere in the streets of Tucson, was a god brought into creation by good intentions.

***

(It was brightness and then a darkness and then brightness again. It was hot, ever so hot, and when she stood up her tongue lolled and it felt like the best thing that ever happened. She took two steps forward and then four steps. Everything smelled so good. She wanted to experience everything, all at once, and she wanted it all right now. She walked the length of one block and then she found the boy. Or the boy found her. Either way, the boy was wonderful and she was wonderful. He bent down and picked her up and he said, *Oh, I love you.* She thought, *yes, love, that's wonderful. It's wonderful to be loved.* He said, *I'm going to name you Rainbow.* She thought, *Yes, Rainbow. That's who I am. My name is Rainbow.*)

***

Kimmie learned the hard way that you can't look like she did in Southern Arizona and say, *I'm a shaman,* and still have people take you seriously. It only invited the same disdain a tourist buying dreamcatchers would get. Or worse, one of those crystal-loving, vortex-seeking New Agers in Sedona. And it was too much work to say, *not that kind of shaman; the Korean kind,* since, really, that wasn't any better. Even if they knew there were other kinds, she would still have to explain about her mom, and then bear through some kindly-meant variation of, *Oh, you can't tell at all.*

So she didn't call herself a shaman, not out loud, but instead fashioned herself as a private investigator. Sometimes a youth pastor, depending on the situation. To the old woman who saw her standing at little Sarah Atherton's shrine, she said she was a guidance counselor. *Not at Sarah's school you see, but one near here. It hits kids hard, you know? When someone their own age dies. Even if they didn't know her.* The old woman nodded like those lies made sense. It gave Kimmie the opportunity to ask the important question: *Did you know Sarah?*

I feel *like I did*, the old woman said. *It's just like you said. It hits hard. I work in the coffeeshop right over here, and I come here every day to pay my respects to that poor little girl. I talked to her mother right here on this corner. I left these candles here. I brought roses. I've been praying for her poor soul. I just feel like I know her, like she was my own little girl. I pray for her.*

Kimmie stopped herself from saying, *I bet you do.* The old woman wouldn't understand. Instead, she thought about how the old woman approached her with the promptness of a security guard in a shopping mall when certain groups of teenagers linger for more than two minutes. The woman was proud of this shrine, proud of her proximity to little Sarah Atherton's tragedy. *Did you see any kids her earlier today? They might be one of my clients.* A boy, the old woman was quick to tell Kimmie. A teenager—maybe too old to be one of yours? But he had a dog. Just like Sarah. *Right. Just like Sarah.*

***

(Rainbow was put into a basket and everything was just a little less wonderful. She didn't understand why. The kid—her kid? Or was she his?—was still bright and full of love. He had a basket on his bike and he carried pizza in the back. She could smell it clearly and a stirring that was not quite a memory made the scent familiar. He talked to her in soothing soliloquies with a cadence that was almost hymnal in its glory. The world flew past as they moved together like one creature, her tongue lolling to one side with instinctual joy. Yet—. Not everything was joy. There was something deep inside her. What was it? Elegy?)

***

Kimmie Jones spoke with the dead. After talking to the old woman, she went inside the nearby Trader Joe's and bought offerings. Large chocolate chip cookies and a can of iced tea. The street was too busy to do a full-on ritual, (and, anyway, people would have thought she was insane if she started the dancing and singing her ancestors would have insisted upon), but she was able to find a nearby plaza that was empty enough for her to sit comfortably on a bench with the cookies, the tea, and the dead.

Lazy, said the ghost. He looked like he was in his early twenties and had for as long as Kimmie knew him. He was one of the only ghosts who regularly came when Kimmie called who could speak English. Kimmie still couldn't hold conversation in Korean and her daily Duolingo lessons had yet to provide the vocabulary she needed to ask, *How do I help the restless dead?*

They didn't have rice cakes, Kimmie told the ghost. *And anyway I need help. The mourners created a god and I have to find it. Since the god wasn't at the shrine, it must be hiding in a body. That can get real bad. You know that.* The ghost did know that. He'd helped her with the god-ridden before. This knowledge did not induce promptness. Instead, the ghost took one of the chocolate chip cookies and broke it in half. He broke the cookie again and again until it was just little crumbs so small they disappeared into the dirt. The dead didn't eat, not that Kimmie had ever seen. Stripped down to the bare essentials of ritual, the dead simply valued the offer of food. The tea remained untouched, but Kimmie knew that after the ghost left the can would be empty.

Small gods die after the shrine is dismantled, the ghost said. *Even if they're riding a body.* But Kimmie already knew that so she just stared at him. Then the ghost shrugged. *You could just wait it out.* Kimmie had to close her eyes, breathe in and out. On a day like this, you could almost smell the heat. Not just the creosote and the earth, but the very heat rising off the asphalt. The scent helped Kimmie ignore what was better left repressed (shame, anger, memory). *No,* Kimmie said, when she could trust herself to speak. *I can't wait.*

***

(The boy carried her in his basket but Rainbow lost herself. It was getting harder and harder to maintain that original thought: *I am Rainbow and everything is wonderful.* It was harder to think of anything at all. Much easier to concentrate on what was happening to her. The basket jostled with uneven rhythm, the boy talked to her with a comforting cadence, the day was full of loudness and interesting smells. The boy carried her in his bike; she was lifted with the momentum. It felt like a ride, one that she only dimly remembered, and it lifted them both to greater heights, up, up, up to air she dimly remembered as divine.)

***

When she was fourteen-years-old, Kimmie wanted to die. Twenty years later, that defining characteristic still seemed so vivid and acute. Like a jagged stone caught in the throat even now. At fourteen, she wanted to die. It still seemed like a miracle that she hadn't.

At first, it was just the physical sickness wearing her down. The loss of appetite, the insomnia, the constant pain in her stomach, and no one could really explain why. There were so many doctor's appointments and tests. They all became really good at saying, *you're perfectly healthy,* in a way that made it clear that it wasn't their fault their tests didn't have answers. *I want this to end, I want this to end, I want to end,* became Kimmie's constant mantra. At one point, Kimmie burst into tears after a healthy diagnosis. *Then why do I hurt so much? Why can't I sleep?*

Then the hallucinations started. The people who weren't really there. The voices that no one else could hear. The dreams so real she swore they actually happened. Kimmie's mom took her to different doctors then, who asked a different set of questions, and left Kimmie feeling like she was fundamentally broken inside. That was when she started thinking about death in a different way. Not as a way to stop hurting, but because she might as well. *She might as well.*

Church ended up saving her life, but not in that way church usually did. Kimmie's mom liked going to the Adventist church because that's where the other Koreans were, and it was an easy way to get food and conversation similar to her childhood. Eun-ae Jones took Kimmie there not as a way to find god but community. It was there that Kimmie met the old woman who said, *This is* shinbyeong. *Your daughter is experiencing self-loss. She is a shaman and needs divine wind. Her sickness will not end unless she accepts her calling.* Eun-ae didn't like that. *Mudang* weren't much better than cheap fortune-tellers in her mind, and anyway, this was America and that didn't happen here. She married a white man, for God's sake, her daughter was practically white. It didn't make sense. But the old woman insisted, *Do you want her to get better or not?* Kimmie's mother did. So did Kimmie.

***

(When the ride ended, she was lifted again. The kid slid her body onto a soft pile of clothing among the boxes in the garage. He pulled an old coat over the top, creating a cave that emanated the sweetness of old ladies who frequently powdered themselves—a light rose motif that played ironically well in the deep recesses of Rainbow's ancestral brain. The pizza kid lifted her head to help her lap water from a hubcap. He broke bits of pepperoni and crust into bite-sized pieces and left them where her tongue could reach them. Much later, she heard him practicing his orations like songs. Like monks chanting in the distance, they were a comfort.)

***

I can't wait, don't you see? There's a god out there who doesn't know what's happening. They're in pain and they need help. And I have to help. Kimmie shouldn't have to explain herself to the dead. The ghost should know. (He should *know*.)

The ghost remained stubborn. *Do you know how many small gods are born* every day? You'd think the numbers would lessen in this modern age, but people don't ever stop worshipping. They've just changed the objects of adoration. It used to be saints' bones, now it's internet memes. It's dead celebrities, or social media influencers. Or it's a dead child and her dog at the corner of a busy intersection. The worship has to go somewhere.

Kimmie twisted a ring around her right thumb, the only piece of jewelry she consistently wore. A college boyfriend once tried to give her a promise ring and she'd laughed in his face. But the thumb ring was a reminder to mourn. A reminder of a higher calling and a promise and a grief no one will ever understand. Slowly, she said, *You know where she is.*

You shouldn't even exist, the ghost said. Kimmie didn't understand why he was so mad this time. He helped her with a dozen different exorcisms and purifications before. He stood up, and paced back and forth. The air around them dimmed, and she could taste ash in her mouth, the flavor of the angry dead. *A* tuigi *like you shouldn't have this kind of power. Stop meddling.* The insult for mixed-race children was like spitting oil in her face. The slur sat there between them, pungent and acidic, gnawing at the edges of silence between shaman and ghost. Then Kimmie asked, *How did you die?*

***

(It was the smell of roses that did it. For a moment, there was a melody and a memory, and it was roses that carried something faint and full of grief. The boy carried her in his arms and tried to entice her with a stick. *But the roses*, she wanted to tell him. *It was always roses. The people came singing and carrying roses but the roses always died. Why did no one ever save the roses?* It seemed very important that the boy should know that. He put the stick under her nose and she bit it. Her tail thumped. There was something beautiful in that stick.)

***

Oh, shove off, the ghost said, collapsing onto the bench again. Kimmie persisted. *It was a hit and run, wasn't it? Like little Sarah Atherton.* The ghost said, *no you stupid* tuigi, *I was a drunk driver. Hit a pole. Died on impact. No one mourned me. Christ, and who would have? But dead isn't so bad. You never wondered about me before?*

It seemed rude to ask, Kimmie said. All the other ghosts Kimmie met had been dead for a very long time. She never knew why it was only Koreans, except that it probably had something to do with belief. The ghosts who didn't expect to talk to shamans never did. (Although Kimmie is pretty sure she'd have decent success with a Oujia board, if she ever dared.)

I was three-years-old when we moved to America, the ghost said. *My mother would tell me about the* **mudang** *on the island she grew up on. They always seemed like such incredible people. I like helping you. Even if you're not like the stories.* Kimmie didn't say anything. She only thought about how her own mother had never told her any shaman stories. Her own mother still didn't believe in that sort of thing. Once Kimmie miraculously recovered, Eun-ae Jones never mentioned Kimmie's illness, the old woman, or the word *shaman* ever again. She stopped going to church, too.

Finally, the ghost said, *It was one of those Uber Eats guys. He took the god somewhere west of here. Go back to the shrine, pick up one of the dead flowers, and then go where it tells you. The god is connected to the shrine, don't you even know that much?* The ghost didn't wait for an answer. He disappeared, knocking over the can. Tea puddled around Kimmie's feet. An offering rejected.

***

(At some point, she split apart. There was the Rainbow with the stick, and the Rainbow filled with roses. The Rainbow filled with roses was thinking about the brightness in small acts. Suddenly, it felt like she knew a secret about the world that others did not. A timeless, antediluvian knowledge that if only everyone knew, then there would be nothing horrible. It was a oneness and with it came peace. The boy throwing the stick, who would bend down and run his hands through her fur, he carried in him that same brightness that Rainbow did, that the ground did, that the clouds did. If only he knew about the brightness in both of them, then everything would be just fine. The Rainbow with the stick thought about how much she loved that moment when the stick was in the air and she had to devote her entire being to catching it and bringing it back.)

***

Kimmie chose one of the dead roses. There were so many roses around the shrine it seemed like the best choice. She had to glance around before she bent down and picked it up. For a brief paranoid second, she thought maybe the old woman from the coffee shop would come running out and yell at her for stealing. Surely, no matter the context, it was not illegal to pick up a dead flower from the ground. (That logic didn't matter. Kimmie Jones possessed an overly heightened respect for the law and obedience, so anxiety always made her sick when she had to do anything that might not be proper.)

It would not have surprised her if the dead rose actually started talking to her; stranger things had happened through the course of fulfilling her calling, but as soon as she picked it up, she knew the ghost hadn't been literal when he'd said, *Go where it tells you.* The memento mori acted like a compass in her mind, and by the time she climbed back into her ancient Subaru she knew where to go. (When she was nineteen, new to university and taking her first Korean Literature class, she asked her mother, *Should we be driving Japanese cars? After what they did?* And her mother just snorted and said, *They're the best cars. What else matters?*)

West, the ghost said. The dead rose also sent her west. The streets of Tucson were long and straight, in nice parallel and perpendicular lines that made it easy to navigate. Not being a particularly enthusiastic driver, Kimmie always appreciated that. The speed limit that never surpassed 40 mph allowed her mind to drift during an otherwise tense activity.

The worship has to go somewhere. That's what the ghost said. *Small gods are born every day.* Most people weren't religious these days, and if they were, they kept it to themselves. Kimmie had a coworker who read the bible during her lunch break and had the good sense not to bring it up in conversation. But people *do* worship, Kimmie thought. It was instinctual, like breathing, like falling in love. People lived their lives finding and cherishing so many infinitely precious things. People never stopped needing solace. Like the word on the concrete wall: Rejoice! People would always find reasons to rejoice.

***

(*Hey, are you okay?* The kid said, when they collapsed together in the driveway. *You have to be okay. I know we just met, but I love you.* Rainbow's tail thumped in response, and she looked up at the boy adoringly. Inside, the music of the spheres sent reverberations that touched the deepest part of Rainbow's soul.)

***

Driving along Tucson's grid, Kimmie thought about the early years. For Kimmie, the only early years that mattered were those years after she became a shaman, as if she wasn't really a person until then. At fifteen, she made all the stupid mistakes with the divine that a four-year-old might while playing with scissors. It wasn't like there were books she could read to tell her what to do. Any more than there were books that could tell her how to be properly Korean. She had one mentor, the old woman who helped her through the *shinbyeong*, who quickly left her to her own devices.

It was easier to talk to gods and ghosts than her classmates. In those days, Kimmie thought she was redefining loneliness. Everything was so intense at fifteen, and she was convinced that she felt an isolation that no one had ever experienced before. Growing up where the majority of the people didn't know the difference between Japan and Korea and China, and living with her ability to talk to ghosts and gods, some might forgive young Kimmie for feeling like she had a proprietary hold over *lonely*. Some might forgive fifteen-year-old Kimmie, but thirty-four-year-old Kimmie could not. Her young self was insufferable.

The best thing that could be said about young Kimmie was that at least she was on the sidelines. If she'd had the slightest bit of charisma, she probably could have started her own cult. As it was, that fell to Claudia Padovano. Kimmie tried not to think too much about Claudia anymore. Except she still wore Mary Mary's silver thumb ring, and she couldn't think about Mary Mary without thinking about Claudia Padovano, who had, after all, created the god.

The worst thing that could be said about young Kimmie was that she was desperate for anyone's approval. So when Claudia Padovano came to her and said, *hey, you're into all that freaky ghost stuff, right? Do you know how to cast spells?* Kimmie didn't tell her to go away. Claudia Padovano wasn't the kind of person anyone told to go away. It was such a flattering thing to be noticed by her, that Kimmie couldn't help but brag a little. *I talk to ghosts, actually. I'm a shaman.* Claudia surrounded by a group of people would have laughed at that, but Claudia on her own just smiled and said, *Really? What's that like?* No one had ever smiled and asked Kimmie what it was like to be her before, so she told Claudia everything.

***

(It was coming closer now. Rainbow didn't know what, but it felt familiar. It was at the same time a homecoming and a final departure. The kid touched her nose and she ran her tongue under his hand. There was love here, Rainbow thought. Right here. The same as what was carried with the roses. She was beginning to understand something just as it was getting too late for revelations to matter.)

***

Claudia enjoyed the story of being a shaman so much, she told everyone she was one. Claimed she was descended from Italian witches, and she talked to a ghost called Mary Mary. She took everything Kimmie had explained about Korean culture and then got it all wrong by making it her own. It was all over the school by the time Kimmie heard it, and by then, it was far too late to do anything about it. Claudia never talked to Kimmie again. The rapid network of high school rumor ensured Kimmie still heard all about what Claudia said. *Mary Mary told me when you're going to die. Mary Mary told me you're going to marry Brett Hendricks. Mary Mary told me that we're going to win the football game this weekend.* If it had been anyone but Claudia, maybe nothing would have happened. Since it *was* Claudia, the whole school fell in love with Mary Mary. Girls in Kimmie's math class would say, *Mary Mary came to my dreams last night. It was so freaky. She wants me to cut my hair.* It was a perfectly normal thing to hear someone say, *Mary Mary told me I shouldn't talk to you.*

Of course, it was only inevitable that Kimmie started seeing Mary Mary around school. Their own patron god, created by a dozen different private rituals and prayers. *Wear these bracelets, it will connect us to Mary Mary. Leave out a cup of cranberry juice under the full moon, and Mary Mary will bless you.* At first it was horrifying, but then it was sad. Like all high school legends, Mary Mary lost her glory. The rumor network started circulating the possibility that choir sweetheart Laura Jenkins was pregnant, and that was a much more interesting thing to talk about, and so eventually people stopped talking about Mary Mary.

Walking past the diminishing body of Mary Mary every day and pretending not to see her was the cruelest thing Kimmie had ever done. The god didn't understand what was happening. It was born, it was worshipped, and now it was fading away. Kimmie could feel her pain like a thorn embedded deep in the flesh of Kimmie's palm—constant but ultimately ignorable. Mary Mary would sit at the center of the quad, tears streaming down her eyes, hands out like cup, begging apathetic students to worship her. When she was all but disappeared, Kimmie finally approached her. *Hey,* she said. *Do you want to go somewhere?* As a shaman, she could be possessed by gods as easily as she could ghosts. Her terms only. So she let Mary Mary inside, thinking she could just take her somewhere else, somewhere gods could be happy.

But Mary Mary just wanted to go to school. She went to Kimmie's classes, she took notes, she raised her hand and answered questions, and ate cafeteria pizza at a crowded lunch table. For about three months, the school had worshipped Mary Mary. So for one day, Mary Mary experienced every mundane task at school and made it a precious, reverent act. When the day was done, Mary Mary bought the silver thumb ring. It was on mark-down at a pop-up tent vendor near the school; only five bucks. She liked the look of it on Kimmie's hand. Then she said, *Thank you,* and disappeared forever.

***

(The revelation was this: that if the love brought in roses meant anything, and if the love gloried to the skies above meant anything, then the love right here, carried in a stick thrown in the air, carried in the arm around her body, meant the exact same thing. If anything was worthy of being worshipped, then all things were worthy of being worshipped. Rainbow wished she could tell that to the boy, because she thought he would like to know.)

***

Kimmie pulled up alongside someone's dirt driveway, and then sat in her car for about a minute before it got too hot to be there without the air conditioner on. There was a teenager sitting with his dog in front of his open garage. In a couple years, he'd be just like one of the college students she often saw around town: young, budding intellectual, sure of himself. He'd probably carry Neruda in his back pocket and hang around coffee shops. He had an array of rainbow bracelets around his left wrist, and his right arm slung around the dog.

It took her a minute to realize where the god went. Not little Sarah Atherton after all. Or at least, not just her. The worshipped came back and found a nearby body. Usually a messy circumstance, but not this time. Kimmie looked down at the dog, who looked back at her, panting and thumping its tail. *You lost or something?* The guy said, wary. *I was visiting a friend,* Kimmie said quickly. *Cute dog. She looks sick.*

I just found her today. Do you think she's going to die? And Kimmie, quick with lies, said, *I have a little vet training, can I take a look?* If their positions had been reversed, Kimmie would certainly object to a stranger approaching her like this, but the guy didn't seem to mind. Kimmie bent down at the dog, who licked her palm. The ghost was right—away from the shine, the god was already fading away. More beast than divine at this point, but still in pain. Silently, so only the god could hear, Kimmie said, *Do you want to go somewhere?*

To this day, she didn't know how to explain why it was important to her that she remember and mourn for Mary Mary. She had no doubt that all the students that created her with their mock rituals and rumors and irreverent reverence had long since forgotten. Just like the people who lit candles for little Sarah Atherton would eventually forget the tragedy ever meant something to them. But, Kimmie thought, someone should remember the cherished. Like honoring the ruins of cathedrals, someone needed to preserve the divinity in the small but infinite and precious things. It seemed appropriate that a *tuigi* shaman helped out abandoned gods. The god leapt into Kimmie, filling her with confusion and settling into a comfortable oneness with her surroundings. The dog got up and barked, just a dog, and Kimmie said, *She'll be fine now.* Taking the god with her, she got back into her car.

***

(It was a simple question: *Do you want to go somewhere?* And Rainbow realized that she didn't want to go anywhere. She loved the boy that loved her and she loved the sun and the ground and the stick. If she could choose to be anywhere it would be right here. But even as she knew that this was exactly everything she could have wanted she knew it couldn't last. It was already fading. There was solace offered and solace accepted. It wasn't what she wanted but it was a brightness, and beautiful nonetheless.)

How We Watch What Is Burning
By Emily Polk

Beyond the cracked sidewalk, and the telephone pole with layers of flyers in a rainbow of colors, and the patch of dry brown grass there stood a ten-foot high concrete block wall, caked with dozens of coats of paint. There was a small shrine at the foot of it, with burnt out candles and dead flowers and a few soggy teddy bears. One word of graffiti filled the wall, red letters on a gold background: Rejoice!

"Rejoice my big fat ass," the old man whispered to his dog, a mangy-looking mutt who looked not unlike the old man—gray mustache and gray skin and hairy in the ears and nose. "Who writes this crap? Half the town gone, kids burned alive, so many still missing and you want us to rejoice? I'll show you rej— "

"It's not about the fire," the girl with the blue hair stopped in front of the old man. She pulled her earphones out of her ears. "That graffiti was here before everything burned down," she said. "This used to be the 'Tabernacle of Praise.' Well, on the weekends, anyway. During the week it was just the Boys and Girls Club Rec Center." She looked at the dried brown grass, remembered how it felt under her feet the last time she was outside the gold canvas tent. A month before the fire, the Tabernacle had held its biggest revelry yet, a celebration of the meteor that had just crashed in an uninhabited forest a few hundred miles north of them. She was riding her bike home from her job at the pizza place when she saw the lemonade light spilling outside of the tent. People were praying and prostrating inside. Somebody who looked like Elton John was in the front shouting and others were moaning. The meteor was a message, they said, a sign their Lord was returning. How could anybody have known that a month later another biblical act would destroy their town, their farms, their houses? How could they have known that six boys would die in that very spot? How could the girl have known that her brother would be one of them?

The old man squinted at her. She had brown eyes and big cheeks and bigger knees on skinny legs. He thought she couldn't be more than fifteen or sixteen. "My brother Camden died here during the fire," she said. The man tried to say he was sorry, but the blue-haired girl kept on talking. "The funny thing is," she said, kneeling in front of the small shrine where she began to sit the teddy bears upright and arrange the roses that had dried and scattered their petals. "He was an asshole to me all my life. And now I can't remember that. I just picture him playing basketball, choking on smoke, trying to leave, not knowing it was no use, the fire was everywhere. He was dead before he could run. But I keep thinking if I come here every day, one day I'll see him. I've been here every day for seven months, hoping." She stopped rearranging the petals and looked at the old man. "You look just like your dog."

"I'm sorry about your brother," he said. "And you're not the first person to notice the handsome resemblance between me and my dog. It's the only reason my wife stays with me." The girl smiled and reached over to pet the dog, who was now sniffing the teddy bears. "His name is actually Professor Abraham Van Helsing. But we just call him Professor Abe. So how long have you had that blue hair?" he asked. "Not long. I needed some place to put it," she said. She took a cerulean lock in her fingers. "Put what?" he asked. She let the lock go. "Put the blue. It was so big. This big dark blue thing hurting down in my chest, keeping me from breathing. I needed to get it out. I'm Mia by the way." She stood and held out her hand.

"Walter," he said. "My wife calls me Wally." He said it without thinking and immediately regretted it. He hoped she wouldn't ask where his wife was. He didn't want to say that she just moved to the hospice in Chico; that her mind was loose now, like the clouds; that last winter she fell and broke her neck and after she woke up, all she wanted was to talk about was meteors. He didn't want to tell the girl that he was tired and scared and so he left his wife every morning to drive over an hour across the scorched earth so that he could smell the suffering of other people. How this made him feel less alone. How the smoky smell of charred buildings and homes and the dead trees that stood like burned ghosts made his breath catch in his throat. How he liked that feeling.

But the girl only asked, "What's her name?" And it was a gentle kind of asking. The kind of asking when you know there is a whole other story underneath the question, but nobody needs to tell it if they don't want to. "You want to know her real name or her stage name?" he asked. "Her stage name," Mia said. "Rainbow Salem," he said. "Rainy to me." And this is what he *wanted* to tell her: That half a century ago his wife was the greatest jazz singer in New York City; that she sang under the chandeliers of the Rainbow Room on the 65 floor of 30 Rockefeller Plaza every other Saturday night where he played the piano, and it took him two years to ask her for a drink and by then everybody knew her as the "Rainbow Girl" and she loved this name so much that she always wore a rainbow scarf when she sang. He would have told the girl all of this, but just then, Professor Abe trotted over to the concrete wall, lifted his right leg and relieved himself right over the "oi" in 'Rejoice!' "OI!" said the old man who looked just like his dog. The girl with the blue hair laughed, and then they were friends.

He came back every day after that at the same time and so did she.

Sometimes Mia gave Wally her other earpiece and they listened to her music while they walked around the wall. Sometimes Wally told her about his life with Rainbow in New York City; the way the sidewalks sweat in the summer, how his mother wanted him to be a classical pianist but jazz was what made his fingers move; how Rainy always came home smelling like the flower perfumes of the fancy ladies who came to hear her sing, how she came from a long line of singing women, how she sang in her sleep, just like her mother and her mother's mother. The couple had moved out west 20 years earlier to take care of Rainy's father and didn't plan on staying. But things were different when they visited New York. Fewer and fewer people remembered the Rainbow Girl. There were better piano players in the clubs. "Better not to go back," Wally told Mia. "Leave the memories alone. They do better when they have their space."

"Someday I hope to have a place not to go back to," Mia said. She had lived her whole life just down the street from the Tabernacle, in a small cabin spared by the fire. Wally smiled and winked at her. They walked around the concrete wall for nearly an hour, before Mia had to leave for work. "How come the pizza joint didn't burn down?" Wally asked her. "It did," she told him. "But not all of it was ruined. I think the walk-in freezer saved it." Mia had hid in the freezer during the fire. Everything happened so fast she could barely remember how she found her way in there, except that the pizza kid had pulled her in. The pizza kid was the most *good* person Mia knew. He was famous in town for delivering a pizza and then staying to fix a leaking sink or prune a fruit tree or keep somebody company while they ate. Mia once heard him tell a customer that he was saving his pizza money to go to seminary school. The truth was she didn't actually know if he was *truly* good or just longing to be good, but his longing felt familiar and stirred in her an affection that made her run in the other direction when she saw him. His real name was Rowan and he wasn't really a kid even though the customers called him that; at 18, he was two years older than Mia, the same age as her brother.

During the fire they had squatted on the ground of the freezer inches from each other. She could feel the warmth from his body as they huddled, shivering. Everything smelled like frozen pepperoni. "I was going to see the meteorite tonight," he whispered. He folded his knees up to his chest and rested his head on them. Mia thought of the photos all over the news. Most of them showed hundreds of flattened trees and beige dust clouds, not unlike a bomb explosion. She was struck by how something so beautiful could also look so violent and had wanted to see it for herself. "How were you going to get to it? There are no roads and the government isn't letting anybody near it," she said. "None of that's true," the pizza kid told her. "My neighbors work for the forest service. They say there *are* trails out there—old logging roads that aren't public. One of them goes right near it. There's an old garage not too far from it that the forest service uses to store old equipment and uniforms. People have parked there and hiked out to it. I was going to try tonight." Mia was about to ask if she could go with him when she remembered the fire burning outside.

Her thoughts turned anxiously to her mother and brother. She hoped they were okay. The pizza kid felt her shivering and began to sing quietly. *"Oh Come Oh Come Emmanuel, And ransom captive Israel, That mourns in lonely exile here, Until the son of God appears."* His voice was a soft tenor that weaved a blanket of sound over her, lulling her into a cold, uneasy sleep. She dreamed of falling stars and of a boy who wanted to know God. Only later, after she woke and the fire was gone, did she wonder at what point in her dreaming did her brother die.

One morning Mia found Wally staring at the concrete wall with a bemused expression. Professor Abe seemed to be staring at it too. Underneath the red-lettered "Rejoice!" somebody had written, "Jesus Hates Meateors!" Wally turned to Mia. "Could it be true? Are meteors made out of meat? Does Jesus hate them?" Mia took a deep breath. "I've been meaning to tell you. Our meteor is made out of a pig from outer space. Jesus hates pigs from outer space."

Wally pretended to look devastated. "Well, Rainy won't be happy about this," he said. "That meteor is the only thing she talks about. She's got the nurses reading her every book they can find about comets, asteroids, shooting stars, who knows what. Last week, I was pushing her wheelchair outside and she noticed a silver hubcap the shape of a star and she's convinced it was once part of the meteor. Now she makes me fill it up with water so she can drink from it. She thinks she's drinking from her star." The image made Mia smile. "She's got us listening to all the astronomy podcasts—Skywatch, Astronomycast, StarDate. Do you know meteorites strike different places on earth about once every five years? This is serious business here, right Professor Abe?" Wally's dog looked up at him for a moment and then went back to sniffing the brown grass.

"Wally, we can take her there! To the meteor. She can see it for herself," Mia said. "If you think she can make the trip. I know a way." Wally frowned. "Nobody knows," he said. "Those are rumors; there aren't even roads up there." Mia told him what the pizza kid had told her. She knew he hadn't made it up there yet and might be willing to take them too. Wally shuffled his feet. "I don't know if she can make it," he said. "She'll need to be carried, she's paralyzed below her neck you know, and her mind, it's not all there, what if she—" Mia put her hand on his arm. "We can try," she said. Later, she thought that was all anybody had no matter how young or old or sad you were. The trying.

On Sunday night, Mia carried a large pepperoni pizza and a large cheese pizza out to the delivery truck. Then she climbed into the passenger seat and waited. The pizza kid was closing the restaurant and then he would drive them to meet Wally and Rainbow at the hospice. From there they would drive nearly five hours to the garage hidden in the woods. At dawn, they would hike out to the meteorite. The truck, which didn't need to be returned until Tuesday, had an open cargo bed in the back where they could fit Rainy's wheel chair, bed, food, and any other supplies they needed.

It was well past 10 p.m. when the kid climbed into the truck. Mia was struck by the wildness of his brown curly hair; as though a small untamed part of him was escaping through the civilized container of his carefully restrained body. As they drove in silence through the darkness it was impossible to see the charred ruins left from the fire or the green buds that had grown at the feet of blackened trees, and now more than half a year later, were nearly a foot high, spindly green petals reaching toward the sky. "Did you know Cam?" she finally spoke and her voice sounded strange to her. "I'm really sorry," he said. "I didn't know your brother. I didn't know anybody who died in the fire." A pinching that felt like envy squeezed her stomach. "I figured you didn't," she said. "He probably would have hated you. Almost as much as he hated me and my mom. But not quite as much." She was trying to sound funny, but her words came out sad. She fiddled with the zipper on her jacket. "It'll be a year this fall," she said. "But everything inside is still burning. I wish somebody could tell me when the burning stops."

"I don't know when the burning stops," Rowan said. "But I know he didn't hate you. I know that for sure." Mia looked at him. He looked older than 17 to her, but his face was still innocent, not quite a grown man. "You already sound like a priest," she said. "Is it true? You're going to seminary?" He flinched a tiny bit. "I wasn't trying to sound like a priest. But I'd like to go to seminary school. It's hard to get into and I don't know if I'll be good at it—" he said. "Oh, you'll be good at it," she interrupted him. "You're the closest thing to a priest I've ever met." His face was serious. "I didn't say I wanted to be a priest," he said. "I just want a way out. A good way." He didn't say anything more. After a while he started to hum the orations he was studying for his entrance exams, and the night made a story of their small truck on the quiet road, enveloping them in the dark ink of a starless night. When Mia spoke again, they were just pulling into the hospice and she could see Wally standing next to a frail woman in a wheelchair. A small dog was curled up on her lap. Mia's voice was low, almost a whisper. "Thank you," she said. "Thank you for taking us tonight and thank you especially for pulling me into the freezer."

Mia studied Rainbow intently. She was sleeping, a black shawl around her shoulders and another gray blanket over her legs. Her olive skin looked golden in the light of the parking lot street lamps. "You're a good kid to do this for us," Wally said to Rowan, holding out his hand. "This blue-haired mashugana speaks very highly of you." He turned to his wife. "We'll both ride in the back together," Wally said. "If I'm sleeping when we get to the garage, please take her in for me, make sure she's warm. She'll be thirsty I'm sure, and maybe hungry too." They all lifted Rainbow onto the back of the truck in her wheelchair and tied her in. Professor Abe nuzzled himself into her lap as Wally threw a backpack and some blankets into a corner of the truck's bed. And so it was that the old man who looked just like his dog and his wife who could not move her arms or legs, were securely fastened in the back of a pizza delivery truck while a girl with blue hair and a holy pizza kid drove into the night toward a meteorite that crashed into the earth and quietly soothed itself into rock.

Mia watched Rainbow through the truck cab's window and thought of her own mother who had gotten pregnant twice by men as angry and drunk as her own father had been. Her mother who had been alone for as long as Mia could remember. How different it must have been for Rainbow. All of these years with a man who loved her. Did it change a human to be loved for so long? Did it help to shape the voice that made her famous? Did it keep her alive now? "I think that might be it," the kid interrupted her thoughts. "Way over there, do you see it?" They had been following the forest service map, riding slowly on a dirt road that was taking them deeper and deeper into the forest. To the left at the far end, nestled in a small clearing, was a wooden structure. "Let's let Wally sleep for as long as he can," Mia said as they inched closer to the clearing. "We can take care of Rainbow for him." The kid nodded. Then he said in a whisper so gentle it could have been the wind: *"Even to your old age, and to gray hairs I will carry you. I have made, and I will bear; I will carry and will deliver…"*

When the ride ended, she was lifted again. The kid slid her body onto a soft pile of clothing among the boxes in the garage. He pulled an old coat over the top, creating a cave that emanated the sweetness of old ladies who frequently powdered themselves—a light rose motif that played ironically well in the deep recesses of Rainbow's ancestral brain. The pizza kid lifted her head to help her lap water from a hubcap. He broke bits of pepperoni and crust into bite-sized pieces and left them where her tongue could reach them. Much later, she heard him practicing his orations like songs. Like monks chanting in the distance, they were a comfort.

She never asked where she was or where Wally was. Mia watched the pizza kid take care of her and thought that his actions were their own kind of prayer; a kind of answer to every question Mia would ever have. She drifted to sleep among boxes, and the musty smell of old things, listening to his orations and Rainbow's quiet shallow breaths. When she woke a few hours later to a lavender light, the old woman's head was tilted toward her.

"Wally never liked kids," she said. "But he really likes you." Mia smiled. Rainbow's voice was hoarse on top, but smooth with ridges of history underneath. "I'm sorry about your fall," Mia said. Rainbow closed her eyes. Mia thought her eyelids looked like the wings of lightning bugs. "Oh it's alright," she said. "My body's been old and on the way out for a long time. I think I was meant to trade places with that star we're going to see. That star came in, I'm going out." She started to chuckle. "Just don't tell Wally." She turned her head away from Mia and toward the garage door. "Now, if you wouldn't mind, I'll need that old man to help me with a few things. Wally? Wally are you near?" The pitch of her voice rose when she called out, and for a second Mia could hear her singing. She ran out to the truck to get Wally.

Rowan had procured a long thin wooden board from the back of the truck, and right before they were ready to leave he tied an inflatable ridge rest on top of it. Wally laid Rainbow on the ridge rest with her head resting on top of a pillow. He and Rowan fastened her in with multiple cords and ropes and then placed a blanket over her. Professor Abe jumped onto the blanket. "Look at this Casanova here, trying to hitch a ride," Wally said. "Not so fast, Professor Abe. We only carry the Queen."

"Wait, I almost forgot," said Mia. "I brought my brother's compass." She pulled it out of her pocket. "I found it in his room. I thought it might be useful but I'm not sure how to read it." She offered the small circular object with numbers and an arrow to Wally who took it in his hands and looked at it closely. Then he handed it to Rowan. "Do you want to tell her or should I?" he said. "Mia, this isn't a compass," Rowan said. "It's a scale." Mia could see he was tightening his jaw so he wouldn't laugh. "Like a scale for measuring drugs," he said. Mia snatched it out of his hand. "It is?" She looked at it closely. "Dammit, I should have known." She stuffed it in her backpack. "Are we ready to see this fallen star or what? Okay you can laugh now, stop trying to hide it."

Rowan led the single file line with Wally in the middle and Mia at the end. They hoisted Rainbow up and carried her on their heads. She wasn't more than a 100 pounds and between the three of them she wasn't very heavy. They found the trail easily in the wooded area in back of the garage and almost at once they moved as one body—Rainbow was the torso and she and Wally and Rowan were her legs. Mia lost herself in the comradeship of her companions and their shared pilgrimage. She felt as if they were carried along by a current she could not name, but which was strong enough to hold each one of their deepest longings and most secret grief. She could see nothing but the overgrown path and the back of Wally's gray hair and white t-shirt, wet now with sweat. Their feet crunched the dry, brown earth in a steady rhythm, a singular beat comprised of six different footsteps. Professor Abe disappeared into the bramble of oak tree roots and pine needles and fallen bay leaves, reappearing every now and then to scramble between their legs.

Nobody could be sure they were headed in the right direction, but Rowan led them through the dense forest with quiet confidence. Rainbow slept intermittently and let them know when she was awake because she always said the same thing, as though reciting a favorite verse to a long cherished poem. "We are getting closer. Can you feel it? The star feels us, I am sure. We are almost there now. Easy does it, we are almost there."

At some point, Wally turned his attention to the pizza kid's future. "After you get out of this divinity school, are you still going to be able to finagle with the ladies or will that be out of the question?" Mia responded from the back of the line. "He is going to be able to finagle with anybody he wants to, women, men, others, whoever. Don't be so heteronormative." Wally proffered a gasp. "Hetta? Norma? Never liked any of them. Rowan, she's always busting my chops."

The kid's voice came from the front of the pack. "There's a lot you can do after seminary. I'm still trying to figure it out," he said. "Well, if it's allowed," Wally said, "There's a real firecracker here who would make a very entertaining minister's wife." His voice was playful. "I mean she does have blue hair but underneath it, she's a real superior plum." Mia grunted. "You know I can hear you back here. And what does that even mean? What the hell is a plum?" Rowan said nothing, but turned his head back for a second to grin at Wally and Mia. Mia smiled back and quickly looked at the ground.

They stopped to eat the rest of their pizza at a clearing when the sun was high enough in the royal blue sky to turn the land a honey almost-Autumn hue. Mia could not say for sure what she was feeling, except that she had felt something sacred in the walking. Her mind was clear for the first time since the fire. She had a purpose and she knew how to fulfill it. She was cared for and could care for the others. What would happen when they got to the meteor? Part of her never wanted to get there. When she looked up the air was vibrating, as though it were being lit by a kind of electricity. Her body tingled and when she closed her eyes, small white crystals fell behind her lids.

The afternoon took on the faint smell of burning sage and cedar and the air seemed to get drier the farther they walked. Even the bird and bug song sounded dry and dusty. Mia wondered if the trail were not disappearing behind her back, if they were not being swallowed whole by this wild land, sizzling under the late summer sun. Was there a reason the meteor landed in this spot? Was it pulled here by something they would see once they got to the site? They were getting tired. The more tired they got, the heavier Rainbow became, and the closer they had to pay attention to each step.

Nobody would have seen the gun if the man standing behind the pine tree holding it hadn't shouted, "One more step and I'll shoot the shit out of all of you!" Rowan stopped short and Wally and Mia stumbled, almost losing their grip on Rainbow. A man with dried apple skin, dressed in a torn ranger's uniform and a broad-brimmed hat aimed his rifle at the group. "Y'all mind telling me what it is you are doing out here? The forest service closed this land to the public more than 9 months ago." Wally, Rowan and Mia placed Rainbow gently down on the ground. Her eyes were closed. Professor Abe came running out of low-lying bushes and growled at the man. "That a person you were carrying on top of y'all?" The man leaned in to get a closer look. "Yes," Wally said. "She's my wife. She had a bad fall right around the time the meteor crashed here. She can't move her arms or legs." His words came out in quiet gasps.

The man lowered his gun but held it firmly. "I suppose you're trying to make it to that meteor you speak of? The meteor that landed in my backyard?" He spit on the ground. "I've been living out here for over 43 years and now…" He closed his right eye and opened his left one wide. "NOW, since that damn meteor came, I have to deal with hooligans and vagrants trampling out here like it's some city carnival. THIS AIN'T NO CITY CARNIVAL!" He spit again and wiped his mouth with his sleeve. "You people leave your beer cans and drugs, your firecrackers and food, every kind of dirty plastic wrapper and tissue. Who do you think you are?" Mia stared at the gun in his clenched hand. She thought about making a run for it. She couldn't die out here; couldn't do that to her mother.

Wally stepped forward. "My wife is dying," he said. "This meteor is the last thing she wants to see. If you let us pass, I promise we won't be any trouble." The man looked over at Mia and Rowan. "I can't carry her myself. I need their help," Wally said. "Please, sir. We've come all this way." The man walked over to Rainbow. It wasn't clear if he was going to kick her or let them pass.

"The meteor's just over a mile from here, due east," he finally said. "I haven't let anybody pass by here in months," he said. "So you understand I'm breaking very important rules here?" Everybody nodded, except for Rainbow who was still sleeping. "If you promise you won't stay long, and won't do anything stupid, I won't stop you." He picked up his gun and watched the group hoist the sleeping woman on top of their heads. Professor Abe growled softly. The man sighed as they passed and then as an afterthought called after them. "It sure is something to see, a real miracle. Just you wait."

Nobody spoke as they ventured deeper into the woods and Mia's thoughts returned to her mother. She had left a short note for her on the kitchen table and now wondered if that had been enough. Her mother had been stoic since her son's death—accepting condolences with a calm reserve, nodding patiently when others told her how strong she was, what a brave mother. But Mia shared a bed with her and knew everything was different at night. During the mandatory evacuation, Mia and her mother had slept in the basement of the Motel 6 on the outskirts of town after it was converted to a temporary housing shelter. Each night Mia pretended to be asleep as her mother quietly cried herself to sleep. Mia had wanted to touch her, to say something that would soothe her rising and falling body. But she never did.

"Got to take a sentimental journey… Gonna set my heart at ease…Gonna make a sentimental journey…To renew old memories…" At first it seemed as if the melody were coming from deep inside Mia's memories. When she realized it was not coming from her mind, she thought the song must be coming right from the land itself. Then she realized, and her heartbeat quickened. *"Got my bag, got my reservation…Spent each dime I could afford… Like a child in wild anticipation… Long to hear that all aboard…"*

Rainbow was singing. Her voice sounded to Mia like a mama lion licking her cubs; like a swollen cloud right before it rained; like strawberry jam on a fresh baked biscuit. The sound her body made was strong enough to hold the sharp sadness of a girl who lost her brother; of a husband about to lose his wife, but still gentle enough to hold the longing of a boy who wanted to believe in something bigger than himself. Her voice was all of them, but mostly it was a tide pulling them to the shore of a fallen star. "Sing it, Rainy," Wally said, and his own voice faltered. "Nobody sings like the Rainbow Girl. Isn't that what they all say, Rainy? Nobody sings like the Rainbow Girl."

And then there it was. The small dirt canyon through the trees, an open mouth a few hundred feet wide that sucked in all the life around it.

From the angle they were approaching, it was impossible to know if it was a wound or a womb in the earth. Thousands of trees burned and ripped from their roots leaned into the canyon. "Can you just imagine what that meteor must have looked like falling from the sky?" Rowan asked. "The force of so much light and energy in the universe heading right to this one spot."

But Mia couldn't picture it. The closer they got to the canyon, the harder it was for her to breath. Her mind spun with images of the man with the gun and her brother choking on smoke and the melancholy stillness that settled on everything and everyone after the fire. She felt dizzy. Her face had turned a deep shade of rose, freckled with beads of sweat. Rainbow and the wooden platform felt impossibly heavy on her head. Wally heard her labored breathing and turned to her. "Alright, alright, let's take a break here," he said. But Mia didn't want a break. She tottered back and forth. "No break here. We are almost there, keep going," she said.

They veered off the trail and began to walk straight toward the canyon. The light changed from a dappled gold to a brighter yellow. Mia wondered if they weren't walking toward something alive, something from outside their universe that was still breathing down there, with its own history, down in the earth where it had come to rest. Finally, they stopped at the rim. Just below them, a few hundred feet down was their star. It had congealed from its fiery liquid form to a hard gray rock about the size and shape of a leatherback turtle, unevenly rounded, sometimes a rusty red color toward the center but mostly gray and black. It seemed to contain an infinity of undulations, waves that froze as they rose and fell across its thick surface.

They stared down together as one body, holding Rainbow above them. A crow squawked in the distance. "Well, will you look at that! Just a big, giant rock down there!" Rainbow said. She started to laugh. "But I can still see it in my dreams. Oh it was beautiful once. Before it made that big, terrible hole. Before it fell, while it fell, I know it was beautiful once." Wally reached his hand up and put it on top of his wife's. "I know it was," he said. "I remember."

They put Rainbow down and Mia fell to her knees. She put her face in the cold, hard dirt and tried to catch her breath but she couldn't. She started to weep. "I know just how it felt," she whispered. Rowan knelt and put his hand on her back. "The meteor?" he asked. "No," Mia said. "The land right here. I know just how it felt having something so big and sharp and unbearable suddenly smash into it."

She raised herself up from the dirt and walked to the edge. She stared for a long time at the meteorite and then reached into her pocket and took out her brother's scale. Cam would have just graduated high school. He would have been so angry at her for going into his room and taking it. But he wasn't here anymore. He would never know. She opened her mouth and howled, swung wide and threw the scale as hard as she could, aiming for the center of the canyon. It landed a foot in front her with a small thud. "Well…" she said, clapping the dust off her hands and wiping her eyes. "That was anticlimactic."

Rowan walked a few steps and picked it up. "Come with me," he said. "Let's go down to it. Let's go touch it." There was no clear way down to the meteorite, but it wasn't a hard scramble past loose dirt and rock, now that they weren't carrying Rainbow. In a few minutes, they stood before the gray space rock. They both kneeled and put their hands on it. It felt warm to Mia's fingers. Not quite alive, but alive enough to take in some of its sister sunlight and hold it.

"I thought God would be out here," Rowan said and then he laughed, as though there had never been a more stupid idea. "I don't know what I was expecting. I don't even know if I would know this was a meteor if I came upon it myself, it looks just like a big rock in the woods."

"When I was six years old, my mother had a new boyfriend who took all of us camping," Mia said. "We camped along a river, probably not too far from here. Except that when we got there, he only wanted to be with my mom. He told us to get out of his way, go play down at the water." Mia kept her hands on the meteor as she talked. Its hard waves were a comfort to her. "So we did. But the current was really strong where we were swimming and I got caught under a rapid. I couldn't get above the water, I couldn't catch my breath. My brother saw me and pulled me out. He grabbed me under my arms and yanked me onto the bank. When I stopped choking and caught my breath, the first thing I saw was his face. His eyes looked so worried. I had never seen him look like that." Mia looked at Rowan. "That's the only good memory I have of my brother," she said. "It's the only time I've ever had a feeling of God. Before today. I felt that same feeling out here. Not here at the meteor, but while we were walking."

Rowan smiled at her. "Wally was right," he said with affection. "You really are a superior plum." Mia feigned a scowl. "Dude, what does that even mean?" As if responding to the mention of his name, Wally's voice came suddenly from above them. "KIDS!" he called down into the canyon. "We need to get moving out of here! It's getting late and we've got to make it back to the garage before sundown. I don't want to get shot by Ranger Danger. Come on out of there!"

Rowan grabbed Mia's hand and together they climbed back up to Wally and Rainbow, who was sleeping again, and Professor Abe, who was looking a little worn out. The four humans would become one body again, moving steadily through the dust, away from their fallen star and back to the place from where they had come.

In the fall, Mia and Wally stopped meeting at the concrete wall. Instead, she visited him at his home, on evenings when she didn't have school or work. After Rainbow died, she helped him to dye his hair blue and they had laughed for a long time leaning over the kitchen sink, while Professor Abe looked at them with his head turned to the side. She liked to sit with

Wally on the radiator underneath his living room window and watch for shooting stars. Sometimes her mind would wander back to when the big meteor had crashed and she would imagine what it might have been like to actually see it falling from the sky. It wasn't the meteor she liked to imagine, it was everybody *watching* it. Alone together.

Sometimes she imagined her mother and her brother and her whole town looking up at the sky on the night that it fell. She thought this might be the thing that united them all in life and in death: after the fires and the burning, the counting of dead and the soggy shrines with candles and teddy bears, the exaltations to rejoice and the cries to grief—maybe this is what they had left. The memory of a few minutes of kneeling underneath a window, while the draft put goosebumps on bare arms; the air smelling of cut grass and thunderstorms, and brown pine needles that crunched under your feet; the silence amplified by the hum of insects, by relief that for a few minutes, there was nothing to do but stare up at the sky. Everything was quiet because you couldn't talk when the whole weight of the world was crushing your chest, and you weren't sure if you would see anything, or if any of this sky-searching was worth anything at all. Mia imagined Rainbow before her fall, wearing a colorful scarf, holding Professor Abe in her arms, going over to her side porch for the clearest view of her slice of sky and her mother in the kitchen watching through the window next to the sink and her brother Cam, rising out of his bed, walking to the bathroom and sneaking a look out the window, while Mia sat in the dark of her bedroom, looking back and forth between the night sky and the shadows cast by the moon, not wanting the moment to end, knowing that a meteor couldn't save anybody, but still hoping for salvation in the sight of it, as though redemption was hidden in the orange flesh of a shooting star; as though the miracle of its presence was enough to carry them through the burning.

The Reign in Spain
By E. Michael Brehm

Beyond the cracked sidewalk, and the telephone pole with layers of flyers in a rainbow of colors, and the patch of dry brown grass there stood a ten-foot high concrete block wall, caked with dozens of coats of paint. There was a small shrine at the foot of it, with burnt out candles and dead flowers and a few soggy teddy bears. One word of graffiti filled the wall, red letters on a gold background: Rejoice!

Not that she registered any of this at first. Hung over, exhausted, and getting pelted with the last fat drops of an autumn rain, she found just hanging on to consciousness difficult enough. It would take almost no effort at all, she thought, to simply let go of it, to drift away into blissful ignorance of everything around her, to let her mind go wherever it would.

"My dear Iris," he was saying. He crossed the room with a cup in each hand. His silk trousers billowed as he walked, the fabric loose and flowing. The robe he wore was parted enough to reveal the gleaming dark skin of the hairless chest beneath. She knew she shouldn't—ambrosia was a tricky substance in the best of circumstances—but when he handed one of the cups to her, she took it willingly and brought it to her lips. "It seems we have this argument at least once a century, though the rules have been clear since the Harappan Council of 3,146,927: You get the rainbows west of Samarkand, and I get the rainbows east of Samarkand." He paused to take a drink, so she took one, too. "I weary of this discussion. I suggest we solve this between the two of us." He took another drink. She didn't wish to be rude, so... "I propose a wager."

There was more of that story she needed to know, but she left it behind in the ether and returned to a square of sidewalk near the concrete wall, dragged back into awareness by the most unforeseen of circumstances: Someone was chanting to her. In her present condition, that was an obligation that was not entirely welcome, but one simply did not ignore a devotee, however unfortunate their timing. She rolled over, coming off of her back and onto all fours. She tried to stand up, but that was a mistake; all fours it was, then.

"'The RAIN is a PAIN/'bout to drive me inSANE/and if it don't stop soon I'm gonna open a VEIN' and okay, no," the voice said, jarring her awake as it shifted cadence to become normal speech. "Too violent and off topic. Um… 'They say it's no PAIN no GAIN in this here camPAIGN,' and that's a 'pain' sound twice, as well as cliché. 'Gonna bust out of Shawshank like Andy DuFRESNE,' annnnd no. Clever, but no. 'The RAIN in SPAIN stays MAINly on the PLAIN/I'm dumber than Rodgers and his boy HammerSTAIN.'"

Despite the irregular pattern of the orations, the chanting gave her strength. The priest—or whoever was the cause of the rhyming cantos—remained out of sight. His voice was clear, but she could not ascertain his location. She still didn't think she should risk standing up, but she glanced about her, taking stock of her surroundings. She spotted the patch of dry brown grass and crept toward it. Thick foliage from a maple that hung over the wall sheltered this small stretch of ground from the elements, for despite the recent rain the grass was arid and spiky, its blades cracking beneath her feet. She felt a sudden urge and lifted one of her legs, sighing contentedly as the grass turned verdant and green beneath her. *Better*, she thought. She lowered her leg again, then turned and moved toward the shrine. The candles had been useless even before the rain, and drying out the teddy bears would take forever. Still: It's the thought that counts. The 'Rejoice!' was a nice touch, though no part of her felt like rejoicing. Her favorite bit was the rainbow, which ended directly in the center of the bear-candle circle. It not only brightened up the place, but it explained how she got here. She could have sworn the flowers had been dead when she first arrived, but they bloomed now. Whether that was because of the rainbow or her work on the nearby grass was impossible to tell.

"Spain, rain, pain, main," the voice continued, though it sounded more like a grocery list than a chant. "Wait, that's it! Not R-A-I-N rain; R-E-I-G-N *reign*. 'The REIGN in SPAIN GAINED the Christians TERRAIN/ swept down from the Pyrenees and over the PLAINS/ Ferdinand had IsaBELLA/ was one lucky FELLA/ hottest chick in the world since Eleanor of AquiTAINE/ she was a cool fashionISTA/ and a fine-looking SISTA/ he said, Hey, yo, girl, how 'bout a reconQUISTA?/ Aragon and CASTILE/ we could be a big DEAL/ bring the Muslims to HEEL/ make 'em SQUEAL and FEEL Spain has lost its APPEAL.'/ She said 'For REAL and for SURE/ I'm so sick of the MOORS' and wait a minute," the voice said, breaking its rhythm again. "Does 'moor' rhyme with 'for' or with 'sure'?"

"Sure," she said aloud, her first word since her arrival. The priest's voice seemed to be coming from a small hut of some kind, glass walls supported by a metal frame. The rain had fogged the glass, so while she could make out the shape of him, she couldn't see *him*. She needed a better vantage point, so she meandered back across the sidewalk and began to climb the pole, easily grasping both the soggy paper flyers and the wood underneath. "Try something like, 'She said For REAL and for SURE/ I'm so sick of the MOORS/ All this learning and culture is hard to ENDURE/ Your idea has ALLURE/ Keep Christianity PURE/ Our own Garden of Eden in miniaTURE,' or something like that."

She saw the shape of him get even bigger; he must have been seated, before. Then he came out of the hut, appearing unobscured—which *also* rhymed with 'moor,' come to think of it—and the sight of him surprised her. He was just a kid. Honestly, he could not have been a day older than sixty-five. His face was chubby and appeared to be melting, with jowls like wax sagging off his skull. Despite a profusion of hair jutting forth from his nostrils as well as his ears, the top of his head was bare and speckled like a brown egg. He wore a grey overcoat and open galoshes, carried a pizza box in his arms, kept a pencil tucked behind his right ear. She thought he should carry himself with more dignity, if he was truly a priest. And of course, he should have been at least a couple of centuries older. Maybe he was some kind of priest-in-training.

"Say, that's not bad," he said. He shifted the pizza box into his left arm only, then brought down the pencil and began to scribble on the lid. "I mean, it's a little racist—or at least, *religionist*, if that's a thing—and I don't know about the Garden of Eden being larger than all of Spain, but really, that's not bad at all. I—" he paused, suddenly looking around. "Wait. Where are you?"

"Right here," she said, and after that things began to happen very fast. She waved at him from her place on the pole, and as she did she realized she wasn't waving an arm with a hand at the end of it, but rather a front leg that split into two distinct parts, both of which ended with claws. At almost the same time, he gave a quick yell of fright and instinctively struck at her. Luckily for her, he dropped the pencil or she might have been speared with it, but the force of his hand was enough to dislodge her from the pole. For a brief moment she spun and flew through the air, her eyes rolling backward to look at herself. For the first time she registered how colorful she was, bright purple and blue and pink and green all at the same time. It really should have been one of the first things she noticed; she blamed it on the hangover. He probably hadn't seen her because she blended in so well with the flyers on the pole. That was what she was thinking when she hit the wall with a surprising amount of force, her body going *splat!* almost exactly in the center of the 'O' in 'Rejoice!' *A friggin' chameleon*, she thought to herself as her reptilian body tumbled down the wall and settled into the formerly-brown grass. She had a fleeting memory that she had peed there not that much earlier.

Jesus, she thought, but then immediately corrected herself. Not Jesus—he had been a self-righteous little prick ever since the Evangelicals got a hold of him—but *Indra*. She vowed then and there that she would never spend the night drinking with the God of Storms again, and consciousness slipped away from her once more.

"I wish to be summoned," Indra was saying. "Despite my immense power and strength, few call upon me anymore. I have become the stuff of legend, though my storms are every bit as terrifying and my rains every bit as beneficial as they have been since the Dawn of Time. You are a messenger, a conduit between the humans and the divine. My wager, therefore, is simply this. I will send you to a place of my choosing, in a form of my choosing. You will select any human you believe shows promise. You may train them however you like, but before one mortal day has passed, they—alone, and unaided by you—must attempt to summon me. If they succeed, you will have given me what I wish, and in exchange, I will give you the rainbows. All of them: north, south, east or west."

That, she thought as she took another drink of the truly sensational ambrosia, was a prize worth fighting for. If she won, there would be no more errant rainbows, no more messages she tried to deliver where she ended up fifty miles away from where she had planned because he had bent the rainbow to fire lightning. Certainly her power would increase. Not only would she gain strength in the East, but unlike the rest of the Greek Pantheon, she would also gain in the West; as the undisputed Goddess of Rainbows, the LGBTQ contingent alone should elevate her status. Of course, with Indra there was almost always a catch. She reclined further on her divan and looked him directly in the eyes. "And if this mortal I choose fails *to summon you?"*

"Oh, my God!" the kid yelled, bringing her back to the present. That clinched it, really; he had to be a priest-in-training, or he would have known enough to say god*dess*. Still, he dropped the pizza box and ran toward her. He almost lost one of his galoshes—was it possible that was called a *galosh*?—but in three steps he was by her side, kneeling on the damp sidewalk. "Oh, I'm so sorry! I didn't see you! My eyes, they're not what they used to be. Are you all right? How do you talk, anyway? What's your name? Do you have a name? Can you tell me you're all right? What do I call you?"

For someone whose chants had once given her strength, his speech rather annoyed her. She would have preferred he go back to the rain in Spain, or the reign in Spain, or whatever. Her head had hurt *before*, and smacking into the wall had done her no favors. She kept seeing colored spots before her eyes, and she could not tell if they were imaginary or her own skin. "I'll call you Rainbow. Is that all right?" he went on, though he never paused long enough to let her answer. Rainbow was closer to the mark than a lot of other things she had been called, but names hold power, and should not be assigned so lightly. His priestly training had either not progressed very far or was in the hands of incompetents. Still, he seemed genuinely sorry about what had happened, and atonement was a significant part of worship. And she supposed she *had* spooked the kid; certainly she would have tried a different tactic of introduction had she realized she was a reptile. Though her head still hurt and his questions continued to fall on her like the recently departed raindrops, his hands were surprisingly gentle as they cupped her tiny form. She felt herself being lifted, carried across the sidewalk, and then lowered once again as he stooped to collect his discarded pizza box.

She noted the smell of diesel fumes, which suddenly covered her like a damp rag. *The glass hut is a bus stop*, she thought. *Really should have figured that out.* Not for the first time, she tried to recollect just how much she had had to drink the night before. By the time the kid stood up again the bus had departed, but he didn't seem to mind. He carried both pizza and her around the bus stop to the other side, where he had parked a Schwinn bicycle that looked to have been manufactured in the Fifties or Sixties. He had probably only stopped to get out of the rain. The bike was outfitted with a huge wire metal basket on the front, with one of those thumb-push bicycle bells near the right hand grip and an automatic garage door opener near the left.

"I'm sorry about this, Rainbow," the kid said, "but I don't know how else to get you home." He set the pizza box on top of the bike and propped it against the side of the bus stop so he could open it. He laid her down inside on a portion of cardboard that was slick with grease, surrounded by warmth on both sides courtesy of the remaining three-quarters of a large pepperoni. *I'm cold-blooded*, she realized, lazily rolling around to coat herself with the grease. *And what the Hades, I've been called worse than Rainbow. Fine, kid: Rainbow it is.* Then he closed the lid of the box, leaving her in warmth and semi-darkness.

It took the kid a while to get moving while he figured out the balance of the bike and the box. She didn't imagine his clothing helped; a large overcoat and open galoshes were not exactly your standard biking apparel. Nevertheless, after a couple of start-stops and one hard pull of the handlebars that rolled her over and left her back coated with melted cheese—which felt *fantastic*—he managed to find his rhythm. After that, traveling by bicycle-propelled pizza box wasn't that much different than flying. She found it peaceful, and felt herself drifting away into sleep once again, but she shook herself, vowing to hold on as long as possible.

As they picked up speed, the lid of the pizza box opened slightly, allowing her to sit up and peer outside. They rode through a modest residential neighborhood of a vintage that matched the bicycle. Back in the day, it had probably been a sign of success to move here, a chance for new homeowners—or at any rate, new *white* homeowners—to get out of the city and own a two-bedroom, one-bathroom, no-basement, one-car-garage slice of heaven. Now it was trapped in no-man's land, the more affluent either moving further out into more distant suburbs or back into the city to gentrify it. She felt the bicycle veering left, and they turned into a driveway where the garage door was already moving upward. It was a *two*-car garage—this family had been loaded, once upon a time—almost completely filled with wall-to-wall boxes except for an area that contained what at first glance looked like slightly more than half of a Chevy Corvair.

When the ride ended, she was lifted again. The kid slid her body onto a soft pile of clothing among the boxes in the garage. He pulled an old coat over the top, creating a cave that emanated the sweetness of old ladies who frequently powdered themselves—a light rose motif that played ironically well in the deep recesses of Rainbow's ancestral brain. The pizza kid lifted her head to help her lap water from a hubcap. He broke bits of pepperoni and crust into bite-sized pieces and left them where her tongue could reach them. Much later, she heard him practicing his orations like songs. Like monks chanting in the distance, they were a comfort.

"Found myself a RAINbow/working on my MAIN flow/left her in PAIN, though/she never once comPLAINED, yo," the kid went on. She heard him rummaging about in drawers and cupboards, though if the garage was any indication she had no idea how he hoped to find anything. Still, his voice soothed her. She matched her breathing to the rhythm of his words, and soon enough she drifted away once again.

Indra leaned over and poured more into her glass before refilling his own. Three hundred places to sit in this room, but of course he reclined on the divan closest to hers. That simple gesture caused his robe to part further, revealing more of his chest as well as the outline of his upper abs. She could smell his scent—all wind and rain and damp soil and earthworms—which she found every bit as intoxicating as the contents of her glass. "If he fails to summon me," Indra said, smiling, "all is not lost; we will simply settle our disputes in a different fashion. You will marry me, and we will share ownership of the rainbows as husband and wife. It has been lonely since Indrani left me. I also believe—and I hope you won't think me rude to suggest this—that the position I offer is an increase in status for you. You are a companion of Hera: if you become my wife, you will be her equal, Queen of All Eastern Gods. Now you are a messenger who travels by rainbow; married to me, you will become the Goddess of Storms, the Lady of Lightning. You will wield rainbows as weapons to hurl thunderbolts, in addition to sending them as signs of peace when the storm has passed. The power I shall give you as your bridal gift is much greater than that which you now wield. Therefore, as your wedding gift to me, you will give me your word to submit to my will before utilizing that power."

She practically choked on her ambrosia. She broke into a fit of coughing, which only seemed to subside when she took a second, longer drink. "Dude," she said, and it was possible she slurred the word. "First of all, Indrani left you because you had sex with an ape. *I can't exactly say I blame her; you make Zeus look like a guy with high moral standards. Second: Submit to your will? Are you kidding with that?"*

He smiled again. His teeth were gleaming white, nearly perfect except for a tiny gap between the two front ones that she found herself tempted to fill with her tongue. "That is my wager, but you are of course free to decline it. However, my loneliness is real, Iris. I think we have both enjoyed our periodic dalliances, but I find I yearn for companionship on a more regular basis. If I cannot have you as my wife, I will be forced to find another. And it would not do for a new husband to dally with other goddesses, however tempting they may be. So if you choose not to accept my wager, we must be quit of each other, forever. You would leave this night, and we will never see one another again. Shall I fill your glass, while we discuss this further?"

That was how he had done it, the son-of-a-Purusha. He had kept her there all night, plying her with cup after cup of ambrosia until the evening had become a blur of amber-colored liquid and coffee-colored skin and that fabulous smell and all the divans all over the room that they explored one right after the other. At some point—she could not remember precisely when—she had accepted his wager. She *did* remember finally pushing his robe from his shoulders and licking his chest. She had both wanted and enjoyed everything that followed after that, but while she was merely having fun, he had been rigging the odds in order to increase his chances of winning the bet. It was only that morning, after *way* too much to drink and a night of exhaustive lovemaking, that he slid her down the rainbow to the center of that homemade shrine. To top it off, before she left he had changed her into a chameleon—she vaguely remembered him saying something about a form of *his* choosing, not hers—and she had been too hung over to even notice.

"...he said, 'Hey, yo, girl, how 'bout a ReconQUISTA?'" the priest chanted in the distance, but his voice grew louder with each line. "'Aragon and CASTILE/ we could be a big DEAL/ bring the Muslims to HEEL/ make 'em SQUEAL and FEEL Spain has lost its APPEAL.'/ She said 'For REAL and for SURE/ I'm so sick of the MOORS/ All this learning and culture is hard to ENDURE/ Your idea has ALLURE/ We'll make Spain good and PURE/ 'Cuz if Islam's the sickness Christianity's the CURE—"

"I thought you said *mine* was racist," she said. She rolled onto all fours and walked across the pile of clothes, then climbed the box until she could peek over the edge of it. She had no idea how long she had slept, only that for the first time since showing up at the shrine, nothing hurt. "And aside from that, what you're saying isn't really true. Spain wasn't even Spain, at the time. The Moors referred to it as al-Andalus, and it just might have been one of the most tolerant and cosmopolitan places on the planet, back then. Islam wasn't the sickness; the Iberian Peninsula flourished under Muslim rule. And Muslims, Jews, and Christians were mostly getting along OK before Ferdinand and Isabella went on their land-grab."

"Hey, you're awake!" he said, stepping into the garage from the house. She noticed he had changed clothes, the overcoat and galoshes replaced by the pair of bright red Chuck Taylor high-tops and a sensible cardigan in a matching color. "I've been checking on you all night. I was worried. You didn't eat anything at all, and other than the little bit of water you had when you arrived... Well. I didn't know if you were going to make it. I'm glad you did. And you're right about al-Andalus, of course; the Reconquista might have been good for Ferdinand and Isabella—at least after Chris Columbus starting having his way with the New World—but driving out the Muslims and Jews destroyed the Spanish middle class, severely curtailed education, and made certain Spain was never going to be a long-term world power. But that's OK, I'm just getting the conversation started; next week I'll do the whole thing over again, from the Muslim side. I'll probably have to do the Jewish side the week after that. I might even have to do India's side, and then China's side, since most of Spain's wealth ended up there. Anyway, sorry I had to leave you alone for so long; I was filming."

She supposed that others would find his smile grandfatherly, but to her it was impish, like a kid who just made up his own joke and was therefore the only one who found it funny. Still, she had to admit, she was happy to see him. "What is the purpose of all this chanting that you do?"

"I rap about historical events, and I upload them to YouTube. I'm actually a bit of a thing. Online, they call me M.C. JewTube, which is *also* a little racist, but if it gets kids to watch… So I pick a time period or event, and then I write about it. When I think I've covered every side of the issue, I pick a new event and start over. So the purpose of it is education; it's cultural understanding. Most of us don't know our history, and it might solve a lot of conflict if we did. For instance, there was a time when Islam, Christianity and Judaism were considered by many to be very slightly different approaches to one and the same thing. Though I imagine a talking chameleon with excellent working knowledge of the Iberian Peninsula in the late 15th century is probably already well aware of that. So, since I answered your question, is it all right if I ask what exactly is going on here?"

She sighed, which in chameleon form involved an awkward amount of tongue. "That's fair. Put me on the ground, will you?" she said, and he moved forward, holding out his cupped hands while she left the box and climbed onto them. Just as had happened at the bus stop, he lowered her gently to the garage floor, leaving her on all fours between a portion of the Corvair's front fender and a line of five lug nuts. She could only imagine what this might look like from his perspective—a flash of light, she supposed, followed by a rainbow slowly growing from the garage floor until it assumed the shape of an extremely attractive and nude young woman—and concentrated on the transformation itself. Whatever Indra could do, she could undo, now that her head wasn't addled by too much booze and too little sleep.

"My goodness, young lady," he said; she found it cute the way he tried to avoid looking at her nakedness. He turned most of his back to her, his right hand shielding his eyes while his left began to rummage through the boxes nearby. "Do you want me to keel over? At my age, I'm likely to have a heart attack. Here," he said, tossing a dress back over his shoulder, which she caught on the fly. "You're Myra's size, or close enough. Just what are you doing here, anyway?"

The dress was vintage, probably mid-70's, short-sleeved with a narrow waist, long enough that the hem dragged against the lug nuts on the floor. She twirled in it once, the multi-colored fabric a fitting tribute to her demesne, though the polyester scratched a little. "Thank you," she said. "You can turn around now, if you like." He did, glancing at her directly once again. "In answer to your question, my real name is Iris. I'm the Goddess of Rainbows, at least west of Samarkand, and I'm here because I bet Lord Indra that I could find someone who could summon him, so that I might win control of *all* rainbows, all over the world. If I lose, I have to marry him. Sorry to hit you with the truth like that, but I figured you could take it. I don't know what your life story is, but I've seen you talk to a chameleon and then watch it transform into human shape, and it seems like you're a guy who's somewhat comfortable with the miraculous."

"Well," he said, pulling absently at some of the hair that sprouted from his left ear. He caught himself doing that and stopped. "My life story. First, I'm afraid I don't have quite so glamorous an introduction. I'm Herschel, high school history teacher, Internet sensation, and sentimental packrat. I am here because this is the house I grew up in. You are standing in its garage, which now houses nothing else aside from my bicycle, all of Myra's things I cannot bear to donate or throw away, and a classic convertible I once promised my father I could get running, long before I discovered I didn't know how to do that. By day, I teach history at Chester A. Arthur High School. By night, and during the weekends and summers, I post my videos, where young people tell me in the comments section that they learned more from me than they ever learned in school, and that makes me feel good.

"What is perhaps more important is that I am a man whose life can divide by twenty-one. Nothing special happened to me—I was born, grew up in a nice place, went to school, and so on—until I was twenty-one years old, and that was the year my father died. As the eldest son, I had responsibilities, but I was afraid of them, so when enough relatives showed up I snuck out of saying *kaddish* and walked the four blocks to Petrovsky's Deli for a cup of coffee, and the waitress who served it to me was the seventeen-year-old version of Myra. A year later I started teaching, and a year after that we were married, and then life went on, the way it does, until a day came when I was forty-two years old, and Myra was thirty-eight and pregnant for the very first time in our marriage, and not for lack of trying, I can tell you. Like Abraham and Sarah we were, way too old for this, a miracle baby we thought would never come. Then Myra died in childbirth, which I didn't even know was a thing in the late 20th century, but it was. That was also the day Myra gave me my son, who of course had to be named Isaac, and from then on I didn't do anything all that special except try to be a good father to my boy, who grew up to be both smarter than his father and more beautiful than his mother, and who now goes to school in California and makes me proud. And *now* I know that when he finishes his degree next year, I'll retire from teaching and do YouTube full-time, and the *reason* I now know that is because I'm sixty-three years old, and until you came along, nothing special had happened to me this year, so while it's fair to say I didn't know you were coming, it's also fair to say I knew *something* was, and I've been so grateful ever since you showed up because until you did I thought this was the year I was going to die. So I don't know about comfortable. But I'm a 63-year-old man with a beautiful son and two hundred thousand subscribers, and I'm still alive: I know miraculous when I see it."

She hadn't realized, at the bus stop or on the bike ride or when he put her to sleep in a box, how beautiful he was, but she saw it now. She saw his whole life ahead of him, not just this fragile human shell, but everything beyond. She saw him grow from being this young, scared, 63-year-old kid until he flourished—well before his second century, she noted—into a herald of the gods, a messenger like she was, a conduit between the divine and the mortal. She took two steps toward him and cupped his face in her hands. She kissed him on his left cheek, tasting the salt of his tears, and when he made no move to stop her she also kissed his right. But then—"Wait a minute," she said, drawing back to look at him. "You said you've been checking on me all night?"

He shrugged and wiped at his face. "Off and on, yeah. I mean, I slept, also, but I set an alarm and got up to check on you every couple of hours. I don't know much about chameleons. I got on the internet, but that was mostly feeding and environment, so I didn't know what to do for you. I just kept checking to make sure you were still breathing—"

"No, it's OK, Herschel, really," she said, her mind working frantically. What time had she arrived, yesterday? What time was it *now*? "You did everything right. But my bet with Indra only gives me one mortal day. Either I need to get someone to successfully summon him, or I have to marry him. Which, really, might not be all that bad—I mean, he's powerful, and good-looking, and it would make me Queen of All Eastern Gods—except that as part of my marriage contract I have to submit to his will."

"Submit to his will? Are you kidding me?" he said, taking a step closer. His cheeks were still damp, but his eyes showed no sign of his recent tears. "You can't do that, you're a goddess. If you go around willy-nilly, submitting to the gods, what kind of role model would that be? How are women ever going to get equality here, if they can't have it where you come from? No. Screw that: you're going to win this thing. I found you yesterday at around 11. It's just past 10. We've got a little under an hour. I recognize I may not be what you came here looking for, but I'm what you've got. So tell me what I need to do."

She kissed him again, this time on the mouth, her hands playfully tugging on each of his earlobes. "Thank you," she said, and was pleased to see him blush. "All right. We need an astra," she said, and she saw his look of confused surprise get replaced by plain old confusion. "It's a weapon, of sorts, or at least it's something that can be *used* as a weapon. You hold it in your hand while you summon. So let's see... *Vasavi Shakti* was a magical dart. Do you have any kind of dart, Herschel? Bar darts? Lawn darts? A *Dodge* Dart?" He shook his head. "OK... The *vajra* is just a bolt of lightning, that's no help... The *Anjalika Astra* is largely undefined... The *visoshana* is some kind of drying device..."

"That's it!" Herschel cried. "I can do that!" He moved away from her, toward the back of the garage, chucking boxes toward his left or right. "Myra got it for me years ago, as a sort of joke—you should have seen the infomercial, we laughed and laughed, the guy was so funny, but then of course he got in some trouble, but—here it is!" He held up a package emblazoned with a red badge that said *As Seen on TV* in the upper right corner, next to a large single word in a funky orange font: *ShamWow!* "Look," he said, moving back toward her as quickly as he could through the mess. "Original packaging, all eight of them, each one guaranteed to hold twenty times its weight in liquid!"

She couldn't help but smile. "Well, it's unconventional, but I suppose it will have to do. Now, I'm afraid there's no real time to train you properly, but you're a teacher, which means—technically speaking—you're a rabbi. You have your rapping, which is close enough to a chant or incantation. The main thing is to realize—and I promise you this—

nothing is going to happen to you. If Indra doesn't show up, then that's it; I'll leave, and your life will go on as before. If Indra *does* show up, then he owes you a favor and he's not allowed to hurt you, even if he tries to play all high-and-mighty. Now, you summon in two ways, either by praising him so that he wants to show up and hear more, or by insulting him so that he wants to show up and see who's insulting him. Since you don't know a lot about him and I don't have time to teach you much, I'd go with the latter. He's the God of Storms and Lightning, but he's not widely followed anymore due to shifting ideas within Hinduism that won't matter to what you're trying to do. His wife left him, he slept with an ape… You get the idea. Just hold the astra in your hand and whatever you do, don't let it go. Once you start, I can't help you anymore or I lose the bet, so if you have questions, ask them now."

"Please, Goddess," he said to her, and his smile was nothing short of beatific. "I teach high school in the public school system; I know a thing or two about insults. Just… Whatever happens next, I want to say that now that I know you're all right, I have to admit this whole thing has been kind of fun."

He took a step back, distancing himself from her. He nodded to her once, then lifted the package of ShamWows in his right hand. Finally, he tilted his head back, and his incantation began, words spilling forth from his mouth. "Indra, God of STORMS!/ I know this ain't the NORM/ I'm here playing around with the summoning FORM/ It ain't DEformed/ It's FREE form/ /And I aim to REFORM/ Cuz you think you HOT but boy, you barely LUKEWARM/ Rap is the ART FORM that I'm here beSTOWIN'/ But you don't need a weatherman to know you got no wind BLOWIN'," he chanted, while the ceiling of the garage vanished, replaced by a swirling vortex of blue-black clouds. Herschel's face began to show strain, and he closed his eyes, but kept going. "You mess with my goddess and send her on HER TRIP/ Cuz you sittin' home with nobody who WORSHIPS/ You're lonely and SCARED, unprePARED, or imPAIRED/ Cuz you can't get no homies to offer no PRAYERS," he called, and lightning struck from the ceiling, hitting the ShamWows in his right hand and disappearing. Thunder came like a sonic boom, rattling the windows and dislodging a few of the boxes. A deluge of rain began to fall inside of the garage, but what should have drenched the entire place began to circle like a whirlpool, or like water around a drain; all of it funneled directly into the absorbent cloths. Herschel seemed to grow larger in her gaze, his voice strong enough to be heard over the thunder, though his uplifted hand began to shake. "Got no WIFE, a bad LIFE, so you mess with CLIMATES/ And when you get desperate you're off bangin' PRIMATES!" he yelled, while above him wind howled and a black funnel cloud descended. But all of it, *all* of it—the wind, the rain, the lightning, the thunder—seemed to settle into the orange cloths clutched in Herschel's right fist. "What you call a storm ain't much more than a SHOWER/ Been living too long in your ivory TOWER/ Iris can't make rainbows if you won't ALLOW HER?/ That's a goddess, my man, not a delicate FLOWER!/ So if you want a wife, boy, don't knock down, EMPOWER/ Now get your ass here—YOU'VE GOT LESS THAN AN HOUR!"

 The blast came in the form of a powerful gust of wind, strong enough to lift her from her feet, her borrowed dress filling like a sail, blowing her backward into the overhead garage door, where she stayed suspended, her feet at least eighteen inches above the floor. Every box in the garage took flight, smashing into one another and spilling Myra's clothes, which then swirled through the air like multicolored ghosts. The wind grew in strength until the entire garage shook on its concrete slab and she heard the trusses overhead begin to crack—and then just as swiftly it stopped, and she slowly fell from the overhead door until her feet once again touched the ground. Myra's clothes folded themselves in mid-air, gently floating back toward the boxes from whence they had come. The boxes rearranged themselves in orderly stacks. Herschel had not moved, the package of ShamWows held aloft. Only now, directly in front of him, stood Indra, looking angry, and surprised, and yet somehow—she hoped—happy to see her.

Today he wore a long shirt of pale blue silk, the color of the sky whenever one imagines a perfect day. White trousers completed the ensemble, except for the sandals on his feet, which seemed to be made of clouds. She couldn't help it, she *still* found him handsome. But handsome as he was, he had tried to cheat her and failed. She would not go easy on him just because he was gorgeous. "You owe me my rainbows, God of Storms," she said, slowly walking toward them, "*all* of them; north, south, east, and west. And you owe Herschel a boon, for he has summoned you, as you wished." For just a moment, Indra's eyes flashed lightning, but just as quickly they faded again. He nodded to her. He nodded to Herschel. He turned back to her again, and he *bowed*.

A short while later—while Indra muttered and cursed and made a general racket inside the garage—she and Herschel stood together in his driveway. He took the Shamwows—the original packaging had fallen apart due to moisture—and twisted them between his two hands, sending a torrent of water down the asphalt and into the street. For almost fifteen minutes water shot forth from his hands like a tapped fire hydrant, drifting downhill until it fell away into the city sewer grates. He, whose words had summoned a god, had been largely silent ever since, but he turned to her, and took her right hand—which she allowed him to do—and brought it to his lips. "I'm going to miss you," he said, smiling at her. "With you gone, I'm due for another twenty-one years of ordinary."

She smiled at him, and once again took his face between her hands. "I'll let you in on a little secret, Herschel: In no way, shape, or form, are you *ordinary*. I cannot thank you enough for what you did." She could *feel* her new power, like a spring coiled and waiting, but in many ways it felt a lot like finally coming home after a trying journey. "In fact, because of what you did, I'll let you in on *two* little secrets. You're not going to die this year. You're *never* going to die. This," she said, patting him on his collarbone, "this body will give out. And you're quite right: you'll be eighty-four when it happens. By then, you'll have five grandchildren, and the youngest one, Leah, will steal a handkerchief out of your dresser drawer and hold it during *kaddish* because she thinks it smells like you. But that's just Phase One, Herschel. The universe has a lot more in store for you in Phase Two. For example—and only if you're interested—I'm going to need a herald. I would be honored if you would come work with me."

Before he could answer, the automatic garage door began to rise, seemingly of its own accord, but as it ascended she noticed Indra near the button, his lovely silk clothes stained and tattered. He would no doubt view that as something humiliating, but Herschel had asked what he had asked, and she had no control over such things. Still, dirty or otherwise, the God of Storms had fulfilled his end of the bargain. The garage was nearly bare. Not only had all of the boxes been removed, but the space had been swept, washed, and cleaned until the grey concrete gleamed. The only things that remained—in what now seemed like an enormous amount of space—were Herschel's bicycle, in pride of place on one half of the garage. The other half held a fully-restored 1963 Chevrolet Corvair Monza Spyder Convertible, its body a pearl white that looked like sunshine on a cloud, its interior the blue of a bright summer sky, and its ragtop striped like a rainbow, as a reminder of the god and goddess who had entered his life that day. Indra stepped forward and gave Herschel the keys.

"Satisfied?" she asked, and Herschel nodded, tears already streaming down his face. "Then this is where I leave you," she said. She felt her power shift, and then a spectrum of light that perfectly matched his convertible top appeared at her feet, slowly lifting her into the air. "Think about that job I was talking about. It's a standing offer. And thank you again, Herschel." She waved to him, and he blew her a kiss, too emotional for words. She prepared herself to soar even higher, but then she noticed Indra, dirty and smudged and sad, standing all alone by the corner of the garage. Even if he *had* tricked her, she could hardly leave him like that. So she slowed her ascent, and then stopped, and finally began to return to earth once again, until she paused directly in front of him. "Need a lift?" she asked, holding out a hand. He paused. He smiled. And then he bowed, and took her hand, and together the Goddess of Rainbows and the God of Storms rose into the sky and sailed over the town, dragging a multi-colored contrail behind them.

Made of Light
By India Choquette

Beyond the cracked sidewalk, and the telephone pole with layers of flyers in a rainbow of colors, and the patch of dry brown grass, there stood a ten-foot high concrete block wall, caked with dozens of coats of paint. There was a small shrine at the foot of it, with burnt out candles and dead flowers and a few soggy teddy bears. One word of graffiti filled the wall, red letters on a gold background: Rejoice!

It was the last standing wall of the ruined buildings—a single giant tombstone at the back of the now empty lot. A high chain link fence kept out opportunists hoping to make use of free space in Harlem—ball dribbling kids or backyard barbequers. Not that anyone would—at least not anyone who knew the history. And the only people around were people who knew the history. Outsiders avoided the neighborhood in general. Gentrification was a few blocks away, yes, but for now, their reputation protected them. Uncut grass fought its way through the cracks—desperate tufts in a rough sea of broken concrete.

Crossing the lot was a risk, but Rainbow doubted her neighbors could see out of the small yellow windows, their view obscured by large window fans or, for the richest, poorly self-installed air conditioner units. Just this morning during her grocery run, she'd seen one fall from a window—a suicidal appliance. She held her breath and lifted her fingertips, navigating the heavy metal unit to the sidewalk where it landed with a sound no louder than the accidental scrape of a backstage tap dancer. A stupefied rat scuttled away under a parked car. No other visible witnesses. Rainbow hoped that the owner would be down to claim it—the summer was hot, and she knew how it was to sleep without an AC. But she didn't stick around to alert them. That wasn't her job.

What was her job, then? To fetch the groceries from the bodega, to pocket the expensive fruit when the thick eyebrowed clerk wasn't looking, to pay with the EBT card, to return with the groceries, to clean, to cook lunch. To go to family prayer. To return to the kitchen. To wash and dry the dishes. To confess to him. To lie to him. To miss her mother. To this. To that. To while away the hours until the afternoon, when it was her job to pick up the little ones from school.

That was where it started: the tiny ounce of freedom that arrived each day like a holiday when he permitted her to walk alone for twenty-five minutes to gather Indigo, Calm, and Mercy from their overwhelmed school. Her brothers and sisters of spirit, but only half of blood. With the freedom came the desire for more freedom. And after months of practice and secret messages, her deliverance was upon her.

She said goodbye to her spirit mothers. After her mother left, they'd shown up at the apartment door like packages. Rainbow sometimes wondered if it was their impending arrival that broke her mother's back. Rainbow slipped down the stairs, averting her eyes in the off chance she encountered a fellow tenant, "the enemies from within." She'd sworn never to engage with them because they'd called the gray haired woman with the clipboard. The woman had marked her paper when Mercy revealed that the children all slept within arms distance of him—curled at his feet with a limb hanging off or on the lumpy trundle bed. Rainbow slept on the floor on the window side, so that once everyone fell asleep, she could roll under the bed and practice. Little Mercy got in trouble for her big mouth. She wasn't supposed to tell outsiders about their lives. But it didn't matter: the gray haired woman yielded no results, and things went back to normal after he punished then pardoned Mercy, citing heavenly intervention for keeping them safe from the government. Next year, he said, homeschool.

But today—today, the day of the falling air conditioner. It was the heaviest object she'd moved without being in direct contact with the wall. It was the sign she'd been waiting for—the note had said that they'd come for her the day she could overthrow gravity on her own. She didn't blame Mercy for telling the gray haired woman how things were—when she was her age, she'd believed the same thing: that hope came from the outside. But the government wasn't God and was limited in a way He was not. All fell before God's plans. Even her father.

Rainbow's father hadn't realized the door he'd opened when he permitted her to pick up the younger ones in the afternoons. Alone. It was a special privilege. He trusted only his oldest daughter to make the trip without supervision. Even the mothers had to go together for drop off. They were still new to the practice and more susceptible to corruption. But Rainbow had been raised in it, he said. Her faith was the strongest. He didn't know. At the corner, just out of sight from the window, she'd run. Rainbow's legs strengthened over the weeks, and her lungs eased into it. It had gotten easier. If she ran left instead of walking right, she could visit God's wall.

Today, she ran faster. The sight of the wall filled her chest with something thick and watery. She climbed the fence, careful not to catch her dress. Who knew how long she'd be wearing it? She hadn't been able to sneak a change of clothes. She landed softly and ran across the lot. She planted her leather shoes below the graffiti and placed her palms on the wall. She closed her eyes. "Rejoice!" The warmth flowed through her.

***

"Wait, wait! Don't hang up," I said into my headphones. That's how it was, wasn't it? Ella could be mad but still answer. "Listen," I said, merging into her traffic jam of words. "That's not my song anymore. I used to be bump and grind, but now I'm 'Take Me to the River.'" I didn't like to stand here where the explosion happened. Bad luck. I remembered it: the building full of moms and kids, then BAM! It shook the street. I thought it was 9/11 all over again, but it turned out it was our own supposed protectors—a bad gas line. Ella breathed, and I took another shot. "I know it's hard to hear, but the strongest battles go to the strongest soldiers. You're over there still drinking milk when you need to start eating meat." Government bullshit. White supremacists. Ella's shrill voice hurt my eardrums, so I took the left earbud—my good ear—out and flicked off the earwax while she went on.

And Ella went on. And on. Her yelling was why I hadn't come home. I paced. Since the explosion, I avoided this block. Unconscious—like the way I walk down the street with my hands outside my pockets. In plain sight. There was talk—after the dust settled from the two buildings, after the eight names had been spoken on the news, after everyone displaced disappeared—of turning the empty lot into a community garden. But that was the government that wanted that. The community just wanted that not to happen to our buildings. Them not to explode without notice. It was bad enough with the roaches, and the way the water was sometimes a little yellow. Legionnaires. The next door buildings taped up their windows and waited for repairs that never came. This block reminded me that we were disposable, that people didn't care, that we were cursed. I usually avoided the shit out of it.

Not today, though. I glanced at the explosion site, wondering how I'd got there. But let me tell you—the sight I saw caused me to take out my other ear bud. There was a girl in a dress that looked like something my grandma sewed out of old sheets for a doll. It was pale and pink and hung all loose around her, her scraggly brown hair grown all the way past her butt. She had her hands on the wall with her back to me, but around her—I kid you not—the teddy bears, the candles, the dead flowers—all the shit that people put out after—was floating two feet off the ground.

Some shit.

"Christ," said a nasal voice behind me. I jumped. A kid holding a mangy looking Chihuahua stood not more than ten feet from me. He approached the fence, watching the girl. The kid was ugly: not even thirty and already a receded hairline, and he kept his hair long, which made him look like a balding Jesus. He was fat too, not solid, but baby fat. Fat, ugly, bald, teenage Jesus. With bad skin. He wore a Domino's pizza t-shirt, but one that made it certain that he was a fan and not an employee. The dog let out a loud yip. Both me and the kid gave it a look, and it wiggled its body with glee as the floating objects fell with a clatter. The girl followed, hitting the concrete like that big Indonesian tsunami.

"Oh shit," I said. The girl fell hard. "Did she pass out?" I asked ugly Jesus. The kid didn't respond. What did he know? I could hear Ella's screech even though the ear buds were in my hand. I clicked the red button, hanging up on her. I'd pay for that. I checked the street. No one else other than the pizza kid. Even though I'd ended the call—shit, what was I thinking?—I could hear still Ella's voice in my head. "Mouse, you better get out of there!" she'd say. No good could come from a black man standing over a passed out white girl in a deserted lot. Better to leave it. But the pizza kid was staring in a creepy way. Like he was going to cut the girl up and eat her. "I'm gonna call 911," I said. I looked down and put in the numbers. But before I could hit the green button, my skull lit up with pain, and my mind collapsed into darkness. Nothing good, I swore I heard Ella say.

***

"Shut up, Pixie!" Jeremy said, dropping the cinder block. It was only a fragment. He'd been able to pick it up with one hand and smash it into the short black guy's head. Even so, it had scratched him up. His hands were soft. The guy was still breathing. That was okay. An old black guy knew to stay out of white people business. Jeremy sucked his teeth and ran his hand through his hair. Pixie paced along the fence as he stepped up to climb it. He fit his toe in the tiny hole and laced his fingers through the fence. He pulled up and the fence to bulged out like a food baby belly. He held on for a single second. Pixie yelped as he slid to the ground. He couldn't get over this fence. Too fat. "Hey! Rainbow!" he yelled. "You playing dead?" They'd told him her name was Rainbow, which was a stupid name. But they were offering a big payout for her—the biggest yet. She rolled over. Good. They'd promised she'd come willingly.

He looked up the fence again. It was tall. When had he gotten so fat? He knew the answer—when he started working for them. He couldn't trust those fuckers with anything. The past two years, he'd slipped enough bad food to women to be paranoid. Sneaky fuckers. Better to get Domino's from Shawn. He nudged the black guy with his boot. Still out. Jeremy banged his fist into the fence, and the clash moved like ripples down the line. The girl stood up, swaying like she'd just gotten off the Tilt-A-Whirl. "Are you coming or what?" he yelled. She waddled towards him. Pixie ran in circles, her goopy eyes popping. "Spit that out," he said to the dog, stooping down. She'd found a piece of food—a pristine chicken wing, all the meat still on. He was gagging the dog when Rainbow—his cash cow, his deliverance—landed by his side.

***

The kid slid the white van door open with too much aggression, and it bounced back. He swore and shook out his finger. Rainbow peaked in. There weren't any seats in the back, just a pile of empty grease stained Domino's boxes. Her hands shook. She'd absorbed everything from God's wall, and it left her buzzing. The kid pulled something out the pocket of his black jeans. He must be hot. "You have to take this," he said, handing her a small orange pill. "It will stop leakage." She nodded. She already felt a kind of deep internal suck, as if a plug in the bottom of her heart was pulled, sucking her energy into a metaphysical plumbing system. She swallowed the pill dry, letting it scrape the soft insides of her throat like fingernails against a child's neck. "Let me check," he said. She tilted her head back, and he peered into her open mouth. "Lift your tongue." She did. She smelled his meaty breath. "Okay, get in."

She lifted her dress, exposing her knees and hairy shins. She was never allowed to shave. Her first try getting into the van, she tripped on the step. "They're kicking in," the kid grunted, and he lifted her from behind, not waiting for her to stumble again. It was the first time a man other than her father had touched her, and his hands were burning hot through the thin fabric of her dress. Demonic. But weren't angels closer to the sun? While he situated himself in the driver's seat, she lay her face against the cool metal of the van wall. Her body felt outside of her control—the drugs? "I'm not what you expected, right?" the kid said, catching her drooping eyes in the rearview mirror. Her tongue was too lazy to respond. The van started. The dog licked her face, and its slimy tongue unglued her eyes. She caught her rescuer's face again as he pulled away: he was so young—a kid really—with long brown hair and a t-shirt. "People don't expect fatties to be competent," he said. "But I am." The dog looked down at her too, its cloudy eyes full of adoration. She fell into a strange kind of sleep.

In her dream, the dull city glow illuminated the dirty bedroom window. Grime frosted glass. Rainbow rolled under the bed where Mercy's small hot body waited for her. The dense girl was hotter than the sun, and Rainbow pushed her away with a foot. But Mercy's little nails pinched her leg, and she wiggled closer. "What's a rainbow made out of?" Mercy mouthed, too little breath to be a whisper. Rainbow gave her a look in the dark—only the stained mattress separated them from him—but Mercy didn't need a response. She'd asked it a million times. "Light. Rainbows are made of light," Mercy said, reaching out for her older sister and clinging. They held each other and inhaled the dust particles.

When the ride ended, she was lifted again. The kid slid her body onto a soft pile of clothing among the boxes in the garage. He pulled an old coat over the top, creating a cave that emanated the sweetness of old ladies who frequently powdered themselves—a light rose motif that played ironically well in the deep recesses of Rainbow's ancestral brain. The pizza kid lifted her head to help her lap water from a hubcap. He broke bits of pepperoni and crust into bite-sized pieces and left them where her tongue could reach them. Much later, she heard him practicing his orations like songs. Like monks chanting in the distance, they were a comfort.

Like a pigeon, you can't trust people just because they feed you. Rats of the skies. Free food catches pests, and the city was all poison and pests. Rainbow Perkins was born on November 18th, 2000. She was ten years old when her mother left. "I'll think of you every day," her mother had said over and over as they rushed past overflowing garbage cans on their way to the doctor. That was 2010, and Rainbow's stomach cramped and strained even though there was nothing left to push out. Food poisoning, her mother said to her father. "I need to take our daughter to the clinic." A smell coming from Rainbow had settled the argument. It used to bother her that her mother poisoned her to get out. Not anymore. God helps those. Mercy would understand some day. Rainbow fought to open her eyes.

The drug was wearing off, and Rainbow wiggled her fingers. She hadn't dreamed the chanting—the kid was still at it. She would not eat with her face like a dog. Her hands needed to wake up. But grogginess pulled her back under to her mother on a summer day. 2007? 2008? Dates didn't have meaning when her mother was still there. Rainbow had stood on a blue plastic stool over the stove, reaching her short arms to the back burner. She was making hot dogs. She could have them if she made them herself, her mother said. The water boiled, and she tried to lift the pot by the handle. It felt heavier through the potholder, and even with both hands gripping, it tilted. The water burned her thighs, and she tumbled backwards. The boiling water, the pot, and the hot dogs came after her. She screamed but no one came. Hours later, when pain became her new normal, she turned her head to the side and ate a hot dog off the floor. She couldn't bear to move more than that. Rainbow drifted back to consciousness. She was free now. She began to eat the pizza, her stiff fingers pushing the pieces between her lips. Salty, crisp, still warm.

***

The graffiti at the explosion site appeared overnight. Before "Rejoice!" took over the wall, there were computer printed pictures of the victims encased in little plastic sheaths taped above the offerings. Some thought the graffiti was a miracle: divine assurance that the victims were safe in the kingdom of heaven. But some of us locals thought it was "very fucked up." All graffiti appeared overnight, we said, and it was more likely a racist than an angel. But us cynics didn't want to spoil it for the believers, and the graffiti stayed. And as the teddy bears rotted and the candle jars filled with brown rainwater, the message floated above the site, reminding all who passed to "Rejoice!" Each interpreted it to their own needs.

***

Indigo, Calm, and Mercy stood in front of the school in ascending order of age but descending of intelligence. The boys—Indigo and Calm—were eight. They stood too still for little boys, staring stupidly into space. The teachers recommended special ed but didn't follow through when their guardian wouldn't sign the form. Between their homemade clothes and otherworldly gaze, speech therapy was needed at the very least. Thank god for their sister, the teachers said. The twins would float endlessly if not for the pull of their small sister's gravity.

Mercy's eyes darted side to side, alert as a songbird. Rainbow wasn't there. She was dead or gone. The only reasons to be late. The other days, Rainbow arrived out of breath, running to them. Kids at recess got out of breath when they ran around, too. Mercy watched quietly on the side. Her breath was soft and slow, barely there. Rainbow, who'd held her hand. Rainbow, who'd brushed her hair in the evenings. Gone. "We're walking," Mercy told the twins. "Come on." They followed her, as lifeless as shadows.

***

I knew they were cops from the sound of their boots by my ear. A hand pulled me up. I forced my eyes open. Open NOW. I touched the back of my head—sticky. "Hey, man," I said, trying to smile. I scanned the ground. My phone was gone. Not in the scrubby grass by the fence. Did the pizza kid take it? Or was it just some lucky guy walking by? And the girl? No, it was just me and the cops. One cop was white, one was not. That made sense. They'd been trying to keep the white cops out of the communities. It was just a PR thing, but it was a good PR thing. The white cop's mouth moved. Did I lose my hearing? This was fucked up. The skin of the cop's shaved cheek melded perfectly into his shaved bald head. Just one big egg. I should tell them about the girl. No, I thought watching the cop's white skin stretch as his jaw moved. I better get home to Ella. The white cop pulled out his notebook.

***

Jeremy sat at the opening of the garage, chanting out into the street like a kind of reverse siren. He bellowed, but not enough to drown out the girl. She still had his attention, and he listened for the moment Rainbow stood up behind him. He'd covered her with a coat, and he heard it fall away. They'd told him to be extra careful with her. She was powerful, they said. Okay. So, a glorified human battery, a religious weirdo. Amish? She had contacted them. No one contacted them. Jeremy's job was to drag them kicking and screaming—that was a brag, they were heavily sedated. It took every ounce of willpower not to stare at her as she slept. She was a bomb, and the only way he could turn his back to a bomb was with chanting. Yelling was calming in a way nothing else was—the universal vibrations and all that crap. Pixie at his side, he sang along to the mediation app.

"We didn't go that far," she said. He turned just his head to face her, a demonic head spin on a Buddha body. A fat human owl. He pushed the insults out. She had a piece of food stuck to her face, and her lips were greasy like from the pepperoni. Lip gloss. "I thought it would be further away. Especially when you had that big old van," she said with a shy smile. She was happy. She wanted to go to them! Jesus. He wouldn't even need to feel bad about it this time.

"The facility is across the island," he said. "I needed to feed you. I can't deliver you all drained and hungry." He'd have to knock her out again later. But she didn't need to know that. She nodded slowly, taking in the garage. It was nearly empty except for the van and the pizza boxes. There were some Goodwill discards he'd salvaged from the dumpster behind the store. "Haven't gotten around to recycling," he said, wiping the spit away from the corners of his mouth. Chanting made him drool like crazy.

Pixie let out a yip from his side. Jeremy scooped her into his lap and felt the wetness. Her small rancid mouth was foaming. He'd fed her—when? This morning? No, she'd eaten that trash outside the fence. At the pickup site. The wall. "The wing," he muttered. "Those fuckers." Pixie started hacking, a wave passing through her small body. They'd gotten to her. The past two years, the number of foods he considered safe diminished each day. No street food. That was obvious. A small financial incentive would be all it took to slip something in there. Then the grocery store. That food wasn't attended. Anyone could go in and mess with it. He'd done that for them. Soon, Jeremy only ate Domino's because Shawn worked at Domino's, and Shawn was incorruptible. Shawn paid child support for a baby he never legally got to see. Without Shawn and without the chanting, Jeremy would be nonfunctional from anxiety. And without Pixie. But they had easily set the trap: a nice juicy wing on the ground. She was a dog—she'd go after it. His chest tightened. He'd been so focused on his food that the hadn't considered hers. It started to happen. His throat closed, and he squeezed Pixie to his chest harder than he wanted.

"Get on your side," Rainbow said from somewhere above him. He obeyed. Her strangeness—her open plain face, her antiquated clothes, her freakishly long hair—gave her the feel of an old timey healer. She rubbed his back firmly and medically. A rhythmic circle that calmed the tornado in his lungs, as if she pulled the speed out of him. He lay for a long time, it felt, holding Pixie. He'd adopted her—her little gray face, her little black nails—the day he graduated high school. Shawn's girl, Cassie, hadn't wanted the dog anymore and planned to put her out for the city to swallow. Cassie told Shawn they couldn't keep the dog—not with the baby coming. So, Jeremy stepped up. Pixie'd been the one little body distracting him from his paranoia. But they knew that, didn't they? They knew everything. After a thousand too fast breaths, he slowed, only to find that Pixie had slowed, too. Rainbow removed the dead dog from his arms. He pressed his finger and thumb into his eyelids, and the tears would stay in. Message received. He'd get them Rainbow as soon as possible.

***

Mercy didn't know how to read a clock yet, but they were late. She ran up the stairs using her hands like a cat—hands on the step, then feet bounding behind. Four legs were faster than two. The twins lagged. She knocked quietly on the door, hoping one of the mothers would hear it. Please, she prayed. The way the doorknob turned—slow and angry—she knew it was him. But it wasn't her fault! It was Rainbow. She'd tell him about the nights—the way she made small soft pieces of fabric scraps fly in the space between the floor and the bed frame. And the spoon. Once, Rainbow'd lifted a whole spoon out of a bowl. She'd even lifted Mercy's curls from the back of her neck, tickling her.

***

I didn't walk fast, but I didn't walk slow. I kept my hands out of my pockets. The had cops let me go with a "verbal reminder" that public intoxication was a crime. No shit. I even showed them my head. Drunk, they said. I didn't argue. Did I want to go to the hospital? I should, I thought, but no. I wanted to go home. The cops didn't offer me a ride, not even the black one. I didn't ask for one. I wanted Ella with a warm washcloth, dabbing my blood away. She kept a stocked first aid kit in the bathroom—salve, bandages, peroxide. It amazed me every time she brought it out. She was prepared for whenever for whatever. Not a lot of people like that. And her soft sure hands. I wanted them. I heard their radio buzz as I turned the corner. In the pit of my stomach, I knew someone had reported the girl. Instincts. For what? I didn't know. But I turned under the train tracks and picked up my pace.

**

The pizza kid let her sit in the front seat, and she bounced up and down like a kid. She didn't have to be afraid anymore! He wouldn't leave the apartment to search of her. Or at least he hadn't when her mother left. "Where are we going?" Rainbow asked. The kid recovered quickly from his attack, but his face was still splotchy. There was something urgent, and he'd hustled her back into the van. She felt bad about the dog, but it looked old. Older than either of them. And it was just a dog. But God created all creatures. Still, this was her future. Her future outside! She tried to look less happy. For the pizza kid's sake. With God's wall trapped inside her, her skin hummed. The pill had worked—it kept it in this time.

"They told me you contacted them," he said, his voice thin after his chanting and crying. She nodded. "How?" How could she tell him that she dreamed of the wall? He should know all this. The first chance, she went there. She found the red flyer tacked to the pole. She came back the next day with a pen. She signed her name on a Friday. She returned on Monday to see a new yellow paper with instructions. God was speaking. Finally! She followed the steps, draining the wall into her hands. Not the wall, no, but whatever was stored inside. She recorded the results on the yellow page, hiding her pen in her hair. She went home. Her powers faded over the night. She returned. They wrote more instructions. She practiced. She responded. She got stronger. Then, after months, they wrote a date. And here she was. "Never mind," he said.

He turned left. "You're going back the way we came!" she said. They passed a closet sized salon where a woman named Rita did eyebrows. Rainbow remembered the sign: the long arc drawn in ink, the blue cartoon eye looking seductively from under the arch. She'd passed it three or more times the day her mother abandoned her at the clinic. She had tried to get home after her appointment. But she was alone and lost. Would something she knew from the inside be familiar from the outside? She stumbled back to the eye over and over again, her stomach aching, her throat swelling, her fear rising. It was dark when she found the cracked step at the entrance and climbed the stairs to their apartment. Her legs were small then, and she'd desperately wanted to sit and rest. Her father was surprised to see her. She had been too young to recognize her missed chance at freedom.

The kid shifted his weight in the seat, and the old thing creaked under his weight. "Did they tell you want they wanted you for?" he asked. She'd expected someone older, yes, infinite, and blonde, maybe. Someone from "The Agency." That's what they'd called themselves on the flyers. But she knew divine intervention when she saw it. But maybe He disguised His angels. Jesus dressed in rags, didn't he? The van had rust spots. Rescuing must take a toll, she thought. "Did they tell you?" he asked again, stealing a glance at her with his bloodshot eyes.

"To deliver me from evil," she said, folding her hands in her lap. He gripped the oversized steering wheel, and she saw that an angry red rash covered his knuckles and hands. A thought hit her: what if the notes weren't from God?

***

Mercy knew he had a phone, but she'd never seen it. He called the police. The police! The door was shut, but she could hear. The twins stared out the window. Mercy listened. She heard him say he couldn't go down to the station because he had three small children at home. Mercy stared at her hand on the door. She hated the mole on her arm. It was on the left side, just above the wrist. It was big and lumpy like a small brown mountain. Rainbow had said it made her special. Mercy left her post and climbed on the toilet seat to reach the shelf. Her small fingers closed on the nail clippers. She spun the top part the way Rainbow had showed her, and the tiny piece of metal grew an arm, and she could push, the two sharp pieces coming together. She snipped the top of the mole, just a small chunk. It bled. She hadn't thought it would—thought it was more like how food stuck to Calm's face sometimes. Not a part of herself. She unrolled a piece of toilet paper and blotted the blood away. The chunk was gone, a small uneven crevasse in the smooth mound. The crevasse flooded red. Her songbird eyes darted to the door. She lifted the clippers and cut away another piece of herself, slippery with blood. Get rid of it, she thought.

***

Like most careers, Jeremy hadn't chosen his. Specialized human trafficking was not a special calling. It started with Cassie. Jeremy and Shawn were best friends since middle school. They planned to sign up at Apex for mechanics after graduating, then go on to work in a garage. They'd only discussed it once, at age fourteen, but they weren't the type to review things over and over. They said it once and that was enough. Plan set. But then Cassie was too stupid to take her birth control—how hard is it to set an alarm on your phone?—and she got pregnant, and then she had the baby, and then she got mad at Shawn and took all his money. He got the job at Domino's, and Jeremy started hanging around the back of the Goodwill until a guy in a suit asked him if he owned his van. He did. He and Pixie slept in it. Could he work for cash. He could. He could absolutely. The girls were never any kind of way—black, white, ugly, pretty, fat, thin—young, but not always. He got a picture, a name, and a pickup site. He gave them a tainted bagel, a candy bar, a drink, whatever.

The fear came like the spring—anticipated, but surprising just the same. It was only a matter of time until his employer took him out. But he had to eat. The pizza was safe for now, but they'd get Shawn eventually. They already got Pixie. Rainbow would be a big payout, and once he got that, he'd peace.

Rainbow was a career first. They'd told him not to hurt her, for one. They told him she'd come willingly. She did. She looked both ways at every intersection as he drove, a mixture of joy and apprehension on her face. Her nose was too straight. "This is Mercy's school," she said. "She's my half sister." Jeremy didn't ask. Of course, she had to have a sister. He glanced down at the dashboard clock set deep behind the steering wheel. His chubby fingers at ten and two. It wasn't fair to say he was a human trafficker. He didn't know what they did with the girls. He'd pull the van up to the back of the hospital. The freight elevator went up and down.

They weren't there yet, but he could picture it: the hospital spanned several blocks with walking bridges reaching across the highway like metal cobwebs. He'd pull the van underneath the oldest building. The lot was mostly for broken medical equipment and out of commission ambulances. Junkyard cemetery. He'd back into where the fresh gurney sat. It was there for him, just like they'd promised, and he'd drop the girl onto it, covering her with a sheet. He'd call the elevator. He'd imagine the pulleys straining to lower his weight down and down. LL3 was somewhere deep—below the river, maybe. The door would open. LL3 was under construction and lit by a single clip light. He'd roll the gurney past the drop cloths and sawhorses to the pristine metal door in the back. Light escaped around the edges for the frame. Then he'd leave the girl like a baby on a doorstep—unknowing and unprotected—and go back the way he came. The money would be on the driver's seat of his van when he returned. Once, he'd heard a sound within that room, a sound like—

***

The movement caught the corner of her eye. The kid caught it too, but he was too slow. A black car accelerated, and Rainbow raised her palms and pushed from inside. The car moved faster than the falling air conditioner and it was heavier, but she was charged. The car halted without a sound. The glare from the evening light hid the driver, but something inside told her to push. She did. The car shot backwards out of sight. Glory to God. She dropped her hands. "Are you okay?" she asked, turning to the pizza kid.

"Jesus Christ," he said finally. "Jesus fucking Christ." What kind of angel was he? Angels couldn't do that, couldn't swear like that. She watched him as he looked after the car. Gone. He punched the gas and ran two red lights before pulling under the train track.

Up until the day her mother disappeared, Rainbow didn't know that there was anything beyond unhappiness. Life was just that way. There was death, yes, but that came after the suffering. "She doesn't love you," her father had said, the skin of his hands on the coarse fabric of her shirt. "She doesn't love us." He'd smelled sour and lemony in his closeness, and Rainbow knew he was a liar. If there was nothing else, why would her mother leave? Later that night, he had slammed her pinkie and ring finger in the silverware drawer. Because, he said, Rainbow should have stopped her. The man the mother feared transformed into a man the daughter barely survived. Mercy, the twins, him—they were all inside the unhappiness, but what lay beyond? Angels or demons? "All paths to the Lord are Mercy and Truth." What was she doing?

***

Jeremy's temple throbbed. She had *options*. Unlike him. "You can stop a car with your mind," he said. "What can anyone do to you?" Her plain face stared. "These people—I mean, they killed my dog. And she was just a small, helpless, whatever." He tried to control his breathing. His hands shook. "She wasn't hurting anyone," he said, the sobs coming. "People who hurt defenseless animals don't deserve to live. They have no mercy." He dropped his head to the steering wheel. He heard her pull the door handle, and jump down, light as air. She ran back beyond the underpass. He didn't chase her. Okay then, he thought. At least he did something right before the end. He tried to picture the faces of the women he'd brought in—he couldn't. The gas tank was full. He opened the mediation app on his phone, sliding the volume all the way up. He pulled out and turned east. He would cross the river tonight. He couldn't eat pizza forever. He chanted with the windows down as the smoky wind caught his hair.

***

I was a block from Ella's when the sirens caught up to me. "Paranoid," I muttered to myself. I jogged. Not too fast. There were a million reasons for sirens in New York. A billon. The cop car pulled around the corner and skidded to a stop just across the street. The doors slammed. I started running. They ran, too, and shouted. Two sets of feet behind me. I wasn't young anymore. Forty-five-year old bones. Forty-fucking-five. What was I doing running around? I tripped.

"Don't shoot!" I screamed, throwing my hands up. I needed to show my hands. That was the clearest moment of my life: I knew everything inside me, and I saw everything around me. I saw the way God sees—everything all at once. If I lived, the only thing I ever wanted was to wake each day in Ella's bed. Why hadn't I known that? I heard another set of legs running, not from the cop car, from somewhere else. The gunshot. How can I explain it? I opened my eyes, hoping Ella was there. That it was her legs, and I'd get to see her one last time. But it wasn't Ella—it was the girl from the explosion. The girl was fast. Here's what I can say. The gun fired. The second gun fired. My eyes were open, I swear, and there, standing in front of Rita's big eye, stood the girl, her arm extended, her fist closed. The cops turned; their attention pulled away from my kneeling brown flesh. They shouted and raised their weapons. She stared them down, slowly flipped her hand, and two small pings echoed on the sidewalk. Two bullets fell from her palm. She'd snatched them out of the air. Her face was. Well. She was a meat eater. This was not a soldier drinking milk. The cops froze, but I was up. I was running. And I didn't stop until the door closed behind me, and I collapsed into her lap, apologies flowing from my lips like air. And Ella held me and listened.

***

Up the stairs, eyes up. Two at a time. Rainbow could smell their dinner—something rich and meaty. She planted her feet before the door. His voice passed through the thin walls, and she placed her palms on the door. She couldn't hear Mercy, but she knew she was inside, looking down at her plate, ducking his anger. Rainbow cleared her lungs. Nothing could scare her. She was made of light.

Rainbow's End
By Curtis Clarke

Beyond the cracked sidewalk, and the telephone pole with layers of flyers in a rainbow of colors, and the patch of dry brown grass there stood a ten-foot high concrete block wall, caked with dozens of coats of paint. There was a small shrine at the foot of it, with burnt out candles and dead flowers and a few soggy teddy bears. One word of graffiti filled the wall, red letters on a gold background: Rejoice!

When the councilman came to paint over the graffiti the first time, he gave the message no weight. He assumed the word was a grammatical mistake; as if the writer had meant to say *RE: Joyce*, as though he were informing any passer-by that this memorial was in regards to the abducted girl—as if anyone in town was to think otherwise. As if anyone was unaware of the latest tragedy to befall the Cummings family. As he brushed another coat of gold across the wall and the misunderstood missive, the councilman thought it could only be meant to inform: these flowers and candles are in regards to Joyce Cummings, the graffiti said. That had to be it. Couldn't possibly mean what it said. A thirteen-year-old girl was missing, assumed dead. There was nothing here to celebrate.

***

The Cummings family couldn't find anybody to charge, partly because they never found the girl's body. All the Sheriff's Department had was grainy CCTV footage on a three-second delay, the snapshots of which formed a mosaic showing the last known recorded eighteen seconds of the young girl before she was disappeared. Joyce in her school uniform, with her purple scrunchie and matching shoes, reading the missing dog posters and piano lesson flyers stapled to the telephone pole, before that 2010 Cadillac Sedan (with no rear plates) crept into frame, crept because it knew it was being watched said the Sherriff, and opened its rear-drivers-side-maw to swallow up the schoolgirl and to never spit her back out.

Nana Cummings looked pure, like Mrs. Claus. She was how grandmothers in storybooks looked in your mind. Cancer had taken her husband, a drunk driver had taken her daughter, and now a dark shadow in a Cadillac had taken one of her grandchildren. Life had heaped itself upon the old woman, but she never allowed her old bones to buckle. She still had her virtue, and she still had Alistair. He was her responsibility, and to be responsible for him was enough to keep her going. He was enough to keep her physically mobile and mentally sharp, and that was worthy of praise. And despite all the tragedy that befell her name, her good rapport never diminished. She was as just and lovely as ever. The responsibility towards the boy pulled her in the mornings from the warm covers, it hammered her toes into her sensible shoes, and it had her powdering herself in preparation for the day ahead. She was forever ensconced in that rosy-sweet scent. Alistair told her she looked like a cake, dusting itself with icing sugar, that's why she was so sweet. She powdered herself too with duty, and commitment.

In the unnecessary stacking of difficulties, Nana Cummings couldn't anticipate how challenging it would be to tell Alistair—Alistair who had difficulty understanding so many things already—Alistair, for whom even when the explanations were simple, was never easy. It was a challenge getting him to understand years ago how he'd lost his mother and father on that same road, but to a different, larger, vehicle. Nana Cummings found it hard to transmit to Alistair that Rainbow Street had now taken the boy's baby sister, because the old woman could hardly accept it herself. This was the dreadful reduction of the Cummings clan. Alistair, who now only had Nana Cummings, and Nana Cummings who now had only her grandson left. Her grandson Alistair, who some argued, never really arrived.

They said Alistair was *touched*. That was the softest way they could think to put it. The Lord had just stirred the boy a little too long when cooking him up and some of his stuff got scrambled. If they were feeling mean they might go so far as to say some chunks of the shell got left in the batter. They were indeed on eggshells when little Joyce came into the world—both for the question of her mental capacity, and for young Alistair's ability to process just who she was and what it meant to have a sister. But whatever trepidations the family had buried within were soon assuaged when the family pediatrician gave the infant a clean bill of health. Again all were relieved when the big (usually clumsy) brother held his baby sister in his palms as though she were precious glass, and tried to hide his wet, shining eyes.

As she grew, it was immediately obvious that the girl was brighter than most. The brother and sister were both far from normal, but in opposite directions. If they were feeling spiteful they might say Joyce pinched some of the smarts meant for her brother. Most afternoons Alistair would meet Joyce at her regular school and together they'd walk home along that same cracked sidewalk, down Rainbow Street. Stray dogs had colored the grass with their number ones, and had left number twos to calcify and turn chalky in the sun. They'd take this street maybe four afternoons a week, neither one possessing the possibility to intuit how pivotal that stretch of road would be to their family's lives. And how could they? How could anyone not in possession of the world's darkest crystal ball understand that, for the Cummings family, Rainbow Street was a curse? Sometimes Joyce would hold her big brother's hand as they walked, more for Alistair's sake, though he'd deny it. They were a team, balanced, some yin/yang energy about them. Alistair once bent down by the ten-foot high concrete block wall, pretending to tie his shoe, crumbled the ghost of a dachshund's defecation in his palm, and jumped up to blow the dust at Joyce. She screamed. He giggled.

Mrs. Kimble was the speech pathologist at Alistair's school and she had the boy working on his diction by reciting Shakespeare mostly, some other old stuff too—antiquated works that may as well have been written in another language for how well he could comprehend their meaning, but laid out in such a pristine form of English that (his teacher reasoned) if Alistair could wrap his lips around *these* texts and fling *those* syllables off his tongue, he would therefore never struggle with any words ever again. It was Nana Cummings who decided to further his studies and introduce her grandson to The Good Book. Not because she was an overly religious woman (atheist-adjacent after discovering the driver who killed her daughter had four times the Blood of Christ as was legally allowed on his breath) but she gave her grandson the King James version because if he wanted to master the English language, then these pages were the foundation for how we communicate—or so she told Alistair.

After Joyce was taken, Alistair spoke even less; yet another piece missing. No one was particularly worried, or shocked, or upset—because it seemed natural. He had enough difficulties with the minutia of life, so how could he possibly be expected to process a real tragedy? He was kept occupied. At school he'd continued to read texts Mrs. Kimble (the speech pathologist) presented to him. Like a glistening fish breaching the surface of the water, saliva catching the light, his masticated fingernail skimmed along under another unintelligible soliloquy; but he wouldn't speak the words. Not in public. Not anymore. It was obvious to anyone watching that he was reading, his lips folding in on themselves and popping out the plosives. Tip of the tongue slipping past teeth on the sibilants. He would will himself to read along, able to mouth the words, but lacking the strength to back these mouth shapes with voice. And no one pressed him. Best to let the kid speak up in his own time. Make himself heard when he's ready.

It didn't matter at work. At the pie place, Alistair's employment was more symbolic than necessary. He was more a store mascot than he was a useful member of the team. When he first started the job, to gussy it up, the manager told Alistair his title was as an *Underwater Ceramic Technician*, which made the kid giggle and repeat the job description to anyone who cared to ask. It didn't matter now that he wasn't talking to anyone, because it didn't matter if the dish-pig spoke or not. Dealing predominantly with take-out pizzas, Alistair hardly had any washing-up to do. If it were a quiet night he'd hang around and help out with odd jobs in the kitchen, and if it were busy he'd be sent home to make sure he didn't get in the way. At the end of each shift he was allowed to make himself up a pizza with any toppings he fancied. Most of the time he'd have finished the pie before he reached home, but having always saved two slices for Joyce. Pepperoni was her favorite.

The local folk banded together the weekend after Joyce was abducted and linked arms to march across the barrens on the outer limits of the town proper. To walk side-by-side across the spoilt land behind the tinned-fruit factory and to look down the banks at the edges of the creek, half disgusted, half excited for anything they might find: a scuffed Velcro-strapped shoe, a ripped hair-tie, tiny tarnished underpants - anything maybe belonging to a small girl … anything with blood on it. Instead the volunteers were half relieved, half bored when, as the sun went down signaling the end to that first week, they'd come up with nothing. Worst of all was waiting. Waiting for anything. There were stretches of time that warped and warbled and seemed to go on and on and on, but Alistair would be shocked when he realized that it was still the same day. Equal parts distraction, distress and desperation left him discombobulated. He was helpless, and nothing he did could make things better. By the following Wednesday everywhere that was close enough to search had been scoured, with no sign of Joyce. It was as though that 2010 Cadillac was a black hole and could only absorb, completely, anything that went inside. Not even the light of a child was bright enough to escape. All anyone could hope for now was a miracle.

Nothing needed to be explained in any unsettling detail for Alistair to understand he wouldn't be seeing his baby sister again. In an attempt to shield the kid and his fragile understanding of things, the particulars of his sister's abduction were denied the boy. All he was told was that Joyce had gone away, she still loved her big brother very much, and she didn't want to leave, but she was gone now, and she was in a happy place. But Alistair didn't need spectacular powers of comprehension to see that they were all telling lies. The exhausted, distressed pressure ringing the adults' eyes let Alistair know that these people were not happy, and if the adults weren't happy about what happened to her, then there was no way Joyce could be either. There were no answers—and Alistair was accustomed to not knowing many things, but he was certain there was always an adult somewhere close by who could explain away all the confusion ... but not this time. Not about Joyce. There were no kisses or cuddles to make everything better. And although he knew immediately things were wrong, it still took Alistair a week before he could cry for his sister.

That night while Nana Cummings was sleeping (passed-out really after a handful of something helpful from Dr. Konkoly) Alistair crept, crept in case he was being watched, into Joyce's room. The door and windows had been kept closed. Nothing had been touched yet; the smell of shoes beginning to ripen against the cloying scent of floral deodorant. Dust was collecting along the windowsill. Nana Cummings had made the bed. Because who doesn't love coming home to a made bed? But that was all. Nestled amongst the pillows was Joyce's teddy, a silly toy with a tape player in its body that would move teddy's mouth when you played a cassette so it looked like it was speaking or singing along. She'd had it for years now, but still couldn't admit how much she loved it. Gingerly, and in the semi-darkness of the late evening, Alistair sat down on the bed, and soon slid in under the covers. He didn't turn it on, but hugged his sister's coveted teddy bear and, before he fell completely asleep, had mottled the synthetic fur with his tears.

The bear was as close a pet as Joyce could tolerate before sneezing. Nana Cummings had floated the idea of a dog for the kids before. Lord knows she couldn't tire those two out the way some goofy, energetic Labrador could. And who was she kidding pretending she wouldn't love a little extra companionship around the house herself? They made it all the way to the pound before tiny Joyce let her allergies be known. At about the third cage down, whilst looking at an unkempt Malamute, the young girl began to sneeze, and then sneeze again, and again, over and over until Nana Cummings called the whole thing off. In the car on the ride home Joyce tried to protest, explaining that *her* puppy wouldn't be so scraggly, would be clean, washed regularly and therefore hypoallergenic. Though where on earth the young girl plucked that word from was beyond everyone. Nana Cummings gifted Joyce the Teddy Ruxpin instead.

It was the day after he spent the night in his sister's sad bed that Alistair took the teddy down to *the site*. This was how they referred to that block on Rainbow Street where it happened. The *scene* somehow made it sound worse. There were still fresh wreaths and bouquets, and paper images of Joyce someone had photocopied from the school yearbook. There were letters from strangers calling her an *angel* and a *blessing* and a *treasure*, letters promising she would never be forgotten, even though most scribbling the messages had never before known the girl. There were too a few dolls and toys that were already weather-beaten before being offered to the roadside shrine. The mismatched thrift-store toys made the whole site look more like a curbside pickup. After lunch Alistair brought the Teddy Ruxpin down without Nana Cummings knowing, without anyone seeing him. He swapped her real, cherished, teddy bear for the unknown hand-me-downs that strangers had dumped. He tried not to throw the random and wrong dolls too hard when he tossed them into the closest bin.

The week he found the puppy dog was the same week he began to peruse the King James Bible Nana Cummings had gifted him. He'd completed the readings at his school, and since the speech pathologist and therapist were still not pressing him to vocalize (essentially deferring all his assessment for a semester) he could read through the assigned work much more quickly. At home the boy opened, by chance or by providence, on *Philippians* and began to labor through the verses. It was mid-afternoon he began reading, and between turning one page to another it somehow grew dark outside. Alistair got caught up not so much in the message as he did the language itself. *Whereof, thou, spake*: these ancient, hocus-pocus words seemed to resonate in silence and make the pages tremble under his wet fingertips. It wasn't until Nana Cummings knocked on his door to ask if everything was okay that Alistair realized he'd been reading aloud.

He was following his feet home after work when he found himself again by the site. It wasn't that he sought out Rainbow Street in any masochistic way, it just happened to be a quick route between home and school and the pizza shop. A Bermuda Triangle. Her flowers were all but wilted away and the candles now looked, from the sun and rain, like something Dali had painted. Alistair stopped chewing the slice he held to watch a stray, a puppy, come waddling around from behind the concrete block wall. The pup was a female, a mutt with no collar; forgotten or abandoned, it didn't matter. She bounded in amongst the letters and flowers of the memorial, sniffing everything, lost to her senses, her wrecking-ball tail knocking over more than the photos. Alistair smiled a greasy peperoni smile at the demolition doggo because he was sick of Joyce's shrine too. He was sick of getting sad every time he saw it; though now watching the pup innocently destroy everything started to feel like some kind of antidote. But as the dog approached the Teddy Ruxpin, Alistair straightened up. He was ready to step in should the pup decide

Joyce's bear be a good place as any to lift the leg and go pee. But the pizza kid didn't interfere because the dog was a girl, and girl dogs don't lift their legs to go pee. Instead, the puppy crinkled her nose at the teddy, had a good sniff, and then sneezed.

There was no decisive moment where Alistair knew he would adopt this stray. He simply knew it was time for *them* to leave, like when he and Joyce used to both silently know it was the right moment to move. That yin/yang energy. He was cautious to pick her up lest those puppy teeth needle into his palm. But she was a good dog and didn't bite, or even whimper any objections. She surrendered in his hands with complete trust, the way Joyce used to rag-doll atop him when they were play fighting. Even though the pup was small, she was lighter than he expected. His fingernails thrummed along the pup's ribs. She must be hungry. Alistair took a slice out of the box that was sitting in the basket of his bike and held it to the dog's mouth. Every muscle in her face seemed to flex and she began to paddle the air, like she was stroking her way through water. Straight away she took a round of peperoni and snaffled it up, her tail like a conductors wand during a crescendo. Peperoni was Joyce's favorite. So he lifted the puppy up and sat her atop the near empty pizza-box in the basket of his bike and walked the two of them home.

The bike gears ticked loudly as he wheeled the dog along the road. He'd found her on Rainbow Street and decided on the ride home to name the puppy Rainbow, to avoid confusion. Because it was not that Alistair thought the dog *was* Joyce exactly, but the dog made him think *of* Joyce, and for now, that was enough.

When the ride ended, she was lifted again. The kid slid her body onto a soft pile of clothing among the boxes in the garage. He pulled an old coat over the top, creating a cave that emanated the sweetness of old ladies who frequently powdered themselves—a light rose motif that played ironically well in the deep recesses of Rainbow's ancestral brain.

The pizza kid lifted her head to help her lap water from a hubcap. He broke bits of pepperoni and crust into bite-sized pieces and left them where her tongue could reach them. Much later, she heard him practicing his orations like songs. Like monks chanting in the distance, they were a comfort.

The sound of Alistair's recitations lulled the dog into a slumber, though the boy didn't yet want her to hear his speech. When he came to check on her after dinner, he gave the pup a poke at the neck to make sure it was exhaustion that had the dog lying so still, and nothing worse. Alistair knew he didn't want to keep her in the garage overnight. Despite ensconcing her in Nana Cummings' winter coats, he thought it might get a little too cold out here once it got dark. Plus it must be scary for her (for Rainbow, her name **now** was Rainbow) to be alone in the garage for so long. Even Alistair didn't like the garage at nighttime. And Joyce hated it. So while Nana Cummings sat on her recliner and watched her stories, Alistair slipped the pup up into his shirt and smuggled her from the garage to his room. The high walls of his laundry hamper would keep Rainbow safe, and the clothes themselves would keep her warm. The clothes smelled like him, and this comforted her, helped Rainbow fall back asleep just about as fast as did Alistair.

Alistair saw the shadow man in the 2010 Cadillac. He was a magician. Alistair saw him hop out of the car wearing a top hat and white gloves. He performed a tableau to the CCVT camera, in its strange three second staccato, as though they were a paying audience. He started pulling flowers from out his sleeves. He fanned out a deck of cards and puffed his cheeks like he was blowing out a candle, and the cards vanished. Alistair knew magicians made people disappear and reappear all the time. They could, with the flick of a satin cape, have their assistants' outfit change cut and color before your eyes. They could saw people in half and then stick them back together like it was nothing. As Alistair dreamt he thought maybe this was the driver's big magic? Three seconds. Magic men are scary, and mysterious, and you don't get to peak behind their curtain; you don't get to peak in the backseat of their car to see how they do their tricks. Two seconds. Maybe the magician driving the car disappeared Joyce the girl, only to reappear Rainbow the pup? One second. That would be one hell of a trick. Reveal.

By the end of the week there were pizza boxes cheesed together in Alistair's room. Nana Cummings kept a clean home, and she'd taught her grandson those principals of hygiene and tidying, so hoarding these greasy boxes was out of the question. And it wasn't until she noticed the old hubcap under Alistair's desk holding a puddle of water that she decided to confront the boy for what she suspected to be his depression. There was a smell too about the room. Not the *boy* smell, to which she was accustomed. This was animal, yet milky sweet, a little off but not overly unpleasant. She looked the room over briefly for anything tracked in on a careless shoe, or any spoiled meat that may have fallen under the bed. Nana Cummings found nothing and so decided the stench must be coming from the moldy pizza crusts. She placed the boxes atop the laundry hamper by the door, leaving them near to hand so she could talk to Alistair about them as soon as he came home; all the while deaf to the squeaks coming from the self-same hamper.

Alistair knew that the dog needed space, so he snuck her out of the house and took Rainbow to the creek. There was a clearing out by the banks where teenage couples went to neck and younger children came to play Army, and where he and Joyce came a few times to picnic. But today it was empty. On hot days the smell of rotten apples from the canned fruit factory would be nauseating. But today was not too bad. So Alistair dropped Rainbow down by the tranquil waters to stretch her legs while he practiced his orations in the gentle solitude; humming the speech really, so as not to disrupt Rainbow and her play. The dog barked at her own reflection in the water, jumping repeatedly towards her two-dimensional liquid twin under the water's edge—that bamboozling edge between wet and dry paws. She was too busy to listen to Alistair, throwing feints at her puppy reflection like she was a boxer feeling-out her opponent. Her own shadow, shadowboxing back. Alistair thought it was funny she couldn't recognize herself anymore, and then conceded that her new look was quite different compared to how the Cummings clan normally saw the girl. He clomped over to where she was and splashed his foot in the water, stamping out his own reflection in case it started tricking him like it was … Rainbow. He splashed the water again for stuttering on her new name and the arc of the spray wet the dog, and so she ran off to scratch about in the thick growth behind the fallen logs.

He could practice his orations by the creek because he knew them now, knew them *off book* as Nana Cummings would call it (she used to be in the theatre) but still the words didn't slippery-dip down his tongue the way Alistair knew they should. The consonants got stuck coming out, like they were clinging to his teeth, caught between his molars—maybe this was why he needed to floss more? He spat out one line at a time, repeating the verses while Rainbow sniffed and scratched **around in the thick scrub**. Alistair repeated lines, smoothing them on every pass, and it was around the same time he lost count of the repetitions that the puppy came across a girl's shoe. It was small, dirty purple, with a Velcro strap. It looked familiar, but then again all little girl's shoes looked the same, didn't they? Plus the council volunteers and the Sheriff's Department had scoured the banks and barrens back here, so Alistair told himself the shoe couldn't be that familiar. He picked up Rainbow to pry the dog away from her investigative sniffing. She scrambled in his hands and managed to hold the shoe firm between her teeth when she was lifted.

The reveal of the dog caught the old woman unprepared. She couldn't be mad at the boy for trying to look after the pet with old pizza crusts and dirty water, but she could certainly be mad at him for trying to sneak the dog home in the first place. Aside from the responsibility, cost of food, vet bills, time to look after it, and someone to exercise it properly

... mostly, didn't Alistair think it was perhaps too soon to be adopting something new after something so precious had so recently been lost? Shouldn't they all give it more time? But Alistair explained that they didn't have to give time any longer! He didn't need to wait and waste another day, that none of it mattered any more because of Rainbow. Nana Cummings wasn't exactly sure what her grandson was saying, but then again it wasn't often even *he* was sure of what he was saying. And the old woman could see that the boy was happy, and chatty, and bright—bright like none of them had been since the smallest, most glittering light in the Cummings Clan had been extinguished. Nana Cummings couldn't be mad, but she could let him keep the dog.

Mrs. Kimble sat beside the boy and watched his mouth move; trying at least to read his lips and discern whether his enunciation was improving, to say nothing of his diction. Her leg bounced up and down so much she made the page flutter and Alistair's vision vibrate. Presently she excused herself but told the boy to continue. Nature calls, even for education professionals. She exited her office, leaving Alistair alone with his work, her humming old desktop, and the sky-high shelves of medical books; those tomes that intimidate even the most seasoned reader. As soon as she was safely down the hall, Alistair lurched over to his satchel bag and dug his fingers into the strategically sized opening of the zipper. His fingers were met by a damp *boop* from the dog's nose. Taking some sandwich crusts from his pocket, he dropped a whole-wheat wedge into the bag and watched Rainbow give it the obligatory sniff. What she really wanted was water. Alistair knew this and gave an exasperated apology, promising to get her a drink after recess.

Mrs. Kimble returned while he was still petting Rainbow on the bridge of her snoot. She didn't lose her temper—other children behaved truly shockingly, Alistair had merely snuck a cute little puppy into the school. Adorable, if still wrong. Nana Cummings was called in to come collect both dog and boy. She was none too impressed, but again principally at having had her afternoon shows interrupted as opposed to her grandson's indiscretion. Both women half-heartedly chastised the boy in Mrs. Kimble's office, and Alistair felt that so long as he kept his head down, supplicated, it didn't feel too bad, and it seemed enough to make the women feel they'd done enough. After he'd learnt his lesson (only twelve minutes apparently) it was Mrs. Kimble of all people who suggested to Nana Cummings that maybe it wouldn't be a half bad idea to possibly get the pooch registered as a support animal, if that didn't sound like too wild an idea; that way the boy could take Rainbow anywhere he wanted and he'd be perfectly allowed to have her there … just a suggestion.

Once Rainbow got her assistance card in the mail (complete with puppy-mug-shot-license-photo) it felt nice to know things were now official. There was no need to hide her; more than that, he could have her close, with him all the time. Nana Cummings got a second-hand carrier with a soft mat and mesh front where the dog—sorry Rainbow—where Rainbow could rest when Alistair was busy learning; because he had to remember he was a very lucky boy to be able to have Rainbow as a support dog, and it wasn't an excuse for him to slack off, or get distracted. And Alistair couldn't be mad that Nana Cummings kept calling her *the dog*, because she didn't really understand … not yet. And how could she until she'd spent time enough with Rainbow to be reminded? But Alistair *could* be a little mad with himself for not explaining things to his grandma properly … though only a little. The time wasn't quite right. Still his smile unfolded itself as he imaged how Nana Cummings was going to be once she heard. Once she knew. Her elation, her joy. Her Joyce. This was as much a privilege as it was a responsibility, and Alistair was very aware. He knew this was a blessing. This was a real one, and one that kept unfolding itself. He wasn't about to slip up and neglect his studies and thereby threaten his connection to Rainbow.

If anything, it worked completely to everyone's plan, and beyond their hopes. Alistair improved greatly with the dog close by. What started as a bit of a sneak move to soothe a wounded boy, in turn became an actual panacea for the young man. Soon he was back up to speed with the curriculum and his focus had restored itself. The dog was help, difficult to measure, but there was a definite exercise of will on Alistair's part that contributed greatly. He explained to Nana Cummings that he needed to have her close by and would do whatever he had to, to make sure he didn't lose her … and here the boy stopped himself from saying *again*. But Nana Cummings, like Mrs. Kimble (like Joyce) all too accustomed to reading the lips of the boy who was often reluctant to speak, could interpret the word on which he'd bitten his tongue and translate, understand that he was speaking of his departed sister.

Eventually, he let slip her old name. Nana Cummings heard it, the knell, and let it linger. He was by the back door feeding the dog more pizza crusts, even after the old woman had bought a sixteen-dollar bag of specialty puppy food, and a teething toy for the damn thing. While Nana Cummings did the dishes, Alistair fed the pup and mumbled *peperoni is your favorite, isn't it Joyce*. It came unprovoked. Was his mind somewhere else, thinking about his sister? Peperoni *used* to be the girl's favorite. What was he saying? But Nana Cummings heard it plain and understood it straight away. She still let it linger for a moment longer, to see if the boy understood it himself. He kept smiling and feeding and petting. No one had spoken her name. Not in this house. Not after the old woman ran herself ragged keeping together what few things they had left. Not after Alistair had gone near mute in the immediate weeks following. But why wouldn't he be talking about her again? Talking to her. Talking to his dead sister. Through a dog.

It made sense now. It was something anyone could grasp. It gave the whole tragedy meaning this way. That cursed road, that damned spot on the Cummings clan, was the end and beginning of everything, the same point. You only get rainbows without rain, and there's a pot of gold at the end of all of them. Everyone knew this. The rain was Alistair losing his family, but the gold was getting Joyce back, re-Joyce, the return of his sister. And as a puppy too! The thing she always wanted but couldn't have. It was the only way to ensure everything wasn't meaningless. The peace, which passed all Alistair's understanding, kept Joyce's heart and mind through Rainbow. If there was any virtue … if there was any praise.

She knew this couldn't possibly be healthy. That the boy was now, what? Using this dog as a medium to commune with the other side? Blasphemous was the wrong word, but there was something improper about it all that Nan Cummings couldn't quite define, but also couldn't completely square away. Couldn't reconcile. Certainly not the way Alistair seemingly had. It was as though everything were back to normal for the boy. This dog was a definite tool, and it appeared as though it was used for healing. But it looked too like a crutch. Nana Cummings knew her poor grandson couldn't lean on this fantasy (canine reincarnation was too brittle). He couldn't hold this story and its magical truth forever. But at the same time the grandmother felt helpless to correct him—no, she felt it would be unnecessarily cruel to burden the boy with the unbearable weight of reality. So she powdered herself with more of that rosy-scented duty and commitment, and let the boy look through his rose-colored glasses.

They got a cat-harness, because it was the only thing small enough to fit the puppy. At the pizza shop he could tie her up out back, make a box fort for her to rest in, and watch her through the window above the sink and his work. He'd be sure to exercise her properly on the walk home. Now that Nana Cummings knew about the dog, his responsibilities towards the pup increased. But he was happy to see that Rainbow was cared for properly, to see that she was welcomed back—though he wouldn't admit as much to Nana Cummings. He wouldn't admit all of it to Nana, not to anyone at the pizza shop either, nor to anyone at school.

He walked Rainbow by the site, because why not. It wasn't as though he'd decided; it was simple muscle memory now, and if anything, the place no longer held that thick, maudlin atmosphere it once had. Rainbow knew this place well and pulled on the harness, nearly choking herself to get back to the shrine and the memory of her scent. Alistair nodded to himself as he let the leash zip out of his palm and smiled as Rainbow barreled through the leftover memorial, its remnants looked sadder and creepier as its tangibility deteriorated: ink on cards running like blood, deflated balloons like spent prophylactics. Dead flowers for a dead person. But Alistair saw none of this. Rainbow saw none of this. They were free from it now. This wasn't for them any more. Rainbow seemed to prove it by rag-dolling herself amongst the detritus, legs and tail akimbo, sending well-wishes flying. She knocked over her Teddy Ruxpin and the robotic mouth moved, though no sound came out, and the eyelids closed over, though they were blinking away no vision, and Alistair understood that the thing still worked. All he need do was change the batteries and he could play any cassette he wanted. And so he picked up the teddy, its ear green with mold spores ... a change of batteries and maybe some *Febreze*.

He never bothered to dry himself after a bath; Nana Cummings just chalked it up to forgetfulness. Trivialities were easy forgotten, but he was normally pretty good on the important stuff. This was the first reason why the little girl's shoe so much unsettled the woman. Having snatched it off Rainbow, the dog confused and upset and apologetic and cranky all at the same time, Nana Cummings satisfied herself that it was her missing granddaughter's shoe and couldn't have stopped her distress boiling over into frustration, even if she'd tried. She didn't wait for him to even drip dry before the old woman began questioning Alistair. Why had he gone into Joyce's room and not told her? Did he forget to close her door? How could he be so careless as to allow this mutt, this stray dog to munch away at his sister's things? Had he no respect for Joyce's property? Had he no respect for Joyce? And Alistair was formulating answers and explanations for these questions when he remembered a truth that encompassed the lot (as only the truest truths do): Alistair remembered that he'd found the shoe.

Even after he'd corrected himself and told her that, actually, it was *Rainbow* who'd found the little purple Velcro-strapped size 4, it still didn't calm Nana Cummings down. If anything, it agitated her even more. She had on her face, upon discovering the shoe, the same mix of bewilderment and chagrin that Rainbow showed when the shoe was removed. He explained that they'd found it at the quiet spot at the creek, behind the tinned fruit factory. This information now showed on the woman's face as anger and distress, the reason behind which was difficult for Alistair to understand. It was no matter for Alistair, because before he could seek clarification, the woman dashed towards the telephone muttering that *they'd already searched the creek*. Alistair had never seen her move so fast. Almost made him giggle.

He knew they'd come up with nothing. Apart from them already having searched there, and apart from it not even looking like Joyce's shoe, Alistair knew something none of the grown-ups knew … there was nothing to find. The Sheriff's Department said that the K-9 unit had lost the scent because the shoe was contaminated with house smells once Alistair had removed it from the spot in the scrub, behind the old log. Acting as his own defense, the boy reasoned that the sniffer dogs had lost the scent because the shoe was contaminated by the scent of Joyce. Of Rainbow Joyce. The puppy cops could smell Joyce, they could smell the girl missing, but only because they could smell the dog, the girl returned. The dog: rejoiced. And before he could elucidate his further deductions to the Sheriff's Department, Nana Cummings had placed herself between Alistair and the befuddled Deputy. She was pleading again and Alistair didn't like watching that, so he instead watched as the breeze corrugated the surface of the creek. The only thing Nana Cummings said to Alistair in the car ride home was that if he didn't stop this nonsense she'd get rid of the damned dog.

Nana Cummings had spent the afternoon sobbing. She was asleep before it even was dark out. There had been a phone call. Alistair could only hear his grandmother's side of the conversation, and only then from his bedroom. *How do you mean it's gone cold? Can't we canvass suburbs further out? Knock on more doors? No, there must be. There has to be more.* But even if there was more, he wasn't interested. He listened to the chime of the phone as Nana Cummings dropped the receiver. He listened as the crying began afresh. He listened to footfalls down the hall and then the slippery metallic lock of his grandma's door. And even if there was more, Alistair didn't care to hear it, because it was pointless. None of them realized. And the boy took it upon himself to help them realize. And so Alistair did something novel ... he wrote.

By full dark, Nana Cummings sobs had stretched out to become snores, which let Alistair know the coast was clear. The boy had stayed up late into the night, scribbling his missive, scratching some parts out, starting again, moving words around like those old men who wrote his orations must have done all that long time ago. It was the first speech he'd ever written; therefore he allowed himself sufficient time to see that it came out good. He wanted it to be clear, and to make sure he was understood. Not mixing up his meanings. He wanted it to explain to the town (and to the world) that Joyce was back! He wanted to tell everyone that they could stop being so sad all the time. She was here! She was Rainbow. So after hiding the paper and putting Rainbow in her carry-case (with some greasy pizza crusts to snack on) but before sneaking out of the house completely, he ducked into the garage to fossick through Nana's scrapbooking box, which held a number of art supplies. He left once he'd found the paint.

***

No one had any clue what to make of the graffiti. *Rejoice!* Was this some perverted joke? The council were quick to paint over it, but it appeared a day later, then they painted over it, and it appeared again. Whatever was happening, it was interesting. What was most compelling, initially, was that the word came with a time and date. Some of the more religious folk murmured (with no true conviction) that it could be a prophecy? Counting down. End of times maybe? Likely just some head-case. No one bothered to stake the site out and see who was the vandal of the little girl's shrine, but some local residents gossiped that they saw the handicapped brother loitering about after dark. Though he did often walk his dog by the scene—poor thing, probably trying in his own way to reconnect. So the council painted over it, and it appeared, and they painted over it and now it was just those big red, dripping letters. The date and time were gone. That didn't matter though, because anyone interested had committed them to memory; hard to forget because noon on Sunday September 1st was only a week away.

He gave himself seven days to finish and practice his speech. Being sure he had time enough to polish the words, but also being cautious of the unfinished work being critiqued before it was ready, Alistair took the scrap pages to school, but hid them underneath the padding of Rainbow's carry-case. Mrs. Kimble didn't ask about the graffiti because she hoped to God the boy hadn't seen it, it was too awful. Better than being back on track, Alistair was making real progress. She didn't want to jeopardize this development by telling him about someone's sick prank. She'd offered the idea of registering Rainbow as a support dog as a joke, but it truly seemed to help the boy, and Mrs. Kimble didn't wish to stunt his growth by digging up the painful and the buried. Alistair asked the speech pathologist if he had permission to do some independent work, now that he'd completed everything assigned. She of course obliged him, then pulled a curious face when the boy produced the King James Brick and clapped it on his desk. Mrs. Kimble noted the fourth verse in the fourth chapter from *Philippians*, across which the boy dragged his finger as he read, but the teacher curiously neglected to pay attention to the rivulets of dried red paint caked down his middle and index fingers.

Nana Cummings saw it straight away. There was a part of her that knew Alistair had done it as soon as she was told about the graffiti. After the possibility of any development from finding the shoe had evaporated, similarly did the woman's hope dry up; her soul a salt flat, nothing wrong or bitter—just empty. When she confronted him about the graffiti, he stuttered, but pushed through enough to confess to his grandma that he had written it, and that he was going to explain to everyone why. She didn't understand how he could have done it, and said there was no possible explanation he could offer. She said, her voice flat, that she would *not* be going back there, ever again. That she couldn't possibly. The site was just too devastating. She said she'd lived many, many years and enjoyed a number of good decades, but felt as her time was nearing its end, the world seemed to be throwing a lifetime of suffering at her; one thing after another, and she didn't know if this was maybe punishment for something she'd done, if it was terrible luck, if fate and circumstance were trying to finish her off more quickly than was planned, or if the capricious gods were laughing, keeping her alive, so she (the oldest—ha ha ha) might just outlive her entire bloodline? As Nana Cummings wept in front of Alistair, something she'd never done before and wasn't even aware she was doing now, the boy took her hand, as though he was some kind of pastor or charity worker, or like *he* was the grandparent, and cupped the woman's arthritic fingers, knuckles knotted like kindling that pops in a fire, and brought the hand to his face and caught a rosy whiff of some of that duty and commitment and sweetness she never ceased powdering herself with, and smiled at his nana; her palm with its thin skin and thick bones against his cheek. She *must* come, he told her; he was going to show her that everything was back to the way it was. Rainbow barked because she knew Alistair was right.

The guys at the pizza shop didn't say anything to him really. As the days wound down to judgment, they gave him a few sideways glances—a few more than usual—probably just to keep eyes on him and make sure this wasn't the week he finally decided to snap. The kid washed lots of knives in that sink of his. The manager, without making it conspicuous, scheduled Alistair an RDO for the coming Sunday. Gave himself one too, because he had no clue as to what was going to happen at noon on Rainbow Street. Though he knew he wanted to see it, whatever it was. Were they bringing the girl back? Was it a taunt from the kidnapper? The store manager held that same dormant germ in his gut that only becomes active when tragedy strikes, and has one filming a person in distress as opposed to assisting. He wanted to slow down for this car crash—in fact there were many in town who felt the same thing, and decided upon a similar idea.

It was done. Alistair had never written anything meaningful in his life before, certainly nothing better than this, and there was part of him that knew he'd never put as much of himself into anything again. It wasn't easy for him to do, but he found it was harder for him to *not* do. It was sad work, but he felt achievement like medicine once it was done. He read and reread and altered and tweaked and it was exactly what he wanted to say to everyone. He started with the bible quote (because all great writing has an epigraph). The speech explained that Joyce *was* Rainbow and that he was grateful for that. So grateful. He had his sister back and everyone could stop being sad. The town could exalt in this miracle and be happy again. The proof was in the chronology: Rainbow appeared just after Joyce left, the timing was perfect. The proof was in the shoe Rainbow sniffed out: she'd discovered her own (Joyce's own) old sneaker, even when the police couldn't. And the proof was in the way Alistair felt. He knew enough to know he didn't know much, but his relief, his joy, was undeniable. This was the only explanation he had, and the only explanation needed. When things were tough you had to persevere with fortitude and to find the silver lining and to get up one more time than you fell down, and while something bad had happened, something really very bad, it was now all over. The tragedy had now reached its end. Dirty, evil Rainbow Street had a pot of gold at its end. They could all now rejoice in re-Joyce!

Nana Cummings hadn't woken up yet, so Alistair tiptoed about the house as he prepared breakfast for her. Between what she'd taught him about cooking and his time at the pizza shop watching the guys on the line, he was comfortable in the kitchen. He made for her an omelet with spinach in it, sliced some tomatoes on the side and toasted that gross grainy bread she loved—plenty of butter. The Sunday morning breakfast-in-bed caught her so off-guard she forgot to wake melancholy. He could still surprise her, and she treasured those moments. As she ate her eggs and sipped her tea, Alistair sat on the edge of the bed and beamed up at her, Rainbow in his lap. He was positively illuminated. She noticed he'd donned his nice button-up shirt and someone (Lord knows who? Maybe the dog?) had run a comb through the boy's hair. He was looking very smart today, smart and pleased, and even as she realized that this was *the* day, that today was *the* Sunday, that once she finished eating he was going to ask her to come to the site with him, even then she stayed bright. How could she possibly mope about when there was such elation on her grandson's face? She almost wanted to snatch some of it off him before she discovered it was contagious and she'd already contracted trace amounts of his felicity. He didn't need to say anything to convince her, for, autonomous of her own decision-making, she knew she'd go with him. Today she would stand tall and brave the place where she swore she'd never return. So she asked Alistair to fetch her sensible walking shoes, and the boy yipped because he knew, instantly, that Nana Cummings was in. Scuttling off to fetch her trainers, Alistair sent Rainbow skittering over the hardwood floors as he went. Even after Alistair had left the room the woman's smile remained because she was feeling genuinely ... not *optimistic*, that was too strong a word, but she was feeling *open* to something new, and open to that new thing not necessarily being something difficult. Everyday for this boy was new, was a surprise, and he embraced it, he was happy. Nana Cummings was happy when Alistair surprised her.

At the farmer's market Mrs. Kimble squeezed an avocado with the same tender pressure she used when checking her chest for lumps. She caught a glimpse of her watch and noticed it was nearing noon. The market was beginning to pack up, plus she'd already purchased her groceries for the week. The bishop at her Episcopalian church had led the congregation that morning in a prayer directed towards what was left of the Cumming family, for today, he said, the Lord was testing their faith, and they were brethren in need of support. Little did he know that a majority of his parishioners were planning on demonstrating their support by flocking to the scene as soon as church let out. Mrs. Kimble had told herself during the prayer that she didn't want to participate in the inevitable spectacle over on Rainbow Street, but decided she would go regardless should Alistair accidentally show and need some emotional support after … well, after who knew *what* was going to happen? Besides, she had nothing else on for the afternoon. The avocado was too firm anyway.

Around the same time Mrs. Kimble was perusing the stone fruit, the Sheriff was patrolling aimlessly in his squad car waiting for twelve-o'clock. There was no way he'd be caught out this time. He was certain they hadn't missed the girl's shoe by the creek, so it only meant the sick bastard who took her must have come back and planted it, taunting him and his department. And what was this graffiti then? Was the prick gloating? The Sherriff was resolute in finding out. He flicked the siren on his cruiser and blew through a stop sign. He'd get there early; determined he wasn't going to miss a damn thing this time. And it was this whoop of the police siren that woke the manager of the pizza shop who was still passed-out, nursing a wicked hangover. Thank God he'd given himself the day off. But when he remembered the reason why he'd scheduled himself the RDO, he dragged his aching limbs out of bed and slipped on last-night's crusty Levis. To not feel like he was somehow scamming the pizza shop, he decided he'd use the day off for the original reason he'd scheduled it. He put on sunglasses and a hat, grabbed a bottle of water from the fridge and started towards Rainbow Street. His phone told him it was 11:22 a.m.

Though it was completely dry out, things looked somehow cleaner today; fresh, like the morning after a night shower. The sun seemed to have scattered diamonds on the foliage all along Rainbow Street for Alistair and Nana Cummings. Rainbow trotted ahead, leading the way, tugging on her cat harness. She sniffed the sweet air and knew that today was for her entirely. But, oddly enough, she only felt nervous on Alistair's behalf. She'd been listening to him practice his orations these last couple of nights. He'd been recording himself on an old cassette player, playing it back, and re-recording the speech. Listening, then changing. He wanted to get it exactly how he heard it in his mind. My gosh he had worked hard on this, and she was so very proud of him. As she raced her little paws down the road, eager to get to the vigil, she turned and looked up at Alistair. His left hand held Nana Cummings to steady the old woman on the uneven sidewalk; her brilliant smile something unseen for weeks now. In his right hand Alistair held Rainbow's lead, and her old Teddy Ruxpin. He didn't end up spraying the bear with *Febreze*, but instead with that rosy-sweet scent that touched Rainbow on an ancestral level. She was here with her family, and she was comforted.

His heart dropped when he saw the throng of people by that telephone pole, the same pole with all the old flyers, directly in front of the memorial and the ten-foot high concrete block wall. The latest coat of still-damp paint resplendent and sun kissed, golden in the perfect noonday light. He stopped, but only for a moment, because while there were lots and lots of people here, waiting for him and what he had to say, he saw they were all familiar faces. They were the faces of his teachers and workmates and school friends and their parents and the police and all the many people who had helped his family. And all the fear left his body. He had something for them all and was thrilled to be able to share it with everyone at once. Nana Cummings gave his hand a playful squeeze; she then kissed him on his forehead and told him he was her best boy. Alistair handed Rainbow's lead over to his grandma and gave the little girl a scratch behind her ears. She barked her pleasure, and it was only then that people noticed Alistair and his grandmother and the dog. A murmur rippled its way through the crowd; some people covered their mouths in shock, others looked away shaking their heads. Many were surprised, many were confused. Mrs. Kimble took a step towards the boy but was halted, taken aback when Alistair saw her and gave her an exuberant wave, all elbow and splayed fingers. He looked anything but distressed; he looked a way she'd never seen him look before. As Alistair made his way towards what was left of the memorial, the crowd parted for him, and their conversations ceased. Everyone was watching him, so he made sure to walk tall. In his right hand he held the Teddy Ruxpin, and in his left, a cassette tape. Once at the wall he stood amongst the burnt-out candles and spoilt flowers, then turned to face the crowd. There were no nerves anymore, only certainty. He flicked on the switch underneath the animatronic bear's waistcoat and the toy powered-up; its animatronic eyes blinked, and the mouth began to open and shut. From the dozens of spectators, now, not so much as a sigh could be heard. Alistair took a breath, and scanned the faces before him. Nana Cummings had tears spilling down her cheeks, but it was okay because they were slipping back past her smiling lips. Rainbow spun on the spot clockwise, then counter clockwise, her tail waging so excitedly it threatened to helicopter her off the ground. He felt it was time. Alistair opened the tape deck in the body of the doll and slipped in his cassette. He adjusted the volume setting to HIGH and lifted the doll up above his head like a trophy, his smile threatening to overwhelm the rest of his features. There were a few seconds of dead air on the tape before Alistair's voice could be heard, coming out of the teddy, his voice booming confidently like no one had ever heard him speak before ... *Rejoice in the lord always: and again I say, Rejoice!*

We Manifest How and When We Can

By J. Stuart Croskell

Beyond the cracked sidewalk, and the telephone pole with layers of flyers in a **rainbow** of colors, and the patch of dry brown grass there stood a ten-foot high concrete block wall, caked with dozens of coats of paint. There was a small shrine at the foot of it, with burnt-out candles and dead flowers and a few soggy teddy bears. One word of graffiti filled the wall, red letters on a gold background: Rejoice!

Mary **O' Donoghue** approached the shrine, her ancient bones, arthritic and **cranky**, testing her every step. The memorial was the pizza kid's doing. To her left, about twenty yards away, said kid's mountainous bulk leaned on a long-handled broom, resting. The kid, whose given name was Danny, had been sweeping between the dumpsters at the back of Joe's Pizzeria, allegedly the oldest pizza palace in the city. Danny had started working at Joe's nearly thirty years ago. And despite encroaching middle-age and his enormous size, to the locals, he'd always be the kid. She waved to him, and he briefly touched the rim of his bright-yellow baseball cap, like an old-time gentleman. She refocused on the shrine, aware the kid remained motionless, staring at her. No doubt about it, hands-up, he was the stariest individual in her part of New York City. Always had been, even as a child, an itty-bitty scruff. An odd one, for sure, the kid. Didn't scare her, though; not in the least. Not then, not now.

A tap on her shoulder made her jump. She turned around. The kid. She hadn't heard him. For a big man, he'd the tippy-toed grace of a ballerina. "Missy Mary," he said, "do you like?" In the borough of Eastchester, if a roadside shrine materialized, you could be sure it was one of the kid's. This altar, like all his impromptu creations, was dedicated to Mary. And while the shrine displayed no specific image, photos or otherwise, she knew he'd done it for Mary O' D's greater glory. "Very much, Danny,' she replied, raising her arm, sharing her umbrella with him. "You know, Danny," she added, "you don't have to keep doing this." For reasons mysterious, the kid liked to acknowledge her in this way. Although what he saw in her as a cause for rejoicing and celebration, she'd never fathomed. As for the kid, bless him, even if he had a reason, the poor fellow wouldn't be able to articulate it. **His early diagnosis— vague and inconclusive - of some species of intellectual impairment, meant that he found it troublesome articulating pretty much anything. She** sighed. He'd been doing it for a long time, now, the shrine thing, since he was an *actual* kid. Mary tried to do the math in her long-retired teacher's head. He had to be in his forties now. At least. Hell, she'd babysat him. Lordy. How old did that make her?

Surrounding and framing the shrine, a gloriously colored rainbow arc. The kid was the only person around here who could've created a rainbow like this. Tears swelled. She couldn't help it. "Danny," she said. "This is amazing."

What the hell is this boy going to do with himself when I'm gone? Who's he gonna trail after with puppy-dog eyes when I'm gone? When. I'm. Gone. And I will be gone. Pretty damn soon, according to Doc Jackson. Should she point the kid in the direction of her equally-aged friend, Moira? If anybody needed the salve of veneration, honestly it was she. Mary studied the flyers on the pole, their multi-colored collage, the rain-soaked images bleeding into each other. Something about those colors, the way they pulsed and vibrated. *My eyes*, she thought. *Damn eyes are going now.* Everything was changing. She hardly recognized Eastchester, *her* part of the Bronx. It wasn't any worse or better, just different. Too different from what she'd grown up with;

the borough had left her behind. At least the developers had left Seaton Falls alone. She wished she could get to her favorite park and sit and think. Damned knee joints put the kibosh on that little pleasure. If it weren't for this alley shortcut, even the grocery store would be a no-no. And now cancer had gate-crashed the party. Okay, not much of a party. But, still. "Missy Mary, it's time," Danny said.

Mary studied the boy-man. "Time?" *What the heck was he yabbering about now?* Years ago, when the kid first moved into the shrine business, and the Mary-worshipping began in earnest, it'd agitated her. *I'm not dead*, she'd wanted to scream at him. Goddamit, *I'm still here*. But over the decades, she'd come to appreciate his efforts to mark her existence. *Because I* do *want my life to mean something*. Trouble was, she hadn't achieved anything of note. She hadn't married, no kids. It had been an empty old existence. And now the world was becoming quieter, its colors less keen. *Stuff* had lost its mojo. What on Earth was there about me warranting such devotion? Besides, other folks around here were more deserving of a shrine. The Soup-kitchen guy, for starters, he who tended to the homeless. Or the cop, doing his duty, shot to death a hundred yards or so from where Mary stood.

All her life she'd been waiting for something, something significant, profound. But stupid destiny had been a no-show; it'd stopped for fries and a burger somewhere, forgetting all about her. Fate hadn't done its Fate thing, carried out its obligations. Should be somewhere to complain. And now, too late. The doctor had said. Funny. She didn't feel any different. *Because you've been dying since the day you were born, you silly old fool. Why should you feel different? Mary O' Donoghue, what the hell have you been waiting for all these years? And now, here you are, on your way out. And, yes, girl, this time it's really happening.* She'd had a few health scares recently, but that's all they'd been—*scares*. This was the real deal, the deal that was going to carry her off. *I don't want to go. Not yet.* She had nothing, but it was her piece of nothing, and earthly nothing was better than the other kind of *nothing*.

"Missy Mary," Danny said again. "It's time." The rain pounded on her umbrella, and wind whisked up the leaves and garbage into miniature tornadoes, swirling around her feet. It was cold, but she didn't care. *Might as well get used to it*, she thought. *Soon gonna be frozen for eternity*. She wondered if the kid was Death come to her; the grim reaper sporting a yellow cap and a Joe's Pizzeria work jacket. She clutched the goods from the grocery store closer to her narrow chest. In the distance, the whooping siren of an ambulance whirled around her head. 'Lordy, Lordy,' she said out loud into the alley, the rainy New York night.

When she'd babysat the kid, he always liked to draw rainbows, the only thing he ever drew. Big ones, small ones, images so dazzling, it was doubtful the paper they were drawn on would be able to contain them. She'd kept all Danny's paper rainbows. If she'd a mind to take 'em to some hotshot gallery on Fifth Ave, they'd probably be gobbled up like Johnnycakes. Naïve art was the coming thing, don't you know, and rainbows didn't come any more naive than the kid's. "We got to go, Missy Mary," Danny said. "We got to go to the garage. I made everything nice for you."

She was only half-listening. "Nice? Thank you, Danny." All those years ago, when the kid was knee-high to nothing, a lot of nosey parkers thought it unhealthy the way he hung out with her; the sixty-year age gap the biggest, chewable bone of contention. Yet, his babysitting days long past, the kid had still regularly visited, gawping at her, drawing and coloring rainbows; ofttimes leaving her small offerings, votive stuff. Lego bricks, fluff he'd picked off a blanket, toy soldiers. The bread phase also began during this period. The kid would steal bread from his Mom's larder, concealing it in his pockets. Unleavened bread, it had to be. Any flatbread, come to that. As long as no raising agents were involved, as far as the pizza kid was concerned, it would do. To stop him pinching stuff from home, Mary told him she'd provide. She didn't want him getting into trouble. It was amazing how many exotic flatbreads were on offer in the neighborhood. Tortillas, roti, matzo, pita, kitcha. And that was just for starters.

"Yeah, real nice, Missy," Danny said, shifting from foot to foot. "But we got to go now." Mary tuned out the kid's ramblings. An idea had occurred to her: *Was it because of the unleavened pizza dough used in Joe's that encouraged the kid to hang out there in the first place, helping out, getting in Norm-the-manager's way?* Norm, only ever baked his pizza crusts without yeast; said he had been put on Earth to provide *the crisp*.

The kid tugged at her sleeve. "Missy, *please*." Again, she ignored him. The past was a far more delightful place than the present. Yet, despite the damp and her throbbing knees, she was enjoying her flatbread-related ruminations. As a junior-high-school teacher and Sunday school veteran, Mary had recognized immediately what the kid was about. With the bread. He was *breaking* it; officiating at his own kiddie holy communion, a whippersnapper priest, changing yeast-free bread into the blood and body of some unknown deity. It took her a while longer to realize that the object of this strange, rough Eucharist, the deity to whom he was acknowledging, was none other than her good self; that the bread he swallowed was *her* body, the water he used to consume it with, *her* blood. It made her feel queasy and empowered at the same time. But mostly queasy.

He'd sing, too—if that were the right word - as he broke the bread, before placing it onto his tongue, chewing and swallowing; an eerie, ululating, falsetto; kind of comical, yet oddly potent. Strange, nonsensical orations. Over and over. Break. Chew. Swallow. Warble. Break. Chew. Swallow. Gazing at her all the time, in awe, ecstasy. What must it be like to have a regular *grown* male be this attentive?

Mary breathed out slowly. There was always a significant minority of teachers who got so pumped about their vocation, they forgot to have a life. Indeed, a recognized occupational hazard. Mary was one such. After all, why be the mother of two or three kids, when you could be in loco parentis for a thousand? Besides, there was always next year. Some guy would come along. He would see beyond her metaphorical thick stockings and tortoiseshell spectacles, her folksy school-marm act.

But no one did. No one ever tried. And sometimes she'd get angry with Danny convinced he'd usurped her chance of love and replaced it with something empty, vaguely blasphemous. These black-dog moments were infrequent but, man-oh-man, when they came, they hurt like a bastard; and always on long winter nights when the Atlantic rain beat on her window and the wind off the Hudson howled around the rafters; when there was nothing on TV, and she just wanted someone to hold her hand, tell her everything was alright.

Sometimes she dreamt of running wild, of cave-living, mating, *rutting* strenuously—nothing so flabby as *making love*, oh no—out in the open, on vast plains that lapped at the foothills of towering mountains. And afterward, bathed with sweet-smelling sweat, she'd kill her lover, tear his recently satiated flesh apart, claws glistening, all the time howling at the heavens. Other times, her dream-self revealed a different side. *She saved, bestowed, gave*. And she was magnificent in her beneficence. Naturally, she attributed her raucous nocturnal adventures to her repressed self, expressing and breaking out. But dear God, the sheer *aliveness* of the fucking and the killing.

What's more, the vigor she felt, post-dream, followed her into wakefulness. It was on those days, those mornings that she pleasured herself without inhibition, in ways that shamed her default, everyday self. And she knew, just knew, that if Mr. Right had seen her on one of *those days*, she would have got her man. But her come-and-get-me if-you-dare days were few and far between, and her man never showed up, never appeared in those hours when she was her true self, fresh from the kill, from distributing divine grace.

The kid grabbed her arm, and her groceries dropped to the ground.

Like a lot of things these days, his presence had slipped her mind. "Missy, Mary," he said, "Missy, Missy, MISSY! We gotta go, we gotta." Alarmed, she tried to step away, but his grip was implacable. Holding on to her, he grabbed her umbrella with his free hand, and laid it next to the soggy furries, spent candles. "I'm sorry, Missy Mary. We gotta go. We gotta." He guided her away from the shrine, his grip gentle, yet firm. She had no choice but to move with him. "Danny," she said. "Danny, you're hurting." He wasn't, but she thought it might get through. It didn't. Instead, he continued to propel her along the alley, until they emerged into a quadrangle of neighborhood lockups. Stopping next to one of the garages, the kid fumbled in his jacket pocket. "Danny," she said, struggling. "Danny, what are you *doing*?" The kid found a key, and unlocked the roller door, wrenching it open and upwards, tugging Mary into the gloomy interior, flicking on a light. "Missy, Missy, don't struggle. It's time. Please don't struggle. Gotta be done. Gotta be." She was shivering, freezing, legs shaky. He propped her up against the sidewall, started unbuttoning her coat. "Danny," she said, unable to move, some distant functioning part of her understanding she'd slipped into shock. Next, he removed her sweater, over her head, her arms up, more efficiently than he had business being. Underwear joined her blouse and dress on the concrete floor. Without hesitating, as if he'd been thinking this through for a long time, Danny swept Mary off her feet; holding her emaciated body in massive hands, above his head, like a weightlifter. 'Jus' a little ride, Missy Mary. A short ride."

He turned around—widdershins - slowly at first, then speeding up, spinning, faster and faster, like the carousel cussy old Dad had taken her on a million years ago, its velocity magnified to the nth degree. The garage and its contents blurred, darkening, becoming night-black, and from that infinite night, an explosion of color. Primal colors, divine colors; as they were in their pristine and original form before being filtered by the sensory limitations of humankind. The kid staggered, fell, dropped her. She opened her eyes, her body a lightning rod for all kinds of pain. The kid lay nearby, on his back, breathing heavily, sobbing. "I can't, I can't, *Rainbow*. I'm so sorry." In her head she still rode the kid's carousel, hurtling through time, space, her arms stretching, stretching outwards from Earth, reaching for the heavens. And then she was wholly in her body again, the kid's homegrown fairground ride already slowing, coming to an end.

***

When the ride ended, she was lifted again. The kid slid her body onto a soft pile of clothing among the boxes in the garage. He pulled an old coat over the top, creating a cave that emanated the sweetness of old ladies who frequently powdered themselves—a light rose motif that played ironically well in the deep recesses of Rainbow's ancestral brain. The pizza kid lifted her head to help her lap water from a hubcap. He broke bits of pepperoni and crust into bite-sized pieces and left them where her tongue could reach them. Much later, she heard him practicing his orations like songs. Like monks chanting in the distance, they were a comfort.

As they'd always been, she remembered. After the kid completed his orations, he gazed at her, still devoted, it seemed. But the sadness in his eyes was deep and immoveable. "Rainbow," he whispered. 'Rainbow, Rainbow." Rainbow gazed back. Without knowing how, Rainbow knew the millennia-long thing going on between him and her, the worshipped and the worshipper, it was coming to an end. Just like the kid's little ride, his one-man carousel, the Big Ride, too—the one that had carried them through eons—was nearing its conclusion.

She opened her mouth to ease his pain, to share it, to let him know that she knew and loved him, like she always had, even though it was a love doomed to remain unsatisfied. Congress between a goddess and her priest would not do at all. But all that issued forth from her throat was a pitiful mewl, weak and thin, lacking any substance; about as far removed from the transcendent a girl-god could get.

The kid shook his head slowly, tears streaming freely down his pockmarked moon-face. With some effort, he stood, moving listlessly around the garage, shuffling through the debris, occasionally examining a piece of junk that caught his eye. Rhinestone studs, Christmas tree baubles, anything that had once shined, or still shone. She knew *he* knew she liked cheap and chintzy. *Yes, as goddesses go, I am, in many ways, low maintenance*; it was the thought behind the offering she was more interested in, the *intention*. Moving back to her, his arms filled with booty, he knelt down in front of her once more, his joints creaking under his immense weight. He let the gewgaws tumble to the floor, picking up an individual piece, one at a time, and then carefully placing it in front of her cardboard cave. A pattern of protection, she realized. *Too late for that*, she thought. Yet he still offered, still whispered: *You shine in glory, like the sun, Queen of color, ever the only one*. Over and over.

At that moment, he did something he'd never done before; something he wouldn't ordinarily dare. He touched her. Hesitant, tentative. Lightly at first, resting his fat sausage fingers gently on her head, stroking her multi-colored fur. If he'd done this a thousand years ago, she would have killed him instantly. Yes, to spite herself, she would have murdered her priest, though it would've meant the end of her.

She let out another mewl. Of pleasure this time. The kid's touch, his caress, was … *agreeable*. She nuzzled into him, surprised how small she'd become in this, her final iteration. She was tiny, her head fitting comfortably into his hand. Emboldened, the priest stroked her silken mane. Softly. Oh, so softly. The kid-priest smiled a lovely smile. In all their incarnations, it was always his smile she looked forward to.

What would happen to him when she died, *passed*? She paused, caught in a moment of powerful and sudden déjà vu. She'd had the thought before, recently. *What will he do when I'm gone?* She sighed, trying to bring her memories into relief. *Who or what had I last been?* She'd been human, she knew that. *Ah, yes, Mary. Mortal Mary who favored rose powder, not because she liked it, but because it was what aging females were supposed to dust themselves with.* Might as well have been the dust of bones. Poor Mary had lived a life doing what she was supposed to, never what she wanted. Of course, *as Rainbow*, she'd already *died* a thousand times over, glorious deaths; departures that had Earth trembling, the heavens shaking. Once, her presence on the Blue Planet was impossible to ignore; the events leading up to her imminent absence no less so. This time, only the priest would note her passing. Would death mean oblivion? She knew there wouldn't be another renewal, that there wouldn't even be another fallow period, a mortal incarnation.

And what had been the kid's name, the priest's? When she had been Mary? *Not that it matters.* Rainbow closed her eyes, willing her failing, yet still-divine neurons to take her along the trackways of the recent past. She arrived at his name like a traveler arriving at a yearned-for destination. Ah, yes. *Danny.* Danny boy. She drew back, staring at the kid's hand, rivulets of her rainbow essence running down his mighty palm, his fingers. Just like the colors on the telephone pole in the last moments of the Mary-life. The kid-priest cupped his hand over his nose, inhaling deeply of pure, undistilled rainbow-light. His smile grew bigger. Another first, she realized - she had given to *him*. The priest had received from his goddess. But, yes: What would befall him when she was gone? Not just gone from this life, but gone from all possible existences? Would he pass at the same time as she? Heartbroken, bereft of purpose? Meanly, she hoped so. She didn't wasn't to *go* alone. She pushed her furry head into his hand again. *Don't stop stroking, priest.* The kid resumed his tender ministrations. Rainbow purred.

Mortal Mary's thoughts strolled around Rainbow's head, gaining traction now that she, Rainbow, had remembered the nature of her host body's name. Mary had been right to suspect the world was quietening, its once splendid colors greying. The diminishing, the lessening, of the world was a real thing, really happening. As a discernible process, it had been in operation for some time. Rainbow knew *how* the world was declining; had known for a while. She just didn't know *why*. And she certainly thought—hubristically, and stupidly, it turned out - it would never, ever happen to *her*; that she would fall victim to the slow, inexorable exodus of her kind from this earthly realm forever.

She wished she could talk, communicate with her priest. She'd a lot to say to him. And, she knew, he had much to tell her. About herself, her *nature*. In her glory days, she'd never listened to him. Why should she? *Too busy being a goddess. A goddess, dammit! Didn't have to listen to anybody,* anything. But now. *Speak, priest. Tell me who I am. What is it in me you are devoted to? Before I die, I need to know.*

As if he'd heard her, he whispered, "You shine in glory, like the sun, Queen of color, ever the only one." She whimpered into his palm. *Tell me again, tell me who I am.* Danny, louder, said, "You shine in glory, like the sun, Queen of color, ever the only one." *Again kid, again.* He breathed in, said powerfully, "You shine in glory, like the sun, Queen of color, ever the only one."

Somewhere, hiding between his words, lay the answer to the mystery of her existence. Rainbow, knew, *knew*. But she couldn't figure it. Try as she might, the scaled-down brain inside her tiny skull just wasn't equipped. *If I could only see myself, perhaps, I'd better understand what I am.*

She mewled once more and the kid's brow furrowed. She grizzled again, pushing forward on shaky paws. The kid, bending forward, lowered his huge head level with hers. She rubbed her nose into his, and he rubbed right back, carefully, mind. He sat up, nodding. He understood his mistress. *Well, so he should*. Thousands of years of attending to her needs ought to count for something. He stood up and left the garage, noisily rolling the door shut. Outside, it still rained.

Returning, he carried something wrapped in cloth. Undressing the object, he placed it carefully in front of her. She stared at her reflection.

At first, she thought there was something wrong with the mirror, or her eyesight. Because what she saw, the creature she had become, couldn't possibly contain all Rainbow was, all that she had been. It didn't seem possible.

She tapped the mirror with her paw, held it there. Saluting, acknowledging herself, what she had been. *What had I been? Why can't I remember? I was glorious, yes. A goddess, yes.* But what had it all *meant?* To her? To the priest? The people who'd revered her?

She closed her eyes. Enough of the picture the mirror painted. It told lies. It didn't speak the truth, its reflection failed to present her reality. Whatever it captured, it wasn't her. Perhaps sensing her distress, Danny removed the mirror, placing it at the back of the garage, behind some boxes.

Thirsty. She lowered her head and lapped at the water in the hubcap, too weary to consider the inequity of her reduced circumstances. Despite its rough container, the water was sweet and warm. It had been blessed, sanctified by the priest. The water was her blood now. *I'm glad I taste so sweet.*

He once more knelt before her, his body now shuddering with sobs. He didn't know what to do, she realized. He didn't know how to help her anymore. She let out a strangled cry of frustration, scrambled to his feet, and scuttled back to the door. Shaking his head, he turned and lifted the door, stepping out of the garage into the rain, shutting it behind him. *Am I abandoned? Is this is where I die, in a cardboard cave, among the castoff detritus of humankind?* No. *I will see myself. My true self.* One last time.

She stood on unsteady legs, trembling. Her old strength and power a far-off dream. Still, she moved forward, out of the cave and across the garage floor, toward the garage entrance, moving to the narrow slit of light at its bottom. Outside the rain pattered hard on the asphalt.

She was baffled at the kid's disappearance. He should be with her, in her last moments. After all, they might be his, too. *Rejoice!* He'd written on the wall of her shrine. Where was the rejoicing now? Had her current incarnation disappointed him? Could it be, that after all these years, her priest, her shaman, her interlocutor between goddess and humankind, was … embarrassed by his lady?

She reached the garage entrance, the gap between door and floor tight. Experimentally, she pushed her head through the opening, the sharp edge of the door's base rubbing against her fur, pushing her ears down. She flattened her body against the concrete floor and commando-crawled forward, convinced the weight of the door would force it to descend, slicing her in half. But it didn't, it held, despite the ominous creaking and groaning of wind-caught metal. And then she was free. She looked upwards. Raindrops fell on her face, whiskers.

Behind, the garage door clunked to the ground with a sharp thud. Rainbow shook her head. She needed to think. Using Mortal Mary's memories, she tried to get her bearings. She required a green space, grass under her paws, trees, the smell of wet earth. *I will not die here*. The park. *Yes, the park*. Where Mary had gone to think her sad little thoughts.

Rainbow pressed on, away from the lockups and out into the alley, already drenched, bedraggled. She padded over the cobblestones, weaving through plastic garbage bags, dwarfed on either side by impossibly tall buildings.

Despite the rain, it was warm. Warm like jungles, the daytime deserts, the South Sea Islands. When she had been in her prime, and her priest, sometimes shaman, officiated at her clawed paws, supplicant and willing.

To her left the shrine, the one Mary had been so impressed with before her dizzying ride began. To Rainbow, it looked forlorn and abandoned. Appropriate, really. *Apposite*, teacher-Mary might have said. Already, it was a shrine to a fading memory. Rejoice! *Huh*. Not this time, Danny. Pizza kid. My priest.

She knew where she was now. *I can do this*. But even in this diminished incarnation, she would still attract attention. So she kept to the backways, to the secret paths of urban wildlife, away from human eyes. Bearing west, she crossed silently through the yards of residential houses, first off Light Street, then off Conner, before trotting across the four lanes of Pratt Avenue. Then into the woods. And silence, albeit relatively. The softness under her paws, the odors, mulchy and earthy, succor for her dying body.

A brief rest and Rainbow headed deeper into the woods, toward the glade in Mary's memories, again avoiding the well-trod ways, away from people. Except for the occasional drop of rain slipping off a leaf and exploding on her head, the rain rarely penetrated the tree canopy.

Her ancient senses told her it would cease raining. And soon. She sniffed the air, smelling the sun's imminence, its promised heat, and light, an odor she'd never forget. Not while she lived. She had to reach the glade, though: To see the sky, have the sun at her back.

Surely, I'm owed this. Please. Let me dance in the reflection of my sky-born image one last time. I need to see what I was. I need to understand what I was for. I am Rainbow. Rainbow. *The priest knew. He did.*

Behind her, deep within the woods, a twig snapped. Then another. Exhausted, she couldn't be bothered to turn and look. Whatever was coming, there was no stopping it. Footsteps pounded closer, someone running. Above, the rain ceased, and behind, the sun emerged, warming the skin beneath her multi-colored fur. Over to the north, straddling the whole of New York City, a rainbow, its colors seeming to coalesce; for one brief moment, to solidify.

Scooped up from behind, Rainbow ascended rapidly, held high in one hand, even now facing the rainbow, finally understanding, grasping the meaning of her essential self. "You shine in glory, like the sun, Queen of color, ever the only one," the kid shouted. And as the rainbow evanesced, Rainbow melted into the kid's hand, her colors liquefying, running down his arm, until he held nothing, until rain washed the colors away. And the world became quieter.

Rejoice
By Elsa Cruz

Beyond the cracked sidewalk, and the telephone pole with layers of flyers in a rainbow of colors, and the patch of dry brown grass there stood a ten-foot high concrete block wall, caked with dozens of coats of paint. There was a small shrine at the foot of it, with burnt out candles and dead flowers and a few soggy teddy bears. One word of graffiti filled the wall, red letters on a gold background: Rejoice!

My previous self would have probably lifted my camera without a thought and carefully framed the inspirational graffiti, making sure to crop out the sad stuff. I could have added it to one of my more "urban" photo galleries. Young couples love that stuff. My photos used to be full of frameable moments in time like that—candles that still had flames, flowers without the wilted brown edges, and...well, not that many teddy bears, except from that one wedding when the ring bearer insisted on bringing his Whinnie the Pooh down the aisle. We had all said how sweet it was that to him, the stuffed animal was the most valuable object in the room.

That's how my photo gallery used to be: living children and happy people only. Moments in time that people actually wanted to think about. And the inspirational graffiti here and there to attract the clients who wanted something different but not really.

That was two years ago. I don't take pictures of weddings anymore.

And I try to avoid photo shoots involving children. Half the time I don't bring my camera on days like today and then wish I had later. But I'm not wishing I had my camera now. Now I just stand and wonder which came first: the graffiti or the shrine? If the shrine came first, what sick person would write "rejoice" over something that almost assuredly had something to do with a dead child? And what parents—or parent—with empty arms would choose this spot for a shrine? Unless this was the scene of...oh god, this is getting depressing.

When I walk into Dwelling Grounds, the first thing I see isn't Dani with a blur of blonde hair ready to make my Americano. Instead, I see two old guys playing chess while they each drink a hot chocolate. Now that's something I wish I had my camera for. I could snap a quick photo. Nothing posed. Nothing too intimate. Just me, an outsider looking in for a moment. Not saying I am part of anything. Not promoting any kind of life, just observing.

Dani confirms my order as usual, even though I haven't changed it since she started working here. She's one of those people who would have liked my old Instagram gallery. She would have wanted something different but not really. When we first became friends, she asked if I could do her supposedly upcoming engagement photos. But I told her I don't take happy photos anymore. I can observe the world, but I can't make a world that's not there. Or that might not always be there.

"They come to play chess every Wednesday at 11:15 on the dot," says Dani as she hands me my Americano and a smile. I turn away from the chess players and smile back. She probably thinks I'm depressed. But I take neutral pictures, not sad ones.

Next Wednesday I walk out my door at 11 a.m. sharp. I had even set my alarm so that I can make it out of the house in time. I've been up since 7:45 editing for Royal Real Estate. They wanted everything—even those laminated countertops to look "a little newer than they are." No one has known exactly what I do at home every day since I was married. I don't know what's better—to be mostly seen or mostly unseen, because people can always just decide what they want to see.

Dani smiles when she sees me and makes a silly, somewhat subtle pointing movement towards the chess brigade. They look exactly as they did last week, exactly as I expected and hoped. I pick a table on the opposite side of the room, and set up my camera on the table so that I can snap away without all that obvious crouching and squinting. I quickly duck to measure the framing, and then I can just take pictures with all the appearance of looking through previous photos. The old guys are way too immersed in their game and probably too unversed in modern cameras to guess I was taking their candid portraits. There's something freeing about photographing people who aren't looking straight into the camera, who don't even know you are there. They aren't looking at me to make them appear, and then later feel, a certain way.

Moving to my laptop, I change a few of the photos to black and white and mess around with the lighting. I'll need a name for this photo collection when I post it on my blog. Something that might invoke long lives coming to a close, but not too morose. Something that reveals a distant kind of respect. After a quick thesaurus search I find "Orations," and I like that. I have a feeling that there would be a lot to say about these guys. A lot of life that had been lived. I realize I'm hungry.

"By the way, I think I have a job for you," says Dani as I order a bagel. I doubt it, unless she has a lake house for rent or a new line of blenders for sale. Dani is usually trying to drop hints at un-neutral photo shoots. But there isn't a new ring on her finger so I listen. And for some reason, I agree. After all, there wasn't an endless supply of laminate countertops to edit. And I certainly won't be buying groceries with today's work.

When I get home, Rainbow greets me as usual with two huge paws on my shoulder. Her eyes—one blue and one green—look like little blazing planets in her grey and white galaxy of fur. All this combined with the splash of pink on her nose got her the name Rainbow. Lindsey used to say it sounded like a five-year-old girl named her.

I Google "divorce photography" and sure enough, there are some very artistic shots of smashed photo frames, and half-naked women giving the finger to piles of burning mementos. There are some cute chalkboards that said "Established" and "Finally Free" with the respective years. Lots of trash the dresses involving booze and black thongs. No husbands in sight. Oh no wait, there are some couples shots...with divorce papers, bare fingers, and big smiles. I guess I can shoot a pissed girl with some torn photos. I've had plenty of experience with that.

Two days later, I ring the doorbell, bracing myself for fake eyelashes and spilling out boobs. But the woman who answers is normal. Pretty, but normal. She's wearing a simple black dress and heels. Something Lindsey might have worn to a dinner date at one of those speakeasies downtown. There's no booze or shattered glass in sight, so I ask, "What did you have in mind?"

"We disagreed about almost everything," she says, "He wanted to adopt and I wanted a sperm donor. I'm not keeping anything we owned together. How could I? We couldn't even have a kid together. I just want to remember these things and this place. I want to look strong moving on, but I mostly just want to have a record of something that was good for as long as it was. And I...wanted to get some good shots of this dress. It was his favorite. Like I said, we disagreed on almost everything, but he did try."

I follow her around, room to room, while she poses quietly on chairs and couches, and looks out of windows, and examines travel photos on the wall. The click of the shutter seems too loud. She says she asked me to take the pictures because she thought I would understand. All I can think about are Rainbow's wide planet eyes orbiting around us as we screamed. I never wanted kids and Lindsey never liked dogs. Funny how we ended up together, disappointment making us hoarse.

On the way to Dwelling Grounds today I pass the graffiti shrine again.

There is one bouquet of fresh flowers in the mess of wilted ones. Do you call it a bouquet when it's there because someone died? Or maybe this shrine wasn't about someone who had died, but about someone who had never been alive. After the photoshoot yesterday I had a dream that I can't shake out of my head.

In the dream—in that vapor of the subconscious that either floats away while you're trying to grasp it or sticks to you like sweat on a still day—we were in a car accident. It was when Lindsey and I were married—and Rainbow was in the back seat. We both just looked at each other, shocked, and then back at our shattered windshield. And then this kid on a bike came up beside our car. He had one of those insulated backpack things for pizzas on his back. He stopped and leaned up to the passenger window and said, "I think your dog is dead" but it took us a minute to understand. And then we looked back and Rainbow was bloody and twisted in a strange position in the corner of the floorboard. Lindsey started screaming and crying—which was weird because she never liked Rainbow—and I just stared.

Then the vapors of the dream sped up like cold sweat and we were trying to take Rainbow to the vet—I don't know why we were taking her to the vet if she was already dead—and then somehow instead of being in our arms, she was on one of those medevac cage things. Dreams change without warning—that's the realistic part I guess. And the medevac dropped her into an amusement park ride, like one of those little teacups that spins around. And the pizza kid was there, like some kind of afterlife guardian—very solemn and ceremonial. And in that uncanny way that you will believe anything in a dream, I realized that the amusement park was actually our garage. We always said we were going to organize the garage into a more usable space. And in that realm of dreams where the world itself is a shape-shifter, the garage was also the scene of the accident. It had been all along. And the pizza kid was standing like a medieval sentinel watching Rainbow's body on that tedious, slow-spinning ride, ready to lift her out with much gentler arms than the medevac cage. But how many times would her body need to be moved before she could just rest?

When the ride ended, she was lifted again. The kid slid her body onto a soft pile of clothing among the boxes in the garage. He pulled an old coat over the top, creating a cave that emanated the sweetness of old ladies who frequently powdered themselves—a light rose motif that played ironically well in the deep recesses of Rainbow's ancestral brain. The pizza kid lifted her head to help her lap water from a hubcap. He broke bits of pepperoni and crust into bite-sized pieces and left them where her tongue could reach them. Much later, she heard him practicing his orations like songs. Like monks chanting in the distance, they were a comfort.

That's the part of the dream when I realized—in the cloud of dust from our garage, and the musty pilling on the wool coat that had belonged to my grandmother, and the debris from the crash—that Rainbow was still alive. And we hadn't taken care of her or been her guardian up to the very edge of the afterlife or whatever. And we weren't even thinking about orations to speak about her. But she heard the pizza kid preparing to say something nice about her, and that made her feel better. But in the dream I knew that even at the edge of death she wasn't thinking about me. Why should she be? I hadn't even looked in the back to see if she was okay until the pizza kid told me to. I had just argued with Lindsey for two years while Rainbow watched.

When I arrive home—my mind still colored with the memory of the dream—Rainbow jumps up to greet me as usual, her eyes flashing different colors at once. Maybe one eye was her ancestral eye and one her present-day eye. I wonder if she knows I would neglect her during a near-death experience, that I wouldn't pass the test as her afterlife guardian. I wonder if she wishes I was the pizza kid—nicer, and less self-absorbed.

Once, when Lindsey and I argued like normal couples, we watched a documentary about animal instinct. The narrator had said in a British accent how animal knowledge gets passed down subconsciously from generation to generation, even species to species, and that's why dogs can sense fear. Because they used to be wolves hunting the weakest member of a herd. Lindsey had turned to Rainbow and asked in a laughing fake accent, "Hey doofus, what's going on in your ancestral brain?"

"What's going on in your ancestral brain?" I ask again, holding onto the memory like mist. I even remembered the vanilla candles Lindsey used to buy to cover up to "dog smell." Vanilla and her lavender shampoo. Rainbow twitches her ears like little wings going the wrong way. Maybe her ancestral brain was only thinking about a walk and food after all. Maybe she didn't hold all those years against me. Against us.

Once, I made the mistake of telling Lindsey that I had a dream that *she* had died. She snapped back over a pan of scrambled eggs and said, "So you want me dead?" No, I had tried to explain, because dreams come out of nowhere. She had disagreed of course and said she only dreamed about getting the divorce finalized.

My fingers drum the table with an itch to call Lindsey. And then I start picking the dry skin off my lip, annoyed at the urge. But I want to tell her what I really meant when I told her about that dream. Or if she was in one of her incredulous moods I could at least tell her the weird dream about Rainbow and the pizza kid. She used to get a kick out of my subconscious. I could also ask her how to write this blog post. She always liked giving me advice.

When I was a wedding photographer, I hated writing the text part of my blog posts, or the captions for social media. It had always seemed fake, like I was caving into something we all knew wasn't real. But this time it feels different. Writing about someone's divorce seems real. And ironically, I am more afraid of getting it wrong.

Getting it wrong echoes like someone saying they took a wrong turn in a huge dark cavern. I questioned Lindsey's desire to have kids and she questioned everything about us. What do I have to lose if I get my portfolio wrong? I already got my life wrong. I add "Divorce" to the drop-down menu in my photo gallery. Something about Dani's friend helped me feel the pictures before they even happened. Because she didn't think she had everything right. Like the chess players who never saw me taking their pictures, she was just making the next move. So am I.

Time to update my "About" section. *I've grown a lot as a photographer over the last few years. I used to focus on photoshoots where everyone felt like they needed to smile. Now I try to observe what is really going on and capture that. The results are images that are more raw and powerful. Moments in time. If these pictures help my clients discover their happiness or the way to get there, then I will have accomplished my purpose as an artist.*

My next divorce session was different. They wanted one last photoshoot with both of them and their kids before everything changed. We went to the zoo. The couple held hands even when I wasn't looking through the lens. I asked if there was something specific they didn't want to forget about the good times together and they just looked at their kids and said, "You already took pictures of them."

The next day, I go to Dwelling Grounds to edit the zoo session. The clatter of people meeting and laughing about nothing seems disrespectful to the images of people saying goodbye because of so many looming somethings. I add a reddish filter to try to match the boy's hair with the Indian elephant in the background. What did color tone really matter when his world was falling apart? But how would I know? I never liked kids.

"I saw your new blog post, looks like your photos aren't neutral anymore," a text comes out of nowhere from Lindsey. At least they're not fake, I think. At least they feel something. At least some people know how to say goodbye. At least they could still hold hands at the end.

"I like pictures that allow for anything to happen," I reply. That's what I mean by neutral. That's fair. Instead of saying those people will always be happy, because they won't. Instead of saying they're ready for anything, because they aren't.

"Sounds like it's going well," she says. I hear her voice filling in the blanks: It's going well for me too because I have a baby now. And a partner who wants it. And I'm not neutral at all. I'm happy.

It's funny you texted, I say in my head. I've been wanting to call you. I had a dream, but that's not the reason I wanted to call. It's because it reminded me of another dream, one that you never let me explain. And I haven't called because you used to laugh at my dreams or just get mad about them. But I miss your laugh. All this welling up and I just text, "I had a dream that someone important was dead."

"Sorry to disappoint you," she writes back without a beat. *I'm still here,* I imagine her saying with a sudden tilt of her head. She always shrugged one side of her mouth and raised both eyebrows when she was turning something I said into something I said against her. She always believed I wanted out. Saying I dreamed about Rainbow would just make Lindsey say something about how "that dog" was always more important. But I would have given up everything for Lindsey. I don't know why I just didn't.

I don't respond. In that empty space under her last message is everything I think about telling her. How writing blog posts for the new photoshoots seems easier now because I'm mostly talking to myself, not saying what they want to hear. How if potential clients don't like it, they don't have to hire me. How there's no future forced on anyone. No strings attached.

"I know you always say you're just observing," says Dani when I get a refill for the walk home, "but I think taking pictures of someone or something is kind of like saying there's something valuable there, something worth keeping. And by the way, I haven't seen the chess players this week. It kind of makes me worried and sad."

I walk outside and call Lindsey. While the phone rings, I think back to all those years of reading between the lines—between sarcasm and silence. All the time she spent looking away at nothing instead of at me. And all the times she looked right at me as if she had always known what I was thinking, from the beginning of time. It's all building up in my head, the things I want to say. I know I said a lot of dumb stuff, but I just wanted to say, remember when I told you that I dreamed you died? I know it was one of my many mistakes. But I realized what I should have told you that day about the dream.

"I miss you," is what I say when she answers. There is a long pause, like those pauses that come after asking the question that's been lingering in the air like humidity on a cloudy day. I can hear the smile in the silence. I can hear a joke growing like a snowball in her head, maybe something about how she doesn't miss me but she misses Rainbow. But no, the snow melts. She would never say she missed Rainbow, even if we both knew it was a joke. Sure, people change, but isn't that why all of this happened?

"I miss you too," she says. We both laugh, not content anymore I guess with just the smiles in our voices. But it would never be enough to miss each other. Because we missed what could never last. That's why our conversations now are mostly quiet. Even if we're smiling.

We used to talk about everything—how our days were, what did we think about Vanessa's baby, does the kitchen need repainting, was this what we expected? But eventually we stopped talking, saving our breath I guess, for the arguments that we knew would explode the silence and became the normal. Now we just observe each other. Neutral.

"Hey," she says, "I wanted to ask you, would you take some pictures of Ben? It's his first birthday." Really Lindsey? You want me to be your son's birthday photographer? Is this some kind of validation? I thought I never validated you? Or do you want to just prove that we can be in each other's lives without tension?

There's no smile in her voice. For a second, I wonder if she's trying to prove that she wouldn't be bothered if I showed up to take pictures of her kid. Or maybe she wants to rub something gritty and sharp like gravel in my face—to show me what we could have had. But she should know that I of all people wouldn't feel like I was missing out on something when it came to kids. To answer her question and all her possible intentions I just say, "Okay."

If anything, Ben reminds me that I didn't want kids—then, now, or ever. But the way she looks at him is different. I never saw this Lindsey when it was just us. It makes me miss something—something I had never even had.

With wide planet eyes, Rainbow watches as I edit the photos of Ben and his cake. From the pictures I had of Lindsey holding Ben up to blow out his candles, I finally believe that this—that he—is what Lindsey really wanted. Her smile in these photos is different, different than any photos I had taken of her before. It made her old smiles—the smiles with me—look like she was missing something.

Rainbow twitches an ear and looks at me in expectation. I see her in the corner of my eye, raising her eyebrows as I move my hand to raise the exposure on a photo. What about Rainbow? Is this what she wanted? Her wolf ancestors used to rule the land somewhere in Siberia and now she has to sit here and watch me stare at a screen. I turn to her. She lifts her head as I ask out loud, "What's going on in your ancestral brain?"

"Probably just a walk and food," I answer to myself, and she opens her mouth to show sharp, harmless teeth and a pink tongue. I stand up to get her leash and her modern-day brain clicks with ancestral instinct. She knows. She barks and gallops towards the door. I bring my camera too. After the chess players, I started bringing my camera everywhere like the ancient days. Rainbow and I burst out onto the sidewalk with the world waiting for us.

It's starting to drizzle, so we run. I imagine her ancestor wolves running beside her. Like an arctic chill, my dream about Rainbow and the accident rushes in to fill my chest and drench my mind. But it doesn't stick there. The vapors of the dream-memory seem to push me, as only vapors in a dream could. Warm rain hits my face and I feel the real world rising in me as I shout, "I promise to feed you pizza and write your orations as you journey to the afterlife," and Rainbow barks. And I realize she will never die. Like love and separation, birth and death, everything will just happen over and over—like instinct passed down from our ancestral brains.

The shower passes as quickly as it came. Like a sign in the sky, I see the shrine wall rising to my left. Rainbow pulls at my arm but my instinct grounds my feet. I raise my camera to the graffiti, and then zoom out, capturing that moment in time. Through the lens I see sputtered-out candles with unusable wicks standing in little puddles of water, brown petals plastered on the ground, soggy teddy bears, and over it all—a shade darker from the dampness seeping into red and gold stained concrete—Rejoice.

The New Adventures of Rainbow and Friends
By Phil Dyer

Beyond the cracked sidewalk, and the telephone pole with layers of flyers in a rainbow of colors, and the patch of dry brown grass there stood a ten-foot high concrete block wall, caked with dozens of coats of paint. There was a small shrine at the foot of it, with burnt out candles and dead flowers and a few soggy teddy bears. One word of graffiti filled the wall, red letters on a gold background: Rejoice!

Rainbow did not have time to rejoice. Rainbow was on a mission. With the briefest pause to sniff a votive flower and share a glance of solidarity with a one-eyed teddy, she hurried past the marker shrine and off towards the tumbled suburbs. Just one untimely pilgrim, one persuasive out-of-hours supplicant and they'd find her bed empty. The border watch was meant for human people, not little chimera dog-things, but Rainbow didn't move too fast these days. A forewarned sentry might still head her off.

Little claws scrabbled on upheaved asphalt. For the Following, rejoicing was a specific doctrine, a choreographed meditation intended to project general approval and goodwill across the border. Bells were involved. For the Transcendentals, the act was rather more free-form, but carried the same intent. Rainbow had been venerated by both in her time. The Transcendentals had better biscuits.

Not far now. Rainbow scrambled between concealing rubble in calculated bursts of effort, bobbing her head out of cover to map the next stretch with her good eye. Pink petals trailed behind her sprints like breadcrumb trails, glowing in the evening sun. Another reason to hurry. She clambered awkwardly over the lip of a crater and peered out over the last stretch of open ground before the border. The fur and leaves on the nape of her neck began to bristle. The kids were close.

There was a patrol, of sorts. Volunteers from the two dominant churches made regular circuits- in pairs, for fear the other might stumble on some advantageous revelation. Rainbow smelled them before she heard them, sandalwood and the nose-scrunching soap the monks made in the ruin of the old jam factory. She flattened her flowers and slunk behind a pile of bricks to watch them pass. The pair were in their early forties- as young as people anywhere these days- a heavyset man in a red Following sash and a woman with a hard hat sprayed Transcendent purple. A few meters away over the border, in a trailing crowd that piled up against the invisible boundary, the mirror kids followed.

They were small but fluidly proportioned, straining their shapes to keep pace with the adults. Both the man and the woman's face occasionally slid across the glassy bowl of their own, often as a blend of both, a hard hat occasionally emerging on top. The impression of clothing swam on translucent bodies. The patrol mostly ignored them. Every so often the Transcendent monk would glance over and her face would instantly bloom across a dozen kids in greater detail, the outlines of her grubby boiler suit immediately reflected in the mass. Sometimes the mirror kids spoke in echoes, but mostly they just followed, watching and changing in silence.

Shouts in the distance. As Rainbow cringed deeper into the rubble, a runner from the camp came skidding over the scree, waving to the patrol. Across the border, a flurry of mirror kids simultaneously mimed for attention. Rainbow's ears were too full of roots to catch the conversation from her hiding spot, but adults and their shadows alike immediately spread out, on the hunt and looking low. Rainbow growled some words not fit for church and ran.

They nearly caught her. In Rainbow's early years, she had been fit and strong and the flowers that grew from her crown were as bright and vivid as the children's cartoon that she had been made to imitate. She had been a beacon then, an ambassador of the new powers, full of cheerful advice and oh so quick. They were strange times, yes, the children…gone, the world adrift, all things uncertain, but Rainbow had been there for everyone. Always boil the water, she would say, trotting up and down the queue for the well. If amoxicillin isn't working, why not try a quinolone? Remember, fallen satellites may contain hazardous materials! She didn't always understand it herself, but people had been grateful.

Now she was tired and her body was a bag of worms. The flowers that had been her pride had never quite stopped growing, sinking thin white roots to steal her breath and one eye and probably some of her brain, if she was honest. Now she spent her days dispensing worn-out wisdom from embroidered cushions, wringing the final drops from her significance. Taking turns as a relic for one cult or the other, while her creators tamed new lightning beyond the border, their baby toys forgotten.

Well, no more. Rainbow ran as she hadn't in years, racing away in a flurry of hair and petals. Her lungs clenched, her pulse hammered in her head but her legs kept going. The big man gave up almost immediately, settled for yelling her name as the runner and the purple hat went after her. They moved to corner her in an odd half crouch, the one people used to reassure an animal too far to grab. Rainbow wasn't fooled. As the runner broke into a sprint, she juked under a fallen lamppost, scrambled up a short embankment and tumbled over the painted line of the border. A faint resistance tugged at her fur, as if she was passing through the film of a bubble. The mirror kids were there as she rolled to her feet, all of them the runner reaching out, but she snapped at their half formed fingers and fled. They didn't copy *her*. There were gardens here, untouched suburbia gone feral. With the cries fading behind her, Rainbow wriggled under a fence and disappeared into engulfing green.

The flying fish were new. They bobbed in clumsy shoals along the darkening streets, glimmers of frivolous phosphorescence reflecting in house windows as they passed. The intact glass was almost as strange to see. In places the grid of houses, roads and gardens twisted into theme park craziness, hedge mazes and flumes and tangled fields of fairy lights, teetering monoliths that were just a dozen bungalows ripped up and stacked together. In others the suburbs were preserved pristine, as if the last twenty years had missed them completely. Manicured lawns. Bicycles abandoned on the curb. Rainbow heard noises from a house and climbed up to look into a front window. A television set illuminated an empty sofa. Rainbow half expected to see herself, but it was all nonsense, shifting colors and gibberish sounds.

Also new; towards what might have been the center, a great pyramid rose high above the neighborhood, smooth sides aglow in the last of the evening light. Heat haze trembled at its apex. Joints grumbling, Rainbow set off hopefully towards it.

She didn't recognize the first kid she came across, but they recognized her. They were sitting cross-legged on the curb, looking up at the emerging stars. They were small and slight with a mane of curly hair and when Rainbow approached they rose giggling into the air and disappeared in a burst of the bouncy theme song from her cartoon. We'll sing and laugh and learn, we've a long long way to go! Damn right, Rainbow thought, but she plodded on vaguely encouraged. Other kids began to manifest at the corners of her vision. Nature kids trailing clouds of beetles, party kids darting between rooftops, shy kids whispering in the darkest corners. As she crossed a street near the base of the pyramid a bad kid came right up to her and growled, seething heat and cigarette smoke. Rainbow held her ground, even when they jabbed a clawed finger into the asphalt and dragged a steaming line in front of her nose. They weren't angry at *her*. Eventually they slunk aside and there, looking down at her with gentle curiosity, was her maker.

None of the cults that clung to the ruins outside could really say what had happened to the children. The most coherent guesses revolved around a secret weapon, that the opening salvo of that last brief war had deployed some monstrous prototype, something that stripped the thought from human flesh and left more precious things untouched. That was plausible. Perhaps at the moment of dissolution, the plasticity of infant minds had allowed them to survive united, clumping by like and soul into the gestalt entities that were the gods inside the border, the unlucky unmatched scattered as the mirror kids. This too was plausible. The kids were hard to count, but everyone agreed there were far fewer than there had been children. It didn't explain why there hadn't been any *more*. What was known for sure is that a few months after the apocalypse, a thing that looked like a kid had emerged from ground zero, carrying a real life version of the most famous critter in children's cartoons.

Rainbow's creator looked somewhere between ten and fifteen years old, a tall thin kid of indeterminate sex. They swung their long braids out of the way and crouched down to look over Rainbow's battered old body, tutting at the strangling weave of vegetation. They stroked her brow. Rainbow beat her tail against the ground. There was no need for words. The maker understood her pain. The maker would make her better. The kid's eyes glittered and Rainbow was rising up, up, slowly spinning in a snow of petals. There was a shifting within her, a numb, tugging discomfort as endless capillary roots withered and withdrew. Unwrapped muscles twitched and jerked. Something pulled loose in her bad eye. Through her good one she saw the whole assemblage pulled away, almost a Rainbow-shaped net in places, flowers crumbling to ash and billowing away into the dark. Then her maker set her down, patted her absently on the head and disappeared. The other kids followed, and then it was just Rainbow, hollowed and alone in the middle of the street.

It didn't hurt much, though the smell of blood was overwhelming. She tried to get up, tripped on slack limbs. This was a mistake. They must have been distracted for a moment, but they'd be back. They'd come back and make her better, make her what she was meant to be. She got one paw braced beneath her, slipped again into pooling stickiness as it gave way. Maybe they'd give her wings this time. Someone did it for the fish, after all. Rainbow had often thought she should fly. She thought of her empty cushions in the temple, remembered eating dinner in her sanctum and listening to the Following rejoice in the yard. We are ready, they chanted, as she growled down goat and chewable vitamins. We are ready for you to lead us. Show us your power. Show us a sign. Show me my wings, Rainbow thought, and fell into a dark and sticky sleep.

Rainbow was woken by the most wonderful smell she could imagine, meat and bread and steaming fat. It must be a feast day. Had she forgotten? Maybe the temple had received an extra special sign and she would need to be on top form to interpret it for them. She prised her eye open and coughed some blood. To her crushing disappointment, she was still lying in the road. The edges of the looming pyramid glimmered faintly against the night sky. She didn't feel any wings, although she couldn't feel her legs either. In the orange wash of a nearby streetlight, a kid stood eating a slice of pizza.

Rainbow knew about pizza. Outside, the settlements grew tomatoes and herbs and enough grain to make something that was at least reminiscent of the immortal illustrations on packaging and blasted billboards, impossibly healthy people raising beautifully lit triangles to their smiling faces. This kid could have stepped from one of those pictures. Unusually for a kid, he looked unambiguously male, a lean young boy with light skin and neatly styled hair. His clothing was immaculate. He heard her whimpering and immediately ran over, face full of handsome concern. Rainbow tried to nose at the half eaten crust in his hand, but he tossed it aside to touch her sunken wounds. It vanished before it could hit the floor. Rainbow groaned.

The pizza kid spoke. It was a beautiful sound, though Rainbow couldn't pick out the actual words. She understood their meaning. She should not be hurting. She should not be alone. She should be strong and sleek and full of life and as he said it she could see it, felt the spray on her face as she ran through surf on a sunlit beach. She should eat vet-recommended foods beneath laden tables and ride in brand new pickup trucks through empty, unspoiled natural wonders. It should always be summer, except when it was Fall and she romped through leaves with her beautiful family, except when it was Christmas and she was watching ecstatic children unwrap plastic toys. At some point she became aware the pizza kid was carrying her body, crunching up a gravel drive to one of those perfectly preserved houses with the lawn and the swing-door garage. He laid her out on a concrete floor and as she danced between A Healthy Treat For Glossy Coats and The Best For Your Best Friend she became aware of things moving inside her, of wounds twisting shut and flesh swelling out to fill the hollows the roots had left in her body. When her bare patches started to itch unbearably with the emergence of new fur, she turned away and back into the carousel of wonders, spun away in a tumble of perfect lives and endless comfort.

When the ride ended, she was lifted again. The kid slid her body onto a soft pile of clothing among the boxes in the garage. He pulled an old coat over the top, creating a cave that emanated the sweetness of old ladies who frequently powdered themselves—a light rose motif that played ironically well in the deep recesses of Rainbow's ancestral brain. The pizza kid lifted her head to help her lap water from a hubcap. He broke bits of pepperoni and crust into bite-sized pieces and left them where her tongue could reach them. Much later, she heard him practicing his orations like songs. Like monks chanting in the distance, they were a comfort.

Rainbow didn't recognize herself at first. Her dinners at the temple were delivered on a burnished platter and she had spent considerable quality time with her blurry reflection. In a mirror propped among cobwebbed junk at the back of the garage, she found a brand new Rainbow.

She wondered if her coat had ever been this fine. In the dim morning seeping through a grubby skylight, her muscles bulged beneath russet fur. Her right eye was still blind, but when she squashed her nose against the glass it looked just like the other, twinkling and astonished. Strangest of all, her head was bare. Not a single shoot broke the smooth fur of her scalp, sleek and unscarred. She sat looking at herself until her haunches went numb. She looked good. She looked strong. Rainbow was not entirely a dog, but she could certainly pass for one now. An odd mongrel, yes, with expressive eyes and slightly wrong paws and obviously the distinction of speech, but still a dog.

The temple had other dogs. Rainbow got on fine with them, but no one came to the dogs for advice. No one asked the dogs what they thought of the latest revelations, or sought their blessing for a daring expedition. No one cooked for dogs, except when Rainbow got sick from eating rats and didn't finish her plate.

These were uncomfortable thoughts. Rainbow got up and paced around the garage, nosing at heaps of improbably preserved curios, smells of the certainly-long-dead mingling with old paint and pizza crumbs. There was a door leading into the house, but the handle didn't turn. The big swing door might open with a button on the wall, but Rainbow couldn't reach. She licked at a grease spot and considered dragging things over to stand on. It might be impolite to leave without eating more pizza, but who knew where the kid had got to. She had what she came for, she supposed. Time to move on. She got her strong new teeth into a sack of second-hand clothes and began to methodically heave it across the concrete floor. Something shifted in a pile. With a warning creak, an avalanche of clutter crashed and scattered, old tools and electrical miscellany spinning away from a landslide of garden toys and bike parts. Rainbow yelped and hid behind a sturdier looking stack until the dust settled. When she emerged, guiltily, a much more familiar Rainbow was looking back at her.

It was on a box, a big plastic tub of Outdoor Fun for All Ages. Beneath a grey patina of dust, the cartoon Rainbow held a garden hose in her mouth. An assortment of cartoon children looked on in awe, as leafy shoots erupted from the furrowed soil before them. Her laughing eyes locked with the real Rainbow's one, beneath her glorious, blossoming mane. This was the image of the life bringer, the guide in troubled times, the voice of reason for the masses.

Rainbow stared for a while and then, with the very tip of her nose and tongue, she traced two spreading wings in the dust on the cartoon's back. The grimy plastic tasted awful. Rainbow sat back and looked at the angel and wondered if her rejuvenated eyes would cry.

Suddenly the garage door was clattering upwards of its own accord, morning light and air pouring in. Rainbow drew back, squinting in the glare. The pizza kid ducked inside. He didn't seem perturbed by the mess, but crouched down to inspect her, patting the ground and grinning hugely. Gratitude was clearly in order. Rainbow pulled herself together and licked his face obligingly. His skin was warm, but the kid tasted more like glass than anything else, a slick nothing overlaid with the machine-fresh cotton of his clothes and a lingering residue of fast food. He held her head gently in strong hands, turned her this way and that, peering into her eyes. He made a small noise of irritation. With a gesture and a brief tang of ozone, a disc of pepperoni appeared in his palm. When Rainbow ducked to snap it up, he clapped a hand to the back of her skull. There was a momentary jolt of pain behind her brow and she struggled, but the kid was holding her tight. Something shifted in her brain and suddenly unbearable light bloomed on her right. Her head spun with overlapping images. She thrashed, the kid let her go, the pictures swung back together and she could see, she could see from both of them!

The expanded field of view was dizzying. Rainbow blinked and stumbled, licking furiously at the kid's hands as he laughed. He ruffled her head and began to speak again. The visions washed over her, the carousel spinning up. They would run and play together in the streets, frisbees in the park, lazy afternoons on the porch. There could be a wood nearby, he could easily make one, where she could chase squirrels and run and bark to the fullness of her heart. Long walks in the evening sun. Jumping through sprinklers. A bowl with her name on it. The perfect child and the perfect pet, forever and ever, amen.

Rainbow shook herself free. The visions faded. The pizza kid looked at her with confusion. She looked back into the handsome face of the lonely god-thing. How many vaporised children had combined to make him? What shared understanding had drawn them together? The temple had recorded so many archetypes, distantly observed and argued for, perpetually redefined. There were nature kids, the theory went, children who'd lived for the green places of the old world, now conjuring jungles from the ruins. There were party kids, adrift in continuations of childhood games. There were shy kids, still in hiding. There were bad kids, still angry.

The pizza kid was a fiction from a fiction, a dream of a world they'd never grown to see through. Behind those eyes were children who'd grown up knowing they were the ideal, who'd seen themselves reflected perfectly in screens and magazines. Now the world was inside out, and all they had was the memory of those assurances.

"I'm sorry," said Rainbow. Her voice was raspier than she remembered. "Thank you for fixing me. Thank you for the pizza. But I can't stay here." She cleared her throat. The pizza kid looked utterly bewildered. "I'm very important. People need me."

The kid didn't move for an uncomfortable length of time. Then he got up and walked past her into the garage. Rainbow looked on uneasily as he picked up the box with the cartoon. There probably wasn't much point in running. She had the horrible thought of him withdrawing his gifts, of withering away, the kid looking on blankly as her vision went and her wounds reopened. But he just pointed at the cartoon Rainbow, at her silly dust-drawn wings. He spoke and suddenly she felt the wind in her fur. She felt her pinions snap open, saw the world laid out before her like the map in the temple council's hall, saw the pilgrims gasp in wonder as she swooped into the muster yard. She clapped her wings and opened her mouth to offer new, great wisdom. The vision ended. The pizza kid was staring at her.

"Help me," he said. His voice was beautiful, and completely independent from the movements of his mouth. Images flickered through Rainbow's mind. The pyramid. Her maker. The border. The pyramid again. Outside, the sun emerged from behind a cloud. Beneath the skylight, the pizza kid shone, a haloed sculpture of youth. "Help me. And I will give you wings."

The day was well underway as Rainbow trotted out into the street. The flying fish appeared to be sleeping, tucked beneath the eaves of houses, shoaling up in the gently swaying treetops. Rainbow imagined chasing them and made a mental note for later. That might be beneath an ambassador for transcendence, but no one had complained very much about the rats. She stopped to assess her gravitas in the waxed door of a parked car. Her flowers shone in the morning sun.

She shook her head experimentally. They stayed secure. Every so often she felt she had to check that they weren't growing into her skull, but so far so good. These were plastic, more vivid and durable than the original, snug to her scalp. The pizza kid had taken great care with them. With petals bobbing at the edges of her vision, she felt more like herself. Confidence was critical. The pyramid was waiting.

It blotted out the sun as she crossed into the road where she had lost her first flowers, and for a moment she hesitated, remembering the blood, the mild curiosity on her maker's face. Rainbow didn't think her creator had wanted her dead. They just hadn't thought about it. Rainbow thought of the churches, thought of the vigils, the observers at their telescope perches day and night, straining for a glimpse of the power over the border. Maybe they could even see her now, and she drew herself up a little taller. But they were looking for answers, looking for guidance, and the kids…they were only kids. It wasn't them who'd torn the world apart. It seemed unfair to hope they'd put it back.

The neighborhood near the base of the pyramid was one of the theme park zones. Rainbow wound her way between a forest of endless legs, occasionally hop-skipping nervously at the misapprehension of movement. For miles around, the streets were packed with statues, countless life-size sculptures of the adult human form, naked and clothed alike. They queued, they laughed, they fought and argued, they danced, they cried. Some were barely identifiable, abstract mannequins in rough-cut stone. On others she could see the hairs on their ankles. Rainbow hurried along and avoided looking up. Every so often she heard noises from roofs, or caught a flicker across the shoulders of distant giants. When she finally clambered up onto the first step of the pyramid's dizzying stair, a dark-eyed kid popped up beside her and played her song again. She wasn't sure if it was the same one. Tentatively, it reached out a hand to her muzzle. She accepted the touch; its hands were cold and very light. Another kid appeared, this one dressed all in pink from head to toe. Another and another. As a procession formed around her, Rainbow began to climb.

In her old body it would have been impossible, now it was merely hard going. The stair was made of the same material as the pyramid face, each step a seamlessly extruded block about a meter high, ridiculous even for an adult human. Rainbow wondered why they were there at all. Perhaps it was just for the look. The kids flickered abruptly from point to point, pausing to bravely stroke her fur or sing snatches of the cartoon theme. The surface was warm underfoot, some kind of porous ceramic, with hard edges that hurt to haul herself over. Every so often the pyramid groaned, a rumbling that rattled Rainbow's bones and made the kids shiver and giggle. She hoped she wasn't too late.

The pizza kid had told her that it was a machine, a project of some of the older kids. He didn't understand how it worked, or maybe he just couldn't explain it to her. He'd shown her pictures. She'd seen the lightning crawl its flanks, seen the ground quake, the houses crumble. Seen the whole absurd edifice slowly rotating in its moorings, tearing from the bedrock and rising inexorably into the air, and- the kid was very clear about this- never coming back.

Rainbow wasn't sure why anyone would want to live in the sky. Obviously flying looked amazing, but you had to come down some time. Clouds probably got boring after a while. The kid said no, they want to go further than that. They want to go and never come back. They're tired of this place. The pizza kid could never cry, but a kind of horror had flickered behind that handsome mask. Who could be tired of perfection? But the forces of their creation had bound the kids together with more than fellow feeling. If the others chose to leave, he might not be able to stay.

The other kids hoped that they might find something out there, maybe other things like themselves. That didn't seem likely to Rainbow, but it wasn't her pyramid. She paused to pant for a moment, looking back over her shoulder. The ground seemed very far away already, the crowds of statue town a sprawling, tangled mass below. The older kids probably knew what they were doing. There had been a episode of the cartoon where Rainbow went to the moon, and although that didn't look much more promising, perhaps the plan was something like that.

In any case, Rainbow didn't like it any more than the pizza kid. What was the point in being an expert, if the whole focus of her expertise disappeared into the sky? Even once she had her wings, it sounded like they would be a pain to follow. This wretched stair was quite hard enough. The kids were cheering her on now. It helped. But even with her theme tune chiming from a dozen little gods, uncomfortable thoughts were creeping in. If the pizza kid was right, if she could somehow talk them out of their plan- and they'd already built the pyramid, Rainbow hated to see wasted effort- if they turned around and promised never to stray again, where did that leave them? She turned to look out over the border- beyond the jumbled wilderness, beyond the patches of perfect suburban grid, out past the bubble of the boundary, the red and purple tents of the temple clustered like ticks. Where did that leave anyone?

The top of the pyramid was a trembling plateau lit by unearthly energies. At the center, an open pit plunged to the howling depths of the structure; across the platform, antennae like broken weather vanes sucked lightning from the prickling air and spun electric webs that clung and fizzled. More kids than Rainbow had ever seen together were gathered by the pit in two main groups. Before the smaller of the two, the pizza kid stood proud, somehow more visible and definite, more real than any of the assembled host. Rainbow staggered towards them, huffing and panting. She bet he hadn't climbed.

The other group was headed by her maker. Rainbow wasn't surprised. They didn't look pleased. The pizza kid seemed to be wrapping something up. As Rainbow drew closer, she heard his voice and slipped into the vision. The ground fell away below her, beneath them all, and now they were floating in an endless darkness scattered with stars. It was cold here, colder and more alone than anyone had ever been. There was a tiny spark below them, a little blue dot. Somehow Rainbow knew that everything she knew and loved was on that dot, but it was too late. They were drifting far away, off in the endless dark to who knew where. There was nowhere safe to play in the dark. There were no sunlit streets. There was no ice cream. Something shifted in the scene, and suddenly Rainbow knew that she was the focus of it. Unseen eyes dug into her. Here she was, Rainbow, their Rainbow. Look at her floating, shivering and fearful. Rainbow didn't like it here. This wasn't a place for her. It wasn't a place for anyone. Rainbow cleared her throat. That was probably her cue.

"Hi everybody!" she called into the darkness, feeling silly. "Today we're going to talk about…home!" Rainbow hadn't actually seen much of her cartoon, though sometimes the temple had indulged her curiosity, hooking up a salvaged screen with precious generator time. She had been made with the knowledge built in, the lyrics, the bright clear tones, the friendly waggle of the ears, all instinct. "Home is a very special place. There's nowhere else quite like it!" She looked around at the eternal void. "This isn't my home! Can anyone show me where home is?" There was a pause. Little shapes wavered and vanished in the black. Then, haltingly, warily, a few of the kids appeared, floating beside her. Little fingers uncurled, pointing down at the little blue spot. "That's right!" Rainbow cried. "That *is* my home!" She was on better ground now, there was a song for this. "Home is where we know the best. Home is where we come to rest! Home is where it's best for…me. " She frowned. "Home is with…my…fam-ily." The song trailed off into the blackness. The thoughts were back, and before she or the pizza kid could recover, the scene was wrenched away.

Her maker's visions lacked the flair of the pizza kid's, but they compensated with variety. Here was the world, choking and blasted. Here was their little domain, a bubble in the wastelands, and look how small it was. Here were the machines that killed them. Here were the adults who let them die. Here was the world, and look how small it was. Here were the stars, glittering with promises. Here was the ultimate adventure, the ultimate escape. Here was the pyramid. The pounding atmospherics settled to a conciliatory tone, panned the communal view across the manicured lawns of the pizza kid's estate. There was a compromise on offer here. Here was the pyramid, wreathed in power. Here it was, extending the tiniest fraction of its capabilities. As seen from great remove, a ragged sphere of force erupted from the monolith, slicing miles through rock and earth to encapsulate the kids' domain entirely. With the barest suggestion of effort, the whole assembly shuddered, spun, lifted in its vast entirety out of the barren wastes, a perfect sphere of rock and land and atmosphere, the pyramid resplendent at its centre. In its enormous shadow, temples and tents began to slide and tumble into the crater of its leaving. The vision ended. At the top of the pyramid, still rumbling with potential, the maker extended a hopeful hand.

"No!" screamed the pizza kid. Suddenly there was a wall between the groups, a thunderous collision of immense forces, visible only by its distortion of the world. The pizza kid extended a finger, his eyes aglow with a light to match the pyramid, and that wall ground forward towards the maker and her supporters. The maker slid backwards, rallied, forced him back in turn. The crackling energies of the antennae trembled and streamed away like smoke in the wind, the smallest kids stumbling, flickering with incoherence. "I won't go!" howled the pizza kid. "You think you can just cut out the parts I want, but you can't, you can't!" Around the shifting line of collision, the mystery material of the surface was beginning to score and warp. Rainbow whimpered in terror, flattened against the floor. "It's our world, all of it! It was made for us! You can't just leave!" Rainbow felt the pressure building. This was only the shoving before the fight. Both kids were going to hit out for real at any moment, and they were going to do it on top of an engine that could cut the world in two. She thought of her cushions. She thought of wings. She thought of stars, and the cold and distant blackness. She thought of something else. Rainbow straightened the flowers on her head. They were melting a bit, but they'd have to do. She struggled to her feet, electricity crackling through her fur. In the loudest, bravest, most Rainbow voice she could possibly make, she sang the best idea she'd ever had.

Beyond the cracked sidewalk, far beyond the border strangely absent of mirror kids, beyond the paint and candles and the sad old teddies of the marker shrine, there was a watchtower made of rickety scaffold and scavenged old planking. There was a telescope mounted on a bracket and an uncomfortable wicker chair at the top, with a battered old notepad to write down any miraculous happenings that might be observed. The telescope swung loosely from its mounting, and the notepad had been dropped in haste, but on the open page a single word filled the space, shaky in a disbelieving hand: Rejoice!

In the main courtyard of the dominant temple, lit only by the scattered light of a few sputtering oil lamps, monks in red and purple stood staring at the night sky. Some wept. Some laughed, but it was the sort of laugh that wasn't easily stopped. Some prayed, although it wasn't clear to whom. A terrible light shone on the horizon, towards the centre of the place beyond the border. That wasn't where people were looking. As the assembled multitude gaped up in awe— as rumbling earthquakes shuddered through their bones, the ruined city, the entire planet— the lonely stars slid inexorably across the sky. The world was loose and setting sail, and where it would go now no adult could say.

The beat of wings from darkness. As the moon fell away behind her, Rainbow descended upon the congregation, enormous wings spread wide. Atop her head there was a bouquet of melted plastic, and in her eyes there gleamed a new and precious wisdom, much as it had in the earliest records of the church. Somehow, someone found the presence of mind to bring a cushion. She settled down graciously, folded her beautiful feathers, and then, as the flock huddled in, with a knowing glance at the rapidly shifting sky, she began to speak.

The Best Most Excellent Farm
By Carnegie Euclid

Beyond the cracked sidewalk, and the telephone pole with layers of flyers in a rainbow of colors, and the patch of dry brown grass there stood a ten-foot high concrete block wall, caked with dozens of coats of paint. There was a small shrine at the foot of it, with burnt out candles and dead flowers and a few soggy teddy bears. One word of graffiti filled the wall, red letters on a gold background: Rejoice!

Rainbow strutted atop the wall, as much as a fat chicken could strut, her head held high, the sheep below gazing at her with devotion, the rising sun illuminating her from behind, giving her head a saintly glow. This is what she thought, that she was strutting in such a fashion as to define elegance and grace and humility and a certain angelic aura. In reality—a part of the world Rainbow seldom ventured willingly—her strut was more of a waddle; a waddle with extreme, misplaced confidence. In reality, she was lazy, with a gluttonous streak and a propensity for self-aggrandizement. At night, Rainbow would sneak into the farmer's house and flower garden and trash can and steal teddy bears and candles and flowers and place them at the base of the wall, later saying the items were left by her admirers. Rainbow believed this, that the items were left by her admirers, and you might think this odd, that she would do something, and attribute that very thing to someone else, but

Rainbow found it not odd at all. In fact, she found it very convenient, and she knew, in her brain (She had the best brain, she told herself) that her followers would have placed all those things there if she hadn't, and by the comfortable logic of the logically unfit you could admit that if they could have, would have, placed such things, they actually did, even though they didn't.

The sheep below were mesmerized by Rainbow, gazing at her with a hunger and longing starving sinners often horde and then release upon an unlikely and unworthy savior. They noted there was another candle at the wall this morning, proving Rainbow was admired and loved. Rainbow understood them, really understood the plight of being a sheep, even though she was an eagle, had never been a sheep. Had never given wool, nor milk, nor meat, slept out in the field, been ridden by mischievous farm-boys. "I am the greatest eagle of all time, believe me," Rainbow said. (Rainbow was not an eagle. Rainbow was a fat chicken who never gave an egg—losing her feathers so she appeared bald in spots. I am afraid you may have forgotten this fact.) "I can fly higher, and faster, than all other birds." Rainbow screamed this, her feathers bouncing in agreement, and she smiled and accepted the adulation from the flock below. (Rainbow could not fly. In fact, to ascend the wall each morning and evening, when she wanted to give a speech and bask in admiration, the sheep had to pile onto each other so Rainbow could walk upon their backs to get to the top of the wall.) "I'm the best flyer," Rainbow continued, and the sheep cheered while Rainbow stopped to let them admire her. Some of the other animals often told the sheep that Rainbow was not an eagle. That she was, in fact, a chicken, who had never given an egg, and could not fly, and lied to them constantly. When the goats and cows and cats and pigs and other animals communicated this the sheep quickly turned their backs and quit listening to those animals who obviously did not love the farm. That is what Rainbow said about those vile creatures who said she was not an eagle, and other disgusting lies. The sheep loved these daily rants. Well, they each felt the others loved the rants, and because they were sheep, they each in turn followed along, including a young Hampshire named Exverity, who often chanted last, and with a quiet voice, from the back of the flock.

Rainbow waddled across the wall and stopped, waiting for the sheep's full attention. "I am making the farm the best most excellent. Believe me. Before me, do you remember before me? Before me it was terrible. There was no food, sheep were starving, there were coyotes coming in every night, tearing your throats open, vicious coyotes. It's true," Rainbow stated. It was not true, but the sheep were bleating now with a malignant fervor at Rainbow. Rainbow was just like them, they thought, but much better, because she was an eagle and could fly and she built the wall she stood on each morning and night, the wall that protected them from the vicious coyotes.

"I built this wall, and now you are safe from the coyotes," Rainbow said. She didn't build the wall. The wall was twenty-feet long, built years before for the farmer's son to have something to throw lacrosse balls at and for a few feeble attempts at graffiti and to hold one rock concert in front of in order to impress Wendy Studer. (His band was called Hiding in the Coatrack and he played the bass guitar, and to his credit he stapled many brightly colored posters of this concert on the pole next to the wall. Unfortunately, few attended the concert, and Wendy Studer was unable to make it because of a sick Aunt, but that is not the point of the story.) A coyote, if there was one in the vicinity, could easily walk around the wall, as it was, as stated, twenty feet long. On either end of it was bare ground and crabgrass and a couple of weeping nasturtiums planted by the farmer's daughter. "Now, those crazy other animals are not like us," Rainbow continued. She liked to refer to any of the other animals as crazy and not like us, because the sheep loved that, the sheep knowing they were the best animals, and the cows and goats were taking their jobs of giving milk. "You know," Rainbow continued, "Those cows and goats want the coyotes to come in here and rip your throats open, they do. But I won't let them. That's why I built this wall, and that's why I'm making this farm The Best Most Excellent," and Rainbow stopped and let the sheep admire her. Some of the sheep started to cry, so moved by Rainbow's speech, the greatest eagle that ever lived. One of the sheep fainted, and the other sheep, seeing this, fainted as well, because it seemed like the appropriate thing to do. Exverity watched the fainting around her, and pretended to collapse, thinking that is what true sheep did in such circumstances, though she felt quite stupid lying there, wondering how long her faint should last and when it would be permissible for her to rise and wander off into the low hills and chew on grass.

Across the farm, the other animals were busily being milked, and patrolling the farm for danger, and pulling plows so the fields would grow feed for the long winter, and laying eggs. They could hear the occasional cheer from the wall and the chants that Rainbow often led, "Starve the invaders, Starve the invaders," the invaders being any animal not born on the farm, which included almost all of the cows and many of the chickens and three of the dogs, and half of the goats, and eight of the pigs and some of the very sheep who were gleefully chanting, apparently unable to do the simplest of analysis to determine they were, in fact, chanting in support of their own starvation.

Rainbow stopped pacing and turned slowly to her flock below, and said in a mock whisper, as if sharing a tasty secret, "Maybe we'd be better off if those other, *different* animals, weren't around anymore. Many in the flock say it; maybe it would be best if they were gone." She stopped and waited and when one of the young sheep yelled, "Kill them," Rainbow laughed and said, "I like your spirit. I can't get away with saying that, but many others are saying that's a solution!" and Rainbow waited for the rest of the sheep to take up the chant, "Kill them! Kill them!" as she strutted and preened and basked in the anger and angst propelled from her sheeply-followers' mouths.

That night, in the cool of the main barn, the other animals discussed what they could do about Rainbow. The sheep had taken to sleeping in the small barn on the hill, as they had been told by Rainbow the other animals were unclean and hated the farm and wanted to take their jobs and let the coyotes in, and the best thing would be to never associate with such vile, disgusting animals. So the sheep left the main barn and camped out on the hill in the small barn, leaving the other animals to themselves.

"Perhaps we could encourage a coyote to get Rainbow," one of the goats said. He was new to the farm, and when he arrived on the farmer's truck the sheep told him to go back to where he came from. When he tried to introduce himself to Rainbow she made fun of his accent and yelled, "Invader!" and the sheep bleated at him and spat on him and turned their backs on him. The other goats and cows and chickens explained, in embarrassment, the situation then, and they recoiled at his suggestion now. "The coyote doesn't come around anymore," the dogs replied. They bristled at the idea of allowing a coyote to do harm to any animal on the farm, even though Rainbow often stated they were friends of the coyote, wanted the coyote to kill the other animals.

"The kid is our only choice. He knows Rainbow isn't pulling her weight and is making the sheep nervous and afraid," the first cow said. She was brought to the farm almost a decade before, when all the animals stayed in the same barn and worked and welcomed the new additions and mourned the death of any farm animal. She loved the farm, what it was and what it should be, and only wished it was better now. "I will speak to the kid," she offered, and the other animals nodded in agreement. Let the kid deal with it.

The kid and the cow discussed the problem of Rainbow, both amazed such a stupid, ugly creature could get the sheep to follow her so easily, preying on their fear, while ignoring her constant lying and made up words and incoherent rants. They discussed this while watching Rainbow ride along the backs of her flock, pointing out gardens she said she planted (she didn't) and structures she said she built (she didn't) and ponds she said she dug (she most definitely had not) the sheep cheering her with each grandiose lie. The flock of sheep moved in unison during these tours of the farm so Rainbow could more easily move from one sheep to another. Exverity positioned herself to the rear of the flock during these wanderings, not wanting Rainbow on her back. Most of the other sheep positioned themselves near the front, eager for the honor of providing Rainbow a ride, often jostling for position, trampling the slow and weak in the process. The kid and the cow watched this as the sun set, and they agreed Rainbow should go, for the sake of the farm.

A trap was to be set. Rainbow had become increasingly paranoid, and was seldom alone, preferring the company of extremely complimentary sheep to accompany her. At night she slept above them in the small barn on the hill, the sheep below her intended to be a barrier to any invader. She was happy to sacrifice those stupid sheep, and she knew they would lay down their lives for her, as she was so much better than them.

The kid knew this and did not want to frighten the sheep, who were remarkably sensitive to any perceived threat, by snatching Rainbow while they all watched. It was impossible to grab her during the day, as she rode on the backs of her followers, touring the farm and laying claim to the toil of others. No, she would need to be lured away, quietly, and the kid knew there was only one way to do this.

Rainbow loved food (You will know this already by the rather skillful deployment of the term "gluttonous streak" in paragraph two), all food, but was especially adoring of pizza, and McDonalds french-fries and McNuggets. (Yes, we know what McNuggets are made of, but to be honest, Rainbow did not seem to care.) Rainbow also absolutely abhorred anyone eating such delicacies before she had her fill, and it was only when such food was available would she leave the protection of her sheep.

The kid waited until the sheep were sleeping, and he placed a line of french-fries and McNugget pieces from the barn on the hill to the open rear-door of his car, far enough away from the small barn so the sheep would not hear the shutting of the door. On the backseat of the car were piles of fries and McNuggets and a large sausage and anchovy pizza—Rainbow's favorite.

After the path of food was ready, the kid climbed up the outside of the small barn's wall, until he was inches and a few thin barn boards away from where Rainbow roosted and rested, and he whispered, "Rainbow, we love you, we adore you. We have left a smorgasbord of food for you. Please, let us reward your intelligence and leadership by honoring us, and eat the food outside the door."

Rainbow awakened to these whispers, and it seemed perfectly logical to her that some adoring fans or perhaps angels (She often said she was the Chosen One) would leave a trail of food for her, and whisper about it through a wall, even though all of her followers were fitfully sleeping on the barn floor below. She could detect the aroma of french-fries, and she quietly departed the barn, and was happy to see the trail of food, and began eating and chuckling to herself as she ate, and ate, and ate. When she reached the car she spied the pile of food on the seat. She did not like cars, or trucks, or anything that allowed animals to be moved from place to place, but the pizza was calling to her, so she hopped, but her exceptional girth kept her many inches away from the seat and she fell. She righted herself, caught her breath, and tried again, with similar result. She tried a third time but came no closer to success and she rolled down the small hill where she stayed for many minutes beating her wings against the dirt in frustration, like a petulant child being told it was time for bed.

The kid watched his plan fail before his eyes. Rainbow was too fat to get up to the backseat, and he chastised himself for not building a ramp for the rotund chicken. He considered what to do next, afraid if he grabbed her she would squawk and alarm the other animals. As the kid pondered what to do, Rainbow looked up and noticed him hiding by the front of the car. Rainbow waddled over to him, pecked at his foot, and began to yell. "Hey, stupid kid. Pick me up, would you, so I can finish that food on that seat. I love me some nuggets. Come on, be quick about it," Rainbow said. The kid obliged, gently lifting Rainbow and placing her on the seat, and then shut the door, Rainbow barely noticing, as she was beak-deep in gooey mozzarella and anchovies. She expelled a rather loud chicken-burp, and returned to the pizza.

The kid hopped into the front seat of the car and drove over the field, to the service road. Rainbow complained about the bumps, a french-fry sticking out of her beak, and admonished him to slow it down. She did not ponder why the car was moving, where the kid was driving her, or anything beyond the sphere of fries and nuggets and pizza on the seat. She was accustomed to everything being fine for her, and after she had finished eating, she fell asleep, tired from her exertions. She enjoyed the deep and peaceful sleep of the truly stupid.

When the ride ended, she was lifted again. The kid slid her body onto a soft pile of clothing among the boxes in the garage. He pulled an old coat over the top, creating a cave that emanated the sweetness of old ladies who frequently powdered themselves—a light rose motif that played ironically well in the deep recesses of Rainbow's ancestral brain. The pizza kid lifted her head to help her lap water from a hubcap. He broke bits of pepperoni and crust into bite-sized pieces and left them where her tongue could reach them. Much later, she heard him practicing his orations like songs. Like monks chanting in the distance, they were a comfort.

Rainbow dreamt that—the chanting monk-like orations, and the bit-sized pieces of pizza and the smell of old ladies coats, and the tender lifting of her head for a sip of water with her chicken tongue—while locked in that garage. While she dreamt, morning came, and a sheep awakened in the barn on the hill. When Rainbow was not to be found, that first sheep to stir assumed some other sheep and Rainbow had already left for the wall. She quickly departed, wanting to get to the wall early and cheer Rainbow. When this sheep arrived at the wall, she found no Rainbow and no other sheep, and she became frightened and began to bleat. The other sheep in the small barn on the hill heard this agitated bleating and followed it to the wall, where they all wandered around and around the wall aimlessly, wondering where Rainbow was and what they should do and concerned that the coyotes would come to rip their throats without Rainbow's protection.

One of the sheep tripped and hit the wall with his head. The sheep next to him noticed this, and thought maybe it was intentional, that the head-butting was out of a frustration that he should also feel and act upon, and so he butted the wall. The rest of the flock noticed this, and thought maybe they should butt the wall, until soon the wall was surrounded by head-butting sheep. Eventually, their heads began to hurt, and the head-butting lost its intensity as the various sheep looked to their neighbors on either side, hoping their neighbors would stop, so they could stop as well, but none of them did. An older sheep, tired of the head-butting, pretended to faint, and the rest of the flock, seeing this, pretended to faint as well. The first sheep that fainted then pretended to awaken, and wandered a few steps away from the wall, and looked up at it, trying to determine what time it was by the shadows. The flock, seeing this, did the same, all of the sheep looking up at the wall expectantly. The first sheep, determining it was probably three walks from the barn and back before the rising of the farmer, (The traditional way animals tell time) continued to stare at the top of the wall, thinking, because all of the other sheep were now staring there, it must be important. The flock stood there, wallowing in idiocy and peer-pressure, looking at the top of the wall, waiting for something that was not happening.

Exverity, who you know little of, but that is about to change, was an orphaned sheep who arrived on the farm when she was but a lamb a few months before Rainbow's rise to power. When she first arrived, she would play hide and seek amongst the farm implements and hay bales with the piglets and calves and ducklings. They were her friends, until the older sheep, under the influence of Rainbow, told her the other animals were not to be trusted, that they were taking the sheep jobs like giving milk, and that she should stay with her own kind. "But I thought we didn't like to give milk," Exverity said. The other sheep replied that wasn't the point and she needed to only associate with sheep and listen to Rainbow. Slowly, she did just that, spending more time with the other sheep, and trudging down to the wall each day to listen to Rainbow. On this day, Exverity watched in alarm as the other sheep stood and stared at nothing and she worried, if Rainbow did not show up, that this would be the way they all died; staring at a wall idiotically until they fell exhausted, eventually perishing from starvation, or dehydration, or other -tions.

As Exverity stood amongst the other sheep, pondering a death of dehydration brought on by stupidity, she wondered where Rainbow had gone. One of the sheep beside her said, quite sheepishly, "Perhaps we should look for Rainbow," and waited, until another sheep said the exact same thing. The idea rippled through the flock, each sheep repeating the phrase identically, all agreeing with each other with great vigor. There was so much agreement in fact, that no one moved, because while they all agreed they *should* look for Rainbow, no one said they *would* look for Rainbow. The old sheep, who had pretended to faint to stop the headbutting, grew tired of the constant agreement amongst the flock, so she said, not quite sheepishly, "What did you say? We should send a small group to the barn to look for Rainbow. I agree! Send a small group to the barn!" Soon, the entire flock was repeating this, yet no one was moving. Exasperated, the old sheep finally said, decidedly not sheepishly, "The three largest sheep should go? I agree. Good luck!" The other sheep began to repeat this, and the largest sheep began to look at each other, to see if one or the other would actually depart. This took many moments and quizzical glances and raised eyebrows and small, almost imperceptible nods, as none of them wanted to be the first to go, until through the power of inaction they stood still. The other sheep, growing tired of the chanting with no clear ending nor action, grew quiet, the entire flock looking at each other through the thickness of a cognitively-challenged stupor, eyes wide, minds filled with a quaint sort of comfortable vacancy sheep are known for.

After a while, one of the three largest sheep took a tentative step backwards, and the other two largest sheep, sensing a breakthrough, did the same. They all looked at each other and wondered if this was what they should be doing, and they all took another tentative step back, in unison, so it was in very slow motion, none of them interested in looking like they were acting singularly. After many minutes of this they eventually had turned themselves toward the barn in the field and had gotten into a rhythm so that they were almost walking towards it. The rest of the flock stared after them. One of the remaining sheep, in an act of unguarded rebellion, let escape a sigh, and the rest of them, hearing this, thought such a sigh must be the proper response to this particular situation, and so they all began sighing, until there was nothing left at the wall but a flock of sighing sheep.

When the sighing had run its course and slowly petered out the flock stood in silence, slowly turning back to the wall in unison, each watching his neighbor to make sure that was what they were really supposed to do. A bee landed on the leg of one of the sheep, and she jumped and stomped and yelled, and her neighbors, sensing she was exhibiting some frustration that the current situation required, did the same, until the entire flock was jumping and stomping and yelling.

The yelling and stomping went on for a long time, with each stomp growing less assertive and each yell growing quieter, each member of the flock hoping something would change so that their next act would be less physically taxing, when something did change. The three largest sheep returned, and they stood facing the flock, each of them looking to their neighbor, waiting for them to say something, but nothing was said, because no one started it. There was no sign of Rainbow with the returning three largest but frustratingly silent sheep, and one by one the flock began to slowly turn back to the wall, to stare at it. Every sheep, but Exverity.

Exverity, next to the wall and thus behind the flock when the three largest sheep returned, grew tired of the silence and the dumb stares of the three largest returning sheep and she took a step, then another, and realized no one noticed, so she wandered behind the wall. To this point, it had been a most interesting day, and in her heart she was actually quite happy Rainbow was gone, but the rest of the flock was acting rather strange without Rainbow telling them what to do.

She noticed there was a stack of firewood behind the wall. It was mesmerizing, this stack of wood, and she realized with a little rearranging of the stack she could ascend the wall, and being young and suddenly hidden from the rest of the flock and feeling quite free, she did just that, rearranged some of the wood and climbed upon it until she was on top of the wall.

When Exverity ascended the wall and began to scan the horizon the sheep below suddenly looked up at her. She could feel their eyes upon her, felt them attach themselves to her as she walked back and forth along the wall, their expectant faces fixed to her in rapt attention. A small chant began, in the back of the crowd, tentative, then growing, "Starve the Invaders, Starve the Invaders," began to rise from the throats of the sheep, as they watched Exverity.

Exverity did not know what to do. She was a shy sheep, lacking the verbosity of Rainbow, so she stood still, thinking. The sheep below interpreted this stillness as a need to chant louder, and they did, the words growing so strong Exverity could feel them blow back her fleece. They are cheering me, she thought. She did not know what to say, and thought of all of the things Rainbow would scream from the wall, none of which made much sense to her. She was afraid if she said nothing the sheep below would fall dead of perturbation, so she said the first thing that came to her mind.

"I am Exverity, and I am the greatest eagle of all time. Believe me," she said, and the sheep below looked up at her with quizzical expressions that come most naturally to sheep. The chanting stopped, and Exverity waited, thinking perhaps this was the end of it. Perhaps she could depart the wall and walk off into the field and this nonsense would end, because she obviously was not an eagle. Then, from the back of the flock, a small lamb named Alathea, who enjoyed the crazy chanting each morning, thinking it a ridiculous game adult sheep played, yelled, "You are the greatest eagle of all time!" and soon other sheep said the same thing.

The other farms animals, who had watched in surprise the sheep gather at the wall without Rainbow, akin to those crazy Whos, from Whoville, on Christmas morning, had wandered near the wall to observe the sheep. They felt drawn to the wall this morning like people are drawn to natural disasters or especially gruesome vehicle accidents. At first it was funny, watching the confused sheep formulate a plan of action, but now the other animals looked at each other in alarm, clearly confused as to what was going on. They glanced to the wall and saw Exverity looking below her in confusion. Finally, Exverity raised her head and spoke again.

"I built this wall, with my own hooves. I mean talons! I have made it strong and true and it has kept the coyotes out," she said. Exverity thought saying something this ridiculous would be the end of it. That the sheep below would see how ludicrous this gathering at the wall had become. Her spirits lifted when she noticed the sheep looking at each other in confusion, and Exverity could hear whispers, "I thought Rainbow built the wall?" Each of the sheep repeated this question to their neighbor, but instead of it growing into a chant, it stayed soft and quick, lacking in conviction. Exverity continued, addressing the issue directly, thinking first logic, then absurdity, might be a tactic best used. "How could Rainbow have built this wall? Her feet were small. He wings unnaturally small. Though fat, she was extraordinarily weak." (For the Logic) "I built this wall. Believe Me!" (For the absurdity) Rainbow shouted these words at the sheep. Unfortunately, the flock was quite enamored and well-conditioned to absurdity, and they believed her, because she was on top of the wall, and she was the greatest eagle of all time, and who was this Rainbow anyway.

"And I will tell you something else. Something you've always believed in your hearts. Rainbow was not an eagle!" (There were gasps as Exverity said this, she trying to employ logic yet again) "It's true! She was a chicken. A fat chicken, an ugly chicken. A chicken that lied and stole and never laid an egg! She was no eagle, not like me." Some of the sheep looked at their neighbors, to see what they should do, clearly confused, because, well, they did know that Rainbow wasn't an eagle, not really, I mean, they weren't stupid. But Rainbow said she was, with such conviction, and she said it on top of the wall, and all the other sheep never questioned it, and going along with it just seemed like the right thing to do. Plus, Rainbow said all those things about the other animals being different and, well, different animals were scary, weren't they?

Finally, the small lamb in the back named Alathea, who thought this whole thing was some ludicrous and crazy game shouted, "Rainbow was a chicken!" and the rest of the flock followed, yelling disparaging things about Rainbow, about her lies of being an eagle, and her lineage, and her plumage which, come to think of it, was quite matted and patchy and unappealing, and with an artificial orange glow. Not eagle-like at all. In the morning light, it was so clear to see. Rainbow was nothing but a fat, dumb, lazy, smelly chicken! Thank god Exverity had ascended the wall she built and informed them of these truths.

The other animals edged closer, not understanding what was happening at all. How could this be? They knew Exverity since she was a lamb, and here she was, doing strange things and more importantly, getting the flock of sheep to believe her. The flock of sheep grew excited now, enjoying Exverity, who was an eagle, but an eagle that looked more like them, which was even better than that stupid chicken.

Exverity started to pace about the wall, mesmerized by the power of it, but also frightened. She wondered what they would believe, these sheep. She felt she could say anything, do anything, but instead of making her feel invincible, it frightened her. She thought of something preposterous to say. More preposterous than the fact she was an eagle, and had built this wall, which was clearly here before she was even born.

"You are all eagles, and can fly," Exverity said, and the sheep looked at each other in confusion, because they were sheep. But Alathea, the young lamb in the back, liked how this game had suddenly turned and so she said, "We are all eagles!" with such enthusiasm a few of the other sheep took up the chant, and soon the whole flock was chanting this, and believing it, thinking what is an eagle anyway? Maybe a sheep is an eagle, has always been an eagle, and since I am a sheep, I am an eagle. Yes, that makes perfect sense. And I can fly. If I wanted to; a want that has been unreleased thus far in my life, but is surely within my eagle capabilities should I so choose to partake. Yes. I am an eagle, they all thought.

Exverity watched as the sheep's confused faces turned confident the louder they chanted "We are all eagles!" It was ridiculous. So ridiculous she didn't know what to do. How could sheep believe such obvious and crazy lies, and more importantly, how could she stop this madness she started? She scanned the flock but it offered no comfort, just a flock of crazy, chanting sheep, then she looked beyond the flock to the other animals gathered about, animals confused and slightly scared and obviously not believing anything she said except the part about Rainbow being a fat chicken, and this made her feel better. She caught the eye of the old cow, and the cow, sensing Exverity wandered to a place much scarier and dangerous than ever envisioned, realized Exverity needed help.

The cow whispered to the dogs and dispatched them to the garage. She then gathered the other animals and began to explain what she had in mind. Confusing the flock with opposing realities was her plan. There was disagreement from the other animals, and suggestions, and hypothesis, but eventually they agreed on a course of action, the first phase of which was riding on the back of the dogs who were sprinting from the garage. The other animals watched, the dogs running in a tight pack, Rainbow riding on their backs. (If this story had the budget for trumpets, it is here they would be so employed.)

Rainbow, who had a fine night's sleep and a rather hefty breakfast of cold pizza, was at first quite concerned when the dogs burst into the garage, and in typical Rainbow fashion, said "Hey you stupid mutts, get out of here!" and she stomped her feet and crossed her wings and displayed her most condescending look at them. They, being dogs, did what dogs do when confronted with condescending looks and outbursts from ridiculous chickens, and they began to lick her until she started laughing, and then they popped her on their backs and away they went.

When they arrived at the wall, it was quite a scene. There was the young sheep Exverity on top of the wall, pacing and looking a bit frightened. There was a large flock of sheep quite adamantly proclaiming they were, in fact, eagles, and there where all the other animals, many of them laughing at the sheer preposterousness of the whole scene. The old cow directed the dogs to deposit Rainbow on the top of the wall. The dogs did just that, but being dogs, clamored on top of the wall themselves, to better admire the inanity below.

The sheep below, and Exverity, grew quiet as Rainbow looked down upon her flock of sheep and the other animals. Rainbow gave a quick and decidedly unkind glance at Exverity, and turned up her beak at the dogs, and she then proclaimed, "I am Rainbow, I am the greatest eagle, believe me. And I built this wall! Believe me."

The sheep below looked at Rainbow, really looked at Rainbow. She was not an eagle at all. And, how could she have built that wall? She's grotesquely out of shape, certainly unable to lift a small stone, let alone cinder blocks. It was the most ridiculous notion. And another thing…she always said *Believe me* after every outrageous thing she spoke. It was a tip off, really. *Believe me?* If she were really truthful would she need to always implore others to believe her? Of course not. That stupid chicken, always saying stupid things, and then demanding the sheep believe her. Crazy. The flock stood there, all thinking these very thoughts, but none of them said anything. Even when Rainbow started going on about coyotes coming to rip their throats open and other such nonsense, they all stood in silence. Rainbow stopped talking and looked at those idiot sheep below who had somehow forgotten they were supposed to worship every word that fell from her beak. They had forgotten to chant and praise her. She stared down at them, and they stared up at her, a stalemate of stupid.

Then, Exverity cleared her throat. "Ummm, I am Exverity. I am the greatest eagle, believe me," Exverity said, in a rather timid way, but loud enough the entirety of the flock moved their gaze from that rather stupid-looking, fat chicken, to that rather young and quite frankly funny young sheep who had somehow jumped on the wall and started spouting nonsense. Exverity, sensing the concept of a non-eagle proclaiming to be an eagle was finally looked at with a critical eye from the flock, thought proclaiming herself an eagle once again would put a stop to the madness, but it did not. The flock below looked from her to Rainbow, with tilted heads and a rather unquestioning mien. One of the dogs, thinking there was a game afoot, a game to try to capture the sheep's attention, yelled, "I am Clifford. I am the greatest eagle, believe me!" he said, and he did a little hop when he said it, and all of the sheep's faces turned towards him, which was great fun. Bernie, the sheep dog, said, "Oh, oh, let me try!" and he rushed to the other edge of the wall, "Excuse me, Exverity, I mean great and wondrous eagle," he said, because he needed to pass by her to get to that end of the wall, and he yelled, "I am Bernie, and I am the greatest eagle of all time, and this is the best, most excellent farm! Oh, and I created it! Me, with my own paws. No, darn it. With my own fierce talons! Yeah!" and the sheep all looked at him with slightly cocked heads, as if wondering if he was alright, you know, in the head. "Hey, Clifford, do you see that? They're all looking at me. That's kind of cool! And did you hear, I said that bestest farm line that the stupid chicken used to say all the time. Love that line!" Reginald, the chocolate lab, drooling with excitement to enter the game, exclaimed, "I am Reginald, and I like cheese!" and the others looked at him in confusion. There was a rather thick silence, until Reginald realized his mistake. "Oh, and I'm like this really great eagle, and I fly around the farm all the time and I sing in a band on the weekends, and I never quite understood non-Euclidian geometry and the concept that parallel lines are able to intersect. You know?" Reginald said, and the entirety of the gathering looked at him with rather perplexed stares.

Rainbow began jumping up and down (Well, not quite jumping, because she was rather fat, but she lifted her feet with great enthusiasm and placed them down with extreme prejudice) and she began to yell, "I am the eagle, I am the eagle," and as the sheep turned to her, Exverity also began to jump up and down and proclaim herself the eagle, and Bernie and Clifford and Reginald, quite captivated with the game, began jumping up and down, proclaiming themselves eagles, and then the young sheep Alathea, the one from the very rear of the flock, ran behind the wall and clamored up the stack of wood and she mounted the wall, and faced the flock of sheep below, and she joined the jumping and screaming sheep and chicken and dogs beside her on the wall, and she yelled, "Silence!" And there was.

The sheep below Alathea were looking at her with great interest, and the animals beyond the sheep, and beside her on the wall, all stared at her. Alathea thought of proclaiming herself an eagle, of claiming credit for the very wall she stood upon, and the green of the fields and the barns in the distance and the safety and security of all the animals within her sight, but she didn't, assuming the irony would get lost in the absurdity of what she always thought was a game but had just come to realize was something the rest of the sheep did not treat as a silly game at all, which in retrospect was quite scary. Instead, she gave a sheepish glance to her left, and her right, and she spoke.

"I am Alathea, a lamb born on this farm. That is my mother" and she pointed to a rather shy looking sheep in the back. "Mom, raise your head. There you go. That's my mom. Listen, I'm not an eagle, but neither are all these other animals, but you know that, don't you? We've been coming to this dumb wall, a wall that keeps nothing out, regardless of what that fat chicken says." (Rainbow raised herself up a bit, as if thinking of debating this particular point, but lost her enthusiasm under the low growl of Bernie the dog.) "It's a pretty good farm we live on. Not exactly the best most excellent, but pretty good in its own imperfect way. It is made better by all its inhabitants. It is made worse by fear of differences. That stupid chicken, that fat one over there, is most unhelpful, preying on fears and insecurities to raise herself up. We are better than that. Better than to listen to lies we know are lies, but we accept them anyway. I'm just a little lamb, but even I could see they were lies. We said nothing, because it made us feel better about the worst things in our heart, things we know are wrong and bad and we thought maybe if others had those same dark thoughts, well maybe they aren't so bad, but they are. Let's not do that anymore. We are better. We are better than that." The sheep and other animals looked up at Alathea, then looked to their left and their right, and looked beyond the hills. They did not know what to believe anymore. Under the light of day, and the weight of Alethea's words, they felt embarrassed, realizing the only reason they came to the wall and listened to Rainbow was because the bad parts of their soul felt less bad surrounded by others who thought the same bad thoughts. As if there was a comfort in sharing a sin. But the comfort was gone now. A few of them walked a few tentative steps away, and they survived, and a few more walked the other way, and they survived, and the cow and goats and other animals started to mill about, catching up with the sheep they used to like quite a bit actually, before all of the craziness started with that stupid, fat chicken with the very bad feathers and limited vocabulary and a propensity to spout complete nonsense and lies. Rainbow soon found herself alone on the wall, and she busied herself by yelling at the sky and wind about the unfairness of the world, until later in the afternoon the farmer's son retrieved her and carried her back to the garage.

 The wall came down, later that year. The farmer's son pulled it down with a tractor. No coyotes came. The sheep returned to the main barn with the other animals, which was warmer than that barn on the hill they moved to many moons before. Exverity and Alathea became friends, along with a couple of goats, and they often played soccer together in the fields. Sometimes, when feeling quite adventurous, they would sneak into the farmer's home and hide under the farmer's son's bed and jump out after he covered himself for the night. It scared him and was funny. They all became pretty good animals on that farm. Perhaps not the best, most excellent, but excellent enough. And Rainbow. Well, Rainbow was a very fat and stupid chicken, with malice in her heart. She seemed harmless enough at first, a bit of a joke really, but after a while, she wasn't harmless. Well, Rainbow never returned from that garage. She was never to be seen or heard from again. There are rumors, of course, and even today, on that very farm, the young animals, when the moon is full and they can steal away from their parents' protective gaze, will sometimes sneak into the barn on the hill. Those young animals swear, tucked into a corner of the barn on the hill, there is a wooden box, emblazoned with ACME on its side. In it are scruffy feathers of a most curious and some would say repulsive orange. That is all that is left of Rainbow, they say. But it is just a story, after all.

Pack
By M.J. Fahy

Beyond the cracked sidewalk, and the telephone pole with layers of flyers in a rainbow of colors, and the patch of dry brown grass there stood a ten-foot high concrete block wall, caked with dozens of coats of paint. There was a small shrine at the foot of it, with burnt out candles and dead flowers and a few soggy teddy bears. One word of graffiti filled the wall, red letters on a gold background: Rejoice!

She felt anchored here in this place of abandonment and ruin, reluctant to move on, the scent of the man still too strong, tying her to the wall that, though adorned so gaudily, had shrouded the man with a palpable sadness which settled over him like a cloak. She sensed the cloak was woven from grief, a state in which she too had knowledge.

Her gut cramped with hunger. She would be forced to move soon, now the provider was gone her need for food was beginning to override every other bodily urge. She had scavenged for a while but pickings were meagre. Few men came here and the ones who did were ragged and had little to give. Some gave cruelty; though the sad man had protected her as best he could, growling and howling at them in an unsettling manner.

The man had shared everything he had with her: his food, his scant bedding, his body-heat, even his parasites, and had been the first to touch her since she fled the farm. She longed to return but knew it would be the end of her life if she did. The one named Pa would kill her with the gun that had finished two of her male littermates, and a female, as they cowered, bound and pissing, at his feet. A shudder jolted her body at the memory, bringing her thoughts again to the sad man.

Life had leeched from him two nights ago; she became aware only as he had cooled: his death-chill seeping into her flesh as she lay against the length of him. She stayed close to his body for as long as she dared, men driving her away when they came for him, when daylight broke this morning, throwing stones and yelling, one sound repeatedly hurled like a weapon: *'Wolf!—Wolf!—Wolf!'* Several of their missiles connected with her body, ribs bruised and sore now, making it impossible for her to rest on that side.

Alone now, as she had been in the days of journeying far from the farm, following beside a great road, eating what she scavenged from garbage bins and what was thrown from speeding vehicles. She rose and surveyed the vast wall, the mess of grubby candles and offerings, the sad man's crumpled and stinking blankets. She stretched, tautening aching muscles, yawned whiningly long and loud, then turned and walked away up the wide pot-holed street, all alone.

She cowed behind empty wooden boxes as the big man came thru the door and grabbed a crate of vegetables from the concrete yard, one of three stacked amid other boxes and sacks of potatoes, delivered to the diner only minutes before; the third consecutive day of waiting for the opportune time to hunt, even if her target prey was a large cauliflower. She had caught a rat the evening before: small, granted, but flesh it was and it had tasted wonderful.

The big man went back inside the diner and just as he disappeared, she slunk from her hiding place and took a cauliflower from the topmost crate. Its earthy scent had her salivating immediately and she struggled to hold the slick vegetable as she trotted out of the yard.

Her den was not far, yet distant enough that she was away from unwanted attention. She could still hear traffic noise so felt sure that if she ever had to abandon her den she could seek the road and follow it again. Wherever the road went meant opportunity to eat, that much seemed obvious.

Hidden within prickly scrub, the den was scratched from the earth by an unknown maker. She did not recognize the animal's species from its scent, which had been sprayed liberally around, only that the aroma was pungent and eye-watering in its potency, though many weeks old.

She bit into the fresh cauliflower, savoring how the vegetable crunched between her powerful jaws, the sound reminiscent of bones disintegrating. She wished they were bones, sturdy cow bones packed with gelatinous marrow. Too soon the cauliflower was consumed, its leaves also, left till the very last. Her belly was not full, but she was satisfied and relieved that the terrible hunger-pangs of past days were gone.

Sleep filled her days, her body healing from the trials of her journey: bruised ribs from the men's attack now a barely-there dull ache, sore footpads from endless walking had eventually hardened and toughened. Her eyelids drooped, and always memories of the farm began swirling in her head, of her mother and littermates.

Rainbow could not remember being born. Hazy memories began when her eyes first opened at twelve days-old; not the smallest of the litter but certainly not the largest she was one of three females. Without fail her two brothers were first at the teat and, weeks after, first at the food bowl. They were first to be killed too, but that came later...

The farm was warm and safe, once. They were at the beginning of life and slept in the protection of the barn with their mother, away from the house and garage. Others slept in the barn too, each in their own partitioned quarters, filling the air with a myriad of smells and sounds: The very old donkey named Peter, always braying when the sun came up, reassuring and constant; the gentle cows, Sarah and Ruth, always chewing and shitting; an unsexed and untamed black cat was there sometimes, named Shadow, who kept to the shadows mostly, always killing rats and mice and roaches. Lastly, there were ducks and chickens, always pecking and scratching about, none of whom were named save for the rooster, who was called Rooster. Life passed slowly because there was routine at the farm, each twenty-four hours a comforting repetition of the previous twenty-four.

Pa fed the animals early, almost as soon as Peter and Rooster gave voice at the first orange flare of the sun. He would enter the barn and bang feed buckets together, and then shake hay into hayracks, causing a frantic cacophony of barks, moos, brays, quacks, and clucks. The only silent and mostly absent creature was Shadow, who did not get fed, having to survive on whatever it caught. It survived surprisingly well. Shadow was fat.

Sometimes the kid came with Pa, helping him dole out the food, speeding his efforts. The kid would bleat 'Pa' and other noises every so often, and Pa would answer him with his deep gruff voice. Once the puppies' eyes were open, Pa picked each of them up and handled them firmly yet gently, encouraging the kid to do the same—all under the watchful chocolate gaze of Beba, the puppies' mother, a Golden Labrador, German Shepherd mix. On occasion an old woman would visit the barn, bringing the aroma of spring flowers and walking around clucking like a hen, inspecting the barn's inhabitants like an emperor inspecting his servants. Each time she came, she bought leftovers and treats with her, just for the pups and Beba. Once, the old woman bought a thick blanket for them, spreading it over their straw bed and nodding happily as they circled and settled down to doze.

As they grew, Pa studied the pups more and more closely. Often he rubbed his chin and his face would crinkle in a look of puzzlement. The kid's face did not change; he was always joyful when handling and playing with the pups. He was the one who named them all. Two of the females were called Hester and Penny; the males were Hero and Blaze. The remaining female was given the name, Rainbow, because she had many odd-colored patches in her coat made of bluish-grey, golden-yellow (inherited from Beba), and deepest black.

It was when she was around six months-old that Rainbow got kicked in the head by old Peter. He hadn't meant to do it but had lashed out irritably when bitten by a horse fly. Rainbow liked rooting about in his stall, hunting, pretending to look for things in the straw bedding that were not really there, but it pleased her to look for them anyway.

A foggy memory lingered, of being lifted into the truck by the kid and of Pa sounding angry, then consoling because the kid began to cry. Pa drove fast and they came to a place that stank: a pungent mix of disinfectant and cat piss. Carried into a bright room, Rainbow was placed on a table and a man shone a white light into her eyes and made sounds to Pa and the kid. Something sharp scratched her skin and then the kid carried her back to the truck. Later, the truck filled with the scent of pizza, cheese, tomato, and pepperoni fumes radiated in waves and made her feel both famished and nauseous at the same time, an unsettling combination.

When the ride ended, she was lifted again. The kid slid her body onto a soft pile of clothing among the boxes in the garage. He pulled an old coat over the top, creating a cave that emanated the sweetness of old ladies who frequently powdered themselves—a light rose motif that played ironically well in the deep recesses of Rainbow's ancestral brain. The pizza kid lifted her head to help her lap water from a hubcap. He broke bits of pepperoni and crust into bite-sized pieces and left them where her tongue could reach them. Much later, she heard him practicing his orations like songs. Like monks chanting in the distance, they were a comfort.

The pizza kid, or kiddo, as Pa sometimes referred to him, occasionally made the sound when he cleaned the cow stall, forking great heaps of soiled straw into the barrow and wheeling it out to be tossed onto the dung heap. Rainbow loved the chanting and many times she and her siblings would join in, lifting their throats to the sky and offering up their hypnotic howls.

If Pa was around he would not tolerate the beauty of their voices, he raged and banged empty buckets until they stopped; he did not need to bring his bang-stick again, which he had used to terrify them the first time they sang. There was a ragged hole in the roof now, not huge but enough to make a corner of the barn damp where the rain came in. A thud on an empty bucket now, or one gruff retort, was enough to drive them to hours of petrified, eye-darting, silence.

Nothing felt as wonderful as walking the fields with the kid. He took the pups and Beba out across their land three or four times a week to walk the fence-line and check on the crops. Beba stayed at the kid's side all the way, the pups would venture further afar but were always in sight of their mother.

Except one day when a nine-month-old Blaze, at first freezing and sniffing the air, slipped under a railed fence and sped away over a nearby hill. 'Blaze!' shouted the kid, the loudest Rainbow had ever heard him yell; 'Blaze!' He climbed onto the fence to get a better view. Nothing; Blaze had vanished.

Beba whined and went to follow her offspring. 'No,' said the kid, 'stay, Beba.' Well-trained by Pa, Beba obeyed and immediately sat down. Sensing their mother's tense state, her remaining four pups stayed close by her side. The kid leapt down from the fence and ran in the same direction Blaze had taken.

When the kid returned, dragging the reluctant pup, his belt removed from his pants and fastened round Blaze's neck; the other pups lolled in the sun, Rainbow and Hero tried to catch flies, missing the insects each time their jaws snapped together. Rainbow caught a whiff of something that immediately made her mouth water: *blood*.

Blaze's face was soaked to his ears, some of the blood under his lower jaw so thick and cloying that it dropped to the dry ground in jellied clots. The kid looked close to crying. He looked angry too and Rainbow hung back, keeping plenty of distance between herself and her brother.

Beba tried to wash the blood from her son's face but got screamed at by the kid. She also dropped back, letting the kid drag a disgraced Blaze back to the barn, with Beba and her children following at a respectful distance.

Rainbow smelt the spring flower aroma before she saw the old woman. She came out of the barn with her hands on her hips and said something to the kid, who answered, this time giving in to tears. He pointed towards the hill and his voice rose to an unlikely pitch, until the old woman calmed him.

Fetching a bucket and filling it from a tap outside the barn, the old woman set to washing Blaze's face and front paws, and the kid's bloodied belt, changing the water in the bucket three times before she was satisfied that they had removed it all. Even Beba's snout was scrubbed of blood spots.

One day a strange truck pulled into the yard and from the barn, through gaps in the slats of their pen, Rainbow watched a man climb out of it. The other pups came to watch silently too, five pairs of yellow eyes trained on the stranger with unblinking focus.

The stranger spoke to Pa softly, now and again pointing in the direction of the hill in the distance. He nodded while Pa shook his head in reply. The kid stood to one side of the barn doors listening, his expression stony as he stared at his feet.

Minutes later the man climbed into his truck and drove away, while Pa watched him go and shook his head once more. The kid hurried over to the pups' stall and began speaking quietly to them, rubbing their ears in turn. Beba lay on the blanket, blinking and dozing. Mostly he spoke to Rainbow. Though she could not understand every word he uttered, to her he sounded relieved. He caressed the top of her head, which by now was parallel to his waist so tall had she grown. 'That man was Mister Robbins; he owns the land where the ewe was killed. If Pa knew it was Blaze…if he ever found out…Well now, good for Gran'ma, that's all. Shit.'

Pa leaned against the stall; he had been staring at one-year-old Rainbow and her littermates for close to an hour. He sucked a long hay-stalk and twirled it from one side of his mouth to the other. As her sisters and brothers slept, Rainbow watched the stalk twirl side-to-side, and side-to-side, entranced. When he suddenly stood up straight and spat the stalk on the ground, Rainbow blinked at last and panted, her tongue lolling from her mouth like a pink banner. Pa turned and left the barn.

The next day when the kid came out to the barn, without his father this time, Rainbow knew without looking that he was in an ill-mood. He shoved the wheelbarrow about and growled at the cows when they refused to move over as he cleaned their bedding. The kid even snapped at old Peter when he was slow to move.

Rainbow stood on her back legs and rested her forelegs on the partition dividing her stall with old Peter's. She watched Kiddo as he worked. He had grown stronger over the last few months: tall and sinewy with a new thatch of fluff on his chin. It was warm in the barn and she panted to cool down. The kid muttered: 'And you can stop laughing if you know what's good for you. You won't be laughing when Pa sells you to the circus next year…That's what he reckons. Reckons you five are wolfdogs—reckons Beba bred with a real wolf. How'd that happen, I'd like t—? You *know* what I mean!' He finished cleaning the stalls and left without saying anything else, without even taking her out for a run. She lay on the straw and watched sunbeams dance through the hole in the roof.

The chicks hatched the day after, some ducklings the day after that. Pa nailed chicken wire across the bottom of Beba and the pups' stall when the little fluff-balls began to explore the barn. Just for precautionary measures, he did not want the delicate creatures injured unnecessarily.

Rooster's testosterone became turbo-charged once he had chicks to protect. He crowed twice as long as usual in the mornings, even crowing again at midday for good measure, and if any hens wandered off too far he would round them up and give them a harsh pecking as punishment, the ducks too if they were not watchful.

The kid was there when Rooster died, as he had been when Rooster hatched three years before. Pa was there too, and there would be no covering up this death; indeed, there was a veritable audience if you counted the poultry, cows, donkey, humans, and canids. Even Shadow sat atop a stack of hay bales, not unlike Caesar at an amphitheater.

A red hen inched the length of the barn, her three chicks pecking the ground in her wake. Pa and the kid stood next to the feed bins, talking and laughing, not more than ten feet from Beba and her pups' pen. Rooster spotted the hen and chicks and ran towards them, head down, wings spread wide in a noble attempt at flight. He pecked the hen viciously, causing a flapping, squawking commotion. Pa had stepped forward to grab Rooster when the bird dodged and hopped onto the top of Beba's wooden partition. In a blur of reddish-grey fur, Blaze lunged and bit Rooster's head right off, his body fell sideways into the stall where it was devoured in seconds.

No one moved for several heartbeats, human or animal; even the wolfdogs were surprised at what they had done. Rainbow sat and licked her jowls clean guiltily, for in truth Rooster had been the most delicious thing she had ever tasted. He was even warm. Beba cowered at the back of the stall, far from her pups, her muzzle pressed to the wooden boards.

Pa spun on his heel and strode from the barn. The kid was in a state of disbelief and clung to a feed bin for support, breathing raggedly. He knew what would happen now, what his father's rules were on dogs that proved to be livestock killers.

In less than a minute, Pa kicked one of the barn doors out of his way and came back inside with his shotgun broken and resting over his forearm. It was loaded already and the kid saw that his father's shirt pocket bulged with more cartridges.

Wordlessly the kid helped his father though it sickened him to do so. One by one, they led the wolfdogs out behind the barn, where the scrubby grass was high and coarse. Rainbow looked at the sky, cloudless and bright, so bright that she had to squint and her eyes watered. She knew what was happening was bad. It was bad because the kid had not touched her, save to slip a leash over her head. She turned her face to the hill. If only she could run over the hill, she would be safe. There was blood over the hill, warm blood that she could plunge her face right into...

The two males were shot first. Blaze went quietly, until Pa tipped him on his side and bound his four feet together, like a cow ready for branding. He whimpered softly, until Pa pulled the trigger. The gunshot was a catalyst for panic: the kid had to scramble and struggle to tie each wolfdog to a rail, where they leapt and spun in all directions to try and break free. Pa's face was grim. 'Next one, kiddo,' he said, as calmly as he could manage.

The kid led Penny forward, her coat as red and coppery as Blaze's, Pa used to call her Copper Penny sometimes. In truth she was his favorite of the litter, not that he would have ever admitted to the fact. His mouth set in a thin line, he dispatched her as efficiently as the males, though flies were now beginning to gather, drawn by blood seeping into the earth. Rainbow started howling, and then Hester joined her in a song that was mournful, soulful, and full of ancient wisdom. *'Next!'* bellowed Pa over the reverberating sound.

Tears streamed freely down the kid's face as he untied Hester's leash from the rail. He walked forward and the leash hung behind him, limp and useless and devoid of a wolfdog. The kid whirled to see Hester, the smallest of the litter, running back towards the barn, her long charcoal-grey coat making her a dark smudge against the parched, pale, earth. Pa ran then too, in pursuit, long legs stork-like, his shotgun clasped across and against his chest as he called Hester's name again and again and again. Rainbow had never seen him run before; she was not aware that the kid had slipped the leash from over her head, and that she sat next to him untethered, until he bent next to her and whispered: *'Go on, girl.'* She ran up the field, towards the railed fence, and then leapt the fence and thundered towards the hill, over the brow and down the other side…

Rainbow woke to the cool night, her stomach growled but thirst was her biggest concern, she had not drunk for a day and a half, and that water had been stale and stagnant. She left the odorous den and stretched each limb and her spine until the stiffness of sleep left her. A different scent caught her attention. She froze; ears and eyes picking up sounds and movement that no man could dream to hear or see. She knew the scent, as familiar to her as her own. Hester strode out of the darkness and began rubbing her face against her sister's muzzle, sweet excited yips sounding in both their throats. Hester had not travelled alone; yellow eyes appeared from the gloom behind her. Rainbow studied them and recognized those eyes. They were eyes as old as time: the eyes of her pack.

A Girl Could Fall In Love with a Guy Like Jim
By Jilly Funnell

Part One: Never Trust a Woman

Beyond the cracked sidewalk, and the telephone pole with layers of flyers in a rainbow of colors, and the patch of dry brown grass there stood a ten-foot high concrete block wall, caked with dozens of coats of paint. There was a small shrine at the foot of it, with burnt out candles and dead flowers and a few soggy teddy bears. One word of graffiti filled the wall, red letters on a gold background: Rejoice!

Carly Darling thought the flyers smelled lovely and so did the pole. The scent of the grass was tasty too, skunkier than the clean turf at her apartment house, but nothing hummed as good as the inside of her hiding place, right near the Ocean Boulevard Theater. Also, the safety of the disused, plus-size dumpster, with its two old beer crates to give her a little useful height, satisfied the compulsion to see people who couldn't see her. Luna Fairchild, playwright and theatre director, had recently told Carly that such dank, rose-petally fragranced hiding places evoked gratifying memories of death's release, but then Luna did talk a lot of strange at times. To Carly the scent brought a sustaining mental image of her mother's body inside a casket, dead from too much heroin. The woman had been a waste of space and oxygen. Evidently, they found her with a rabble of starving dogs and had to use dental records to ID the remains.

Hands against the inside surface and head supporting the lid, Carly peeped out at Luna and the stage manager, Jim. Carly almost trusted Luna, who she'd known since the playwright found her appearing as Rainbow the Dog-Faced Dwarf in a carnival booth. When Carly told Luna the roustabouts beat her for refusing to be called Rainbow, Luna grabbed her, yelled that she knew her mother and threatened to call the cops. It turned out Luna had a habit of taking in kids with nowhere to go. She used them to dance and sing and act out dramas on a stage but never paid them because she never made any money. Now Carly had her first real role, though it wasn't at all the kind she wanted because Carly had never wanted to be Rainbow the dog-faced anything ever again. However, Luna had written this play and persuaded her that she didn't have to be Rainbow, she only had to act the part because that was what acting meant. The day after Luna convinced her to take the role, Carly borrowed the office typewriter and laboriously hunted and pecked out a statement which she sealed in an envelope and marked "FOR LUNA FAIRCHILD'S ATTENTION. STRICTLY PRIVATE. TO BE OPENED ONLY IN THE EVENT OF CARLY DARLING'S DEATH." She slipped the envelope to Luna who immediately opened it and said, "Well, nobody ever did think your dead father was a dog, silly girl. What are you saying? You're nuts." Carly was mortified. "It said not to open it until I'm dead," she whispered. "Well, sorry," said Luna, "but I don't want to think of anybody being dead today."

Stage manager Jim, a young and easy-on-the-eye Californian, was a more recent and welcome addition to Carly's life. She'd only known him since rehearsals began. Three weeks after he joined Ocean Boulevard, Luna had told Carly to keep in mind that men like Jim always end up hanging themselves. "And," she said, "I reckon this one carries the rope in his own pocket." A few more weeks down the line and Carly sensed a bit of resentment from Luna every time Jim's name was mentioned. It was perplexing. She and Jim got along very well. For example, wasn't it already a given that she could phone the stage manager to come and get her out from this dumpster whenever she was ready? That was very satisfactory although today, for now, there was no need for him to know her location. Only she and the beer truck guy knew, and the beer truck guy had gone on his way. Carly had discovered a while back, if you were a light in weight person who implied some vague detail of cardiac weakness, spoke like an adult and seemed like a child, most people were willing to help you in and out of places.

Now she heard Jim say it was a total waste to put so many of the same flyer on the one pole. She agreed. Then there were the teddy bears. Another bad decision. Okay they were meant to represent lost childhood and funfair goodies, but soft things with shiny black eyes and stitched whiskers were going to worry children, and above all kids needed protection. Still, with the rain forever blowing in off Puget Sound, the bears' damp bodies would soon rot and wow, wait a minute, something was happening. Luna was circling Jim. She ended up behind him, her hands up on his shoulders, fingers splayed.

"So, Mr. Stage Manager," she said. That was kind of provocative, thought Carly. Honest, it looked like Luna was massaging him. A nip of jealousy discomfited Carly's belly as she pictured Jim grabbing Luna's booty and kissing her and sticking his tongue through her Max Factor lips, which was obviously what the woman wanted. Happily though, he seemed distracted. He looked up at the pole and then across at the flapping banner strung high on the concrete wall. OCEAN BOULEVARD PRODUCTIONS PRESENT/ *RAINBOW* / TICKET OFFICE OPEN / PATRONISE YOUR LOCAL THEATER.

"Jim, honey," said Luna, "are you listening? You have to go to the store." She stopped rubbing him and shimmied too close to the dumpster. Now all Carly could see was the middle of Luna and her jacket pocket, and none of Jim. She held her breath as Luna spoke to him again.

"I need bourbon and we got to get peppermint tea for Mrs. Margery Womark, though I don't know why we're running around for Womark. I mean, what does the woman actually do? And I'm the theatre director, the playwright, the creative artiste, for God's sake. Jim, are you listening? Get soft cider for Carly and pizza for the garage scene. Gee. I am stressed." Luna's hand went into her pocket, pulled out a pack of cigarettes and judging by the scent of smoke, she'd lit up. For a moment Carly worried Luna might chuck her spent match into the dumpster, but all was well. It landed on the sidewalk. "I'm thinking," she heard Luna say, "I might lose that bit of business with the coat. I'm unsure about its value. And you know what's thrown me right off balance, Jim? Cleardon Braveman. Coming on our first night. I mean, isn't he just about the most influential critic in the Pacific Northwest?"

"You asked me that twice already," said Jim. "Take it for what it is. A piece of luck. Braveman's on the level. I told you, I know him a little. Anyways, I'll go and buy cider and pizza and whatever and we'll get on with it. Then your little poop heap of a play can turn into a big poop heap of a play." He laughed. "Close your mouth, Luna, I'm joking."

Using the top of her head to push the dumpster lid up a couple more inches, Carly could see Jim and Luna almost full-length. The theatre director threw her cigarette into the bushes and Jim said, "Let's hope your shrine to the poor kid helps ticket sales." Luna didn't reply. She was looking at the scrawled word "Rejoice" on the concrete wall. "Yeah and before you ask," said Jim, "it's too late to get the graffiti painted out. Pray for a miracle, Luna baby, and maybe we'll all get to rejoice."

Carly shifted her position and her gaze. Across the street there was a line of tired-looking people snaking outside the carpet mart, waiting for the adult movie DVDs. It seemed to Carly it might be easy for folk to turn into those people. Compared with losers like that, Jim was such a fine man.

He was still looking at the big old concrete wall, up and down, side to side, probably genuinely pissed by the waste of flyers and the teddy bears. "Anyways, Luna," he said, "if you don't think Mrs. Margery Womark should demand peppermint tea, why not tell her?" Luna sighed. "Focus please, Jim. I need you to commit to *Rainbow*. Whatever you say and whoever you know, I'm nervous about Braveman. You can't ignore an important critic." Carly nodded. Jim had told her a review from the guy was as good as money in the bank. And he'd also confided that he knew Braveman a lot better than he'd told Luna.

Now Carly heard him say, "You know what, Luna, our Carly may become a real visitor attraction. She alone could sell the play out once the word goes around." Carly was so happy at hearing that, she just had to squat and pee in a corner. Her bladder was full, but the copious estrogen-perfumed stream was efficiently absorbed by several string-tied layers of slowly disintegrating newspaper.

The pleasure of peeing was enhanced by her mental images of Jim. She was beginning to think he was the only one who genuinely cared about her. Luna was so preoccupied lately. But Jim understood stuff. When Carly had complained about being called Rainbow in the play, he gently explained that true theatre is entirely dependent on fact and it would be dishonest to use another name, since Rainbow was the one Carly had been given by the carnival people. It was part of her history, the rich fabric of her life and the paying public had a right to know her authentic story because she was such an interesting and beautiful person. Carly had scurried away to tell the box office clerk how brilliant Jim had been. The woman didn't hear her. Now, in the darkness of the dumpster, Carly smiled at the memory. Box office booths probably weren't designed for those under forty inches high to communicate with people inside.

She yawned, pulled up her pants and settled in a dry corner and slept, inhaling her own comforting odor in the curve of her arm. When she woke, her watch said almost an hour had passed. Gently lifting the lid of the dumpster, she saw nobody she recognized, so she took out her phone and called Jim. When he arrived and lifted her into his arms, his fresh meaty sweat was lovely. "Happy now?" he said as he delivered her to the dressing room. "Almost," said Carly, "But I hope Luna doesn't take out the coat scene. I like that coat. It has this kind of rotten flowery smell. It turns me on." Damn. She shouldn't have let Jim know she knew what Luna had said. Or shared that thing about turning on. Her face heated and she opened and closed her mouth and blinked, feeling real foolish. It was a relief when someone knocked and Jim got the door and in came Luna, wearing too much makeup. "Good news, guys," she said, "I've shoe-horned the word rejoice into several scenes. Doesn't mean anything, of course, but we haven't got time to wash down the wall, so I joined up the dots. Darling Jim, I pride myself on being endlessly resourceful at intimating meaning where none exists." Jim nodded. Carly turned her back and ignored them. She didn't like Luna calling Jim darling.

When Luna had gone, Carly said, "Honestly, Jim, she never asks me about anything. Now I'll have more last-minute stuff to learn. And there's still all that lifting and dropping of me. Why does she make that go on so long?" Jim nodded. "I agree, too long. But you manage it beautifully. You're a natural. You *are* Rainbow. Without you, Luna doesn't have a play." He opened a container of soft cider. "Let's make a toast." Carly held out her hands for the filled bowl and Jim smiled as she drank. "Wow, I forgot how fast you take it," he said, pouring a refill, "but cheers to tonight anyway. I know you will do your very best." Carly drank again, then put down her bowl and excitedly clambered on the corner trunk where she ran the back of her hand upwards and across her face, briefly content. She hadn't been so happy since years ago, before the carnival, when she had twelve big, beautiful dogs around her, loving her, keeping her safe. She'd called them brothers and she never stopped missing them. Jim was strong and kind, like her brothers. She sure would do her very best tonight, just for him.

Part Two: Never Trust a Man

That evening the play opened, as planned. Just one long act, the coat scene included and, after the whole thing was over, there came a thin scatter of applause. Within a few hours Braveman's review was posted and Jim sat in front of his laptop with Carly curled at his feet and read aloud. *Ocean Boulevard Theatre: Luna Fairchild's "Rainbow"*. An eager performance from actress Carly Darling as the eponymous heroine, is pretty much the only saving grace in this densely scripted, uneven and mind-bendingly dull piece largely inspired by an interview that took place one time on the TV show *Oh What A Beautiful Morning*. The interview was with a woman delivered of an unusually featured child, the alleged result of the mother's union with one of her many German Shepherd dogs. She explained her practice of indulging in frequent sexual intercourse with the dogs because she couldn't get a date. In the same interview, she claimed to be in ongoing relationships with James Thurber, Paul Newman and Charles Dickens. The woman passed away through a drug overdose soon after the broadcast so one imagines her true history died with her. However, the true history of writer/director Luna Fairchild is a matter of public record. She was a production assistant on *Oh What A Beautiful Morning* when that dog lover's interview went out. Hey. A gal's got to get her ideas some place.

We first meet Rainbow as she sits alone on the floor of an empty stage, nuzzling and gnawing at the arm of a teddy bear. Enter a female character, billed as A Woman and played by Margot Deane, who ignores Rainbow and mouths at the audience as if she is sharing a secret. For an entire five minutes (I timed it), she proceeds to twist her mouth as if she's dropped a double dose of ecstasy. She mimes what appears to be horseback riding for several more minutes, then draws a finger across her throat. Phew. Already I am picturing myself back in the bar, ordering a nice, sane Pinot Grigio. As if to punish me for such selfish thoughts, a narrator in military attire enters, played by Christopher McNamara, from the short-lived soap "Days and Nights". He orders the audience to picture a carnival carousel. Roustabouts in plaid shirts and brown cloth trousers enter and tread around., more bitch than butch. Rainbow chews her bear and gazes. The miming woman exits left. There is a single offstage gunshot.

Our military buddy now informs us that we are in a lock-up garage where a conveniently invisible carousel is stored. Somebody in the wings chucks a mess of cardboard boxes and clothes onto the stage. A pizza delivery boy enters. Not credited, but his arrival is welcome. A pizza's always nice. Two more carnival hands show up as Rainbow crawls around among the boxes and clothes. The workers grab her and repeatedly lift and drop the poor kid. I resist the urge to yell, "I've got it! These guys are mimicking the movement of a carousel, right?" But before I can show off my talent for guessing charades, the pizza delivery kid's gotten hold of Rainbow. He places her on the pile of clothes and pulls a thick coat across two metal stands so that it hangs above her head. Rainbow sniffs, as if savoring the air, and the kid pours water from a jug into a hub cap and presents it to her, followed by lumps of pizza. At this point I was far more interested in the consistency of the pizza crust (is it thick, thin, stuffed?) than the play. I fear such tropes hold little meaning except to direct us further down the rabbit hole and into the fresh hell that is the unexpected arrival of a projection screen bearing the cheery message "The suppurating cadaver will rise no more. Rejoice!" Luna Fairchild, what were you thinking?

Finally, the pizza kid sings and chants for so long my backside turns numb. I am now yearning for the face-pulling woman to come back and rescue us. And the kid's monotonous dirge is assaulting my ears like a baseball bat, though I grant that he does also produce a decent closing riff of pure soprano. At last, Rainbow and the kid exit, and our narrator announces we are in a court of law. Of course we are. And he is about to give evidence. Of course he is. He swears an oath on an invisible bible to prove it and confirms each member of the audience is both judge and jury. This gives me hope that the thing is over, but I'm wrong. Out comes his "evidence" which, to my surprise, is a poetic passage, sufficiently interesting to justify quoting in full:

"When the ride ended, she was lifted again. The kid slid her body onto a soft pile of clothing among the boxes in the garage. He pulled an old coat over the top, creating a cave that emanated the sweetness of old ladies who frequently powdered themselves—a light rose motif that played ironically well in the deep recesses of Rainbow's ancestral brain. The pizza kid lifted her head to help her lap water from a hubcap. He broke bits of pepperoni and crust into bite-sized pieces and left them where her tongue could reach them. Much later, she heard him practicing his orations like songs. Like monks chanting in the distance, they were a comfort."

What a gift this diamond in the dust rendered to the jaded critic. The allusion to a rose motif along with the singing certainly appealed. Regrettably, the modest light shone in my receptors was soon extinguished. I vaguely recalled that, much earlier, someone or something was shot (off-stage) and I got to hoping it was the director, who was surely responsible for not noticing there were two pages accidentally stuck together in every ten throughout her turgid death march of a script. I also got a clear image of Luna Fairchild's cranium up her own rear end when our narrator finally placed a small piece of black cloth on his head and said "Judge to base. Guilty as charged. Rainbow's mother was guilty. She abandoned her young. As God is my witness, I find this was a capital offence and accordingly the sinner has been rightly executed. Rejoice!"

In summary, I am afraid this piece is a gobbling turkey and, while I am no advocate of violence, Ms. Fairchild should at least receive a public slap for staging such a pile of pretentious horse shit. However, her real punishment will be the audience staying away in droves. Apart from that single, pretty speech and the rather sweet boy soprano, the only genuine notable credit goes to the prosthetic makeup people who render Carly Darling, as the dog-faced dwarf girl, totally convincing.

Part Three: Never Trust a Dog-Faced Dwarf

Carly whined with stress as she heard Braveman's closing words. Dog-faced dwarf? Prosthetic makeup? It was clear, without doubt, that Braveman was an evil bastard. "I'm as shocked as you are," said Jim. "I mean, I didn't rate the play, but you were extraordinary. You were wonderful. As for the makeup comment, it's like Braveman's looking at a beautiful oil painting and simply complimenting the frame. We need to deal with this." He appeared to be deep in thought for a few moments, then he suggested a response or two on Carly's social media. "Facebook and Twitter," he said. Carly was unsure at first but something about the clear commitment in Jim's eyes made her tap in the passwords. Then Jim took over and wrote: *For your information, Mr. Braveman, I was not wearing prosthetic makeup.* Carly nodded and panted a little. "Shame him," said Jim as he posted the comments. "We'll make him eat crow, for sure."

Despite Jim's kindness, a kind of wound inside began to expand and eat at Carly and all she wanted to do was hide away from the ugly world exposed by Braveman's review. When she resisted any contact with Luna, Jim agreed that getting past such things can take a little time. Carly duly holed up in the oak trunk in her room at the apartment house, kept the lid open a little with her head and yelled over and over, "Cleardon Braveman is a fucking ignorant jerk!" She timed the yelling so that folks nearby would think she'd stopped, then off she would go again, like the repetitious midnight barking of her long-lost brothers. In the end, Mrs. Margery Womark pulled Carly out of the trunk and told her she was a naughty little girl who must learn to watch her mouth. Carly snarled. *Why the hell are small people treated like children?* She resisted the urge to bite a chunk out of Womark's scrawny leg. Womark began flinging clothes into a suitcase, yelling, "I'm off and I ain't coming back. This is a madhouse. Good riddance to you, freak!" And she slammed the street door behind her. Carly grabbed her phone and called Jim. "It's all right," he said, as soon as he got to her. "The play's just unbalanced because of Luna's script and direction. You know, I did wonder whether she was treating you as you should be treated. Anyways, good riddance to Womark. She never saw how the beautiful Carly Darling is quite unique. What did she do round here anyways?"

Jim was caring and quite comforting, but in the coming days the spreading wound ached and throbbed inside Carly and the public weren't buying tickets. When she worked up the courage to look at responses on Facebook and Twitter, they were cruel and humiliating. People who openly admitted they hadn't seen the play or even a photograph of the character Rainbow, accused Carly of making up stories. They said critics aren't stupid, and she must have been wearing a mask and she was therefore a lying dumbass, though her mother probably was a dirty dog fucker anyway. "But my father was a not a dog. He was a man, a good man," Carly told Jim. "He was a writer. And an actor. Mostly a writer. I never met him. He went to London, England and he died. Jim, I've caused so much trouble."

"None of this is your fault," said Jim. "The ignorance of people is just amazing." He opened his laptop, got Carly to put in her Twitter password and then he typed "Long story short, guys, a human cannot become impregnated by an animal you ignorant bunch of dicks." He sat back and closed the laptop. Carly gazed up at him, feeling full of admiration. "Now," said Jim, "that's the past. Let's look at the future. I've thought of nothing else and I have an idea." He stopped talking and stared at Carly. "You know," he said, "you could walk off the production. Walk off and shame Braveman and the internet trolls." Carly breathed evenly and audibly, head tilted, mouth slightly open. "If you were going to make such a dramatic exit," Jim continued, "I would suggest you wait for the pizza scene, spit out a big chunk and say something like, 'that's for Cleardon Braveman', and then slowly leave the stage. Straight after that I'll talk to the papers and the TV. This way, people will realize they need to buy tickets. And you could be a star, young lady. With a crowd of adoring fans. How about that?" Carly hesitated. "But what about Luna?" she said. Jim smiled. "Leave Luna to me."

When Carly walked off the production, there were only seven people in the audience, but Luna had to bring the curtain down same as if she'd had a full house, and ask for a little time. Hiding in the wings, Carly heard her yell, "Drugstore! Now! We got to get a dog mask for the understudy."

The following day, Carly read a newspaper headline: "Dog-faced Dwarf Leaves Turkey." She howled and wept copious tears. "Jim, maybe it's my dead mother," she sobbed. "Maybe my dead mother is punishing me from beyond the grave. But what for?" He reassured her. "Your mother is not punishing you," he said. "This is Braveman's fault. It's his doing. Papers are just papers. They have to sell copies to put food on their kids' plates." As if to prove his point, several newspapers went on to speculate regarding whether Carly Darling was dog or human or both. And the comments on social media got worse, so much so that when Carly was invited to be interviewed on the TV show *Oh What a Beautiful Morning*, Jim advised her to accept. He promised he'd help her with what to say and repeatedly reminded her that she was a fine actress who owed the world her talent. "You must not be ground down by dumb gossip," he said.

Having Jim to advise her was the nearest thing to perfect Carly could get. And as he lifted her on to a stool in the Dirt Road Diner, after her TV interview, her insides melted like the ice-cream on her hot waffles. There was no doubt a girl could fall in love with a guy like Jim.

The two of them giggled as they chopped their waffles into bite-sized chunks and then Carly drank her coffee from a soup bowl while Jim told her the latest from Ocean Boulevard. The understudy was threatening to walk out because she was sick of being chucked around in front of a near-empty auditorium and the dog mask was too tight. "You see," Jim told Carly, "you were the only person who could play that part. You're a brilliant actress and singularly special."

"Cleardon Braveman doesn't think so," she said. "He did it all wrong. He went too far. And I guess he made people imagine they were going to have to think about stuff. Nobody wants to think. I didn't want anybody to think. I never had a part in a real play before. I just wanted people to come. I wanted fans."

"Well, maybe people will come now you've been on TV," said Jim and, as he raised his cup to drink, a man in a white shirt, tight paisley vest and blue jeans came over and spoke to Carly. "Gee," he said. "I just saw you on TV. You were great." He turned to Jim. "Ain't it clever to eat with a mouth that shape."

Jim told him to get lost, but the guy just stood there, and Carly heard herself saying what Jim had coached her to say. "I know you don't mean to be rude, so let me explain. There is a rumor, started by a sick person, who said my mother couldn't get a date and slept with her dog and conceived and gave birth to a puppy, which is crazy." Jim put up his right hand and interrupted: "As Miss Darling said on TV this morning, she has now left the production. So, for your information, in case you weren't listening as well as looking, she is no longer playing what has been referred to as the dog-faced dwarf." The man smirked and shrugged. "I never said nothing, did I? Can it write though? I mean, can I have an autograph?" Jim told Carly she didn't have to do it and glared at Paisley Vest. "Don't call the lady it," he said. Carly shrugged and smiled. "Heck, Jim, I'm kind of used to that one." Jim sighed and said, "You sure are a patient girl." And Carly felt all good inside. "You kind of learn patience," she said, "in a carnival booth." And then, because she'd never been asked for her autograph before, she wrote *Carly Darling* on a paper napkin and gave it to Paisley Vest who smiled and said "Thanks, honey. Shame you stepped away from the play. I would have bought twenty tickets. My old lady and her sisters love weird."

As the man left, Jim bit his lip, grinned and said, "Twenty tickets, huh? I think you met your first fan." Carly glowed with pleasure. "My first fan," she said as Jim helped her down so she could visit the rest room, where she hurried into a cubicle. She stood on tiptoe, trying to see her reflection in the mirror. She wanted to know whether having a real fan had made her look any different, but the mirror was too high. She scampered back to Jim and he helped her onto her stool, saying that Luna had pinged over a couple of photos of folks outside Ocean Boulevard. They were holding multi-colored banners decorated with teddy bears and "Bring Back the Real Rainbow." And Luna had told Jim that she could sell out the house for the evening performance and the next several weeks, as long as Carly was guaranteed to appear. Luna had also said there wasn't a single person queueing outside the dirty movie place today.

"But," Jim told Carly, "you don't have to do anything you don't want to. You know, your happiness matters to me above everything. Oh, and my memory." He slapped his palm to his forehead. "I keep meaning," he said, "I must just say, before I forget again. Because of us both being kind of lonely souls in this world, I keep meaning to say, I could arrange for the two of us to talk to a lawyer of my acquaintance. Just a suggestion. Gee, I know we're both dirt poor, but it could still be cool if maybe we leave our plenty of nothing to each other. Because lately we seem to be getting kind of permanent." Carly felt her mouth fill with saliva, and she had to grip the sides of her seat to stop from stretching her neck to nuzzle his chin. Did he mean make wills together? That was what married people did. Wow. It could be a proposal next. Her voice came out high and tight with excitement. "Yes," she said. "And yes, call Luna back. I will be on stage tonight." Then a small lurch of guilt came because she'd spoken Luna's name. She stopped the sensation in its tracks. *I don't owe*

Luna anything.

To celebrate, Jim took her to Gentleman Gino's Hot Spot, where three customers straight way asked for her autograph. Something about earlier and the will stuff, and now the way the fans looked at her, made her feel as if love was coming all around from all directions. She relished the whole signing thing and, to add to the fun, she'd never been in a sophisticated bar before. The live band smelled like spiced beef. Delicious. While she checked out the photographs of show business people on the place mats, the waiter brought champagne. Carly had to be careful. If a small girl drank more than one sparkling coupé, she could easily get to licking Jim's strong brown hands and telling him she loved him. A beeping interrupted her thoughts. It was Luna, messaging Jim again. Evidently the play was sold out for the next seven weeks and counting. Jim promptly ordered big platters of Pacific salmon sliders and chicken quesadillas, and later, after they'd eaten, they took a cab to the theatre. "Jeepers," said the driver, "wait 'til I tell my good lady I had the dog-faced dwarf in the back." The fuzziness from the champagne, and the joy of signing autographs, made Carly feel bullet-proof. Sophisticated and powerful. "We'll wangle you a couple of tickets," she giggled, feeling hot in the cheeks and flirtatious as they reached Ocean Boulevard. Then she saw the crowds outside and said, "Oh my days, Jim, look at all the people." And Jim hid Carly in her favorite dumpster before going inside the theater and along to Wardrobe to grab the coat she liked. When he came back, he pulled her from the dumpster, flung the coat over her head and carried her through the stage door. She scooted to the rest room to pee, feeling like she could die, she was so happy.

And there came a night during the third week of sold-out performances when a big-noise producer was in front and he got his people to arrange for him and his assistant to convene with Jim and Carly. At the meeting, the producer talked movie rights, the deal to be based, he said, "entirely on our Rainbow playing her part on film. It'll be great. We don't make the customers think about stuff. We do it all for them. Gee. Real carousels and, you bet your boots, we'll have real horses. I love a horse." Jim coughed and interrupted. "Miss Darling does prefer to be addressed as Carly," he said. "Yeah, sure," said the producer, crouching in front of her. "See, we got to have you, Rainbow, honey. You are adorable, with your big old eyes and your beautiful big soft face. I can guarantee a million fans at least." He patted her head and stood up. "What a good girl," he said. "I just love her. We all love her. But first, Mr. Jim, I guess we need to pay off this Looney Fairchild?"

"No need," said Jim. "Miss Darling owns all rights to the play." Carly was confused but Jim continued. "When Luna Fairchild begged for Miss Darling to come back, I insisted ownership of the play be formally transferred to Miss Darling, in perpetuity." He looked at Carly. "I'm planning to get the same legal guy to draw up that other matter I spoke about." She felt a rush of excited love as Jim went on. "So Miss Darling has entire ownership of the rights. Yes. That was the only basis on which Miss Darling would return. In truth, Luna Fairchild got the benefit of fantastic ticket sales from a mediocre play, entirely dependent on this young lady here for its success." Carly thought Jim was just amazing. She went all wobbly in the belly.

"And it is also true," she said, as if she were included in the conversation, "that I was taken from my mother at a carnival. She did it on purpose too. What kind of mother lets that happen and does nothing? A bad mother, that's what kind. A mother who betrayed me. I was placed in a sideshow booth where people bought tickets to see me. They put a sign up. 30 seconds for 30 cents though in truth they charged a dollar minimum. I hated that booth. It had nowhere a person could hide." Jim smiled and said, "But remember, they wanted to see your rare beauty." Carly noticed the producer glance nervously at his assistant then back at Jim who nodded to Carly. She figured this was her cue to emphasize the horror of her past. "The fear of being defenseless and abandoned never leaves a person," she said.

The following day Carly realized Jim must have taken her words very seriously because he gave her a small wooden box and when she opened it, there was a pistol. A loaded pistol. When he showed her how to use it, she laughed. "No need! I was taught how to fire a gun years ago, by the carnival folk. I gave mine away. Guns can make a person act on impulse and that's bad. But thank you." Jim smiled down at her. "All right. but promise me you will keep it by you always, just in case." Resisting the urge to rub herself against his leg, Carly clambered on to a chair and kissed his cheek and said, "How can I thank you for all you have done?" And he said, "Just stick around. Please."

Within a few months, the completed film was well on its way to becoming the fifth most successful movie ever. Carly was ecstatic when her photograph went onto the latest table mat in Gentleman Gino's. "Success is about money and money is all about power," said Jim. "Now you could buy this place a hundred times over. When a girl gets rich, she can buy anything." Carly smiled, her heart and head full of love for him. As a tribute to Jim, she vowed that she would never neglect her fans and to prove it she made a personal announcement to them on TV and social media as soon as the movie's sequel was commissioned. At the same time Luna Fairchild announced she was giving up on theatre and returning to her home town near Pittsburgh. "People move on," Jim told Carly. "It happens." He and Carly moved on too. They took up residence in an opulent mansion in the Hollywood Hills, situated behind the most immaculate cream perimeter wall. As the pair relaxed on the terrace there in the evenings, him on his favorite cane chair and Carly on her booster cushion, Carly knew nothing could be better than this.

And it was on one such golden evening that Jim smiled at her and told her she looked wonderful as ever and that was particularly serendipitous because a special guest was dropping by for dinner. Someone it was wise to allow into their intimate circle. Jim pulled Carly onto his lap and held her so close she could almost taste the delicately spiced chicken wings the cook had served him at lunch. "Remember," Jim whispered, "Cleardon Braveman is a gentleman of great influence who is actually a really nice guy with your very best interests at heart." Cleardon Braveman? Carly tensed. Her veins throbbed and heated. She forced herself off Jim's knees, bared her teeth and noisily growled her displeasure. She became hysterical. The maid hurried in. "I thought mad dog bark," she said. Jim told the woman to get back to her work. It was nothing. "It is not nothing," said Carly. She moved behind an armchair, then moved again and crouched in a corner, facing Jim. "You have invited Cleardon Braveman to my house," she said. "But Cleardon Braveman will not help me. As a matter of fact, I don't need his help. So how dare you? Without even asking me first?" She still felt that hurt from the past, that untreatable wound of resentment towards Braveman. And now, in the space of a few moments that had ravaged a calm and happy evening, she had the same malignant resentment for Jim. How could he arrange for that fucking jerk to be entertained in her house, the building that had been bought with her poignant back story and her hard work and her massive appeal to the public? Carly growled again. *Why the hell are small people treated like children?*

She moved towards the stairs, feigning resignation in order to give herself time to think. Upstairs in her room, she rang for the maid then, feeling chilled by shock, took out a blue cashmere shawl. "Tell Mr. Jim I will eat supper in my room," she told the maid, and the woman did as she was told and returned a little later with a note from Jim, saying he knew he'd messed up and was sorry. He'd misguidedly planned the evening as a lovely surprise because he wanted to have Braveman personally apologize to her during dinner and now he was begging her forgiveness too. Feeling a little guilty at the content of the note, Carly told the maid to let her know the moment the two men were seated for their meal. As soon as the woman confirmed, Carly pulled her shawl closer around her shoulders, then descended the stairs and concealed herself behind a potted fig tree, near the half-open door of the dining room. She hoped she was in time to hear Braveman's apology. The first voice was Jim's. "Well done," he said, "with your review. You sure helped me make her a star." Carly gripped a handful of fig foliage to steady herself. There was a long silence then a murmuring and a giggle and another voice, presumably Braveman's. "Your kisses are like cocktails, Jimmy Jim, only sweeter. Now, do behave. Ha! Jim, baby. All I had to do was avoid mentioning the freak, big up the imaginary prosthetic and wham bang, jackpot! You, dear boy, then become her all-time hero and a big noise film guy arrives on cue." "Yeah," said Jim. "And the cherry on the cookie? After far too much delay getting the document drawn up, that little gal sulking upstairs signs her last will and testament tomorrow and you, Braveman, darling, are looking at her sole beneficiary."

"Simple justice," said Braveman. "You've been great for her. Christ! She's nothing but side show fodder." There was an "Ah-ha" of agreement from Jim, then "Sure," he said, "our poor little German Shepherd girl. The Shih Tzu from a shit zoo. You name it, I've heard them saying it. I earn my keep making sure she believes none of it. And I'm happy to say she's still making millions, and that's just great, Braveman, my darling, because a fellow needs a nice spreadsheet to turn him on after staring at that ugly kisser. Of course, the biggest and best cherry on the cookie is the life expectancy. It's nice and sweet and low, honey."

Carly heard whining and realized it was coming from inside her own body. She put her hand over her mouth, as if it were possible to push sound into nothing. She panted as she clambered back upstairs. In her room, she took out the pistol Jim had given her and laid it on the bed. Then she climbed on a chair, pushed the window up to open it, and angrily jettisoned the pistol's wooden box down and out and into the bushes near the swimming pool. "Piece of cheap shit," she snarled. Then, forcing herself to breathe deeply, she quietly descended the stairs, sneaked past the potted fig, sniffing as she went, and entered the dining room. Holding the pistol behind her, she came so close to Jim's right hand side that her nostrils were riddled with the stink of his unease. He reached out to her, briefly glanced at his companion, and spoke. "Hello there, Carly," he said. She manufactured her best eyes-and-teeth smile and shoved the gun barrel hard against his chest.

Her hand and arm shook violently, way out of control. She could not pull the trigger. Jim laughed as he put up his arms in pretense of surrender, but Carly could see that he was shaking too. "Feisty little gal, huh?" he said, his arms dropping and his left hand gripping the side of his chair. "For a moment there I thought she was going to show me what she learned at the carnival." Carly clenched her teeth. A growl came from deep in her throat. "Maybe the play tells a true story," she said. "It does deal with selfishness, greed and lies but what am I saying? You obviously know all about that. So maybe I can't rest until another body is cold in a casket, slowly rotting. Yours. That would smell kind of sweet. Luna called it a rose motif, remember? Hey, Jim," she steadied her hand, aimed the gun at him and said sadly, "I guess you're right. Life expectancy is short. If it's yours."

Braveman stood up and sidestepped, one, two three, towards the terrace doors, saying "All this talk of death and caskets! Come along, people. Stop pointing that horrid thing at him, Rainbow, dear. Let's all get some fresh air." Carly turned her back on Braveman. "My name is not Rainbow," she said, and she watched as Jim bit his lower lip and held out his hands, palms downwards, as if to calm her. "Enough," he said. "Silly girl, Carly. You're not on stage now." As the maid came into the dining room, Carly stared at Jim, longing for him to say something, anything to make this less hideous but there came a weakening of her legs. Her heart seemed to stutter, then it beat fast, then faster and she fell, grazing her cheek on the flat-sawn floor. A trace of estrogen momentarily tinged the air in her nostrils as Carly lost consciousness.

Twenty-four hours later, after the medical team checked on Carly for the fifth time, the maid's text arrived. *Dear Miss Darling, hope you are comfortable in the hospital. Hope you did not mind drive to hospital in Chevy. Sorry for humpy ride. Did you notice I put You Know What in your bag? Very sorry but could not find box. Very well soon please. Mr. Jim has packed and left, as you requested. Many people come to outside house. All of your fans love you.* Carly yawned. They sure do, she thought. She got out of bed and grabbed her overnighter from the storage unit. When she reached inside, pulled at the blue cashmere shawl and uncovered the gun, she smiled. She replaced the overnighter and its hidden memento, back into the unit, clambered into bed and returned her attention to the rolling news on TV. All over the world, reporters were talking about her and people were celebrating her recovery. It was proof that a girl with thousands, no, millions of fans could never be alone. She relaxed against her pillows.

"Someone for you, Miss Darling," said a nurse. Carly sat straight up. She scented bourbon, travel fatigue and some kind of a bribe having been handed over. That nurse would be reported to her superiors for letting Luna Fairchild on to the premises. "You're not needed or welcome," said Carly. Luna's connection with Jim might be tenuous but it was still a connection. "There is no problem here," Carly continued. "My heart just beat too fast but I'm fine and I don't want to talk about anything. The doctor says I will live to be a hundred. So get out before I get you thrown out." Luna pulled off her shades and shoved them in her bag. "I told you I never trusted that Jim," she said. "Think of the sisterhood." Carly leapt out of bed and Luna reversed in the direction of the exit. "Screw the sisterhood," Carly yelled. "There is no sisterhood. You would have let Jim fuck you if he'd wanted to." A nurse appeared. "Miss Darling, take care, please. Get back into bed at once." Carly bared her teeth at Luna. "I told you to get out! Gee, can't a person get a little peace around here? Get her out, nurse. I am not in her fucking sisterhood. Luna Fairchild, you are a cheating Judas. You used me, like everyone else does. Only some of them don't stink so bad. My loyal fans would never forgive me if I as much as breathed the same air as you. Ever. Security!" Luna was swiftly removed.

Alone again, Carly got into bed, and gazed at the TV. A reporter was standing outside her mansion, right by one of her elegant custom-made dumpsters. There was so much stuff and so many people. They'd brought candles, greetings cards, teddy bears with shiny black eyes. And makeshift rainbow shrines. "My public. My fans," said Carly. "This is how it is to be really truly loved." For one peculiar moment, she thought she saw Jim on the TV screen, but it was just some guy. She breathed deeply, contentedly. The fans were her true lovers and their hard-earned money, willingly handed over, would never lie to her. Right there on TV was all the proof she needed. This was where life had brought her. Fame. Stardom. Comfort from strangers and the best rags to riches story ever. Now she had no illusions about her body or her luck. She'd learned how blessed she was to have been born this way. And not only had she acquired great wealth but her life had been spared for a reason. However long it took, she would purchase anonymous revenge on all those who had betrayed her. She smiled. Carly Darling wasn't a freak. She was one hell of a powerful woman.

Everything Else
By Ella Kerr

Beyond the cracked sidewalk, and the telephone pole with layers of flyers in a rainbow of colors, and the patch of dry brown grass there stood a ten-foot high concrete block wall, caked with dozens of coats of paint. There was a small shrine at the foot of it, with burnt out candles and dead flowers and a few soggy teddy bears. One word of graffiti filled the wall, red letters on a gold background: Rejoice!

This is the place where people sat with their hands in their hair and remembered Rainbow: black eyes with shiny crescent moons reflected in her irises, and a black braid that danced all the way down her back. In her later years, that black braid flowed with silver, shining and flashing in the sun like minnows sparkling in a shallow pond. I saw many people come to remember Rainbow on that cracked sidewalk. The patch of concrete was known as The Pot of Gold, (because that's where Rainbow had ended) and was in a strange part of town between the pizza shop and the ocean. The mourners would kneel with one hand on the cement and one hand covering their mouth or their eyes or their heart, thinking of how well they knew the woman whose ashes rested here. Strangely enough, I was the one who knew her the best in her last few months of life.

I would walk to The Pot of Gold in the weeks after her death, and watch every person who came and touched the candles and the flowers and the photographs withered at the edges. Every time they slowed to glance at the words engraved in the concrete, or when they turned their eyes away and craned their necks to stop the remembering; I wondered if I had seen them before: in the photo book of Rainbow's life that I had helped to create. My eyes strained to see the faces of the people who I might recall from her memories. I looked for defining features: a fleck in their pupil, a scar on their eyebrow, a locket. I knew it didn't matter, not anymore anyways, but I was curious enough to wonder: were the people that came to visit her the same people I had seen bright and bold in her memory?

I met Rainbow Alesca Poole 8 months earlier in the sterile light and stale air of a tired hospital. Her dark hair was twisted into a thick bun that hung low on her neck, the strands of silver snaking their way from the crown of her head to the wispy ends, her black eyes like ink pools. She held the hand of a broad chested man with thick arms and veins that ran like rivers into his hands. Matty was his name, her husband of the last eighteen years. Matty's parents were woodworkers, Rainbow had told me, and her parents met at Woodstock (hence a daughter named Rainbow) and they had met in Wooden Bakery in upstate New York. If that wasn't fate she didn't know what was, and he had fallen in love the moment she laughed.

But they laughed a little less these days. The couple came in holding one another and expressing their concerns of Alzheimer's at a hospital nearby four years earlier. At sixty years old, Matty sat staring down at his palms, wondering what he had done to be forced to say goodbye to his wife's mind so early. Rainbow told me he bit his lips until they turned white to keep the tears from coming that first day when they sat in the hospital and heard the word "Alzheimer's" spoken out loud.

Everything Else

The technology of deleting memories was new then; we were all still learning how it worked. But people were being told it was the key to staving off Alzheimer's, if caught early enough, and those who suffered (and their loved ones) were willing to try the procedure, albeit cautiously. With reverence. With a bowing respect to the disease that demanded (it seemed) for one to give up past memories in order to make room for the day to day memories. The procedure was this: if we could delete the thoughts and images that took up large pieces of the brain (falling in love, the smell of your mother's perfume) then we would be able to make room for the mundane: how to get to the grocery store. How to spell your daughter's name. Which was the gas pedal, and which was the brake.

"Research has discovered that brains are like a smart phone's camera roll, continually capturing images of the mundane and the monumental, and Alzheimer's, simply put, is the brain's way of saying, 'Hey, we have run out of storage to take more pictures,'" I would explain to my patients, as they sat with their families, arms linked, heads touching, hearts pounding in rhythm.

"We just need to go in and delete some of the pictures that aren't serving you any longer. You know, the boring ones from a long time ago," I would say with a wink, when patients asked how, exactly they could free up memory space. I never knew how to have this conversation, with any type of patient. How to tell a family we could delete pieces or experiences that made their loved one the person they were, and that alone would be the way to save them.

The insignificant memories were deleted first. In a large screen in a dark room, I would scroll through thousands and thousands of images that a patient held in their brain, taking up space and not allowing new memories to populate. These memories were the daily walks to class in middle school, the boss's coffee order at your first job, the way a brother ordered a deli sandwich, though he's been dead for years now. We would print a book of the thousands of sheets of insignificant memories, indicated as trivial by the grayish hue the image took on, the way they blurred on the edges like it was created with poor quality film. In contrast, the significant memories, the ones patients resorted back to constantly, were bright and clear: the colors vibrant. In these memories, each raindrop and leaf were outlined with extreme precision. These were the memories that made the individual who they were. These were also the memories that took up the most room in an already overcrowded brain. Those were the memories we tried not to touch.

When I met Rainbow, we were past deleting the insignificant memories. She had gone to a previous doctor who had already gotten rid of the so called useless images. Now, sitting in my office, she explained that she needed help deleting some of the more significant memories, to free up even more space. Her hope was that by ridding herself of these more remarkable memories would give her the capacity to keep driving to church for Wednesday night aerobics and recognizing her granddaughter when she came over on Fridays with sticky cheeks and fat, dimpled hands. That's all she wanted. To be there for the simple things.

On the day that I met the couple, as Rainbow explained her desires, Matty excused himself, muttered something about coffee and fresh air and walked out of the room, clearly flustered by the situation. I cleared my throat, "It says here in your chart that your previous doctor was not accommodating you adequately in choosing which of these memories to delete, and that is why you are here right now to see me. Can you explain this a little better to me?" I watched as her eyes glittered, either with tears or with inspiration. She spoke her words as if she was reading them off the gray wall behind me.

"I want you to gray everything out when we choose which memories to keep," Rainbow said, confidently, except for a small catch in her voice. "I want Matty to choose my memories with me and I want every single image to look the same so he doesn't know which one's are more significant than the other. I don't want him knowing that my first kiss is more vivid in my mind then our wedding day, or something like that, you know? Are you able to do that? If you aren't, it is no problem, but I am prepared to find a doctor who can." I was silent for a moment and searched Rainbow's face for awareness, to ensure she understood what she was asking. It was true, the bright images that remained had a gradient. It was easy for anyone to see that while the remaining photographs were all bright, some were especially clear and vivid as the day they happened. What Rainbow wanted was all of these images turned to a dusky gray.

There were times when patients made requests about their families' involvement in their memories: but more often than not, it was that certain memories would stay hidden. They were embarrassed to show what they had seen or remembered, all on cardboard photographs glued to an album. It was a strange process, as a family member, to watch someone's life on card stock and ask, "Are you sure you want to keep that one? Isn't this memory of the family ski trip in Tahoe so much more special to you?"

"It's hard on Matty, seeing me like this. He misses me and I am right there. And if my memory is going to be wiped anyway, why not have him choose? If I am losing my mind, why would I ever let him know that my college sweetheart still burns brightly in my mind, that my days as a girl on the ranch are more clear to me than our honeymoon was? I love him. I love him with every ounce possible and that is why I am asking for this, Doctor. I am asking you to shield him from the truth of my priorities so we can finish out these last years of our love in the bliss of not knowing the intricacies of my mind. Let him choose my priorities. I trust that."

I stared at Rainbow for a long while, then paged through the existing memories I had already printed to a photo book. She was a happy child. Same long, thick black braid. Same deep dimples and deep ink pool eyes. Same laughing smile. "You realize he could delete some memories, absentmindedly of course, but some memories that are really important to you. Things that you could never get back…"

Rainbow reached out and grabbed my hand to reassure me, a strange gesture for a woman who would soon have her mind erased, "I know all of this; and I am sure. Nothing will make a dying woman more comforted than the reassurance that the memories I have left are one's that my husband believes are important to me. He will have so much peace in that. And his peace is truly the only memory I need." I closed my eyes, exhaled slowly, and agreed to her plan.

Rainbow told me they knew the Alzheimer's had gotten bad the night of the storm. She had insisted she was fine, taken the car out, and driven to town to get vanilla ice cream, root beer and nail polish remover. Matty had seen signs in the past, the occasional bout of forgetfulness, but nothing like this before. Rainbow said she didn't remember a thing: not the confusion on the highway of which way to turn. Not the red light that her tires spun through with a high rubbery squeak, or the swerve of the pizza delivery truck narrowly missing a collision. Not the feeling of her shoulder blades smashing through the driver's window, leaving Rainbow a crumpled heap on the asphalt, the gravel stuck to her glittering face in the rain.

It was the pizza delivery boy who found her. He was a strange, kind soul, with developmental delays that you could not see in his face, but could see in his actions, in his movements and the same strange songs he repeated over and over. He knew what it was like to have his face pressed against the asphalt, and he called out to Rainbow when he saw the car flip, empathy in his shoulders, but not his words. He was no good with words. He was no good at anything.

But he knew he should help.

The boy did not know where to take her so he rolled her in a blanket and took her to his house. He started the car as she lay, coddled in the back of a station wagon, wrapped in quilts with the heat on high. It was a strangely peaceful place to rest after a car accident. He hummed strange songs in a language, whether real or not, was pleasantly unfamiliar to Rainbow. She let the sound of his voice be a comfort: a piece of newness that felt like the unknown warmth of beautiful things she had not yet learned. Not the strangeness associated with Alzheimer's: confusion, panic, a constant subtle feeling that she was being tricked into something she could not possibly bare. She allowed herself to drift into the strange dreamlike trance in the back of the pizza boy's car.

When the ride ended, she was lifted again. The kid slid her body onto a soft pile of clothing among the boxes in the garage. He pulled an old coat over the top, creating a cave that emanated the sweetness of old ladies who frequently powdered themselves—a light rose motif that played ironically well in the deep recesses of Rainbow's ancestral brain. The pizza kid lifted her head to help her lap water from a hubcap. He broke bits of pepperoni and crust into bite-sized pieces and left them where her tongue could reach them. Much later, she heard him practicing his orations like songs. Like monks chanting in the distance, they were a comfort.

Matty wasn't proud of how he reacted that night. The incident scared him more than anything ever had, including Vietnam mud storms, including the tornado that he ran from on bare feet on the plains of Indiana when he was a boy. He burst through the garage door, frantic and enraged, and shook the thin pale boy, and screamed with a purple face, "Where is my wife, you lunatic? Where have you taken my wife?!"

The boy trembled and began to cry, and pointed a shaky hand to the fort of blankets where Rainbow lie, peacefully sleeping with a pizza crust in her hand. Matty scooped up Rainbow with both arms, her body lighter than he remembered. She shook violently awake and he cried when she opened her black eyes: so dark, he could see his own blue irises reflected in them. "Rainbow," he whispered, "How will I ever be at peace again?"

This is when Matty brought Rainbow into the hospital four years ago. Desperate for help, holding her hands and pulling her through the doors. He led her by the wrists down mazes of doctor's offices and metal chairs and sterile counters and furrowed brows. Alzheimer's. It was the first time they had spoken the words. Treatment option… the first time they heard there was hope in deleting memories. Priorities. The first time that Rainbow considered that perhaps the kindest thing to do in this unkind world was ensure that her priorities aligned with the person who loved her most for the rest of the time she spent on this earth.

We were startled back to reality, back into the clinical chill of the hospital room when Matty came through the doors again, interrupting Rainbow's reflective monologue, and I hastily swatted the tears that had pooled at the base of my eyelids. His voice was soft and he held shaky hands around a steaming Styrofoam cup of coffee, "What have you all decided on?"

He lowered himself down onto the chair with two hands. I wondered about what he dreamt of at night: was it Rainbow when she was young, dancing with long limbs and wild hair under the sun? His inevitable lonely future while he sat tucked onto one side of the bed? Or perhaps he didn't dream at all, simply willing her memories to stay inside her brain a little longer, while she slept and he lie awake and pressed his hand on her shoulder blades at night.

"I am going to need a new photo book of her current memories, so why don't you both stay here for an updated memory scan, and schedule a time next week to come in and decide which memories stay and which memories go," I said briskly, and hurried out of the room before I could change my mind, before I caught Rainbow's eye and shook my head no, I could not, would not, allow every memory to blend into the next.

But when I looked over my shoulder to close the door, I saw Rainbow's head placed gently on Matty's shoulder and the way he traced the veins that ran up her arm and I understood: keeping this image of his wife frozen just as she is was most important. A place where their memories and priorities aligned nearly perfectly was worth more than everything else.

The next day, I stood in the dark room of the hospital staring at the computer screen and surveyed all of the recollections Rainbow held in her mind. It was easy to tell the intensity of each photo, the lines cut crisply through the computer screen. There were several bold images, perhaps thirty, still as fiery and fresh in her mind if they had occurred just moments before.

There was one of her as a child with a dog at her feet and wildflowers in her hands. Two other dark eyed children ran ahead of her in the distance. Sisters perhaps? Childhood friends? There was the one of her past lover, with smooth black skin and kind brown eyes, dancing with dress pants on and grinning ear to ear. He looked so in love, I blushed, looked away, and understood once again why Rainbow wanted the images blurred to gray.

Then, there was one strikingly bold image of a boy wearing a pizza shop hat and polo shirt. Rainbow held his hand and he cried or sang or a mix of the two. She seemed to be comforting him. I looked at the image closer: this was the boy who had driven her away from the accident and wrapped her in blankets and sang her songs. But they were not in the garage, as she explained before. They seemed to be in a park, she was holding a guitar. They must have met up again, the two must have become friends.

I understood, yet again, why Rainbow had chosen to put the power of choice in Matty's hand. She did not want a strange incident with a special needs boy to be brighter than their engagement. Than the first steps of their daughter. Than the sailing trip in the Maldives. But here it was. Brighter than ever.

And then, a photograph of me, standing with a furrowed brow in the middle of the exam room, biting my lip and trying to be patient. I looked so young in her mind: a stern girl with a serious demeanor. Why was a memory of me so bright? I looked closer to see why this memory stuck with her so intensely it was just a doctor's appointment after all. But I remembered the way her head rested on Matty's shoulder that day in the exam room and I realized just how much she relied on this thought: creating peace for Matty mattered more than everything else.

I muted all of the images to a pearly gray with one click of the button, before I could change my mind and printed the images: an entire life reduced to 200 grayed out memories on shiny paper. The ink smelled synthetic and shallow, opposite of the depth the pictures held. I slid the images gently into plastic sleeves and carried the bound book into the room.

The couple sat on hospital chairs with their legs entangled, Rainbow's head once again on Matty's thick shoulder. I looked away for a moment, embarrassed at the intimacy, and kept my head turned while I placed the newly created album at Matty's side. "We need to reduce this group of 200 photos down to 50," I said, working to ensure my voice did not betray me." It is your job to work together and choose the ones you want to delete."

Rainbow sucked her lips in and bit down and Matty gently looked through the pages, flipping each one, viewing the world through the eyes of his wife for the first time in his life, "Isn't there a way to know which one's are a priority to her, so we know which one's to keep?" he whispered.

Rainbow caught my eye, and I turned quickly away so the soft couple would not see the hesitation on my face. "In this particular case, there's not," I lied. "We weren't able to delineate priority within her brain. Unfortunately." I held my breath and waited for Matty to call me out on my lie, to demand a second opinion, to see the original memories and try to find a way to prioritize what held fast and strong in his wife's mind and what was beginning to fade with years and time and the rose colored glasses of age. But he kept his head down, scanned the thick pages and nodded solemnly.

I watched as Matty placed his lips on Rainbow's ear and ask what memories she wanted to keep. She turned the pages slowly: there she stood with long braids and roller skates, smiling broadly, probably seventeen years old. Their sons first day of school, his skin milky against the dark curls that hung on his forehead. There was the couple's wedding, with moody clouds in the background and a grinning Matty with a young and shaved face.

Rainbow gently grabbed Matty's hand and laid her cheek on his shoulder as they paged through the file. "I don't remember…" she began, and closed her wild black eyes. "I don't remember any of these memories, Matty. Why don't you go ahead and choose for me?"

Matty chose all of the memories that day: methodically and painstakingly. He held every image up to Rainbow's tired eyes and watched for the slightest reaction: a dilation of her pupils. A curl in her lips. A furrow in her brow that would give him a hint that this was a recollection he was supposed to keep for her. But Rainbow, true to her word, or perhaps due to strange ebb and flow of Alzheimer's itself, did not flutter and eyelash, did not wince at a pulsing heart at any of the images he showed her. In the end, he chose every one of Rainbow's memories. When he handed the book back, I closed it quickly so I would not know what she would soon forget.

Beyond the cracked sidewalk, and the telephone pole with layers of flyers in a rainbow of colors, and the patch of dry brown grass there stood a ten-foot high concrete block wall, caked with dozens of coats of paint. There was a small shrine at the foot of it, with burnt out candles and dead flowers and a few soggy teddy bears. One word of graffiti filled the wall, red letters on a gold background: Rejoice! This was the Pot of Gold, the place that Rainbow ended, where they sprinkled her ashes, four and a half months after her memories were deleted.

It wasn't the procedure that killed her, or a broken heart due to the memories she had lost. I reassured Matty of this repeatedly while he kept his eyes down: opening and closing his fingers as if he had just discovered his hands for the first time. It was simply her time; an old and tired euphemism that I hated even before it left my mouth. "The memories you chose didn't kill her, Matty. And the most beautiful thing is that you know what her mind was full of on the day she died. It was full of you."

I visited The Pot of Gold one week after Rainbow's memorial, sat on the bench with the chipped paint and closed my eyes and turned my face up towards the last rays of sun. Someone had just recently tagged the wall, red spray paint read "Rejoice!" in rushed handwriting and dripped down the wall like tiny trickles of blood.

To my right, standing in the distance was a dark skinned man in a blazer and dress pants, holding his cap in one hand and rubbing his wet cheeks with the other. His breaths were slow and deliberate, but the tears pooled at the hollow space between his neck and his collarbone. I couldn't be certain, but the way he twisted his hands and the way his black eyes gleamed almost made me sure: this was the first love, the man I had seen in her memories. If he had chosen her memories, surely he would have kept one of her laughing and his dark hands interlaced between her own brown fingers. The thought of her not remembering him caught in my throat.

As I sat and watched as the man slowly walked away, the wind whipped long strands of hair across my face accompanied by a strange new fragrance. It smelled like spray paint and bread and the destructive scent of adolescence. A boy sat down opposite of me on the bench, and stared down at this palms, stained a sticky red. He had clearly been the one to spray the message above Rainbow's grave. A bystander may have found it offensive: the crude letters on private property of a place to pay respects.

But I had seen Rainbow's memories and knew how she would have viewed the boy with the thin shoulders and the polo shirt. This is how he was saying goodbye. The boy nodded to the place where Rainbow's ashes had been dispersed, "She...she remembered me," the boy said, in his sing-songy voice, "She...she forgot about a lot of things, but she remembered me!"

I stood at his comment, overwhelmed at his inaccuracy and hurriedly rubbed my eyes to prevent my wet eyelashes from leaking tears. I pulled my coat around me tighter and walked away from this place where Rainbow was. "It was wrong," I chastised myself, "it was wrong of me to let Matty choose the memories, wrong of me to allow the people who had loved Rainbow to be forgotten. What had she thought about those last few weeks of life? Was she even able to comprehend the breadth and depth of the love that surrounded her, or had I taken that away by putting the happiness in the hands of another flawed human?"

With my head down, I ran abruptly into a thick and sturdy chest that smelled familiar, like bar soap and black coffee. There stood Matty with wet eyes and a tight smile. He had a strange look on his face, not quite laughter, but something close, and we both waited for the other to speak, uncomfortable with the vulnerability that lay between us.

"I kept the memory of you, you know," Matty said finally, "I know what you two were doing. I know she wanted me to choose her memories so we could reminisce about things together. But I wanted her to remember the best and the brightest things. Not just things where I was standing by her side."

I searched his eyes and found Rainbow there, mischievous with laughing eyes. I thought of Rainbow and her quiet whispers, her secret plans to ensure that her husband knew he was loved, all the while, he meticulously undid her plan. Soon I couldn't help myself, I opened my mouth and laughed.

He shook his head and laughed along with me, a real, genuine surge from his throat, "But those pictures that I didn't understand? The ones of the laughing man, or that pizza boy, or you, Doctor? Those are the memories I left for her. I already knew about the memories we had together. I wanted her to tell me everything else."

922 Fessler Ln
By Alex Lee

I.

Beyond the cracked sidewalk, and the telephone pole with layers of flyers in a rainbow of colors, and the patch of dry brown grass there stood a ten-foot high concrete block wall, caked with dozens of coats of paint. There was a small shrine at the foot of it, with burnt out candles and dead flowers and a few soggy teddy bears. One word of graffiti filled the wall, red letters on a gold background: Rejoice!

Lenny stood looking at the shrine with a box under one arm, his hand on the opposite hip, and a modest belly bulging beneath a blue silk shirt whose design featured cornucopias, Thanksgiving turkeys, and steaming gravy-boats. He wore this peculiar number over a dirty, DayGlo-yellow mesh shirt. Sweat dripped symmetrically over Lenny's whiskered lips. He set the box down shaking his head and making *tsk-tsk* noises, and started straightening the bears up again. He stuck a finger in the guttered candles to knock the water out and tried his lighter against the blackened wicks. He took a ragged hand-towel and started drying the teddy bears—which wasn't *especially* effective... Lenny took the old flowers from the vases and put them in his box and took new flowers from the box and put them in the vases. He opened a water bottle, mixed some plant-food in it, and topped the vases off, before drinking the rest of it. Finally, he took one his dozens of framed headshots of Laura Dern (circa 1990) and set it in the middle of the shrine, where he'd set the last one, at the same artful angle.

"That's it, baby," he said, standing again and wiping his hands. He wiped sweat from his brow and pursed his lips together, tearing up a little. A bulbous cloud drifted over the sun, somewhere over his left shoulder from Laura's reflected point of view. "That's it," he repeated, bent with a groan to collect his cardboard box, blew a kiss at the photograph, and went away belting 'Purple Rain' and rattling the various plated chains he wore on his wrist.

Miss Mayva Washington, 92, watched Lenny perform this admittedly bizarre ritual from her son's covered porch where she sat, sweatless as old Death himself. She'd passed the morning swatting at a Junebug and spitting tobacco juice in a Mason jar. Now Mayva scowled after Lenny's elaborately patterned back as he walked musically away, too hoarse thanks to the COPD to holler at him for making such a racket.

When she stood, there was a long procession of joints that, too soft and chalky at this late date to pop, nonetheless strained against her mightily, sending shooting pains up her papery limbs to her wizened brain. But Mayva had sat too long and done nothing. She took the tube looped around her neck and settled it over her huge, folded ears, fitting the twin barrels of the nasal cannula up her cavernous nostrils, twisted the nozzle on the O_2 and stood struggling to get a few good, long breaths of the pure stuff, not unlike trying to get a sip of milkshake that's too thick for your straw. Then finally grasped the wheeled O_2 tank with one arthritic claw and shuffled into the house.

It took Mayva fifteen minutes to find her late husband's nine-iron in the closet, but clarity of purpose never deserted her. If her body had betrayed her late in life, her mind remained loyal, albeit slightly more encumbered than in years past. Half an hour later the screen door slammed shut behind her and she started tottering across the street, her tank tugged along in one hand, her weight resting on the club in the left, held upside down like a cane. The Junebug watched curiously from the screen where he clung.

She made it to Lenny's shrine and glared at Laura Dern, the flowers, candles and mildewed teddy bears. She vented a contemptuous jet of tobacco juice down the sidewalk the way Lenny had gone, stood her tank on end, and got her balance. She raised the club up above her head, withered fingers tightening on the cracked rubber grip, and at just that moment the sun came out again from behind that towering old cumulonimbus. Mayva's silhouette, floating in front of Laura's winning smile, was edged in gold as if endorsed by Heaven.

She brought the club down a little too wide and took out a vase, knocking the picture over facedown and spilling flora and plantfood and glass on the bears adjacent. Mayva brought the club up again, squinting her good eye, and brought it down on the back of the frame, punching a hole in the cardboard on one side of the headshot and breaking the glass on the other. She slung the club away laterally, and the picture flew about six feet to her right and landed in the street, Laura's torn smile protruding between shards of glass. Mayva started kicking the bears and remaining vases over, and smashed out the candles which splashed wax on her slippers like blood. Flower-petals, wax, glass, and teddy bears littered the sidewalk in little arcs from the epicenter of Mayva's nonagenarian wrath. Then in the pitch and climax of her admittedly arbitrary vengeance, she fell, curled like a question mark in the bottom of a crater.

Mayva's son's dog, Rainbow—which in life she'd bitterly referred to as her 'only grandbaby'—nosed the screen door open and shuffled through with that enfeebled-old-dog's-body gait. The gold glinted on the concrete wall above Mayva as the light gradually left her eyes, and the clouds rolled over the sun again, dousing the vermillion call to arms painted there: *Rejoice*. Period.

A curious convergence chanced to happen then, some deadly-sober spiritual mumbo-jumbo in fact. Mayvaline Louise Washington died at 1:15 pm on June 23, 2019, exactly 92 years, 136 days and 21 hours flat after she was born screaming into this world. She was precisely 92.375 Copernican years old; a perfect RATIONAL. Rainbow the dog, bumping her nose on the way out the closing screen door, turned 12 years, 238 days, 17 hours, 59 minutes and 59 seconds old at the precise moment of Mayva's expiry. At the exchange rate of 7.3 Dog Years for every 'Human Year' (said coefficient often mistakenly given as 7), Rainbow turned *exactly* the same age as Mayva in Spirit Time© at *exactly* the moment she died. Mayva enjoying, like the rest of the featherless bipeds on the Chain-of-Being VIP list, a 1:1 solar and spiritual temporal correspondence. *However*—despite a spiritual age of 92.375, the dog's *Copernican* age was 12.654109589041097… This side of the solar orbit, the dreaded IRRATIONAL had reared its mangy head and sunk its infinite teeth in Rainbow's very soul…

Mayva's soul, in solar-spiritual-rational-determinate-temporal harmony, was imbued by virtue of that fleeting concordance with the grace of finite identity; if not perfectly whole (really though, who *is?*) she had nonetheless become, on winning number 92.375, a beatific poultice, the literal 'salve' in salvation. Rainbow's own soul, on the other hand, was in that same rabid instant deformed, fanatically infinite in its irrationally indeterminate finitude. United in the depthless instant of their temporo-spiritual concurrence, in this convex mirror of solar (not to mention special, generic, historic and life-death) asymmetries, they imparted to one another, at this convergence, certain tropes. Mayva, bumping into Rainbow on her way out, imparted to the diminished wolf her salvific, curmudgeonly sense of ultimate justice which it was her dying act to pass on Lenny's shrine to Laura Dern—in addition to nicotine cravings, preference for Salisbury steak, dislike of Junebugs, and old timey erotic fantasies related to butter-churning. In return, Rainbow sent with Mayva's departing spirit a chaotic stasis as much at equilibrium as the molten universe itself—ushering her out the door and into entropic hell, in other words.

Back in the material plane, Rainbow trotted along, as if the instantaneous epic of damnation and redemption (rather like the collision of two atoms) had not even occurred, transformed in this Pentecost as indelibly as only this fickle cosmos can render. It was rather as if God had farted and in the celestial concussion the two souls had been partly *Freaky Friday*-ed together. Not that they had switched places so much as they had switched trajectories, or slopes, if you like. The Junebug, temporally and spiritually discrete (ergo, untouched by the astral lightning bolt) took its chance and darted out the closing screen door. Rainbow snatched it from the air and dispatched it with a swift crunch, spit it back onto the sidewalk, and trotted off licking her whiskers. She cast a sidelong glance at the *Pieta* Mayva had made of herself in the shrine-debris, but something instinctive told Rainbow not to stop by her former cohabitant. There was a scent in the air, and Mayva's ancient hatred in Rainbow's heart.

Meanwhile, Lenny was pulling his pants down in a gas station bathroom. The mesh shirt turned out to be a mesh one-piece, as in bathing suit... He rummaged and pulled a somewhat weathered bottle of Jergen's out of the cardboard box, absently reading under his breath from a Sears catalogue he kept there: "'...fitted, reversible neckline camisole... comfort fit, Jentell nylon, *ooh*... white and damask—'the hell is *damask?*'"

He poured the lotion, which had separated in the summer heat into a thin oil and a thicker goop, into his palm and rubbed his hands together, eyes still scanning 2003's nighttime underwear collection. He started applying the lotion to his bared knees, appreciating the light floral note yet extant in the somewhat expired ointment. "'Tactel… is a… registered trademark… of… Invista,'" he read. "Huh. The hell do they be—AAIEEE!" Lenny had noticed the cockroach that had crawled onto the cracked toilet-tank lid. The lotion bottle clattered onto the tile and Lenny backed up in a panic, kicking over his cardboard box, and finally tripped over his white pants, down-gyved to his ankles, landing on his ass by the sink, still shrieking.

Then the clerk was knocking on the locked door, shouting. At length, mustering all his lip-quivering courage and shouting down the Armenian accent at the door, Lenny was able to slip his right shoe (Adidas 'Predator Pulse' football cleats, 2004) off. Able to walk again unfettered, his trousers trailing across the bathroom floor from his left, still-cleated foot, he approached the menace with his cudgel raised. Lenny smote, but the vermin retreated beneath the lid, so he flipped it off and it shattered on the ground, ceramic flying everywhere. The accented shouting at the door took on something of an edge. But, sweat dripping, heart thudding, ceramic tinkling and clerk shouting all dimmed, drowned before this new terror, back of the bowl, Lenny's own screams mute before this, nightmare incarnate—*the tank was full of roaches*. As in *brimming*.

A few blocks away, Rainbow trotted blithely along the sidewalk, enjoying the breeze and a newfound appreciation of four-legged ambulation, sniffing at beer cans and hamburger wrappers. She went a couple blocks, and then retreated down a perpendicular street from the sound of sirens, looking nervously back over her shoulder at the salmon-colored, klaxon rush of an EMS hurtling down the street the way she'd come (Mayva's last Hail Mary, too late, alas!). Rainbow kept on, panting in the heat, and turned left at the next sun-marbled block, all clarity of purpose and determination. She did stop to investigate, and then greedily eat, a pizza crust she found on the ground. But then onwards, purpose redoubled! At the original street again Rainbow continued, hot on Lenny's trail.

Lenny landed on his bare ass once more, in the parking lot this time, his box of oddities landing on his head moments after and spilling once more. The clerk—Samvel, a full 17 inches taller than Lenny and at least twice as heavy—stepped back inside and locked the automatic doors with a key, calling the police on his cell phone as he did. Lenny rolled, airing his literally chapped ass, weeping pathetically and cussing the clerk. Lenny started gathering his things again, still sobbing and hurling what we may as well go on and diagnose as 'mentally unfit' threats at his reflection in the glass doors. 'Gonna bake you, buggy-bread mufucker, we'll see who big when the tinfoil come, toilet-man, we'll see! Efollet! You gon bake, bitch!'

A pizza delivery kid, Eugene, pulled up into the Citgo parking lot right about then, there being a Don Giuliani's Pizzeria operating out the other half of the convenience store. Eugene was one of those unfortunately employed youths who was occasionally invited into sympathetic frat houses to take bong rips in lieu of a tip (as popularized on social media). This had, in fact, just occurred. Eugene parked in his usual spot and stared, cosmically aghast, at the scene in the parking lot. Lenny was standing now, pulling his sodden trousers up at last and waving the right cleat at the door histrionically, all or most of his odds and ends gathered in his sagging cardboard attaché. The onlookers were dispersing now that the one-man show was mobile again.

She approached with a growl that she considered an *en garde*; moreover, that Rainbow considered a spectacle of bravery, self-assured in her own righteousness, though ranting Lenny didn't hear her. Hence, Rainbow was able to get her teeth well into the flesh of his calf before he even saw her. Lenny cried out at this new injustice and shook the dog off his leg with a kick. Rainbow's nails skittered on the concrete before she rolled, and then she really went apoplectic with the barking as she struggled back to her paws. Lenny sent his cleated foot into the Rainbow's ribs. She yelped and nipped at him again. He brought the other cleat, still in his hand, down on top of her head. Rainbow tried to stand, but he kicked her again, and then again. Lenny screamed something sublingual at her and reared back for another kick. Then Eugene, unable to believe it himself, broke his magnetic Don Giuliani's car-topper in half across the back of Lenny's skull.

***

When the ride ended, she was lifted again. The kid slid her body onto a soft pile of clothing among the boxes in the garage. He pulled an old coat over the top, creating a cave that emanated the sweetness of old ladies who frequently powdered themselves—a light rose motif that played ironically well in the deep recesses of Rainbow's ancestral brain. The pizza kid lifted her head to help her lap water from a hubcap. He broke bits of pepperoni and crust into bite-sized pieces and left them where her tongue could reach them. Much later, she heard him practicing his orations like songs. Like monks chanting in the distance, they were a comfort.

"…Nugs sticky like honey-bee blush, banana-nut-gorilla-glue kush, buds fragrant as your mama's bush, the night she let me in her tusche, back-door vibin', feel me? *En garde* and *touché* my guy, you ain't my tribe, no I don't particularly wanna die, but I ain't afraid to try, dick so good I'll make ya mama cry, and when I'm done I'm gonna buy that bitch a whole *basket* of fries—call me a motha-fuckah, bruh, but don't get mad, you ain't gotta call me 'Dad,' yo ass so fuckin house-broke, bruh, I'ma buy yo ass a pee-pad—ya incontinent *bitch*, ya heard?"

Eugene looked up from his lined composition book at Rainbow, who'd come limping around the corner. He was still somewhat riled from his encounter with Lenny, but the anger melted from Eugene's face when he saw the wounded corgi. He stood, face squishing around his new mood: "Awww*wwwww*, sweet *bayby*, what are you doing up walking around...?" He knelt beside her and scratched her gently behind the ear. She closed her eyes and lifted her chin, appreciating the attention. Eugene stood and looked around the garage with his hands on his hips. Rainbow opened her eyes, peering up at him patiently. "Aha!" he cried, and set off between stacked cardboard boxes and piled wires and tennis shoes. Eugene returned, at length, with a dusty old leash. Rainbow's docked tail started twitching at the sight.

Meanwhile, Lenny. He meandered down Lennox Ave, a lot of what you'd have to call rueful sentiment on his mind. He passed some other residents smoking cigarettes in the street light and leaning against the crumbling brick and staple-splintered telephone pole. Lenny did his best to ignore them. He pushed open the glass door, spidered over with cracks since long before his first day at the Gallagher Restitution House, a gesture of one-time philanthropy which had neither been repeated, revised, nor rededicated. Some of the fixtures worked, some of the toilets. The lockers were rusted and many of the locks broken, insulation was patchy, the windows foggy. Mice were known to wander in and out of frame. In his dorm, Lenny crouched and pulled the rolling locker out from beneath his bunk, entering the combination 666 and pocketing his lock before anyone saw.

There sat, in toto, Lenny's worldly possessions. He transferred the contents of his ruined cardboard box there, changed into his other, comparatively cleaner pair of pants, sniffed himself and then sprayed each armpit in 5-10 second bursts with a can of Axe body spray (Gold Temptation, 2014) he'd found, humming 'All About That Bass.' He pulled small twigs from his hair, crouching covetously over his treasure horde when another resident passed through the room. Lenny didn't consider him a roommate per se. When they finally left, Lenny pulled out his map and a battered, stained little notepad.

He confirmed the location of the shrine—922 Fessler Ln (or across the street therefrom), which was marked with a gold sticker, and then wrote the date and address in the notepad, making brief, professional notes about the state the shrine was in when he found it, his emendations, et cetera. Then, the very soul of brevity: 'Assault at Citgo—clerk, dog, pizza-boy; *buggy*.'

Lenny stared gravely at the entry, this distillate of his day already bubbling like an Alka-Seltzer talisman in the bottom of his murky mind. 'Assault at Citgo' became legendary as soon as he'd written it, finding its place in the epic order somewhere between 'St. George v. Dragon' and 'Bush Did 9/11.' Lenny began to draw the faces of the 3 arch-villains, those Pharisees and Nazis that had perpetrated this crime against him: the clerk, Rainbow, and Eugene. He drew Romans, carrying cat-o-nine-tails, and cosmonauts, and Chinese nationals, and mermaids…

Before he realized it, it was lights out. The others started shuffling in. He found the pack of Camel Crushes with a small 'Aha!' then covered them furtively in his cupped hands and scrambled his combination lock again as his bunkmates went grumbling onto their squeaky spring mattresses.

Lenny went to the bathroom, catching the security guard's eye as the man went down the hall to relieve second shift. Over the sink, Lenny splashed water onto his face and watched it drip off his chin in the mirror. His head aching where Eugene's blow had fallen. The sounds of the cramped, all-male bathroom—flatulent, phlegmatic men late in life and low in fortune—like an orchestra tuning up, eventually faded while Lenny stood staring monkishly at himself. He stole a squirt of toothpaste from a crinkled tube forgotten on the sink and rubbed it into his teeth with an unwashed finger.

He went out into the hall again and down, taking a left into the stairwell where the guard was waiting for him. Lenny produced the cigarettes by way of toll-fare and the guard cursed him. The usual rate was $20, but Lenny didn't have it tonight. After a long stare, shifted ponderously between Lenny and the pack of Camels, the guard took the cigarettes from his hand and pushed the emergency door open. The alarm was long broken. He ushered Lenny out with the warning that it would be $20 to get back in—the door locked from the outside, so getting back in before the Staff figured out you'd been gone was the only obstacle between residents and free run of the night.

'My good man,' Lenny said, affecting a British accent and pinching an invisible monocle, 'you'll receive your fair dues, wares and blues—and *then* some—jolly good, eh? Bob's your uncle!' As the door slammed back on Lenny's reflection, he cackled gaily to the world at large, turning on his heel with a schizophrenically lyrical flourish, 'For all the coins and purses of the purple battery go oily-doily: BAP! SPERM! CRAP!'

Around 3:00 am on June 24, 2019 Lenny found a tire-iron in a dumpster and shortly after set upon some unsuspecting drunks wandering home. Nothing too brutal, just $20.00 worth of highway robbery, and a taste of something like revenge on the addled assailant's tongue. Both the inebriants were stumbling, true to form; the leaner wore a cowboy hat and the other wore an extra 100-150, and it wasn't muscle. As Lenny knocked the knife out of the cowboy's hand with a sharp crack of iron on knuckles, surprisingly deft for someone in a manic fit, Lenny thought only of the three-headed behemoth: Citgo Clerk, Dog, and Pizza-Boy. The drunks ran off after dropping a twenty, a fairly cheap getaway all things considered, dialing the police. Lenny scooped the knife up off the ground and pocketed it without folding it shut.

When he went back to the Citgo, Lenny didn't recognize the clay-like woman behind the counter, so he used the restroom and left. No roaches this time, though the disparity failed to register. It was when he went down the street to admire his shrine—his very, *very* favorite shrine, 922 Fessler—that Lenny got mad. Mayva's schizo-psychic spirit watched from her porch with a Picasso smile as Lenny fell to his knees gathering up the broken icons of his personal religion. He crawled through the broken glass toward the defiled image, crumpled in the curbside—Laura Dern's ripped smile holding through it all.

II.

A year later, Lenny was released from the psychiatric hospital with a mostly side-effect free medication and a healthier worldview. Whatever eccentricities couldn't be reasoned out of him had been doused, like live coals beneath ash, with the 12-Stepper's shame-and-faith 1-2 punch (a respectably utilitarian punch, one would like to note). Rainbow had recovered fully and trotted along now like a dog half her age, some new fount of mystic vitality sustaining her in the face of science's better judgment. At 13 years, 239 days, 5 hours, 23 minutes and 5 seconds (99.68448727…, now Mayva's spiritual senior), Rainbow was the oldest living Corgi in the world, and she was just as spry, playful and amorous of the odd piece of dairy manufacture as ever she'd been. Eugene had a mixtape on SoundCloud that had 11 plays and was taking computer science classes at the community college, trading out the old colors and stripes of pizza delivery for the more auspicious mantle of the

Sandwich Artist. The Citgo clerk (Samvel) had recently welcomed his son to the world, a smiling, screaming, pooping bundle of perfect, rubicund health, named for his proud father. Mayva's ghost still haunted her old porch, grumbling at her immaterial joints and glowering (contentedly) at passerby. This specific moment—as Lenny's newly freed foot hit the concrete again for the first time; as Rainbow snapped after another wayward Junebug; as Eugene excitedly refreshed his browser to review the CSS code he'd just written; as Samvel peeked over his folded hands and cried *boo!* at Samvel Jr.; and as Mayva sent an stream of astral tobacco juice arcing out into space—was the greatest concurrence of actual happiness between the five players that ever was, or ever would be.

The city's fuck-around public, meanwhile, had taken note of Lenny's shrines and, in his absence, had wholeheartedly embraced the cause of Dern appreciation. Dern murals, Dern posters, Dern stickers, Dern graffiti-tags, Dern drinks and God-Dern menu items began appearing everywhere, like maggots from a medieval cheese. There was a smaller, corollary flourishing of *Jurassic Park*-related memes, with the usual Jeff Goldblum adulation (but no millennial love for Sam Neill, save the occasional anomaly 3 to 10 standard deviations from the mean, alas). Ms. Dern had been tagged in a tweet from Mr. Goldblum alerting her to the situation, and the anything-but-false idol had subsequently expressed her puzzled but authentic gratitude. It was widely considered in the city's coffee shops and bars that a visit from the city's patron saint was inevitable.

Lenny, back on the street with a whole utility belt of coping mechanisms that simply weren't up to the municipal-grade Dern-idolatry that had flourished in his absence, never had a chance. He stood shuddering at the bus stop beneath a full blown, Ben Day-dot poster of the old headshot, Laura's familiar smile tugging winsomely at the loose threads hanging from Lenny's tattered mindscape. A caption, apparently appended to the poster after the fact by a spray-paint commentator, read: 'Can you feel the Dern?' Yes, Lenny certainly could.

He thought his heart was going to stop, so Lenny abandoned the bus stop and went on foot, assuring himself there was a rational explanation—that Magic Concurrence of greatest possible happiness between our players now irrevocably lost, obliterated between the grinding teeth of the past...

He made his way to the temp agency on Garry Owen Rd, counting his steps in order to pace his breathing and keeping his eyes trained on the sidewalk immediately in front of him. Nothing but litter. Garry Owen and environs was a far cry from the nearest slice of avocado toast and its correlates (including Dern iconography), and gathering his courage up enough to look around, Lenny was relieved to find nothing to trouble his mind. The ripples were smoothing out into a placid plane again. In line at the agency, Lenny practiced his meditation, skimming the scum off the pond surface, feeding the giant coy fish, trimming his bonsai and raking sand with every breath. When it was finally his turn he gave his information (and that of his social worker) and was directed to an agent's desk. He was going to be a dishwasher at the soup kitchen, it seemed. Lenny sat contemplating this, savoring the idea that he would work where once he'd supped. It seemed like a chance to give back—and to *earn*, not merely receive—a living. Self-respect glimmered at the corner of his vision, not quite distinct enough to definitively label, but *nonetheless*, it glimmered.

But when he stepped out of the agency, a long-boarder collided with him, knocking him clear off his feet. The boarder, apologizing profusely as her cohorts rolled chuckling down the road, was a polite enough young lady, somewhat heavier than she'd like to be, tattooed, dyed, gauged and pierced all over. She helped him to his feet, very concerned, for Lenny had grown quite thin and, you'd have to say, frail-looking in his stay at the Facility. He chuckled in a no-no-excuse-*me* way, deliberately trying to keep the pain from his syncopated exhalations. Then Lenny looked at the girl. There, monogrammed on a tag on the front of her beanie, sat Laura Dern with an Oh-Really-Now? look on her face (frame 00:48:51:19, *Jurassic Park*, 1992) with the caption 'I'm Going to Give You a Dern Talking-To.' Lenny shrieked as his bowels dropped, the blood hydraulically sucked from his head to fill the void in his guts, and involuntarily shoved the longboarder as he took off down Garry Owen, fast as his slender ankles would take him. So much for healing...

***

150 days, 19 hours 34 minutes and 25 seconds later, 102.7 The Crust played Bobby Womack's seminal classic 'Across 110th Street.' The song played over the speakers at the Citgo, where Eugene was buying a Don Giuliani's pie, just $5.00 with his former-employee-wink-wink discount. He was high and bumbling his way through a fairly awkward long-time-no-see with Samvel at the register while his former colleagues spun his pizza dough in the air. Rainbow was in the car, curled in the seat beneath the open window.

Lenny approached the old battleground from the west, crossing Fessler Ln in the middle of traffic, approximately halfway between the two nearest crosswalks. He wore a dirty Simpsons tee-shirt that was all Homer's yellow face, as well as puce corduroy cutoff shorts which were ambiguously near the booty-short threshold, lime green socks with Nike flip-flops. He was carrying a woman's purse full of mace and Dern headshots, singing '110th Street' under his breath, out of earshot of any radio but being, as he was, sensitive to vibes and waves of any length or amplitude.

He passed Rainbow in the passenger seat without noticing her, but her nose twitched grumpily after him as he went, barely failing to recognize the rose-scented Jergen's. Entering the store, Lenny reached into his bag and pulled out the mace-gun, Dern headshots tumbling into space like a kid's baseball card collection. The two ogres, Clerk and Pizza-Boy, leaned against the counter shooting the breeze, evilly as you please. Their fangs protruded from their pierced green lips, their heavy brows with eyebrows braided right into their hair and beards, portentous bellies spilling over belts with crude orc swords hanging in tattered scabbards and money bags and huge iron keys, their clawed feet crossed lazily in gladiator sandals—the blatant villains and dullards! Lenny pulled the trigger, even as Samvel noticed the lunatic pointing a plastic gun at him and tried, too late, to duck.

The trigger compressed and the bolt pressed forward on its hinges, pushing the mace canister against the flat plane of the 'barrel' and engaged the actuator. Liquid phenacyl chloride blossomed from the aerosol nozzle, a staccato, branching cloud of pure bad-bad emerging and vaporizing in the free air, propelled at 210 mph, accurate to a range of 20 feet.

Samvel and Eugene both got a face full and fell to their knees screaming. The pizzeria staff all ducked or ran out the back entrance (though one, hooded in pizza dough, bounced off several walls first) and back of the store, a teenage girl locked herself in the bathroom and called the police. Lenny peaked his head around the corner of a cardboard Frito-Lays display stand at his victims. A shriek of excited giggling escaped his lips when he saw them, and he emerged triumphant as any Caesar, playing the role of his own troubadour and herald (as well as doing a decent Bobby Womack): "I was the third brother of five, doing whatever I had to do to survive…" Rainbow, meanwhile, had worked her way over the windowsill and fallen flat onto the concrete, then risen again to her weary feet in a here-we-go-again sort of way. She ran toward the glass doors, barking.

"I'm not saying what I did was al-*right*," Lenny crooned, dancing theatrically over his fallen foes as the glass doors slid open, "trying to break out of the ghetto was a day-to-daaay *fight*." Rainbow took one look at Eugene, whom she'd come to consider her own grandbaby in a particularly Mayva-influenced ridge of her brain, and then his assailant. Recognition, and all the accumulated balance of Mayva's porch-bound spite, settled over Rainbow in an instant. In the next she was airborne.

Rainbow's teeth sank into Lenny's wrist. The song died on his lips. The gun went clattering on the tile as Rainbow fell to the floor, tugging Lenny down with her and loosing a mild current of blood from his veins. Deep down in the cerebellum where she slept, Grandmother Wolf, hitherto tranquilized with rose motif and marinara, tasted blood and came snarling to life. Hysterical, Lenny wrenched his hand away from the snarling *lupus reduci* and went screaming out the door, leaving a trail of blood and Laura Derns behind him. Rainbow stopped to look at Eugene, who was still lying on the ground, crying and palming his streaming eyes. It broke her heart, but Rainbow turned to pursue her quarry.

The dual scents of copper blood and ammoniac fear stood as starkly against the day as a tarantula in your bathtub at 6:00 in the morning. Rainbow's paws beat a weary hunter's tattoo in the concrete. Her heart thudded in her ears. After a block, even *her* dimmed eyes could see him. He loped along at a considerable pace, but he was starting to lag. A divine calm descended over Rainbow as she began to recognize her old neighborhood—both Fessler Ln and the anticipation of her imminent kill. A homecoming.

Rainbow launched and brought Lenny down again a block ahead of the fated destination, but this time the corgi-missile failed to latch on to its target and they both went sprawling. Lenny stood with terror, recognizing this assailant at last as that third demon from days of yore, and gave a kick. Rainbow dodged the foot, which lost its sandal with the effort, and lunged for his testicles with a ferocious snarl. Mercifully, she missed these too, but not by nearly enough for Lenny's liking, and he was off again. He stumbled and finally fell at the old shrine at 922 Fessler Ln, nothing left now but the portentous '*Rejoice!*'

The November sun disappeared behind a sheet of clouds. Rainbow approached her prey at a trot. Lenny looked at the graffito commandment on the wall, and looked up to see windswept Dern headshots falling down on him like leaves. At last, he looked snarling Rainbow in the eyes and said the magic word: "Rejoice." The dog keeled over dead. She was 14 years 25 days *exactly*, or 102.7, spiritually, which was exactly one Dog-Copernican coefficient from 110. It so chanced, in another astronomically unlikely, mystical fluke, that 102.7's broadcast of 'Across 110th Street' concluded at that precise moment. 110, as we all know, representing a life of holiness and virtue, though often as not a life concluded painfully. C.f. the 22 sufferings of the Word of God (or Hebraic letters, *or* Tarot Trumps, as you like it) multiplied by the 5 wounds Christ sustained on the Cross, and the 5 marks on Mary His Holy Mother's soul, which concatenated in the union of their tragedy yields 55, which likewise doubled in the left and right eyes of its witnesses (*res cogitans*/redshift/*praeterita* and *res extensa*/blueshift/*futuri*, respectively), yields 110 wounds between the two planes to match the 110 thorns that tore His scalp. As we all know.

Anyway, as the last notes of Womack's masterpiece echoed and ceased, Rainbow and Mayva's twin souls were shredded apart from each other like spaghetti in a centrifuge, each restored to her own spiritual identity in a blitz of closure, a full-circle anti-Pentecost, their discrete souls instanced once again as indelibly as speciation, as irrevocably as frying an egg. An eternity of redemption and peace in an instant, and then both were gone, their threads unwound and returned to the cosmos and sleeping mother-consciousness, Abraham's bosom, Nirvana, the Abyss, *et al.*

"WOOO*eeeeee!*" Lenny, jumping for joy. As far as he was concerned, his three greatest foes lay slain, his Cerberus, cowed. Victory bubbled in his glass, though in a just few woops and touchdown dances it went flat on his tongue. He looked around confusedly, the smile receding from his face. He bent and plucked a headshot off the ground, and for the first time since Lenny saw *Jurassic Park* in theaters, the perfect smile pinned in that glossy plane meant nothing more to him than any other white woman's would. In fact Lenny barely recognized his dear Laura. He let the picture fall from his hands and looked back at the dog, unable to recall now why there'd been such antagonism between them—or even, a moment later, that there'd ever been any bad blood at all. Deeds done and battle won, Memory now withered. Speaking of *blood*, Lenny realized with a start that some quantity of it was leaking rather quickly from his wrist. He stripped his cotton tee-shirt off and wrapped it around his wrist. There were sirens in the distance. Lenny, suddenly freed from his own past, walked across the street, coffee or possibly a hot cocoa on his weary mind. He was pretty cold.

Alms for Jasmine
By Arthur Liu

Beyond the cracked sidewalk, and the telephone pole with layers of flyers in a rainbow of colors, and the patch of dry brown grass there stood a ten-foot high concrete block wall, caked with dozens of coats of paint. There was a small shrine at the foot of it, with burnt out candles and dead flowers and a few soggy teddy bears. One word of graffiti filled the wall, red letters on a gold background: Rejoice!

The day of the accident had been cool and foggy but now the Indian summer heat shimmered in the air. Someone had stolen Jasmine's shoes and she winced with every step she took on the scorching pavement. The scent of urine pricked at her nose. She approached one person after another, pointing to the scrap of cardboard that hung from her neck bearing the words, "Please help." People averted their eyes and pretended they hadn't read the sign.

She passed the liquor store and the Armenian deli and the luxury hotel that marked the beginning of the shopping district. She noticed a couple of teenagers talking loudly, a boy and a girl who both had blond hair. A few steps away stood a man and woman who kept looking back at the boy as if they were waiting for him. The man wore a straw hat that made him look silly. The woman had brown hair that was gray near the scalp. Jasmine smiled to herself because she knew that meant the woman colored her hair.

Jasmine came close to the woman, looked up at her with big sad eyes, and pointed to the cardboard sign. The woman grimaced and said, "Oh, the poor little thing." She asked Jasmine what her name was. Jasmine didn't answer because she wasn't supposed to talk to strangers. The man rolled his beady eyes and said, "Somebody ought to call Child Protective Services." Then he turned away, glaring at the teenagers. Jasmine saw a shiny black iPhone poking up from the back pocket of his khakis. She didn't steal things very often but she was very good at it when she wanted to be. The woman clicked her tongue and said, "For God's sake, Michael, what a thing to say." She looked down and opened her purse. As the woman took out her wallet and pulled two singles from it, Jasmine slid the phone from the man's pocket and hid it in the waistband of her leggings, under her *Lion King* T-shirt. Then she snatched the bills from the woman and ran off.

"You see, that's the thanks you get," the man said to his wife. Her name was Ursula. She sighed and told him to try and remember what the pastor had said in church. And if he couldn't do that, could he at least have a little compassion now and then. "After all, there but for the grace of God..." She never finished her sentence, because their son Jared had rejoined them. The other teenager was gone.

"Well, it's about time," she told him. "Who was that girl, anyway?" Nobody, Jared said, just a friend from school. His mother said it would have been nice for him to introduce her. The boy shrugged and turned to his father. "Can I please have my phone back now?" Michael had snatched it away from him while they were at the restaurant because Jared was too busy texting to pay attention to his family.

"Jared, you're so addicted to that thing, it's pathetic," his father said. Michael felt his back pocket and a puzzled look came over him. He checked his other pockets and found his wallet, his keys, and the condom he had taken on his business trip in case he got lucky. But he didn't find the phone, which was very strange because it was just there a moment ago.

Michael glared at his wife. Clearly it was her fault. "What the hell happened to the phone? Did you take it?" She blinked and made a sound like a soft burp. "I don't have it," she said. "You're the one who grabbed it." The three of them looked around, as if the phone might be floating in the air nearby, and then they scanned the pavement. They found nothing. "I bet it was that fucking kid," Michael said, his face red and sweaty. "The little panhandler grabbed it. Fuck."

"That sweet little girl?" Ursula gasped. "No. She couldn't have. You must have dropped it. Maybe you bumped into somebody and it just fell out of your pocket." Michael said that was a stupid idea. Nobody except that girl had come close to them. If it had magically jumped out of his pocket, he would have heard it fall on the ground.

"Well, I guess we're not going to be turning it in to the police," Jared said. His mother asked what he was talking about. Michael said they shouldn't talk about it in public. They should get in the car first. Jared started to say something but Michael shushed him. Ursula said she didn't know why everybody was being so mysterious. They got in the white Audi and Michael asked if she remembered that hit-and-run a few days ago, the one where a woman and her baby got killed. Ursula said of course she did, it was all over the news. They kept showing a security camera photo of the car that was so blurry you could hardly see anything, just that the car was a dark sedan.

"Well, it turns out Jared here caught the whole thing on his cell phone," Michael said. "You can see the driver's face, and when he zooms off you can see the license plate. Ursula said that was wonderful and told Jared she was so proud of him. It was just like Jared to save the day. She reached back to ruffle his hair but he pulled away. She asked why they hadn't been to the police yet.

"Because there's one little problem," Michael said. "The guy driving the car was Vincent Sang." Ursula grimaced and said, "Oh, no." Michael had called the police intending to make an anonymous tip, but the detective kept asking questions. When he found out about the video, he asked for Jared's phone. Michael didn't want to give it up and the detective got testy. "Look, you can get a new phone, copy everything else you want onto that one, and give us the original one." Michael asked if the detective thought money grew on trees. It was a thousand-dollar phone. They would keep the phone and email the detective a copy of the video.

"Well, go ahead and send the copy," Detective Blaine said. "But I have to tell you, depending on what other evidence we can get, we may still need the actual phone. And we may need Jared to testify." Michael snickered and said, testify in open court against Vincent Sang, are you fucking serious? No way. It was too bad what happened to that poor woman and her baby, but getting his son killed wasn't going to bring them back.

Right after taking Jared's phone, Jasmine brought the device to Orangina. If Orangina was able to get into a phone in time, it was worth more. Otherwise, the phone had to be sold for parts. Jasmine watched as Orangina tapped on the phone. The woman was short and stocky, looked like a younger version of Auntie, with puffy lips and a belly that jiggled. Jasmine thought her hair was very pretty. It looked like a sunset. Orangina smiled and said, "Easy peasy." She put the phone down and gave Jasmine a hundred dollars.

Jasmine thanked her and walked back to the spot near the Home Depot that had been her home for the past month. She gave Auntie the money and that night they had a big dinner from McDonald's and she was very full. Uncle gave her a pair of plastic pool shoes he had bought for her from a street vendor. The next day she went out with her sign and stayed out for a long time. The day was not as hot and her shoes felt good on her feet. By evening, she had collected a lot of money and she felt happy. But when she got home, nothing was there. The tents were gone, the shopping carts were gone, everyone she knew was gone. And Rainbow was gone.

Jasmine wandered around, picking through the debris. Amidst the takeout bags and plastic cups she found a few familiar items—Uncle's hat with the bird's head and the letter B, one of Simon's striped socks, a red bandanna that belonged to one of the other children. She picked them up and dusted them off. She started to cry but then she heard Auntie Rayne's motorized scooter. Even in the heat, the old woman had a fleece blanket over her shoulders. A tattered American flag flew from a plastic stick stapled to the backrest. "Sweetie, sweetie, don't cry," the old woman said. "Uncle, find us a new place, much more better. I show you, come, come." Jasmine asked if everybody was okay. Yes, Auntie said, everybody was fine. Then the girl asked about Rainbow, the dog Auntie Rayne had found in a dumpster and given to her.

"Oh, Rainbow, well, well," the old woman said. She waved her hand and started talking about the building they had found. It used to be a body shop but it was empty now, all boarded up. But Uncle found a way in, and oh, it was real good there. They came to the building and Auntie showed her the back alley that led to Uncle's secret entrance. Everybody was there, even the pizza kid. Jasmine didn't know his real name. People just called him pizza kid because he had a cousin who worked at Little Caesar's and gave him free food now and then. He was a strange, gangly boy who liked to read plays. He memorized whole speeches from them, and at night when Jasmine was falling asleep, she could hear him murmur things like, "Now is the winter of our discontent/Made glorious summer by this sun of York…"

It was very dark inside the garage, even with the candles they had lit. There was a hole in the roof and you could look up and see the stars. Uncle showed Jasmine where her stuff was, her bag with the jeans and the extra shirt and the puffy jacket for the winter. She smiled because Uncle Bing was missing some teeth and he could whistle without even trying. Then he took her to see Rainbow, curled up in a corner. Her fur was matted with blood and part of her ear was gone. The little dog tried to get up when she saw Jasmine but she was too weak.

Jasmine bent over her and big salty tears fell on the dog's face. Rainbow felt sorry for her because she seemed so sad. The girl stroked her head and it felt good. Uncle Bing said, "Some big dog musta got her, honey, she in such a bad way. Poor old Rainbow." Jasmine kept caressing her, cooed to her in a voice like an owl. Auntie Rayne said, "Come on, let's give her a ride, huh, sweetie? She always like that." Rainbow thought, yes, it was fun to ride in Auntie's scooter. But it hurt when Jasmine started to pick her up and she whimpered. The pizza kid asked if he could try. Jasmine stepped back and watched as he lifted Rainbow up and placed her in Auntie's lap. Auntie Rayne put one hand on the dog and her other hand on the control knob of the scooter. She drove around in circles and Rainbow's eyes closed.

When the ride ended, she was lifted again. The kid slid her body onto a soft pile of clothing among the boxes in the garage. He pulled an old coat over the top, creating a cave that emanated the sweetness of old ladies who frequently powdered themselves—a light rose motif that played ironically well in the deep recesses of Rainbow's ancestral brain. The pizza kid lifted her head to help her lap water from a hubcap. He broke bits of pepperoni and crust into bite-sized pieces and left them where her tongue could reach them. Much later, she heard him practicing his orations like songs. Like monks chanting in the distance, they were a comfort.

Rainbow wished she could tell Jasmine what had really happened. When the people in the orange vests came to clear out the encampment, Rainbow had stayed behind, waiting for Jasmine. Simon was there, too, passed out under a sheet. And then the bad men came, men with dark glasses and a German shepherd they kept on a chain. They woke Simon up and asked him questions. It was something about Jasmine, Rainbow could tell. Then they started hitting him, and Rainbow tried to make them stop but they let the German shepherd loose on her. Simon passed out again, and the men kicked him a bunch of times. Before they left, they stomped on Rainbow, too. It hurt very bad where they had done that. Rainbow was very glad that someone had come back for her but she didn't know where Simon was.

And she didn't know that the bad men worked for Vincent Sang. The bad men made it their business to know things. From their contacts inside the police department, they learned that a certain Detective Blaine was in charge of the hit-and-run case, and he had a copy of a cell phone video that implicated Sang. They found out that Michael had called the detective to let him know the phone had been stolen. So there was a cop, a kid named Jared who might have another copy, and now there was a thief, who might or might not have wiped the phone by now. One thing at a time.

Blaine came to work in the morning and found a new computer at his desk. There was voicemail from the I.T. people, too. "Hey, Detective. We were doing a routine system audit and there was an issue with your desktop, so we gave you a new one. Found a bug in your email account, too. There's a memo on your desk with your new username. Choose a better password this time, okay? We migrated most of your emails over but a few of them might not have come through."

Of course the email from Jared was gone, and so was the video. And naturally the boss wanted to see him. Blaine sighed. He knocked on the lieutenant's door and the old man waved him in. "I'm taking you off the hit-and-run thing," he said. Blaine said he was sick and tired of seeing Vincent Sang get away with shit. The boss said he was, too. But that's the way the world was. He handed Blaine a file and said, take this instead, it's a nice straightforward bank robbery.

Three of Sang's men showed up at Jared's door and flashed badges that looked real. Once inside, they questioned Jared and his parents just as politely as they had questioned Simon. They had the boy go online and delete everything on his iCloud account, his social media accounts, everything on his computer. They tried to locate the phone and wipe it remotely but couldn't, and they got very angry. They hit Jared very hard, told him to try wiping it, but he couldn't do it either. They asked about the video and wanted to know if he had any copies. They hit him again and again. Michael said look, you're too late, the police already had a copy. Don't hurt him, there's nothing else here, we don't know anything, please just go. One of the men pointed a gun at Jared and said, kid, you were in the wrong place at the wrong time, and then he shot him. The parents were next.

The pizza kid found Simon on a park bench and brought him to the garage. He'd been in the hospital overnight and he had a dirty bandage around his head that was unraveling. Auntie taped it up for him. People gathered around and Simon told them what had happened to him. His voice was slurred because his mouth was still swollen. The guys who beat him up were looking for Jasmine. They had shown him a picture of Jasmine standing next to a guy in a straw hat. "We don't want to hurt her," they said. "She took a phone from this guy. That's all we want, the phone." Simon said he'd never seen the girl before and they hit him. "That's not what we heard," they said. They started beating on him pretty bad. Then they wanted to know where he would go if he had a phone he wanted to sell. He thought that was right about the time he'd passed out.

Rainbow whimpered and Simon said, "Hey, there you are, girl." As he and Jasmine petted her, Simon told everybody how brave Rainbow had been. Jasmine smiled and Rainbow wagged her tail. She was happy to see Simon again and thought maybe now they were safe. But then she sniffed Simon's hand and she could tell he was still afraid. Jasmine was not afraid, though.

"The man in the straw hat, I remember him," she said. It was his phone that she'd sold to Orangina. Uncle nodded slowly and said, "Sure, he must be the one these guys work for." Jasmine didn't think they worked for the man in the hat. She said maybe they should go see Orangina. Auntie thought that was a good idea. They ought to warn Orangina and maybe they could find out why the phone was so important. Uncle didn't like it but finally he agreed.

He took Jasmine to Orangina's place above the card room. She was busy taking a laptop apart and didn't seem happy to see them, especially since they hadn't brought her anything. Uncle told her some men had beaten up Simon and she shrugged. Then he said they were looking for that phone Jasmine had brought her. She looked up and frowned at him. She was always good to them, why were they getting her in trouble now? Jasmine said she would never have brought the phone to her if she'd thought it was going to be trouble. She asked if Orangina still had it.

"Oh, it right here," Orangina said. She told them she had gotten into the phone right away. "Best type phone and worst type passcode, 1-2-3-4-5-6," she laughed. First thing she had done was to turn off the find-my-phone feature and then she removed the device from the owner's account. It had only taken a moment, and it was all done before she had even paid Jasmine. Then she set the phone aside. Anything else she wanted to do with it could wait till later.

"Well, let's see what you hiding, phone," she said. "It belong to this kid Jared. Look kinda dopey." She laughed and showed them one of the selfies Jared had taken. She was still smiling as she swiped through some other things on the phone but then she found the video and her smile disappeared. "Fuck me," she said. She looked at Bing and Jasmine and shook her head. "You guys in deep shit." She showed them the video.

It starts with a fireball that turns out to be part of a street performance, a couple of guys entertaining a small crowd in a cobblestone plaza across the street from Jared. A young woman in the audience turns toward the camera and steps into the street. She's carrying a baby in a sling over the front of her body. A black car strikes them and they bounce off the hood of the car, landing in front of Jared. The camera shows them for a moment and then goes back up toward the car. The driver is an Asian man in his thirties with tattoos on his neck. He looks straight into the camera with eyes like a dead fish. He hesitates for a moment and drives off, gunning the engine.

"That the guy who killed that lady and her baby," Orangina said. "This is it happening right here. You know him? Vincent Sang. Very bad man." Jasmine didn't know the name but it seemed like Uncle Bing did. Orangina slapped the phone down on the table and pushed it away. "You take it, I don't want it no more. Take, take, it yours. It never been here, I never see this thing. Those guys come see me, I tell them you never bring it here." Uncle said, "But you paid for it, it's yours." Orangina shook her head. Sweat beaded on her forehead and her whole body trembled. "No, no, no. I pay you your hundred dollar just to take it away. Go, get out right now, you hear me, and you take that phone with you. You don't come back no more, you take your stuff to somebody else from now on."

Uncle tried to protest but Jasmine scooped up the phone and ran out. Uncle followed her and called out to her to slow down. They walked half a mile to the public library branch that Uncle liked, a sooty brick building that smelled of old people and dust. They sat on the floor in the children's section and Uncle pretended to read a book to Jasmine while they talked about what to do. Jasmine liked it when Uncle listened to her. She knew he loved her, just like Auntie did, but sometimes when she tried to tell him things he closed up his brown leathery face like a purse and acted like he didn't hear a word she was saying.

It seemed like a bad idea to keep the phone on them and too risky to try and sell it. Maybe they should just put it in the garbage and if the bad people found them, they could say they sold it to some guy, they didn't know his name. But what if the bad guys didn't believe them? Uncle said maybe they could just give it to the bad guys, but how would you find them, and wouldn't it be dangerous? It was a tough problem. At no time did they consider going to the police. Only stupid people or rich people trusted the police. Finally they decided to hide the phone in the library. They could come back for it if they had to.

Uncle put the phone in the bottom of a file cabinet that was open to the public. It held back issues of magazines and nobody ever looked in it. Uncle tucked the phone inside an old copy of *Popular Mechanics*. Jasmine chose the issue—it was published the month she was born. Then they walked toward the body shop, passing the spot where the accident had happened.

The memorial was gone now. No more candles or flowers or teddy bears. But the people who had brought those things for the shrine had not forgotten. They remembered the young woman, named Selina, like the moon. Shy smile, beads in her hair, always doting on her little baby. They remembered how quietly she and the baby had died. No screeching tires, just a dull thud and a fancy car speeding away. People remembered the car and the face of the man who was driving, though they didn't know his name. They whispered about what they had seen and their whispers fluttered through the autumn air like vengeful butterflies.

Uncle and Jasmine entered the alley behind the body shop and saw Rainbow coming toward them. She was still limping but she was much stronger now. She barked and skittered back and forth, blocking their path. "Something's wrong," Jasmine said. "Go back to the library, Uncle. I'll come get you when it's safe." Uncle didn't want to go because Auntie was in there, he had to help her. Jasmine pointed to the dumpster and said just hide behind there, then. I'll see what's going on.

Jasmine climbed up the fire escape as Uncle and Rainbow watched. She looked down and felt dizzy but she kept going until she got to the roof. There was a big skylight and most of the glass was missing so she had a clear view of the garage. She saw Auntie on the floor in a pool of blood. Jasmine stared at her and knew that she was dead. She had seen death often enough to recognize it. Auntie wasn't even her blood but it was Auntie who had found Jasmine in that ditch next to the bodies of her parents and taken her in.

Across from Auntie, the pizza kid was tied up in a chair. He was slumped over, bleeding from his mouth, but Jasmine thought he might be alive. Ten feet away from him sat a big man whose head was bent over his phone. He was right under the skylight. Jasmine looked around for something she could use. The roof was littered with garbage as well as pieces of metal and broken glass. Jasmine found a thick piece of glass that was almost as tall as she was. She could barely lift it, but she managed to slide it to the edge of the skylight. It made a scraping noise as she moved it, and the big man in the chair looked up to see what was making the sound. The glass landed right on his head, almost took it right off. The pizza kid looked up at Jasmine and smiled.

She clambered down the fire escape and ran into the garage, with Uncle and Rainbow close behind. She untied the pizza kid while Uncle held Auntie and cried. "The others are out there looking for you, Jasmine," the pizza kid said. "We didn't tell them anything. They left this one behind in case you came here but they'll be back. We need to go."

They covered Auntie with a blanket and Uncle murmured something in her ear. They gathered up a few of their things and got on the first bus they saw, with Rainbow in a duffel bag. The bus was almost empty and they sat in the back, where they shared what they knew. Rainbow nestled against the clothes in the duffel bag, lulled by the swaying of the bus and the sound of their voices. Jasmine told the pizza kid about the phone and Orangina. The pizza kid said he'd heard the men talking about the woman who had been hit by the car, Selina. The people in the neighborhood talked about Selina as if she was a nobody, however sweet she was. But the bad men said she was a Suazo.

The pizza kid had never heard of the Suazos, and neither had Uncle or Jasmine. But the men who worked for Vincent Sang seemed to know a lot about them. They traded stories about what butchers the Suazos were. They talked freely because Auntie was dead and they thought the pizza kid was dead, too. The Suazos made Vincent Sang look like a saint. That was why the video was so important. It wasn't because of the cops, the cops were a joke. It was the Suazos who had to be kept from seeing that video.

It was dark now and they talked about where they should go. They stayed on the bus until the end of the line and got off without knowing where they were. It was better to stay away from any of the places they knew. They followed a dirt trail that led to a creek, where they saw a group of people with tents. They kept going and walked another mile before settling down under a dead tree that had fallen across the trail like a bridge. Its branches formed a canopy and they sheltered there for the night. Rainbow liked the clean air and the scent of pine.

In the morning they hiked back out to the bus stop and rode back into town. They retrieved the phone from the library when it opened. Uncle knew some people who might know how to find the Suazos so they went to the tikka joint where these people liked to hang out. When they saw Uncle, they laughed and smiled and clapped him on the back. Jasmine and the pizza kid hung back and watched.

Suddenly the laughter stopped and the people with Uncle looked over their shoulders. They took him to a back room, kept him there for a long time. Finally he came out and sat next to Jasmine. "It okay," he said. "We supposed to wait here." The pizza kid started to say something but Uncle shook his head. They got something to eat and slipped Rainbow some of their food. Then two very big men with shaved heads came in and sat down at their table.

"Show them," Uncle said. Jasmine started the video and handed them the phone. The men looked very angry and they spoke to each other in another language. One of them handed Uncle a roll of money. Uncle thanked them and the men stood up. They were almost out the door when Jasmine stood up and called out to them. "Wait. I want to help."

They turned around and laughed. "He killed my Auntie," she said. "I can help you." Everybody looked at her like she was crazy. Uncle tugged at her arm and told her to be quiet. One of the men asked how old she was. Eleven, she said. "How you going to help us, baby?" He took out his gun and said, "You got one of these?"

"You don't know where he is," Jasmine said. "But he's coming after me. I can draw him out for you and then you can get him." The man laughed again. "We know where he is, baby, don't worry. But I like you, you got balls. Here, you take this, just in case." He handed Jasmine his gun. It was so heavy she almost dropped it. The other man said, "Anybody try to mess with you, you tell them you a friend of ours."

Jasmine watched them go. She took Rainbow out of the duffel bag and put the gun inside. Rainbow sneezed and shook herself. Uncle put both hands on her shoulders, rocking her back and forth. He sighed heavily. "Don't scare me like that again, little girl. Come on. Let's get ourselves a real nice tent."

Impossible Death
By Rebecca Loevy

Beyond the cracked sidewalk, and the telephone pole with layers of flyers in a rainbow of colors, and the patch of dry brown grass there stood a ten-foot high concrete block wall, caked with dozens of coats of paint. There was a small shrine at the foot of it, with burnt out candles and dead flowers and a few soggy teddy bears. One word of graffiti filled the wall, red letters on a gold background: Rejoice!

And that is why, during a mid-afternoon heat wave in one of the more obvious rundown neighborhoods of Southern California, as she lay next to the exhausted scene of leftover spirituality, Penny decided it was a perfectly logical idea to consider killing herself.

She was a bitter redhead, anger bursting out of each follicle. And yet, after finally finishing her teenage years of scouring disappointments, the red had faded into a wispy mess of orange and grey, floating above her face like a tumbleweed. It may have been the most exciting feature as the rest of her disappeared into a jumbled mess of cigarettes, sunburnt skin, and tasteless hand-me-down florals.

On this particular day, Penny contemplated the red spray paint as it stared back at her, a bloody smile of someone's once joyous spiritual feelings. Her head tilted sideways as it battled the slump of her body against the concrete wall, a tasteless off-white color that danced with the sun in a terrible way. The shrine of teddy bears and flaking flowers laughed along, a jumbled up zombie, having lost the heart of its creator long ago.

"Hey Penz, what's up with the lookie ya got goin'?" A whiff of cigarette smoke settled itself onto Penny, her long braid shriveling from the nicotine. The shadow of a large woman covered Penny entirely, wavering in place so that Penny felt the onset of seasick nausea kicking in. Penny grabbed onto her braid for comfort.

When you're a somebody who feels like dying, sometimes accentuating the living parts makes it seem more reasonable. Henna seemed a logical approach. Dye orange hair orange. Death felt close, and Penny squeezed shut her eyes, tightening her grip, and imagined an apocalypse coming in and hugging her, flames jutting out, a sublime suffocation.

"Wake up baby Penz! I brought along your favorite kitties." Another whiff of cigarette. Penny reached her hand out and clawed for the packet dangling from the fat woman's chubby fingers. Her eyes squinted and she stuck out her jaw in a defiant "gimme" gesture. It was about this time that two little kittens found their way into Penny's lap, meowing pathetically like the end of the world was only seconds away. Maybe it was.

It was impossible to know why the little devils took to Penny so much. She and their owner both reeked of cigarettes, they hardly pet the damn things, and God knows they weren't being fed properly by either of them. Nevertheless, the two scrawny creatures meowed away, until one of the teddies caught their attention. All it took was a scrape against one of the soggy eyeballs and the whole bear melted, the eye rolling against the pavement with the kittens racing after it.

A long sigh came from the giant in front of Penny. Penny finally managed to topple the cigarette box out of the woman's surprisingly lengthy fingernails and lit up shakily. She imagined a quicker death, one where she could just clap her hands and vanish into super thin air and ride on the waves of electromagnetic fabric, a memory of a nobody floating along all the other countless thoughts that roamed human consciousness.

"Let's go, Penz. I'm hungry and you're burning." Good enough for me, I guess, Penny thought halfheartedly. Standing up on bony legs, she took a final tilted look at the bloodthirsty letters that decorated what she now felt was her own shrine.

Despite the creators' seemingly righteous attempts, cracked sections of the the wall broke the pompous red letters, and the paint huddled into the holes like it was trying to disappear. The J seemed the most hammered by the heat, changed into a darker red.

Penny thought about what would happen if the letter J tried to kill itself. What would the English language do without the letter J? What would all the languages do without the letter J? Spanish? Penny's head grew heavier, her sideways glance starting to feel more upside down, until suddenly one of the kittens flew threw her legs at such a rapid speed that she jumped straight up out of her stupor.

The older woman started to move towards the kitten at a glacial speed, breathing heavily, her shadow tilting on swollen ankles so that Rejoice! looked more like Re———oice! Penny felt a fearful pang. No J, no O, what was life coming to? What was her life coming to?

The question lay like a restless poison as she tumbled after the fat woman and the other shabby cat followed suit, the promise of melting pizza calling in the distance. Greta, for the fat woman had a name, was calling up the pizza kid on her ancient cell phone with the regular order of extra.

Extra sausages. Extra pepperoni. Three containers of garlic sauce and don't you dare forget it, kid, because those little cartons barely hold a damn thing. Two liters of Coke. You bring Pepsi, and you know you aren't getting a tip. Did I already say extra pepperoni?

What about sausage? Okay. Good, good. See you in fifteen minutes, kid. Hang up. Stare at Penny. God, this life was like clockwork by now.

The quartet arrived to Greta's rundown apartment just in time to see the pizza kid turning the corner on his bicycle. He had one of those pasty grins forever planted on his face and his bike had a little bell that jingled to some Beethoven tune with every pedal.

Penny sunk into a corner of the apartment complex' garage. Some three old hags from floor 4 had made it their duty to sell their souls to perfume, so that there was only the northwest corner that had any relief.

As Penny let herself disintegrate into the background, she watched as the kittens hiked up their backs and pranced alongside the pizza kid with a combination of pompous satisfaction and unbridled entitlement. He pet each of them dutifully, paying extra attention to Rainbow, who seemed to have the more manipulative genes of the two kittens. Penny imagined climbing into Rainbow's brain, probably a jumble of ignorant happiness. Would Rainbow ever contemplate an end to this bliss? Doubtful. Penny leaned in a bit and squinted her eyes.

Pizza kid took Rainbow by the belly and flew her up into the sky. Her green eyes gleamed and she went limp like a rag doll. He tossed her on to his neck and she gripped his cheese-stained uniform gleefully. With saturated sexiness, Rainbow let herself be carried by the pizza kid down the front of his shirt and up around his head, climbing across his back as he folded over so she could jump on to one of the shelves in the southeast corner of the garage, the part that smelled the strongest of old women's lavender.

When the ride ended, she was lifted again. The kid slid her body onto a soft pile of clothing among the boxes in the garage. He pulled an old coat over the top, creating a cave that emanated the sweetness of old ladies who frequently powdered themselves—a light rose motif that played ironically well in the deep recesses of Rainbow's ancestral brain. The pizza kid lifted her head to help her lap water from a hubcap. He broke bits of pepperoni and crust into bite-sized pieces and left them where her tongue could reach them. Much later, she heard him practicing his orations like songs. Like monks chanting in the distance, they were a comfort.

To be frank, Penny actually rather liked the pizza kid. He had this thing about him, this ease. Life was simple and elegant. There was nothing better in the world than delivering pizza. With him, kittens were the essence of playfulness and garages were palaces.

Even when Greta would get all grumbly, especially when he fed the kittens some pizza, somewhere deep in Greta, too, was this feeling of appreciation laced with jealousy. No matter how much you want people to be slapped with reality, some people are made of jelly and just jiggle with the punches.

Pizza kid was like that. Penny had a feeling he didn't even care that these two melting women were unaware of his name, his family, his education. They never asked, and he never told them. All he seemed capable of was those endless eulogies of poems and sonnets.

He went everywhere from Rumi's cries for love to Shakespearean sonnets, practicing the periodic table for science tests, to memorizing Bible verses. His mouth was always working words through it like a machine. The cats loved it and purred like crazy every time he came around.

Nonetheless, no amount of happy-go-lucky could transmute the sticky resentment that kept Greta and Penny forever stuck to each other like glue. They rejected anyone who could maintain a sense of never-ending enjoyment, and they especially loved when they were able to diffuse some of that painfully bright light out of people's eyes.

And so, after the extra pepperoni's and sausages were gobbled up, mostly by Greta, and three cigarette packets later, Penny gave a grumble and a yell and chased the pizza kid out of the garage, ready for some peace and quiet from all the happiness.

Penny settled into a faded armchair in her favorite corner, the sides of the fabric peeling away and the powdery dust flaking upwards as she slumped into the cushions. Greta joined her on an old mattress nearby, blue and flat as can be. They were both out of cigarettes, and the pizza box had been donated for its slim remains to the kittens who picked at it dutifully at the garage entrance.

"I met a guy yesterday," Greta said, directing her words slightly over Penny's head. It was hard to meet each other's eyes when hatred filled up each of their bones. Penny drooped her head sideways and started picking at her nails aimlessly. Guys. What are those anyway.

Greta continued somewhat hesitantly into a typical tale. The most amazing gentleman who managed one semi-decent act of chivalry (this time it was opening the door for her on the way out of a McDonald's). That lead to a conversation where they both realized they're lonely and down to hang out for a bit.

Smoke multiple cigarettes. End up in someone's bed for the night. Doesn't matter whose. Wake up in the morning. Regret the whole thing together and decide that it's best to part ways. Buy coffee on separate bills. Bid each other a farewell, good morning, good riddance. Leave by way of handshake.

Poor Greta. She made it sound like it was a natural, even good, thing. Penny soaked it in silently, tired and far from any hope of getting Greta to shut up. Besides, the lady probably needed to let it out anyways.

Meanwhile, as Greta's ramblings continued into her time at church last Sunday, the guy she met who plays football, and her son's letter from three years ago that said he would definitely come for a visit "very soon" once he figured out his "passion" and got out of the military, Penny decided to fantasize her perfect death.

After all, this type of thing could be really beautiful if it was executed just perfectly. She'd use a knife probably because how nice would it be to really see blood leaving. But also it couldn't be too gory because then it just gets gross and nobody wants a gross death. Nobody. Right?

Penny remembered one time where she had really just wanted to stab herself in the leg but didn't because that would have been crazy. It was all because of something stupid Greta had said. Now she kind of wished she had done it just to see how Greta would have reacted.

After all, it was kind of hilarious that Greta had no idea what went on in Penny's head and maybe by just randomly stabbing herself in the leg she could get some cool, deep thought into Greta's otherwise substantially superficial soup-brain.

Or maybe Greta also contemplated ending it all, but she happened to be super good at keeping it a secret and aren't secrets so fascinating! Like what if there is someone who is addicted to eating only sand but nobody knows.

Or if this whole time Rainbow had a secret baby that she kept hidden in one of the garage's hubcaps. Rainbow sniffed and looked up at Penny. That cat was definitely a mind reader. Probably knows everyone's death dates. Probably knows Penny better than she knows herself.

Or what if there was a big secret that Greta was actually made of liquid gold but nobody knew and if anyone found out they would rip her apart and probably Penny too just because she was an acquaintance. And they would sell her for money because people are crazy and poor and need stuff.

And what about existence anyways. Like, who has the most important existence? Is Greta's existence more important than, say, sausages? What will all the people who love extra sausages on their pizza do when suddenly God decides that Greta and sausages can't exist together so we have to pick one and, of course, it must be Greta.

And is it possible to die worse than someone or something else? Pain must be the reference for that, but when it comes down to it, all of it ends the same way. Soul leaves body. People cry, sometimes. Ashes, bones, skin crusties. You go the way of the dodo bird. R.I.P.

Penny slumped deeper into her chair and imagined what it would be like if all of the sudden she just deteriorated completely into a tiny little spiral or shriveled up into a dried raisin. Something where Greta had to call in all the great minds of the world to see where the hell Penny went.

And all those fancy doctors would come one at a time to take a long, hard look at once-upon-a-time Penny and they would try to help Greta figure it out and scientists from all over the globe would come to sort it out, too, and then they would realize! They would realize.

That's Penny. That's Penny and she looks like a conch shell. That's Penny and she turned into a pot. That's Penny and her toes turned into french fries wow they really look like french fries I think they must be! Let's eat them.

And then everyone would eat Penny and she would be inside everyone but no one would know. Greta snorted and Penny looked up for a quick moment. What if Greta was to die right now? So many people are dying all the time…

Penny saw Greta's eyes start to haze over. She'd been caught not listening again. It was so funny, because no matter how much Greta talked and no matter how irrelevant the monologues became, Penny was always meant to be avidly listening.

Penny glanced over at the two kittens who had finished the pizza and were lounging in the heat outside. Their eyes were half closed in imminent, lazy serenity. They looked like wise gurus. Or washed up regrets. And yet, no matter what Penny labeled them, they would still just lay there and fully exist until the day they didn't.

"Penny, I'm worried about you. You hardly talk, you smoke like you want your lungs out of you sooner rather than later. You look like a wreck and you don't have a job. I can't keep feeding you pizza and tossing you out on the streets at night hoping to find you again in the morning. What are you gonna do, Penz? Come on, tell me!"

The signs of ending. It's so funny to see how people get so worried. Penny closed her eyes and thought about all the reasons she hadn't killed herself yet. How it wouldn't do any good for the next life. How her energy would always be around, whether she liked it or not. How making a deadly point was almost like making no point at all.

"Penny! For God's sake, at least just be a human! I'm sick of talking to a wall. If you want to be a wall, why don't you just go back to your little shrine and your soggy teddy bears and let me just forget about you!"

Oh, poor Greta. Penny stood up and looked at her with a chuckle. "Come on, old woman. Let's go for a walk and get some cigarettes." Life goes on. The sun kept swimming through the sky down to the two old ladies who couldn't do anything much but burn up with simple existence.

Jasaun and the Apple Flooshe
By Jeffrey Montanye

Beyond the cracked sidewalk, and the telephone pole with layers of flyers in a rainbow of colors, and the patch of dry brown grass there stood a ten-foot high concrete block wall, caked with dozens of coats of paint. There was a small shrine at the foot of it, with burnt out candles and dead flowers and a few soggy teddy bears. One word of graffiti filled the wall, red letters on a gold background: Rejoice!

Few people ever went beyond the wall, which marked the edge of their village, but Jasaun was different. Standing before that great stack of block, he faced the ghosts of thirty-seven brave men. Only their names remained, written on the painted concrete to remember the sacrifice they had made for their people. It had been three years, but nobody had felt the need to clear away the items placed there to remember their loved ones. And those memoirs would sit there for at least two more years before yet another coat of paint would cover the names forever, providing room for a new list. Jasaun sighed, for the next day would mark his sixteenth birthday, and he would be old enough to participate in the next battle. He imagined his own name on that wall within the next two years but quickly shook the image from his head. There was one ray of sunshine, though, he thought as he held onto the worn-out hardcover book he'd received from the old man at the Liberty Library. He had reached the age of bonding and soon would have his own flooshe. The excitement was enough to make him forget the horrors displayed before him. He flipped the toggle switch of his electric scooter into the "on" position and hit the throttle. Dust flew up as he cruised beyond the wall, heading outside the safety limits of his village.

Six of ten LEDs lit up on the scooter's display panel, just enough power to make it to the tree and back home. Glancing up at the sun, he estimated at least two hours before dinner, plenty of time. He'd make it to his secret spot in about thirty minutes if he kept to the upper road which wasn't as overgrown as the streets between the buildings. The higher elevation of the main road provided splendid views of the old city, now empty and overcome with wild vines and shrubs. From this altitude, Jasaun could see into the broken upper-level windows of the taller buildings. No tribes had claimed this area, and many of the buildings were unexplored, hiding secrets of the life they had known centuries ago. Things were different then, much different. Jasaun tooled on past businesses and buildings of which his generation had no memory. The collapsed street signs and traffic lights had no meaning, and the structures were just the skeletons of a forgotten past. The scooter's motor buzzed as bits of broken safety glass crunched under its tires. Jasaun had reclaimed the two-wheeled electric cycle from an old building before nature had had a chance to take it back.

As Jasaun rode along, it appeared that he was the only thing alive in the city, but he knew better than to believe that lie. He was fully aware of the dangers lurking around every corner and kept a close eye on his scooter's handlebar mirror. It wasn't long before something caught his attention. Through the cracks in the glass, Jasaun could make out three creatures running up the road behind him, and they were catching up. "Galawiskens," he scowled as he pushed the throttle to maximum, but his little two-wheeled electric cart was no match for a full-grown flooshe and its rider. The animals were a little smaller than a horse with much larger, muscular legs. They were even able to climb trees but rarely did as long as food was plentiful at ground level. The first rider cruised past him on the right, intentionally missing him by mere inches. The second two passed on the left. Jasaun could feel the wind from their wake as they overtook him, almost knocking him off the scooter. The three boys, each one only a year or two older than Jasaun, spun their animals around to face him as he hit the brakes hard, letting the rear wheel kick out as his scooter came to a sudden halt. "Don't you know anything?" the leader of the little group began. "People gave up riding that junk years ago when they discovered they could tame animals." He patted his flooshe on the side. "I do hope you're not planning on taking your little toy into the next battle," the three of them scoffed. In the guise of intimidation, which Jasaun found to be very effective, they each wore the skull of a wild boar on their head and had painted their faces with the blood of their latest kill. One of them had a deer draped across the back of his flooshe. The young men were from an aggressive neighboring tribe, one of which hunted and killed animals for their meat. Jasaun knew better than to say something that would get them riled, so he kept his remarks to himself. "I'll see you at the next battle!" the leader sneered. "Perhaps by then, you'll have a real ride." The three of them laughed as they turned and rode off without any further incident. Jasaun breathed of sigh of relief and wiped the sweat from his brow.

Looking off to the side, Jasaun noticed a large pumpkin vine that had grown through the windshield of an overturned pickup truck. Two giant pumpkins, one as big as the truck itself, the other half its size, grew from the vine. The lumpy orange behemoths had enough meat on them to feed a man for a year if one could stomach it. They had a bitter, musky taste that left him feeling nauseous, but if one were starving, they would sustain a person with their abundant protein. Jasaun thought one would make a magnificent fort if hollowed out, but there were plenty of old buildings to sleep in if someone needed to spend the night away from the village. He kicked his scooter into gear and continued on his way.

After a trip through the inner section of the abandoned city, the young Jasaun finally arrived at his destination. His little scooter came to a stop before an enormous apple tree, which had grown through the cracks, heaving up large slabs of concrete around it. He had waited all winter to summon his apple flooshe after discovering the tree several miles inside the abandoned city of Manahawkin. Apple trees were just as rare as flooshe, but this tree was big enough to attract everyone that was in the area. He dismounted his cart to study the tree. "Good," he thought to himself as he examined the blossoms. "They're perfect." He took a deep breath through his nose, drawing in the sweet aroma of the new flowers which had a rosy scent. He cupped his hands around one of the clusters and spoke to it, "Now, go ahead and summon your cousins. Bring them here to absorb your pollen." He looked around the tree at the abandoned buildings. "I'll be back tonight. Tomorrow will be a special day."

Returning home, Jasaun was happy to be back in the familiar streets where he grew up with his tribe. There, the town was alive with villagers meandering about, attending to their daily chores. It wasn't empty and dead as the rest of the world he knew. The smell of bread baking filled the air and clothing hung on lines to dry. About twenty families made the little section of the city their home, renovating the local buildings to suit their needs. Children were laughing and running through the street. A little boy about seven ran up to Jasaun as his scooter came to a stop. "You're in big trouble, mister. Father's been looking all over for you. He says to tell you to get yourself into the kitchen and help Mom as soon as you get home." After delivering his message, Stephin ran off to join his friends.

***

"And pick something green!" his mother shouted through the open window as Jasaun walked across the veranda to the grow house. "You need more green in your diet. All you ever eat is that pizza Kalmez insists on making all the time. It's a wonder you're not as fat as your father." Jasaun sauntered through the plants, picking a couple peppers, zucchini, and some string beans as well. Bending down, he wiped the condensation from the outside of the cloning tank. Air bubbled up to the surface, churning the cloudy mixture to maintain an even temperature and flow of nutrients to the meat. He decided on a lump, then reached into the batch, pulling out a slimy pink ball about the size of a cantaloupe. A long, thin stem of flesh reached from the meat to the seeding pod in the center of the tank. Jasaun reached in with a pair of clippers and snipped the cord. "This will do," he thought as he held the fleshy ball of meat out to examine it.

The Chief of the Ramos tribe towered over his petite wife, who flashed him a suspicious look as he swooped into the kitchen, twirling around like a clumsy dancer. He was a tall man, six-foot-two and sported a full beard. His black pants were cut off at the knees, and he wore a thick belt over his shoulder to help hold them up. His shirt, wet with sweat, was torn from the bottom of the V of the neck to the center of his belly, allowing the air to touch his broad chest. The left sleeve of his shirt hung empty from his shoulder, devoid of an arm. "You're in an awfully good mood today," His wife said as she ducked under his right arm, continuing with dinner preparations. She looked down at the ball of meat her son had just set on the chopping block before retreating to his room. "Jasaun!" she called out, annoyed at what she saw. "You cut the cord too far back." She let out a frustrated sigh, dropping her hands to her side. "Now I'll have to reseed the tank." Grumbling, she cut a small chunk of meat off the ball. "Here," she said to her husband, whose playful antics were just adding to her irritation. "Make yourself useful and toss this back into the cloning tank. I'll get it seeding later." Her husband picked up the small cube of meat and headed toward the grow house. "And stop being so happy!" she yelled to him as the door closed.

"I'm sorry, I can't help being happy!" the Chief hooted as he returned to the kitchen. "Tomorrow my son will be sixteen!" He said with excitement in his voice. "He's finally reached the bonding age!" He fumbled through a sack leaning up against the wall. "Did you pack my tobacco? I want to be able to share a smoke with my son to celebrate our victory once we've captured his flooshe." His wife rolled her eyes. "We'll find us the finest flooshe anybody from any tribe has ever seen!" He stared wistfully off into nowhere. "My boy, bonding with his first flooshe." He turned to his wife. "Don't look so gloomy woman, this is a special time for him, a time to choose his life-long animal companion. Show us a little smile." She forced a smile for her husband. "That's my love," he said, grinning ear to ear. "Where is that boy? He should be here helping his father pack. We leave first thing in the morning."

Jasaun sat on his bed in his room, flipping through the pages of the old book. He could hear his father's muffled voice through the walls of the house, boasting of flooshe trolling with his son. Every boy dreamed of this day. They dreamed of what type of flooshe they would find. He should be happy, but he wasn't. He fumbled with the book in his hands. He wanted a flooshe, but he didn't want to obtain one the way everybody else did, taking it by force and subjecting it to disciplinary torture until its will was broken and it succumbed to fear of its rider. The book he held in his hands was an instruction manual from the old times before the ancient ways had been forgotten. A time when a flooshe was tamed in a more civilized manner. A time when they were treated with love and respect.

***

Jasaun waited until evening, then rushed through the village carrying his sleeping bag and flashlight, hoping not to be noticed. "Where are you going?" an inquisitive voice arose from the shadows. Jasaun winced. It was Cyine, a girl his age who lived with her family nearby. She was stunning enough during the day, but in the orange glow of the setting sun, her beauty was enough to make a boy swallow his own tongue when he tried to speak. And even worse, she liked him too, but he had other things on his mind. He didn't want her tagging along, but he knew if he didn't allow her to go with him, she would tell someone, so he let her follow. Together, they walked across the abandoned city to his secret place.

"Watch it! Be careful of the wasps," Jasaun warned as they walked under a tree that was leaning over the roadway. A low hanging branch had become home to a rather large wasp nest. The paper dome was so humongous, Jasaun wouldn't have been able to wrap his arms around it if he had been foolish enough to try. Cyine stepped back and watched as one of the beasts flew around the tree carrying a squirming bug, returning to the nest from a hunt. The wasp was about the size of a hummingbird and sported a stinger that could penetrate a rubber tire from one of the abandoned automobiles lying scattered about. It was quite colorful, with bright red and yellow wings, but very deadly. "That's how my father lost his arm," Jasaun said as the two of them kept a wary eye on the insects. "While out with a hunting party, he got himself tangled up in a vine and was pulled off his flooshe, landing right in one of those nests. He was stung several times on the arm before he was able to run to safety. The hunting party had to chop his arm off before the poison reached his heart. It would have killed him, for sure. He's lucky to be alive, but without his arm, he's not permitted to go into battle." The two adventurers gave the nest a wide berth as they passed by. "That's why they made him chief. He needed something to keep himself occupied since he couldn't do a lot with just one arm." Jasaun kept talking as they neared his secret place. "There," he said, pointing to a large apple tree, just ahead. "That's the tree, near that yellow building. It's the biggest one I've ever seen and the blossoms…" He took a deep breath. "You can smell them a mile away. There'll be flooshe all over this place in the morning. You'll see." Jasaun looked around for ground that wasn't hard concrete and dropped his sleeping bag. "We'll sleep here tonight." Wrapping his knuckles on the side of a large rusty container, he continued, "This will provide us with cover."

***

Cyine rolled over and wiped the sleep from her eyes. The early morning sun beamed through the holes in the buildings, casting rays of golden yellow through the branches of the tree. "Jasaun?" she called softly, but there was no answer. She was alone. Behind her, she heard what sounded like singing. She listened carefully while focusing her eyes in the direction of the sound. Across the sea of concrete, she could see the silhouette of Jasaun sitting under the apple tree, holding his book out in front of himself, surrounded by a cloud of mist which rose from the blossoms in the warmth of the sun. With his hand outstretched before him, he reached up to touch the snout of a beautiful young rainbow-colored flooshe. She watched in amazement. It was working, Jasaun was actually wooing the animal, instead of forcefully capturing it. She watched as he took his time, slowly rising to his feet, chanting the passages from the book, doing his best not to frighten the creature. Suddenly there was a sound, like low, rumbling thunder, and the ground began to shake. The harmonious scene unraveled before her eyes, giving way to chaos as three flooshe and their riders came storming around the yellow building. The rainbow flooshe reared up in front of Jasaun as the three young men from the Galawisken tribe circled it, tossing ropes around its neck. "Get out of there!" Cyine yelled as Jasaun dodged the beasts, trying to avoid being trampled to death. The boys circled the struggling flooshe, wrapping their ropes tighter with each pass, no doubt looking for an animal for a younger member of their tribe, one who had just reached the age of bonding. Jasaun leaped behind the apple tree, just before his rainbow-colored flooshe tumbled to the ground. The young men reveled in their triumphant victory.

Cyine was terrified, but there was no way she was going to sit back and watch a faction of hoodlums take away their flooshe. As far as she was concerned, that animal belonged to Jasaun. Glancing around for some creative idea to help him, she remembered the wasp nest. The tree was close enough, she thought and ran to it, grabbing onto the low hanging branch. Careful not to alarm the beasts inside, she pulled the limb around, as far as it would bend, leaning all her weight into it. Taking careful aim, she eyed the group of boys, then let the branch fly. With tremendous force, the limb snapped back to its original position. However, the wasp nest was not securely attached enough to withstand the centrifugal force. The entire orb of stinging fury left its anchor and flew freely through the air, right into the celebrating Galawisken boys. The paper nest struck the leader on his back and broke wide open, sending the large colorful wasps in all directions. The ferocious insects immediately focused their rage toward what they perceived to be an enemy and attacked the young men. Dropping their ropes and abandoning their catch, the trio took off on their flooshe with the wasps following right behind as Cyine jumped up and down, performing her own little victory dance. But that victory did not last long.

"What kind of idiot are you?" Jasaun yelled as he stretched his hands over the young flooshe now lying on the ground. It had been stung a couple of times by the wasps. Cyine had run up, expecting to hear praise, but instead, all she got in return was criticism. "That was the stupidest thing anybody could have ever done!" Jasaun's eyes flashed with anger, although, he knew that being taken by the Galawisken tribe would have been a much worse fate for the creature. At least the flooshe had a fighting chance with him and Cyine, if they could figure out a way to get a three-hundred-pound animal seven miles back home. As Jasaun paced back and forth, pondering how he was going to accomplish such a tremendous task, he caught the figure of a distant rider on a flooshe coming up to them fast. As if they didn't have enough trouble on their hands, this person was much more intimidating than the three Galawisken boys.

"What's the meaning of this?" Jasaun's father shouted as he pulled his flooshe to a stop. "I woke up this morning expecting to find my son ready to go flooshe trolling, only to find he hadn't even slept in his bed last night. Of all the days…" He stopped mid-sentence when the beautiful Cyine stood up from behind the flooshe lying on the ground. "Had to do it on your own, huh?" he shook his head with understanding. "You didn't kill it, did you?" he asked as he slid down from his animal. "You know, I would have liked to have done this together." He looked over at Cyine. "But I understand." He knelt down and pulled a stinger from the flooshe's side, holding it up in the light. The muscle on the poison sack was still pumping. "These are tough animals, she'll be OK," he said as he flicked the stinger away. "Come, there's bound to be a metal sheet around here we can use as a sled."

Father and son worked together, creating a sled from a sheet of metal and wiring they had found in a nearby building. Within an hour, the makeshift gurney was hitched up to the Chief's flooshe and ready to go. "Don't forget, son, she may be calm now, but she'll be wild when the poison clears her system. She'll have to be broken. That's not an easy task." The three of them worked together, lifting the flooshe onto the sled to carry it back to their village.

Cyine coddled the sick flooshe as the sled began to grind forward, running her hands through its fur. Up close she could see that the fur was actually formed from small, narrow feathers with a long, flexible shaft and tiny barbs forming the vanes. "It's OK, You're in good hands," Cyine said, patting the creature on the side of its head. Gesturing to Jasaun, she continued to sooth the animal by talking to it, "This is the pizza kid." She bent down and whispered to the rainbow-colored flooshe, "He's always eating Kalmez's pizza." Standing up straight, she addressed her friend, "Jasaun, meet Rainbow." She noticed the smirk on his face right away. "What? I can name her. I thought of it first. Besides, I always wanted to have my own flooshe, but since I'm a girl, I can't. So, I get to name her." The ride was a bit rough and slow going, but the trio was home by dinner.

When the ride ended, she was lifted again. The kid slid her body onto a soft pile of clothing among the boxes in the garage. He pulled an old coat over the top, creating a cave that emanated the sweetness of old ladies who frequently powdered themselves—a light rose motif that played ironically well in the deep recesses of Rainbow's ancestral brain. The pizza kid lifted her head to help her lap water from a hubcap. He broke bits of pepperoni and crust into bite-sized pieces and left them where her tongue could reach them. Much later, she heard him practicing his orations like songs. Like monks chanting in the distance, they were a comfort.

The Chief kicked at the bits of pepperoni his son had left for the flooshe to eat. "You're wasting your time, boy," he spoke loudly, so Jasaun could hear him from his room. "They don't eat meat, not until…" He bent down and gently touched the wild animal on her snout. Speaking softly, so only the flooshe could hear him, he chuckled. "That time in battle, huh, girl? When you tear the flesh off your enemy." He patted her side. "You'll do fine. You'll do just fine."

Jasaun stepped into the garage, holding the old book in his hands. "I'm going to do this my way, father. I'm not going to break her like the other tribes do. Their methods are barbaric. There's a better way. This book teaches about the chants the flooshe respond to," he said, tapping his fingers on the spine. "The ancients who built this place, they knew a lot more than you think."

The chief of the Ramos tribe let out a boisterous laugh. "You have no idea what you're talking about, boy. This creature will throw you off its back and trample you into the mud the first chance it gets." The chief made a fist, pointing his thumb back to himself. "We're doing this my way. Do you hear?" he said forcefully as he snatched the book from Jasaun. Holding onto the binding with his one hand, he flipped through the pages using his thumb to turn them over. "What kind of nonsense have you been reading?" he said, as he gazed at the book. "You've been talking to the old man again, haven't you?" Looking toward the door, in the direction outside of town, "I should have had that library building burned down a long time ago. All he does is eat our food and read from those worthless books all day long. They're nonsense, I tell you, filled with nothing but archaic teachings that cloud your mind. When the people darkened the devices, they put all that nonsense behind them, leaving it for a better life." He threw the book to the ground. Jasaun watched it slide across the floor until it came to rest alongside the sick flooshe. "I've had enough of that old fool," the Chief said as he stormed out into the street.

Jasaun reached down to retrieve the book when he noticed

something unusual about the flooshe's mouth. "Teeth?" He said aloud. "Flooshe don't have teeth." He was correct. The animals rip grass and leaves from plants with their tongues, and grind them up with their boney jaws. "Father," he yelled. "You have to see this." Jumping up, Jasaun went to the door. His father was already two houses away, raging down the street, on his way to the library. "Father! Come quick!" Jasaun yelled.

Inside the garage, his father knelt down, inspecting the mouth of the flooshe. "It can't be. It's only been three years." He looked up in thought. "The teeth only appear every six years or more. They've never come in this early. Perhaps it's the poison." He got up and ran across the street to the flooshe house. Several flooshe stood, grazing on grass the children had plucked for them. Flies buzzed about as the Chief grabbed the bridle of his own animal and pulled its mouth over, prying it open with his hand. "It can't be. They're early. If our flooshe have their teeth already, then all the other tribe's will. We're not ready." He quickly went around and checked the other flooshe. "Jasaun," he yelled. "Alert the council. Tell them to gather at the hall for an emergency meeting."

***

"We need riders," the men all agreed, sitting around the council table in the council hall. "We only have twenty-five who were able to bond with a flooshe." Looking up at the Chief, one of the men asked, "We hear your son has a flooshe now, have they bonded yet?"

The Chief shook his head. "The animal is sick. It isn't well enough to break. It'll be wild once it's back on its feet, not ready to bond. I'll ride with you tomorrow." He noticed the looks from the other men as they glanced at the empty left sleeve of his shirt. "We have no choice. I will ride." The others sat back in their chairs without protesting. They knew the situation was desperate. "Gentlemen, we are on our own. Sleep with your wives tonight, so that they might bare children to replace us, for tomorrow, we ride into battle."

***

While concerns about the flooshe getting their teeth early spread amongst the adults in town, the children had other things on their minds, laughing and running through the street. As Jasaun turned the corner, a little girl about seven ran up to him as he rode in on his electric cart. Montly had a crush on the young man. "Jasaun, Jasaun," she called out as her little legs carried her to his side. "Jacoab found a device in one of the old vehicles! He's on his way to the Burn Bank building to solarize it!" She grabbed his hand and pulled. "Come on! We're going to see the knowledge of the world!" Jasaun flipped out the kickstand and stepped off his scooter. This was a serious situation, he never knew of anybody to ever activate a device before. It was forbidden.

Thousands of coins, copper and silver in color littered the floor of the Burn Bank. The children used this building as a play area. It was one of the only solarized buildings around that wasn't inhabited by a family. Jasaun's feet slipped on the loose change as Montly pulled him along. Several small lamps hung loosely from their wiring, lighting the large room. Old desks and overturned chairs surrounded the lobby, and the ceiling tiles had all collapsed to the floor, deteriorated from years of rainwater leaking through the roof. What was left of the lettering that had once spelled out the name of the bank hung on the wall above the teller stations. A faint outline of the missing letters could still be seen, spelling out the name: Woodburn Bank. The children huddled in one corner next to a power outlet. The oldest one, Jacoab, just a year younger than Jasaun, held a small device in his hands and was about to plug it in. Being the eldest, it was Jasaun's responsibility to stop the others from disobeying a tribal law, but his curiosity got the better of him, and he remained quiet. To know all the secrets of the world was too fantastic of an opportunity to pass up. He stood and watched as Jacoab pushed the small white box into the outlet.

It was ten-year-old Vessey who finally spoke up. "Stop!" she shouted. "You can't do that!" The spunky little girl, with faded, ripped jeans and yellow ruffled blouse, stood upon a wooden chair. Her rosy cheeks puffed out, and her face scrunched as her eyebrows turned down toward the top of her nose. Two little wrinkles formed between her brows as she squinted her eyes. "Look around you, can't you see?" She pointed toward the windows where the sun lit up the buildings outside. "Everywhere out there are houses, and in all those houses lived the tribes of people. Even the scrapers, built to the skies were full of tribes. And then came the devices, and the tribes used them to take all the knowledge of the world into their minds. All the knowledge of everything and all the sicknesses too. And they all got the computer viruses in their minds, and they all died. Do you want to die too?"

Jasaun was about to argue in Jacoab's favor when he glanced out the window and saw his little brother leading his father across the street, pointing to the bank building. "Everybody, scat, Stephin's bringing my father this way," he warned the gang.

Stephin let go of his father's hand and ran inside before him, pointing out Jacoab who held the device in his hands. Ducking under some loose hanging wires, the Chief of the Ramos tribe stepped into the lobby. Jasaun stepped back, giving him plenty of room, for he was the Chief, and nobody stood in his way, not even his own son. Ignoring the younger children as they streamed around him to the outside door, his eyes fixed on Jacoab. "What is that you are holding in your hands?" Jacoab didn't answer. "Hasn't your mother taught you the tribal laws, boy?" He turned to his son, "And you?" gesturing to the younger boy, he continued, "You couldn't stop this?" Jasaun started to answer, but his father cut him off with a simple raise of his hand. "To the house with you! I'll deal with you later." Jasaun hesitated, he wanted to speak his mind, but no words came forth. "Now!" his father bellowed in a voice Jasaun knew not to challenge. He went swiftly to the door but slowed as he crossed the foyer so he could hear his father's words. The Chief said nothing as he reached for the device, a slim shiny black metal with a lighted glass face and buttons along one side. He glanced at it for a moment, colorful symbols filled the screen. "Be hopeful you didn't stare into it too long," the Chief said as he set it on the ground. "If you get the fever..." He picked up a rock. "You'll kill us all," he said as he brought the stone down on the device, reducing it to rubble.

***

Everyone was silent at the dinner table. Jasaun looked around at his seven younger siblings. Nobody spoke a word except for his father. "Their teeth are coming in, and we have few riders. If they would have held out another few years, we'd have at least a dozen or two more." The Chief poked at his beets with his fork. "This is not a good time for them to be early, we lost too many during the last battle. We'll never survive another one this soon."

His wife reached out and placed her hand over his. "We can hide." She looked around at her family. "We can all hide. We won't go to battle this time. We can gather everybody in the village together and hide out in one of the scrapers in the city until the battle is over."

"No," the Chief shook his head. "If we don't go to the battlegrounds, the other tribes will come here. They'll find us. Even our own flooshe will smell us out and attack us. That's their way. We have to go to battle, even if we are just a few. The other tribes won't bother the village if we go, even if we lose the battle. But if we don't fight, they'll come and destroy everyone." He glanced out the window where the children played in the street. "Everyone." He cuffed his fingers around hers. "I have to go this time, too. There's too few of us. Every man who has bonded with a flooshe will have to go."

"It's a death sentence, you know that. Nobody ever comes back from those battles, not those from smaller tribes, like ours." The woman dropped her face into her hands and wept. "Why do we have those stupid animals anyhow? I hate them! I hate them all."

"It's the way it is. We depend on the flooshe… for transportation… for bringing food back to the village… for protection. Until that day comes when our army is strong enough." The Chief pounded the table with his fist, "Then it will be our men coming home, and the women of the other tribes will be left to cry and mourn their losses." Comforting his wife, he placed his hand gently on her back. "You'll have the younger boys until they become of age. They'll help with the chores in the village."

The next day, Jasaun stood near the wall at the edge of their little settlement, helplessly watching his father ride off with the other men. Not being able to ride with the warriors tore him apart inside. "Do you want to go with them?" The voice startled Jasaun. Turning around, he found himself facing the old man from the library. With a paintbrush in hand, he had begun preparing the wall for a new list of names. "Have you read the book I gave you?" he asked. Jasaun shrugged his shoulders. "I suppose your father told you that the information in that book is primitive and outdated." The man stumbled forward, balancing himself on his cane. "He couldn't be any further from the truth. It's our own ways that are uncivilized. We've strayed far from the path of enlightenment, making a complete circle back to our old barbaric past, repeating the mistakes we made hundreds of years ago. All because we refuse to believe what had been written to help us along." The old man let out a groan as he sat down on the weathered park bench. "We believe what we know today is more advanced than what we knew years ago. Hogwash! Do you want to know the real way to bond with a flooshe?" Jasaun nodded silently. "You can't bond with a wild animal if it's trying to kill you. You either have to bind it with ropes or approach it while it's drunk with apple blossom pollen." He looked over at Jasaun. "Like you tried. Or…" The old man's eyes widened as he stared into the young man's face. "Let it get stung by a poisonous wasp." He pulled a device from his pocket and held it out to Jasaun. "All the answers are here." Jasaun was hesitant to take it from him. "Don't worry, you won't get a computer virus. They are wrong about that too." He shook the gadget. "Go ahead, take it. It won't bite you." Jasaun reached out and took the device from the man's shaky hand. "Now, I haven't got a power supply, but I think perhaps Jacoab might be able to help you out with that," he said with a wink.

***

The twenty-five warriors of the Ramos tribe crested the top of the hill as the sun was coming up. There must have been a thousand warriors from at least twelve different tribes scattered across the valley. Each warrior was decorated with paint and clothing that established which tribe they were from. Each man rode his own flooshe, bonded together for life, as a flooshe would never let anyone other than the one it bonds with to ride on its back. If the rider is killed, the animal will never accept another. Nobody knew why, but this was the only time in the flooshe's life that it would eat meat, and that meat would be a warrior from a rival tribe, which is why the tribes chose this time to battle for their rights to the land. When the battle was over, only the strongest tribe would stand, and there would be no worries of any other tribes coming against it since all capable warriors would be dead.

As hours went by, the flooshe grew impatient, pacing back and forth, becoming more difficult for the riders to control. Each man did his best to command their beast, but the time would come when one of the animals would disobey its master and strike out on its own. It was just a little afternoon on the second day when that happened. A young man of seventeen had had help taming a rather large flooshe but didn't have the strength to keep it under control. With drool running down its neck, the animal let out a loud, scratchy scream and charged head-on into the battlefield. One by one, all the flooshe started to charge. Warriors scrambled to mount their beasts, but some had broken away and charged without their riders. The battle frenzy had begun.

A young rider from Jasaun's tribe took off into the fight, strapped to the back of his flooshe as it dashed ahead, seeking a target. It took on an older warrior from a rival clan who had black and yellow stripes painted on his face. The flooshe reared up on their hind legs slashing at one another with razor-sharp claws. The flooshe competed for each other's rider just as much as the riders were in competition with each other. One of the animal's claws swiped the leg of the black and yellow-faced man, cutting deep into his flesh. Blood spilled out, but the man clung to his animal. His flooshe blocked another swipe by turning its body and knocked the offending beast onto its side, pinning its rider to the ground. The Chief of the Ramos tribe turned just in time to watch the rival tribe's flooshe grab his fellow rider by the back of his neck and thrash him about like a rag doll. The flooshe began to feast. As expected, the battle was not going well for the Ramos tribe.

All the next day and into the night, the battle raged on, until the following morning only a few exhausted warriors were still standing. With blood running down his face, mixing with the blue and white tribal paint, one warrior lifted his sword with his last bit of strength, bringing it down against his opponent who blocked it with his own blade, then stumbled back to his knees. He narrowly missed being sliced in half, only to find himself being dragged off to be devoured by a flooshe who had lost its rider. Those who were able had limped back to their tribal territories, most getting eaten on the way. Only those who were able to maintain their mount would return to their home villages. After the flooshe had gorged themselves, they sought the dark spaces of the empty buildings where they slept until they gave birth to their offspring.

***

Back at the Ramos village, the women and children anxiously awaited the return of their husbands and fathers. In the morning of the sixth day, families gathered at the wall, giving up hope that anybody would come back home. Names were being added to the wall, and new shrines began to appear, mourning their loved ones. The entire tribe was there except for one, Jasaun.

On the sixth day after his father went off to battle, Jasaun burst from the garage with full gear and saddle, riding on the back of Rainbow. Cyine stepped out of the garage, holding the device in her hand, waving a red cloth into the air. Jasaun tore off through the town, heading out to the battlefield on his newly bonded animal companion. Riding slowly through the dead bodies, he suddenly stopped and jumped from his flooshe, rushing over to his father. The Chief was covered with blood but still breathing. "Father," he said, "I did it. I solved the mystery of the flooshe. He reached for his father. "Come on, I'm taking you home." Unable to speak, the chief reached up with his one arm and touched his son's face. He smiled one last time, then closed his eyes forever. Jasaun held him tight, pushing his face against his father's. "I promise you, father. I promise you. We'll never have to go through this again." He wanted to stay and hug his father, but out on the battlefield, several flooshe were still searching through the bodies for anything that was still alive. In a few weeks, scavenger birds and animals would devour what was left. Jasaun stood to mount his flooshe when a sword came down, missing him by inches. He ducked and rolled out of the way.

"Well, well, if it isn't ol' scooter boy!" the voice mocked. Standing before Jasaun was one of the Galawisken boys. "I don't see a weapon," he continued as he lifted his sword for another swing. "All the easier for me to kill you." Jasaun stepped back, stumbling over the bodies lying on the ground. He had been spending most of his time learning how to tame a flooshe properly rather than learning how to wield a sword. The young warrior with the boar skull on his head continued forward. Jasaun glanced around for anything he could use to defend himself but saw nothing other than a small knife with a four-inch blade which he snatched up from the ground. The Galawisken warrior laughed, "Another toy? What do you intend to do with that little trinket, tickle me?" he taunted as he readied his sword for the final kill. He never saw the blow coming. Rainbow came up quickly from behind and took him out with one swipe of her front claws; the boar's skull flew off his head. Lying on his back on the concrete ground without his menacing headgear, he was no longer intimidating. He pushed himself away, but Rainbow stayed with him, ready to make the final blow.

"Rainbow, No!" Jasaun yelled out, and the animal stopped its pursuit immediately. The frightened Galawisken pushed himself to his feet, and ran off, leaving his sword behind. He had never seen anybody maintain control over a flooshe just as it was about to feed. "Good girl," Jasaun said as he patted her side. He draped his father's body over her back, grabbed the warrior's sword, and together they walked side-by-side back to their village.

***

Chunks of wood flew in all directions as Jasaun chopped at the apple tree. "No, Jasaun, don't," Cyine cried out. "You can't cut down the trees. It won't stop the tribes from fighting. They'll find another way to attract the flooshe. Besides, these trees grow all over the world. What will you do? Travel around the globe, cutting down apple trees the rest of your life? Please don't cut down the tree." Jasaun put down his sword. It was too much work anyhow. Cyine took his hand. "Come on, let's go home."

Back in the village, Jasaun's mother stepped out of the house with a chunk of pumpkin in her hands. "I don't know why I bother with these things. Nobody ever eats them." She sat down beside her son. Rainbow stood in the street. A slight bit of drool dripped from her mouth. "You can't keep her, you know. She hasn't satisfied her taste for meat." His mother looked him in the eye. "She'll eat you. You have to let her go." Jasaun sighed. His mother put her arm around her son as a partial hug. "I guess you'll have to be chief now. It's a big responsibility, you know." Jasaun nodded. "But I'm sure you'll come up with lots of new and better ways to do things around here," she said as she tossed the chunk of pumpkin into the street. Before it could touch the ground, Rainbow lunged forward, grabbing it in her mouth. She devoured it as if it were a piece of meat. Jasaun's eyes widened as he realized the true use of the giant vegetables.

Just outside their village, near the Liberty Library, Jasaun led Rainbow to one of the giant pumpkins growing alongside a building. "It makes you wonder, doesn't it?" The old man asked as he approached Jasaun, sitting on a worn-out bench, looking out over the run-down buildings. "There are millions of them across the entire planet, building after building, after building. Every square inch of dry land has been paved, stoned, steel-plated, solarized, or concreted. Somebody built all that. What happened to all those people?" The two men watched as Rainbow clawed into the side of a giant pumpkin and began to feast. "All gone, due to a silly misunderstanding. Everybody wanted a flooshe, but nobody wanted the pumpkins." He glanced over at Jasaun. "Now that you know you don't have to provide human sacrifices to the flooshe any longer, what do you intend to do about the battles? You know they'll come after you if you don't fight."

Jasaun held the device in his hands. "I don't know, but I have a feeling that the answers are in here. And we have at least five years to figure it out." He glanced over at the memorial wall with its layers of paint and new shrines. "As Chief of the Ramos tribe, that's the first job I plan to abolish." Looking at the old man, he continued. "I'm sure you won't mind a new career." He gazed out over the town with its abandoned vehicles scattered about. "Have you ever tried to get one of those things working?" The old man smiled.

The Cat Girls
By Aaron Muller

Beyond the cracked sidewalk, and the telephone pole with layers of flyers in a rainbow of colors, and the patch of dry brown grass there stood a ten-foot high concrete block wall, caked with dozens of coats of paint. There was a small shrine at the foot of it, with burnt out candles and dead flowers and a few soggy teddy bears. One word of graffiti filled the wall, red letters on a gold background: Rejoice!

Another girl dead, which is how so many of them end up. The prettiest ones get a shrine and a vigil. This used to be her wall. It used to be plastered with a photo of her, smiling with her curls fresh and bouncing, holding a bouquet of flowers like a baby she'd never have. She'd lost count of the years since she'd been transformed, but it had to have been at least seventy. Seventy years a stray, seventy years for that photo to give way to the elements and make room for the next lost little girl. They rejoice when they're found, as if burying the body can bring them peace. Do all little girls turn into something else when they die? Are all of their bodies empty? What they put in the ground isn't the little girl. It's a container.

Her container was buried four blocks from here, decomposed entirely, nothing left but dusty bones. Sometimes she would go visit her own grave, paw at the grass like she could dig herself up and get back into the right container. Curl up in her old rib cage. Gnaw on her femur and carry her finger bones out like prizes, in her little mouth for the entire neighborhood to ignore. No one really fed her anymore. She just kept coming around. The same calico cat, plodding around town for decades, but all calicos look the same in their splotches, so to them she was just the product of a lack of community neutering. She was generations of cats.

All of her mewling attempted a story. At least for the first few decades. *I'm not really what I look like! I was killed by two men and I can tell you what they look like! Don't scratch my belly!* It took her, arguably, too long to give up on trying to tell. At worst she'd get rocks thrown at her or a dog chasing her down. At best she'd get the dregs of a can of tuna. She'd been religious growing up, and her child-instincts told her that this was a punishment. She knew there was a heaven and a hell, and that all that reincarnation business was backwards. She had been punished backwards. Turned into something so fierce and dangerous, but cursed by smallness. Just like a little girl, but hairier.

She visited her old shrine on her walk each day. It had rained last night. The rain always sped up the forgetting. Pretty girls and their teddy bears do not charm as much when they're soaking wet with dirty rain water. And, rejoice! They'd found the body. They'd found the container. Maybe for this little girl, there was a heaven, or maybe she'd been an awful child, and there was a hell. Or she had just been operating under a false certainty that there was either of these things, and she was a chipmunk somewhere in the next town over.

Traffic was light. Maybe that was for the best. People aren't as alert when there are fewer other cars to look out for. That's something she might have learned by driving, had she made it that far. Everything she knew, she had learned as a girl, or by listening to grown-ups talk. In backyards, in classrooms, in supermarkets she would sneak into to steal seafood. It was a worldly education. And at first, learning had given her purpose. But there was no one to talk to.

Not even the other strays, who could only meow and rub their necks against her, unable to say if they had once been a person. She had gained so much knowledge and stored it all in her little cat-girl brain, and she felt she had begun to overflow.

There was a bright red pickup truck barreling down the street at too high a speed, because, she had learned, that is how people who own bright red pickup trucks drive. At that moment, she was thankful. She trotted out into the street, slower and more careful than a cat who simply wants to get to the other side. That was a joke she finally got.

The man behind the wheel stayed focused on singing. She could not help but purr, and she slowed down to a stand-still once the vehicle came within ten feet. She'd done this before, to no avail. She'd learned better methods.

Closing her eyes, she made her peace. That's what cats do when they're happy, they close their eyes to show trust. And she trusted that man to tear her in half and barely feel but a small bump in the road. But too much time passed, and she heard some screeching, and the continued chugging of an engine, getting farther and farther away. She had lived. There were no more cars.

But she felt a strange stinging, and turned her head to look at her tail. The end had been flattened, bloodied, its little, delicate bones and nerves crushed beyond repair. She began to wail, involuntary and shrill. She dragged her useless tail over to the sidewalk, cursing at the sky and at that man and at the two men who put her inside of this cat. She curled her tail closer to herself, inspecting the damage, the small trail of blood and fur she'd left behind. Instinct drove her to lick the wound, and it stung. This had not been the plan. Dying slowly from an infection would be more painful, and it might drive her to change her mind and wander into the vet's office uptown.

She sat a while, on her haunches, pathetic and bleeding. She wondered how many ounces of blood she had, and how quickly she would die, if she would die at all. The blood didn't spurt or gush, but it stung like it ought to flow so hard and so fast. Lightheaded, she eased into the pavement to lay down, and was startled awake, as cats so often are, by the sound of tired screeching again. A second chance, maybe. Maybe next time she'd come back as an insect and it would be so much easier to die because she wouldn't be cute.

But nothing hit her. She opened her eyes and through the blur from the searing pain she saw a squatting boy in a baseball cap. She opened her mouth to show her teeth, but all that came out was a desperate whine. He reached into his jeans pocket, scrambling, and brought out a red bandana.

"Poor kitty," he cooed, fearlessly reaching into the blood and patches of fur to tie the bandana around her tail. She hissed at the tightening, and he clicked his tongue to try and quiet her. He was young, no older than sixteen, a speckled face and greasy hair that fell from his hat. She never got to be that old. It was almost a good thing. She died pretty. "Let's get you someplace safe."

He mumbled to himself as he carried her back to his car. A loud, powder-blue little thing with only two doors, lined with rust. He spoke about how he can't afford to take her to a vet, he's sorry, his mom will kill him for getting blood on the seats. She tried to mewl in protest, to keep him out of trouble and keep herself dying slowly, but he wouldn't listen. He nestled her into the front passenger's seat, wedging her against the leather with a pizza box. Full and heavy, smelling of garlic. She'd make him late.

"It's okay, kitty, I hate this job anyway," he said, putting the car in gear and driving away from the scene of the crime. Stick-shift. She watched as he struggled with the lever like he was just learning how to use it. His hand shook as he gripped the knob, his knuckles covered in scratches and peeling skin. It was something she could have done, but she never really had. Not to a person. She'd killed squirrels, birds, beached fish. Decades ago, when finally she became too starving to avoid it. Amongst the smaller beasts, she was very powerful. Being that she had the mind of a human girl, she found herself far more calculated than other cats. Maybe her new container had given her the gift of feline instinct, but it was certainly bolstered by having played so many games of hide-and-seek.

It was a game of hide-and-seek that got her killed. She was so very good at it, she had climbed up a skinny tree and perched on one of the thicker branches, just strong enough to support her weight. Even then, she had the balance of a cat. Hours passed and no one could find her. The sky turned pink and no one came. Victorious, having hidden and not been sought, she fell asleep. When she awoke it was in a bed of leaves, her head spinning. Something had dragged her down from the branch, and at first she was certain it was a bear. What was is she'd been told? Stay absolutely still. She tried not to move, there on the ground, betraying herself with her shaky breath and shivering limbs.

A man is a beast that's worse than a bear. Bears don't hurt you because they want to see you suffer. Bears don't wrap their fat fingers around your throat until the world goes dark. Bears don't bury you in the muddy delta of a local creek.

"Look at that, kitty," he said, pointing through the windshield. "A rainbow." She couldn't see it above the dashboard. "That's what I'll call you, okay? Rainbow the kitty, because I found you after it rained." She knew that was not her name. She knew she had once had a name, and it had once been fondly called by her parents when she played too long in the backyard. She knew it had once been printed beneath the portrait on the concrete wall, but with the years its letters faded both from the paper and her mind. Rainbow. Bright and colorful, arching back like a tired cat preparing to nap. Stretching wide across the sky, which is where people say angels are. And she didn't get to be one, so she would be a rainbow instead.

She couldn't know how long she sat in that car seat, drifting in and out, letting the entire world smell like pizza, letting herself forget her name entirely. Rainbows are as fleeting as pretty, young girls. She would soon disappear from the sky and the earth.

When the ride ended, she was lifted again. The kid slid her body onto a soft pile of clothing among the boxes in the garage. He pulled an old coat over the top, creating a cave that emanated the sweetness of old ladies who frequently powdered themselves—a light rose motif that played ironically well in the deep recesses of Rainbow's ancestral brain. The pizza kid lifted her head to help her lap water from a hubcap. He broke bits of pepperoni and crust into bite-sized pieces and left them where her tongue could reach them. Much later, she heard him practicing his orations like songs. Like monks chanting in the distance, they were a comfort.

"My sister was wise beyond her years," he spoke, staring intently at a crumpled piece of lined paper. "Maybe that's why she was taken from us so soon." Rainbow had been a wise girl as well. Monstrous men can't stand that sort of thing. "I remember she liked to read. She would stay up all night and, I'm sorry mom and dad, I'd…I'd lie and say she was sleeping." His voice wavered and he balled the paper up in his fist. "It's so fucking stupid, Rainbow," he said, turning to her, getting down on his knees and patting the scruff of her neck. "What am I supposed to say? My baby sister is dead and they think because I get good grades in English I can shit out a eulogy? It's bullshit."

He sat down beside her, cradling his head in his hands. His sister was the new dead girl, the one who had the current spotlight, the one for whom they rejoiced when they found the body. Rainbow studied the pizza kid, noting his black clothes and the anarchist patches. He didn't seem the type of boy to rejoice for much of anything.

She tried to move her tail again, and it ached, but the bleeding had stopped. The kid mumbled something about cleaning it, and he got up to leave the garage and go inside his house. A house tainted like hers had once been. In her daily travels, she struggled to even approach the street where she used to live. Maybe it had been torn down, or at least painted a different color. Not that she would be able to tell; with her cat's sight and in time she had forgotten the color of most things. She wondered if it burned for the boy to go back inside of his house, the house where he protected his sister's reading, and watched her grow, and then know she would stop growing.

He returned with a bottle of rubbing alcohol and a roll of toilet paper. Already his face looked apologetic and hesitant, as if causing pain would kill him. He really was a stupid boy, if he didn't even consider the idea that she might be rabid or otherwise diseased. But, Rainbow guessed, losing a sister could make you stupid, or it could make you not care if you contract something deadly.

It burned worse than it ever had from her mother tending to scrapes on her knees. She could not help the way she hissed and whined. He apologized, furtive and tearful, dabbing at the wound. His touch was rough no matter how clear it was that he was trying to be careful and treat her like the delicate thing she so clearly was. He was not yet a monstrous man, but a kind and gentle boy. Once her tail was cleaned, he wrapped it in toilet paper, his method unsure and his technique sloppy.

"There we go, Rainbow," he said, tender and soft, smoothing down the remaining fur on the rest of her injured tail. "Not good as new, but you'll be alright, I think." And then, all caution to the wind, his heart laid bare and his eyes watery, he leaned down and kissed her flat, furry forehead. She shut her eyes, unable to thank him. Unable to truly wish she'd been flattened by that truck.

He pulled the balled-up paper from his pocket and straightened it out. He stared at it, eyes scanning the sloppy handwriting and the heavy black ink that covered his mistakes and his most hated phrases. She could see him mouthing the words, twisting his brow in disdain as he mumbled through it. She wondered if there was any good way to eulogize a little girl. She'd not been present for her own.

But, since then, she'd heard a lot of them. Searching for mice in cemeteries, sitting in the open window of a stranger's living room while they watch TV at night. They were always sure to mention that she was beautiful, more specifically that her smile had the divine power to control the light. She was special, she was full of promise. She was gone too soon. Rainbow had imagined her own eulogy countless times, but none of it ever sounded right. She would never know if any of it was true. If she would have grown into a beautiful woman, if she was truly special and if her smile would continue to be magic. Maybe she would have been entirely unremarkable, after all.

She realized she'd been meowing, sometimes unable to control it, when she wished she could still talk to herself. She had so many ideas to share with the pizza kid. What to say about his sister, how to make the rest of the congregation take a good hard look at themselves, at this town, at the way we eulogize little girls.

"What is it, Rainbow? Does it still hurt really bad?" he asked, seeming eager to stuff the paper back in his pocket and further procrastinate. "Well, it's gonna hurt for a bit, and I'm sorry. One time I broke my leg during soccer. Well, another kid broke it because he landed on me, and it hurt *so* bad." He scratched behind her ears as he talked, filling the empty space and silence. "And I was complaining a lot but my mom told me to suck it up, that sometimes, things are really painful. They hurt so much, but you…" His voice cracked a little, the distinct wavering of tears and not of puberty.

"...you have to just get through it, Rainbow." He sniffed hard. "You have to...write this stupid fucking thing."

He rested his head on her soft belly, and she felt her fur begin to soak from big, salty tears. Had anyone cried on a stray cat when she died? Had any animals been harmed in the making of her untimely death?

He took out his paper again, flipping it over to the blank side and drawing a pen out of his coat pocket. The paper was already run through with rough writing, threatening to tear at every crease, but he continued to bully it toward disintegration, scribbling words Rainbow couldn't quite make out. Her eyes still blurry from the pain, she worried that maybe she was forgetting how to read. How long do cat containers live when they're filled with the soul of a girl? Do cats get dementia like the many old people whose laps she's laid in, her soft fur subduing them enough to pass away? They did it naturally, like she never got to do. Maybe, someday, she'd be put down with a swift injection to the thigh to save her from further misery.

"How's this sound, Rainbow?" he asked her, clearing his throat, turning to face her as if she were a proper audience. "The day before she was taken away from us, my sister told me she was scared all the time. I told her it was stupid. She told me I was a boy and didn't get it." He paused, fighting himself, blinking his eyes until he seemed certain he wouldn't cry. "I should have listened and been scared too. Now she's dead and we have her body and everyone is telling me that's a good thing because she can be at peace but it's all so fucking s-stupid…"

She wished so much she had proper hands with which to comfort him. Lacking the strength to approach, to give him a caring lick on the face, she reached out one paw, groping into the air for whichever part of him she could touch. Her soft toe pads to his forehead, she purred.

"Would you have been at peace, Rainbow? If you'd really gotten hit by a car all the way?" She closed her eyes slowly, blinking at him, desperate to tell him she just didn't know. To tell him she would probably just have moved down the food chain and gotten eaten by another cat, cycling through until she was a microbe, living a simple life with no brain and no ability to learn. "I don't even believe in heaven, Rainbow," he went on. "She's just dead."

It was then that she made her decision. She would go to all the local haunts, literally sniffing around for the pizza kid's sister. She had to be somewhere. Rainbow couldn't be the only one, as she had never been extraordinary, even as a person. She was not a terribly special cat, either. If she had been, maybe someone would have insisted on keeping her. But she had one glossy eye, patches of matted fur that just wouldn't soften no matter her preening. Maybe all little girls turned into unlovable cats. She would find a cat so ugly and unremarkable she could be certain it was this boy's sister.

He tried and failed a few more times to write the eulogy, each draft more cynical and lazy than the last. Even Rainbow began to grow tired of his nihilism, and she struggled to sit upright and stretch, yawn, show her little teeth and her long tongue. She never got the hang of sleeping eighteen hours a day.

"I'm sorry, Rainbow. I'll figure it out. I have actual homework to do, anyway," he told her, running a hand down her soft back. "I'll check on you later, okay?" She purred then, bidding him goodbye with a forceful rub of her neck on his wrist.

She heard the screen door open and close, and then she stood up, stumbling just a little from having been laying down so long, and losing a little blood. Her tail, she decided, would be just fine as long as she didn't try to get hit by a car again. She ignored the regret. Stifled the sheepish feeling she had, pushed it down into her soft belly until it was buried like her last container. Dying the first time around had been so hard. She knew she was stupid for trying to do it again.

She snuck out of the shed, looking around the yard to make sure no one would see her, that no other, bigger animal would notice her weakened state and try to attack. It felt familiar, like being a little girl, to have to be so careful. Once she was out of the yard, she headed north, toward her old shrine, knowing that at this time of evening the strays would be prowling for food. People coming home from work would sometimes drop the meat from their sandwiches, and the stampede, the competition, would begin. She would look for the loser. Someone who had not been a cat for long enough to know how to get what they need. Someone timid and small.

Amidst the fray, beyond the whirlwind of cats clambering for discarded cold cuts, there was a singular kitten, sitting patiently in front of the shrine. Skinny, hungry, with matted fur, eyes dilated and focused on the rain-soaked portrait. She thought then that maybe she had an instinct unlike any other animal, looking at the wayward kitten, approaching it under the cover of the hungry mob and its desperate meowing.

She sat beside the little cat, her round haunches looking so plump in comparison. At least, she thought, her injured tail would be a comfort to this young vagabond. Rainbow made a low sound, the kind of warbling that precedes a fervent dash across the street, and the other cat turned to her, its massive pupils shrinking, its tail fluffing up as if someone had rubbed a balloon on it.

It had not been so painful in a long time, not being able to speak or ask questions. She was finally face to face with someone, maybe, that knew what it was like to be dead. Had she died painfully? Had she been suffocated in her sleep? The man that did it, because she decided it had to be a man, did she know him? Her fur was reddish-brown, like her brother's hair. Her eyes were a tired green and her claws were caked with dirt in large clumps. Just like a corpse pulled out of the brush, she was so unpretty.

This was their chance to be pretty again, like before they died. Maybe it was *why* they died. Men are much kinder to cats than they are to little girls, she'd found. Rainbow lifted a paw and settled it on the kitten's pointed shoulder blades, kneading her toes into the soft space between them. Even against the wild feasting behind them, she could hear the involuntary purring.

There they stayed for the evening, hungry, but not bothering with the scraps left behind by their more simple brothers and sisters. A new, unloving family that would never eulogize them when they died, even if they had the words. They would rot away like any other container, cycling back into the dirt to become something stupid.

Something brainless like a flower. Pretty and without any consequences. She could grow for one season only and no one would say that her life had gotten cut short. She could be useful for once, a haven for bees and a gift for young lovers. She could be laid upon her own grave and left to wither, dried within the pages of a book, ground down to a fine powder for paints and perfumes. No one would look at her and be overcome with a primal urge to snap her stem. A sprig of lilac, delicate as a little girl and poisonous for cats, she would be too dumb to know that her life had become so much better than the last time around.

Rejoice! She read it and reread it, wondering if the little girl cat beside her had learned how to do that before she died. Rejoice! Syllables her lipless mouth was incapable of making. Rejoice! A feeling in the heart that she had not gotten since she was naïve enough to let it happen. Rejoice! She'd found the pizza boy's sister, and she would soon die of famine and mange, unless Rainbow did something about it.

A car drove by. The passenger threw a half-eaten piece of fried dough from the window, and the powdery sugar cast a splatter over the both of them. With one maternal paw, Rainbow nudged the dough over toward the kitten, bidding her to eat, to survive, even though she knew it would seem like the most foolish thing to do. To go on living, smaller, but far less helpless than you were before.

Side by side, tails swaying together and apart, they walked back to the shed. The kid was still inside the house, loud music seeping out from his open bedroom window, and the kitten looked up at the source, her mouth open to try and talk. Rainbow wished she could tell her that it would become easier. Eventually, she would see the benefit of never having to talk ever again. In the shed, they awaited his return. The kitten sat on the top of a high stack of boxes, claws digging into the cardboard, still unused to feeling safe in hard-to-reach places.

The last time Rainbow had climbed up very high, it had been during an ill-fated game of hide-and-seek. She had avoided it ever since. But, instincts tuned, she saw a clear path up to the top, an easy series of jumps to get her closer to heaven.

Letters from Bahati
By Tyler Nelson

Beyond the cracked sidewalk, and the telephone pole with layers of flyers in a rainbow of colors, and the patch of dry brown grass there stood a ten-foot-high concrete block wall, caked with dozens of coats of paint. There was a small shrine at the foot of it, with burnt-out candles and dead flowers and a few soggy teddy bears. One word of graffiti filled the wall, red letters on a gold background: Rejoice!

Firelight danced across the paint making it look like blood. The sun was setting and shadows crawled across the village. Three men rested around a small fire near the base of the wall. One of them smoked a pipe, an early star in the twilight, while another with a long scar across his forearm searched his bag for food. The third wrote a letter.

"Who you writing to?" asked the man holding the pipe. The letter writer's eyes flicked up and back down, flashing white in the night. "My brother." "He get dragged off to the rebels with the other schoolboys?" The man stopped writing and looked up again. "No Jaafan, nobody dragged him anywhere. The church got him out. He is in Europe." He started to write again.

The man with the scar snorted. "He's going to get lost. That place is too big, too big." "Oh come on Salim, I hear it's not so bad," said Jaafan, "Maybe he gonna find himself a nice little French girl, what you think?" Salim shifted his feet. "Maybe. Maybe we all go to Europe someday."

The third man finished the letter, folded it up, then slipped it into a pocket in his shirt. "Europe is not home," he said. Salim nodded, but Jaafan shook his head. "I don't know what home is no more. This place used to be my home! Now it's empty." The man with the letter stared into the fire. "The war will end soon. Then, this will be home again."

The embers in the shallow pit glowed softly. Burning ashes rose into the air and drifted towards the wall. The three men watched them as they floated. Just before they reached the wall their light would winked out. The candles sat, lifeless. The toy bears rested where they were thrown, abandoned in haste. The word rejoice hung on the wall like a sentenced man.

Jaafan shifted onto his knees and knocked the ash from his pipe into the fire. "We need to sleep. They want us back early tomorrow." Salim put down the bag and wrung his hands. "Akono isn't going to be happy we didn't find anything." Jaafan stood and threw his hands in the air. "Nothing to find anymore! No food, no fuel, no nothing! He gonna deal with it." Salim looked down at the fire. "We're going to deal with it."

"Let's go to sleep," said the man with the letter. The men pulled thin blankets from their packs and rolled over, backs to the dying fire. The man with the letter looked again at the wall and sighed. Jaafan rolled over. "Bahati, go to sleep. We got lots of walking to do tomorrow," Bahati reached into his shirt to touch the letter. He pulled his blanket tight around himself and drifted off to sleep with his rifle cradled in his arms.

I stand across the street from a tall concrete wall covered in bright paints. All around me are shadows from ravaged buildings that loom over my head. "Yamal." My brother's voice echoes around me. "Yamal." I cannot see him. I look back at the wall. At eye level, the word rejoice is painted in scarlet paint and outlined in gold. The letters draw me towards them. I cross the street to stand on the sidewalk. Near the base of the wall is a small fire pit full of cold ashes. I hear boots striking the pavement behind me. "Yamal." I turn and there stands my brother. He smiles sadly and nods at the word. "Rejoice," he says, and I wake up.

It's early morning. Light has begun to chase the night away. My heart hammers in my chest, and my thoughts race behind my eyes. I lie still and breathe deeply, shutting out the world as I close my eyes. Every morning since the arrival of the letter five months ago I wake up early. Early and afraid. I open my eyes and look at the small table beside my bed. In the faint light, I can see the letter lying there.

"My dear Yamal, the war has begun. I have been conscripted, and I thank God in his grace that I am alive. I have not seen Mother or Father for months. Maybe they have been liberated from this mess like you. Our village is no more than ruins now. Everywhere the rebels fight and everywhere we fight back. President Ade has gone into hiding to protect himself from the rebels and their supporters. Some people here treat the rebels like forerunners for God, but if God has a hand in this then I never knew Him after all. Still, I ask that you pray for us Yamal, pray for us all. I am giving this letter to the church, and I hope that it will find you. Your brother, Bahati."

It has been two years since I have seen my family. Two years since I was taken by my brother to the church and they put me into the trunk of a car. We drove many miles across many borders, through Niger and Libya to the coast. Then I was put on a rubber boat that was too small. The boat was tossed by the waves and nearly sank many times, but we arrived at last to the shores of Europe. I know of many others who did not make it.

I don't know if I will ever have a home now. It has been so long since I have had a one, or someone to share it with. In my dreams, I see what used to be my home crumbling to ashes. Family and friends are gone. I see a world that is falling apart, a crumbling country, a home turned into a warring hell. What frightens me the most is that I see my brother in the middle of it.

I look away from the letter and towards the tent above me. The morning light has grown stronger and shines through the fabric. My breathing is normal now and my heart is steady. The fear of the dream has come out of me, out through my breath and into the air.

All around me I hear people are stirring. Down and across the row, on and on throughout the camp, fathers and mothers and children rise. Tent doors flap open as they leave their little shelters and their feet shuffle across the cold earth. It is time to work. Time to report to the bakeries and factories and sanitation buildings. It is time for me to go to work too. I pull on my clothes, my socks, and my boots, and with a sigh walk towards the tent where they feed us.

Breakfast is a small affair. Some beans and rice from dinner last night. I eat quickly and leave. As I leave the compound a dog approaches me from its resting place by the gate. She is gray, medium-sized and lean. Small scars crisscross her back from scuffles over scraps. No one would be able to tell what breed she is. I feed her a few beans from my breakfast. I have named her Rainbow because she is faithful and her affection gives me hope each day. "Come on," I say to her, "we have a lot to do today."

We make the same trip each day, away from the camp and into the city, zigging and zagging past concrete apartments and stone museums. A manager at the camp has got me a job as a garbage boy at a cafe near the city center. Rainbow happily weaves behind me, chasing birds and the quick rays of morning light. But as we near a busy street corner, something across the street catches her attention.

She dashes into the street after it.

"Rainbow!" I yell out. But it is too late. The early morning traffic surges. Drivers angrily rend the air with their horns. Cars swerve and metal crunches. Rainbow yelps in pain as she is thrown across the road. She rises and in the confusion and bolts. I chase after her but quickly lose sight of her in the mess.

Rainbow ran. She ran from the red-hot anger, the sharp shouts, and the pain like thorns. But the pain followed. She ran until it crawled up her leg and into her body and she could run no more. In the deep shadows of a back alley, behind a large dumpster that smelled of spoiled meats and waste, she collapsed. In her aching and fitful rest she did not hear the soft footsteps of the young boy, nor feel his hands that gently lifted her into a bicycle basket that was soft and had the scent of fresh bread and tomato paste. The boy set off, and the smooth motion of the bicycle relaxed her.

When the ride ended, she was lifted again. The kid slid her body onto a soft pile of clothing among the boxes in the garage. He pulled an old coat over the top, creating a cave that emanated the sweetness of old ladies who frequently powdered themselves—a light rose motif that played ironically well in the deep recesses of Rainbow's ancestral brain. The pizza kid lifted her head to help her lap water from a hubcap. He broke bits of pepperoni and crust into bite-sized pieces and left them where her tongue could reach them. Much later, she heard him practicing his orations like songs. Like monks chanting in the distance, they were a comfort.

She slept well until the boy returned again to feed her. He smelled of bread and sausage, a spicy and tasteful aroma that woke her. He fed her more pits of pizza, laying them in front of her, then helped her to drink from the hubcap again. She lapped slowly at the water, tasting the bitter rust and enjoying the warmth on her tongue. The boy reached out to touch her injured leg. She snarled and snapped weakly at him. He jerked his hand back and frowned. He walked back to his bicycle and rode off, the click of gears fading into the distance.

I like to think while I ride. I feel that I am a blessed person. When my family arrived here and I was born they named me Akachi because they knew that God had helped them to escape. I have lived in a stable country my whole life. I have never had to face the open seas in a tiny boat or been held at gunpoint on a dangerous border. My father, my mother, and my uncles made it safely here, and now with their skills they cook and clean and fix to survive. But this is not their home.

The sadness of what they have left behind can be seen in the lines of my mother's face, in the scars of my father's hands, and in the silence that lays itself so heavily on my family when we speak of the past. My father was a pastor and my mother led a beautiful choir. Now we sing and recite our prayers before dinner, chanting out the Gospels and the hymns of our country, but really they have so little time for music or religion. My family lives in a peaceful place, but they are not at peace.

Hard work helps to shake off the silence. We all do our part. After fourteen years of working and saving, buying only necessities, learning the language, and learning how to do business, my mother and father had enough money and courage to open a cafe. I work delivering the little pies and pizzas that my mother makes.

Today the city is beautiful and quiet in the early morning light. But that will not last long. The sun is rising quickly and with it the people. I descend from our little apartment above the courtyard to my bicycle where it stands inside the gate. I mount and begin my journey to the cafe.

I ride quickly down side streets and alleys. The path has long since been set in my memory. But today something new happens. As I turn down an alley I hear a whine echo across the walls. I stop my bike. I see small spots of red on the ground, and when I lean down to look at them, I see that it is blood. I follow the trail with my eyes. It leads to a large dumpster in the shadows. I lean the bike against the alley wall and walk slowly towards the dumpster. The whine has turned to a whimper.

I stop at the corner of the dumpster and look around. There is a dog curled up where the dumpster meets the wall. It is a common street dog, not very big, but not so small it cannot survive. One of its legs lays askew at a painful angle. It is the source of the blood. I step closer. The dog takes no notice of me. It continues to whimper and breathe fitfully.

I take another step closer. Still, the dog does not respond. Its eyes are tightly shut. I reach out and place my hand on its head. The whimper stops. I hesitate for a moment and then reach down and gently lift the dog into my arms. I return to my bike and place it into the basket. I mount the bike and ride back home.

When I arrive I park the bike and lift the dog gently from the basket. I carry her to the back of the courtyard where my father has rented a small shed for our old things. I place her into a box of my mother's clothes and then pull an old coat over the top.

I dash up to our apartment to get a box of small pizzas and croissants. I bring it back down to the shed and break pizzas into pieces. As she eats them I frown at the leg. When I try to touch it she snaps at me. She lays down her head and sleeps again. I leave the rest of the pizza in the box and move the hubcap closer. I look up at the sun, and realize that I will be late. I run back to my bike and ride away.

The small room sat dusty and dark. A small cot stood in one corner, near the window. Bottles lay scattered across the floor. The door swung open and crashed against the wall. Bahati staggered to the cot and sat. He picked up a bottle and twisted the lid off. After a long pull, he took a sheet of paper from under the cot and began to write. Tears fell from his face and onto the page.

It has been three days since Rainbow was struck and fled. I searched until I had to go to work. After work, I went out to search again but I could not find her. The next day was the same, but when I returned to the camp I found a letter waiting for me. A new group of refugees had arrived. One of them said that a soldier had arrived at the church as they were leaving. He gave him my name and asked him to please deliver the letter. "God must smile on you son." The man smiled and patted me on the back. I thanked him and went to my tent to read the letter.

"Yamal, I am drowned in sorrow. Another village has been burned to the ground. The rebels descended and destroyed everything. We have found no one alive. Oh Yamal, Shani lived in that village! I had hoped to marry her when this war ends, but now my soul is empty. The rebels attack and we defend. But it is not enough. Is there anything worth defending now? My only hope lies in you brother. To see you, to hear your voice. I still pray that you are well and that I will see you again. Bahati."

My heart races again. Even deep in sorrow, my brother is still alive. My hope is still alive. I sit in my tent and read the letter again and again. The words make my heart heavy, but also strengthen me enough to bear it. My tears fall to the smears already present on the letter. Thousands of miles apart, our tears and sadness mix.

The next morning I rise early to search for Rainbow, but with no luck. With my eyes down I walk to work. Besides my impatience to return to my search, it is a usual day. I sweep and mop the floor before the cafe opens. I clean trash bins and carry empty boxes to the dumpster. The family that owns the cafe keeps busy. The mother kneading the dough, the father working the register. The boy Akachi, who is my age, dashes in and out with deliveries. We have not spoken to each other much. He is always busy running his errands while I clean.

But in the afternoon as I carry a bag to the dumpster he runs through the door and stops me. "What do you have there?" he asks. I examine the bag. "Old meat and bad bread I think." "Give me the bag please." "What?" "May I have it?" I look at the bag. "But why?" He looks back towards the cafe as if expecting someone to come out.

"I just need the food." "For what?" I am not sure why I won't just give it to him. He looks back at the cafe again. "Listen, if I tell you, you won't tell anyone else?" I shrug. "Yes, fine." "I have found a dog, and I need more food to give it." "A dog?" "Yes, a dog." "What kind of dog?" Akachi shrugs now. "I don't know, a street dog. It has a hurt leg and I am trying to help it." I am stunned. "Is it a gray dog, with scars on its back? I know this dog!" Akachi is stunned too. "You know this dog? Are you sure?" "Yes she is my friend, can you show me where she is?" Another glance at the cafe. "Yes, I guess so. Wait for me here when you finish tonight."

It is almost evening when I take my last load of garbage to the dumpsters. I wait for half an hour before I hear bicycle gears clicking in the distance. Akachi rides up and jumps from the bicycle. "Are you ready? Let's go." We set off through the city into the dusk. We wind and twist through streets and alleys that are unfamiliar to me, but Akachi never hesitates.

He asks me questions as we walk. "How long have you been here?" "Two years," I say. "Do you live in the camp?" "Yes." How is it that you work for my family?" "Someone at the camp knows your father." "Oh, that makes sense. My father knows a lot of people. He is very kind. How do you know this dog?" "She is my friend. She would wait outside the camp and we would walk together." "Oh. How did she get hurt?" "She was struck by a car."

Akachi laughs. "She is tough! I have seen the scars on her back, and when I tried to bandage her leg she almost bit me!" I nod. "I named her Rainbow because every day I would wake up and she would be waiting for me. She is my hope. She is my only friend." Akachi nods slowly. "What is your name? All this time you have worked in the cafe and I have never asked." I look at him. "My name is Yamal." He nods again and is silent for a minute. "Yamal would you like to be *my* friend? Then you would have two friends!" I stop walking and he stops too. I look at his smiling face. "I think I would like that." "Good," he says and grins wider. "Then let's go find our other friend."

The air was hazy and turbulent. The moon threw shadows that quivered and the burning huts made them dance. Shouts and cries of pain in the distance gave a disjointed melody, and gunfire lent an accompaniment. Bahati and his band ran through the darkness towards the center of the village.

Gunfire flashed to their left and two soldiers crashed to the earth. Three of them returned fired into the darkness and the shooting ceased. The remaining soldiers pressed themselves to the walls of the huts and waited. When nothing more happened Bahati spoke softly. "Be on guard. We are close to the center. We must get there and give the signal! You," he said pointing at two of the men, "move around to the south and tell them to be ready. We will send the signal when we reach the square." They nodded grimly and set off.

The rest of the group crept slowly towards the center of the village, keeping close to the walls of the huts and low to the ground.

The shouting and the gunfire grew closer. Bahati motioned for a stop. Around the next corner, the village opened into a small square. It was blockaded with fences and old trucks. Glancing around the corner, the men could see flashes of gunfire across the blockade.

Bahati held out his hand and a soldier handed him a small flare. "Quietly now," he said pulling a match from his pocket, "ready yourselves." Every man in the band held his gun tightly to his chest, their fingers on the triggers.

Fwoosh! Bahati struck the match and lit the flare. It sparked to life, angry and red. He stepped out from behind the hut and threw it high in the air towards the square shouting "Forward!" The men rushed into the square, jumping barriers, and everything collapsed into chaos. Bahati raised his gun and began to shoot. Bullets filled the night, claiming lives for their own. At the sight of the flare, other groups poured in from all directions against the rebels.

The surprise attack did not last long. The rebels, outnumbered and fighting what seemed to be demons from the dark, gave up and fled into the night. The men fired after them taunting their cowardice. In the settling dust, they searched the village, finding food stores and weapons. Bahati released his breath and leaned against a truck. He was tired and afraid, but unhurt. He reached to his chest, felt his heart racing, and then felt the letter that lay in his pocket.

There she lay, resting peacefully. Akachi has bandaged her leg and made her a soft bed. For all her vulnerability now, I know that she is still tough, and will be fine in time. "It took a long time before she would trust me," Akachi says, "but now we are friends. Can I keep her here until she is better?" "I think that would be best." "Good. I am going to get her some more things to eat."

When he runs off towards the apartment buildings, I bend down and gently rub Rainbow's head. She hums softly in her sleep. At this moment, I feel a sense of peace. I have found hope again, and it has multiplied. Akachi returns with sausage. "She likes these." For the first time in a long time, I smile. We place the sausage near Rainbow's head and she wakes and snaps it up. She hums happily as we feed her sausage and let her lick our fingers clean. When she finishes eating, she lays her head down and sleeps.

The third letter crossed borders, sailed seas, and changed hands, carried on the power of the prayer of an older brother. It arrived, dirty and smudged but intact, from the hands of a weary mother into the hands of a hopeful young boy.

"Dear Yamal, I sit on the edge of a battlefield to write to you. Men shout for victory around me, but the only victory I see is that I live another day. Or is it a victory? No, I must believe it is so. Because I must believe that I will see you again someday. God will smile on us again. I am tired in my head and in my heart. It is a heart that is heavy. I wish to remind you of the poem that hung on the wall in what used to be our home. The song that Mother would sing so often. *Should love be the world's lone weapon, then man could wage no war, not for a dearth of knowledge, but lack of arms therefore. And should we give love a voice, then shall all the land rejoice.* I hope that one day we shall rejoice together Yamal. Your brother, Bahati."

Time's Up
By Kate Osment

Beyond the cracked sidewalk, and the telephone pole with layers of flyers in a rainbow of colors, and the patch of dry brown grass there stood a ten-foot high concrete block wall, caked with dozens of coats of paint. There was a small shrine at the foot of it, with burnt out candles and dead flowers and a few soggy teddy bears. One word of graffiti filled the wall, red letters on a gold background: Rejoice!

The screen faded to black, and Em Castle jabbed at the mouse to eject the DVD from her laptop before the end credits could play. Gracie was one hell of a set designer, you had to give the woman that.

The news had hit headlines that morning that a suitable candidate to chair the inquiry had eventually been found. Months of ministerial dithering had led to fresh accusations of an establishment cover-up, and *The Sentinel*'s editorial was implying that it remained to be seen whether they were entirely unfounded.

Em had been forced to quickly turn the page on the photograph of Baroness Mills. It showed a thin-lipped old woman in pince-nez and a pearl necklace, whose clear, steady gaze was apparent even in newsprint and who had a reputation "of meticulous attention to detail".

It was considered impolitic to say it now, of course, but they'd won awards for *Rejoice*. The top brass at National Telly hadn't been bloody well complaining then. If you asked Gracie for a gritty, urban, apocalyptic backdrop with a vaguely Catholic ostentatiousness, you'd get one with enough edge to cut the critics and public.

Gracie was capable of so much more than pissing about in Wales with things like backdrops for stage productions of *Swedish Folk Tales: Queered*. She'd just been underachieving lately, Em had told the suits to get them to hire her for the *Rejoice* set, and hadn't she been right?

Calling it nepotism, like that up-himself MP on the select committee had, was ridiculous. Em lit a Rothmans and hauled herself out of her desk chair to get a large whiskey, because remembering the committee's questioning was making her need one.

It had been a hellish experience, and entirely the fault of her agent (Well, him and bloody Gracie.). Jonesy had twisted Em's arm to get her there, saying staying away would look bad. She was pretty sure that going had turned out to look worse.

The truth was fine, Jonesy had told her. Just stay away from the whole and nothing but. Alright for him to say. It had barely worked in Parliament and the thought of trying it out in front of that wrinkled old tortoise Mills was not a pleasant one.

'It'll be a piece of piss, Em! All it is, right, is political posturing by MPs who need to show how tough on crime' (he rolled his eyes) 'they are, 'specially crime that affects voters' kiddies. Just don't fucking well swear at them.'

Em, who thought of optimism as something like delusion, hadn't been so sure. Five years ago, Gracie had been optimistic that her actions wouldn't have consequences, which had created an almighty sodding mess where thinking about *Rejoice* made them all do anything but.

Well, the next time Gracie wanted a job, or the execs at the NTS wanted talent to compete for the Order of the Brown Nose at

Westminster, they could come to some other mug. They needed Em more than she needed them.

'You were very keen on Grace Rafferty being the one to design the *Rejoice* set, weren't you, Ms. Castle? You demanded, in fact, that the National Television Service hire her.' Em had been irritated from the first mention of the series' title.

'I wouldn't say demanded.' 'Wouldn't you?' George Davies MP had sarcastically countered. 'Other witnesses involved in the production of the show would.' Em wanted to kill Jonesy for making her do this. 'It was just a recommendation of someone I knew was talented.'

'Yes,' interjected Rachel Field MP, 'in fact you've known Rafferty intimately for thirty years, isn't that correct?' 'What the fuck is this, guilt by association?' Em had snarled, forgetting Jonesy's orders not to swear. Flashbulbs popped, tabloid headline writers suppressed squeals of delight, and the committee chair had disapprovingly shifted his huge bulk and instructed Em to please not take that tone with them.

Field leaned forward, eyes glittering. 'Do you seriously expect us to believe that you were unaware of her proclivities when you got her the *Rejoice* job?' Em had suddenly felt very tired, old, and aware she came across as having all the charm of Jimmy Savile's tracksuit, and the same purpose of covering up an abuser: someone she despised.

Em Castle and Gracie Rafferty had always come across as an unlikely pair: the stick-thin, black-clad, chain smoking writer who held that children should ideally be neither seen nor heard, and the flamboyant blue-haired big-bosomed artist who couldn't get enough of the little buggers, thought even their screeching on public transport was cute.

Em had been known, after snorting Bolivia's GDP at dinner parties she found more than usually tedious, to declare that she hoped her lifestyle had damaged her ovaries permanently; Gracie had been determined even as a teenager that being a lesbian wasn't going to stop her becoming a mother about six times over.

In the days of her success, critics had said Gracie's designs created a space in which the innocence and beauty of childhood could flourish onscreen or some such bollocks. They'd gone crazy at the time over an episode of *Rejoice* which, if Em recalled, began with something like this:

When the ride ended, she was lifted again. The kid slid her body onto a soft pile of clothing among the boxes in the garage. He pulled an old coat over the top, creating a cave that emanated the sweetness of old ladies who frequently powdered themselves—a light rose motif that played ironically well in the deep recesses of Rainbow's ancestral brain. The pizza kid lifted her head to help her lap water from a hubcap. He broke bits of pepperoni and crust into bite-sized pieces and left them where her tongue could reach them. Much later, she heard him practicing his orations like songs. Like monks chanting in the distance, they were a comfort.

Gracie hadn't become a mother. Never found the right woman. Maybe that should've told Em something, thinking back. But she'd still made a rather grating point of saying she wanted kids in every interview she'd ever given, which was probably why, Em had said to her five years ago, she hadn't been asked for one in quite a while.

As that cow Field had delighted in pointing out, they'd been best mates for thirty years, so she wished that had really been the reason. But the magazine editors and radio producers of this world let you spout all the bullshit you wanted, of course, if you'd designed a set for anything that mattered in the last decade.

Well, call her a bloody nepotist, but friendship counted for something. She'd wanted to read those annoying interviews again, and as a scriptwriter with considerable clout at the NTS, she'd used it to make sure Gracie got the *Rejoice* gig.

It was no wonder, to be honest, that those anonymous 'other witnesses involved in the production of the show' had gone squealing to the select committee about the hiring process. The cowardly bastards were allergic to straight talking, and Em had given them some.

'Thing is, I don't actually give a damn that you've already promised it to some hipster still waiting for his balls to drop. Sack him and hire Gracie Rafferty or I walk. You'll have precious fucking little to rejoice over without any chance of a decent script.'

And yes, maybe she should have thought harder about the fact that several of the actors would be young teenage girls. Em couldn't pretend it hadn't crossed her mind. But hell's teeth, Gracie had been in danger of having her house repossessed.

She'd shown up on Em's doorstep one soggy, freezing London night five years ago after a characteristic several-month drop off the radar, considerably the worse for wear, which put Em in the unusual position of being the more sober of the two.

It had turned out that the bloody little Welsh thing had folded, which didn't surprise Em. What did surprise her was that Gracie had apparently been stupid enough to invest her own money in it—well, not hers, a payday loan company's.

The woman had a list of negative assets as long as your arm, including her home, which by chance was the subject of a phone call from some bailiffs that very night. Seemed Gracie had forgotten to make mortgage payments for she wasn't sure exactly how long, Em, ok?

'I have no idea what I'm going to do', Gracie had sobbed. 'They all want their fucking money and I can't pay them. I'm not earning anything!' So Em, recently hired to write the script of the NTS' new baby, *Rejoice*, had called the production team.

They'd celebrated that night, downing whiskey after whiskey 'to Gracie finally becoming a gainfully-employed, responsible adult'. Give Em credit where it was due, as come the small hours she remembered drunkenly raising it: 'No bloody funny business this time, alright?'

She'd done her best, nobody could say she hadn't. Did they think it was pleasant, having to bring that up while you were meant to be celebrating a friend's new job? But Em had seen it as her unfortunate duty to face the issue.

'I mean it, Gracie. I just saved your arse, promise me I won't regret it. You were very fucking lucky that that little bimbo's parents- oh, I'm sorry (Gracie had interrupted angrily), you don't like me calling her that? Would 'child' be better?'

'Yes mate she was a bloody child, she was fourteen! It was disgusting and you know what, if you weren't my best friend I'd have gone to the pigs myself! I'm still amazed nobody did. And the rumors haven't gone away.'

The rumors Em referred to were no small factor in Gracie's extended period of unemployment before *Rejoice*, and some (although by no means all) concerned a regrettable incident supposed to have taken place a year earlier at an industry schmooze thrown for *Prediction*.

Em's script for that film had won an award ('I'll have to tell the showbiz editors to start calling you "Emmy" Castle!' cackled Jonesy), and she'd brought Gracie to the do partly so the latter could network, but mainly, she had to admit, to show off.

Em and Jonesy had occupied themselves with caning the free bar for all it was worth, and at some point mislaid Gracie (and Jonesy's then-wife). So the first Em heard of it was when Gracie phoned the next morning. Was she her friend's keeper?

'I hope this is important,' Em had moaned. 'I was asleep.' 'More like passed out, you old soak,' Gracie chuckled. 'I just wanted to say thanks for dragging me along last night. I met this girl, Em, she's fantastic—I'm definitely over Daphne now!'

Gracie, apparently, had spent all night in bed but not been to sleep yet. It was her wont to overshare, and before she could impart too much information, Em interrupted. 'Alright, Casanova, I get the picture. What's she like then?'

To think she'd been glad Gracie had met someone new! And that she'd believed she'd turned a corner, was going to cut all that out! Some hope. The new squeeze, it transpired, was thinking about doing art at GCSE. Em thought at first that she'd misheard.

'What?' Gracie had repeated it. Em's hangover had suddenly seemed a lot worse. 'Please tell me she's one of those mature students retaking exams they were too thick to pass first time around?' 'What?' said Gracie, confused. 'No...' Em, needing comfort, scrabbled for a cigarette.

'Did you mean A levels?' Gracie hadn't. Em half-hoped this was all a bad dream, but if so the nightmare was recurring. She bit the bullet. 'How old is she, Gracie?' Fourteen. That was how old. And Gracie had said it so casually!

There were many things about the British media industry that Em liked, such as the fact that it paid her silly money for what she didn't even think was real work, but the way it treated underage girls wasn't one of them.

If you wanted to sleep at night, there was stuff you had to ignore. Turned out the girl Gracie had met had been at the *Prediction* party because the event DJ had picked up her (and her similar-aged friends) in a nightclub and brought them along.

According to Gracie, she was very mature for her age. Everything had been entirely consensual, no-one was going to report it to the police, and why was Em so angry? 'You're not usually worried about laws—cocaine's illegal!' Em had gone ballistic.

'What exactly is too fucking young for you, Gracie? It's not—it doesn't - you can't just call the legal age of consent 'arbitrary'! If it is, where do you draw the line? Clearly not at fourteen, so where then? Thirteen? Twelve? Eleven?'

She'd eventually managed to persuade Gracie not to see the girl again, pointing out that it was illegal, immoral, and disgusted her, Em, personally. How many people bothered to do that? Most of them just bloody whispered about it and looked the other way!

It was just unfair to say she didn't care about the problem. If that was true, why had she tried so hard to stop Gracie, Em would've liked to know. And it wasn't like she was the only one who'd been aware.

Em stubbed out another Rothmans in the overflowing ashtray. Was it her fault that Gracie had been up to her old tricks on the set of *Rejoice*? And if the girl concerned really felt so bloody abused, why the hell had she taken so long to pipe up?

The bosses at the NTS were now claiming that what they'd watched go on for decades had been rare and was appalling news to them, but parties like the *Prediction* one, where it was best not to ask about the age of the groupies, hadn't been unusual. Neither had the situation at *Rejoice*, where unsupervised children—yes, Em thought, that was what they were - had been left to 'hang out' with Gracie (and others). This was what was rare: society giving a fuck.

The Trans-Europa
By Henry Silvia

Beyond the cracked sidewalk, and the telephone pole with layers of flyers in a rainbow of colors, and the patch of dry brown grass there stood a ten-foot-high concrete block wall, caked with dozens of coats of paint. There was a small shrine at the foot of it, with burnt-out candles and dead flowers and a few soggy teddy bears. One word of graffiti filled the wall, red letters on a gold background: Rejoice!

***

I requested a pause and soaked in the details. What did I overlook last time through? Bears, candles, dead grass. Dead, just like her. Like Rainbow. Are these clues? Exactly how meta was this game? Am I mistaking thematic elements for clues? I need to be better at this.

I fixated on the word *Rejoice*. The color palette of this whole scene was at odds with itself. Golden tones and somber browns of death clashed with bombastic, overly saturated hues of pop. Soda pop, pop music, other Indy-pop games from this publisher. Were they placed there as a red herring, or were they meant to be hints for my next move? There's a fine line between examination of minutiae and diluting one's focus. I must get better at this.

A previously ignored message, serving only as a distraction, had become a nagging, flashing box, center-stage in my field of view. 'LUCAS. DINNER. NOW.' There could be no misinterpretation of this hint. The rest of this game will have to wait. I logged off the server and toggled augmented reality mode on my audio-visual implants.

The real world of today was so different from the old one in-game. Different in more ways than most care to admit. We're often made to feel nostalgia is the worst kind of addiction. I tell myself it couldn't be, what harm could come from seeing our world as it once was? I ask, but I already have my answer. I heard it every night at dinner from my parents and, until recently, my older sister. *You spend too much time in those AR fantasy worlds. How will you ever be a productive citizen with your head in the cloud?* Everything is in the cloud, why not my head? Besides, I *do* have a plan, they just couldn't hear it.

Two mag-lev rides and an express elevator and I was back at our living quarters. I'd call it home, if that word felt appropriate. If there was a chance in Hell, I'd be in my own place, but the waitlist for housing-relocation is longer than a weekend on Venus. A quick retina scan let me in. I stowed my gear in a cubby by the door and kicked off my shoes. The news played quietly on the vid-screen in the living room, something about rebuilding the Musk Spaceport. I toggled AR mode again and slithered to the table.

Dinner started without me, as always. Being late wasn't something I tried to do, but then, I suppose being on-time wasn't either. "Sorry I'm late." I meant it, though it's doubtful they could have believed me after how many times I've had to say it. My father cocked an eyebrow and made sure I saw him look at me and then to my empty seat. Mom never lifted her eyes from her plate. They don't know how else to treat me, other than like a disappointment, like an *addict*. This world has grown so clean, so soft but yet so...rigid. It's hard for me to come out of a twenty-first century world and be anything but disappointed with this twenty-third century one they wanted me to live in.

"You missed Devra's call." Mom took an angry bite of cheesy broccoli casserole, swallowed hard and reached for her glass of water. Even when she did manage to speak to me, at me, she never made eye contact. Tonight, she fixated on her meal. A lot of effort goes into ignoring your son completely. She was adept, but failed at it, on occasion. I suppose chastising me counted as communication.

My sister Devra had been away at university for almost a year. I imagine her time as a psychology major was better spent learning from less typical sources than her own dysfunctional family. Last time we spoke she actually encouraged me to stick with my AR gaming, to focus on the case-studies I had been exploring. She saw merit in my efforts, even if our parents wouldn't.

Society's grown so soft that crime-solving passes for entertainment these days. It's as much a fantasy game for the niche market that plays, as dragon slaying was for the kids of the twenty-first. The publisher of the AR games I play uses historical case data and builds a true-to-life narrative for players. The only way to win is to actually solve a crime based on real evidence just like real detectives did back then. I'm spending most of my free time playing through these games to sharpen my deduction and observation skills. I need to become an expert, all the while knowing today's world is virtually crime free. Technology has made it pretty hard to get away with anything, but that same technology has created a system so soft, so out of practice they couldn't find a whore in a brothel. My father was a part of that system and couldn't see the point. *You might as well be a typewriter salesman*, he would say. I'd always wanted a career in criminology. What would he say of my focus now, I wonder?

"I'm sorry I missed her call, how are things going out there?" I asked, looking first at my visually non-committal mother, then to my visibly disinterested father. It was like this every night, a straight-up throw-down. An uneven tag-team brawl between our two sides, them versus me. I'm not sure which was worse, being their target, or the fact they weren't aware I always was.

"She's coming home on a shuttle this weekend." Dad tapped in and spared Mom any effort in prying herself away from her beloved casserole. "Honestly, Lucas, we told her how much time you're spending in AR and she seems genuinely concerned about it. About you. It's a very long ride from Europa, so I fully expect you to make time to spend with her while she's here." With his breath, he fogged his glasses as he spoke. So opposed to the cybernetic enhancement that provided me with AR, he'd rather wear an appliance on his face than risk letting the benefits change his stubborn mind. He wiped the horn-rimmed bifocals with his napkin and put them back on his face.

Devra coming all the way from Uni just to preach AR abstinence at me is a complete farce. I have no doubt the truth is closer to this; Mom and Dad bombarded Devra with their abject ignorance for several hours and she leveraged their concerns for a free ticket home. She really was brilliant. It would be nice to see her again.

I choked on my words as I spoke them to my dad. "I know you want me there. At the spaceport, I mean. And, to talk to her." Then I went a little off-book, sticking to a script is a slog anyway. "You'll stand there, at the port and tap your foot anxiously. You'll check your watch every thirty seconds or so while you grind your teeth and huff in that pissed off way you do. You'll look around for your absent son. You'll lean into Mom and attempt to entrap her in your frustrations with how unreliable I am. She, in turn, will simply stare out the window, seemingly ignoring you, so as not to fuel your rage, but secretly feeling the very same way. I'll be late, and I'll miss the landing. I'll miss a lot of things." I stopped and searched his face for any sort of empathy. There was none. "I'm going to figure this out, all of this. I promise you, all of you." I could see my words meant nothing to him. He stared through me for a second then resumed eating. Mom never skipped a frame. See what I mean? Analog to our world, soft, but so rigid. I have no one to blame for this predicament but myself.

***

Once you're assigned a case in-game, you're fed information exactly as the original lead detective was. A point of difference here is that when you start to make decisions, game AI generates scenarios based on your input and plays them out in real-time for you. Hell, I could suspect the pope and AI would show me how he might have killed her. I don't have time for any sort of fantasy, though. I study only real, potential suspects, real victims and visit any augmented real locations. I'm not doing any of this for *funsies*.

Back in-game I reviewed dossiers on everyone available to me. Rainbow Curtis was born in 1990 to Chet and Doreen Curtis of Brooklyn, New York. She went missing on August 14th, 2012. One suspect was a local pizza delivery man named Carl Franke. Carl had been arrested once before in 2006 in Florida for possession of marijuana, solicitation and assaulting an undercover officer. Additionally, his prior misdemeanor charges of destruction of property stemmed from what notes described as 'misogynistic graffiti.' Photos showed rail cars tagged with the sort of words for women no one uses anymore, but the striking, and interesting part was the style. Giant red letters on a gold background, it could have just as easily said *Rejoice!*

Having completely ruined his life so early, he was left with very few opportunities to improve upon it. Carl moved back to New York City in 2009 and found work at Giuseppe's Pizzeria folding boxes and making deliveries. As the oldest employee he earned the ironic nickname "the pizza kid." Case notes indicated he didn't care for this moniker.

Sometime in 2011, Carl got religion. He expressed to his co-workers and on-again, off-again girlfriend, Becky Worley, he had embraced the 'Light of Tao.' He was often heard vocalizing mantras when performing menial tasks. His co-workers knew of his record, but never thought him much of a threat.

Letting augmented reality overlay city streets, I followed Carl, aka the pizza kid, on the day of Rainbow's disappearance. This was where AI took over based on my input and rendered a scene fitting the criminal narrative I proposed. I knew Carl left work at six in the evening, shortly before Rainbow Curtis went missing. His drive home tracked with Rainbow's. She walked every day along this same route. Historic weather data showed heavy rain all day. I told the AI to proceed assuming he stopped and offered her a ride. Assume she refused, an argument ensued and despite his more recent Taoism, he reverted to his primal self. The pizza kid assaulted Rainbow and, in a panic, placed her unconscious body in the back seat of his Volkswagen Golf. Records show he had access to his uncle's storage area, a garage about twenty blocks away, the only place he would think to take her.

When the ride ended, she was lifted again. The kid slid her body onto a soft pile of clothing among the boxes in the garage. He pulled an old coat over the top, creating a cave that emanated the sweetness of old ladies who frequently powdered themselves—a light rose motif that played ironically well in the deep recesses of Rainbow's ancestral brain. The pizza kid lifted her head to help her lap water from a hubcap. He broke bits of pepperoni and crust into bite-sized pieces and left them where her tongue could reach them. Much later, she heard him practicing his orations like songs. Like monks chanting in the distance, they were a comfort.

Of course, we can only assume what either of them thought, did or heard. I like to imagine pizza-kid-Carl reverted to his enlightened self through vocalization of his mantras. I like to imagine in those closing moments of Rainbow's life he tried just a little to ease her suffering, but the truth is, records don't show much more than a garage location and a general description of its contents. Physical evidence doesn't place either Carl or Rainbow at the scene. Doesn't mean it didn't happen, just that I can't prove it happened. Most of this is speculation, just me and the game AI filling in gaps.

This is my third time through, but the first time I picked up on the pizza kid as a prime suspect. Even though my reasons for playing the game were not about entertainment, it *is* meant as such. The game is designed to lead players away from the true perpetrator in an attempt to make gameplay last longer.

Having to start over didn't bother me. Like anything in life, failure is part of the learning process. What I glean through multiple play-throughs helps me spot false leads easier when I investigate other cases. There is a case much more relevant to me than poor Rainbow, but I owe it to my family to get that one right the first time.

I was on the verge. Evidence laid out neatly in front of me, Carl was my guy. I found myself growing angry with the pizza kid. He's probably been dead for two hundred years, but somehow the way he treated Rainbow incited me. Something in his profile caused the AI to have him giving Rainbow water from a *hubcap*.

Am I supposed to hate this guy? Was he just misdirection? Why bother, Carl? Why feed her scraps of garbage pizza? Why chant your stupid, useless mantras? Why cover her in old ladies' coats? Why were you always late? Why so much death? Who was to blame?

I caught myself. Off-topic again. One thing at a time, Lucas. I needed to hear Devra's voice again. I toggled AR mode and stepped back from the garage. A quick transitional animation played, and I was looking at a high-rise where the garage once stood. Despite these new interstitials I still got freaked out a little when switching from an AR version of a location to its current, real-world appearance. Thank

God for safety protocols, I surely would have walked off a non-existing bridge or two without them.

"Replay last incoming VM from Devra." Sure, I could have AI simulate her voice, her face and converse with her, but why torture myself? At least with voicemail I know it's really her. She had become my anchor these last few months. I wish I could say my push towards police work was for my parents, but Devra and I had gotten so close... This is for her, I know it is.

"Hey little brother, it's Dev. Obvi. I'm sorry about the last call with mom and dad, I mean, sorry I missed you. I wasn't sure of the time difference. Europa is in some weird century-long wider-than-normal orbit and time is sorta elastic here right now."

She sounded happy. At peace. Things were chaotic at home before she left. I don't blame her for wanting to go away to school, but all the way to Jupiter? Literally the farthest away from us she could possibly be. I wonder, did our parents ever made that connection? I let her message play on.

"Anyway, I know you're having a rough go with Mom and Dad. I'm sorry I had to leave you to fend for yourself. They seem overly concerned about your 'AR addiction.' I guess they're a little too old school to see its benefits for you, but I wanted you to know, I do. We use a lot of AR in psychology here."

Validation. This wasn't the first, or only time she'd said as much, but it was the most important. I never want to think of her as maturing to that stoic place Mom and Dad ended up. I get it, I guess. The world of today is so different from the twenty-first. Individual freedoms are at a premium. The whole world needs to operate efficiently or there's no way twelve billion people will survive here. Every behavior mandated, every citizen indoctrinated and no one really running the show. Autopilot. Rigid, but soft.

"Listen, I'm not sure what they told you, but the truth is I wanted to come home and see you. Well, not a hundred percent you. I do have friends, too, but...you know what I mean. Anyway, we have a break starting this weekend. Midterms were brutal and my brain needs a defrag. I *may* have let Mom and Dad think I was in their corner regarding your AR issue, but trust me, Lucas, it was just a bait-and-switch to get dad to cover the shuttle flight back home. Let's keep that nugget on the downlow, you feel me? Love ya, kiddo, see ya soonsies."

The message ended. I missed my train, standing there on platform six, engrossed in her words. Not especially stellar or encouraging, but in contrast to life as we knew before, it left me smiling, eyes drier than the last few times I played it.

When I got home, the place was dark and quiet. I toggled my AR mode and walked into the kitchen. Mom was standing at the sink scrubbing leftover casserole from a glass dish. "Hi, Mom," I whispered softly. I stood there a minute and watched her toil, but she never acknowledged my presence.

"I think I've cracked the case, Mom. I'm pretty confident I know who killed Rainbow Curtis." In return for my declaration, I received nothing. I knew she couldn't possibly care. Not then, not now. I didn't expect a response, so it wasn't any different than before.

I turned away and walked toward my bedroom. I stopped midway to look at my dad sitting on the couch, watching the news. He turned his head and with a simple glare conveyed all the disappointment he needed to. Yes, Dad, I missed dinner...again.

I spent the evening in console mode, going over my notes and the evidence I'd collected on Rainbow's killer. For the first time, I ignored obvious clues. Angry, misogynist pizza delivery man was probably some programmer's inside joke. I'm sure most noobs finger him as the killer. I know I nearly did. I'm finally getting better at this.

How had I been so bad at this? The last two times I didn't even find him as a suspect, now I can see he's too obvious. This game hinges on your intuition steering you away from Occam's Razor. Just because it's the most likely answer doesn't make it the only answer. Certainly not the *right* one.

I needed to think like a detective, weigh all options equally. If there's anything I've learned in the last year it's the importance of family and the roles, good or bad, they play in your life. These are the people closest to you and despite all appearances, they must be considered regardless of the damage it may do. Truth is far too often stranger than fiction.

Chet and Doreen Curtis were separated in 2001. When Rainbow went missing, Chet was in New Mexico working a construction job. Initially, Chet was cleared as a potential suspect, despite abuse charges on his record from when Rainbow was little.

I decided to dig a little deeper. Game AI has access to historic video data as well as all public records of the time. After hours of watching the most boring footage of men building apartment complexes, I found him. Unmistakable in his hardhat, and coveralls. A thick, dark mustache hid a tired frown and a work permit badge pinned prominently on his chest very plainly read "Chet Curtis."

The problem was, this wasn't Chet Curtis. Yeah, maybe I cheated a little. Today's facial recognition is an order of magnitude faster than what the twenty-first had. Diego Garcia was his name. He was known associate of Chet's from the nineties when they worked day-labor at a lumber yard together. Diego had no green card, no EAD and no work visa at the time. This didn't stop him from trying to provide for his family. It explains why he would need to assume Chet's identity, but not what I discovered next.

If the Chet in New Mexico was actually Diego, then where was the real Chet Curtis? Another three-hundred hours of tollbooth video and the magic of twenty-third-century facial rec proved useful.

Video evidence puts Chet in New York at the time of Rainbow's disappearance. This was the missing link, the clue I needed to push forward with Chet as a suspect. Finally, a break—a break in a two-hundred-year-old case. My excitement was fleeting.

I submitted my findings to the game AI, which led to unlocking video interviews with both Chet and Diego. When faced with the evidence, Chet broke down in the interrogation room, claiming it was all a horrible accident. He seemed sincerely distraught over what he had done. He led detectives to Rainbow's grave, a construction site he had after-hours access to. Her own father… I can't imagine what could bring someone to a place where they kill their own child. Once found out he alternated between semi-catatonic, and uncontrollable sobbing. As one weight lifted, a new one descended. I can relate.

The game was done. I won. It was bittersweet, to say the least. In my momentary excitement, I ran out to the living room to share my victory with my parents. I knew they resented the games, but I needed them to be proud of me. I needed their approval. I hoped, at that moment, beyond all reason, they would simply smile and say, 'well done, boy.' But, no. I toggled off console mode and there sat Mom and Dad watching the news.

"Tomorrow marks the one-year anniversary of the Trans-Europa shuttle disaster at New York's Musk Memorial Spaceport. Of the one-hundred-twenty-three lives lost, eight were crew, seventy were passengers. Many of them college students on break from the University of Europa. Forty-five people on the ground, including families and port workers, were caught up in the blast and wreckage of the shuttle. The port remains closed, the investigation, still ongoing."

I stood at the edge of the couch and watched as Mom and Dad stared blankly at the news playing on the screen. Unmoved, unaffected. But then, why wouldn't they be? This feed is now. They are forever locked into *then*. On location, in front of the barricaded space port, a woman continued the report.

"A year later and authorities are no closer to finding so much as a suspect in this apparent act of terrorism. Plans to rebuild are slated for later this month and the families of those lost are in outrage, left to ask *when did commerce begin to outweigh human life?* Pundits blame complacency of today's law enforcement agencies for a lack of closure, citing lax attention and disregard for classic investigatory procedures in their push for reform within the system. Some speculate that the need for change in the way we, as a society, handle crime, is precisely what precipitated this attack."

The news snapped me back to this dark reality. I stood between projected screen and my parents and told them what I've wanted to say for the past year. "Everything I do, everything I am is dedicated to finding the truth. This, this obscene gesture—keeping you here, reliving these days leading up to the end, it's all to keep me focused. I'm getting closer to figuring it all out. I'm sorry I missed the landing. I'm sorry you were angry with me. I'm sorry you must have felt Devra was only on that shuttle because of me. I'm sorry you all died, and I didn't. I'm sorry I was late."

They just sat and stared through me. Again, why wouldn't they? I haven't programmed them to extrapolate behavior for situations like this. I shut down their AR simulation and went back to my room. Back into console mode where I could add more details to my own on-going investigation. But, first, "replay last incoming VM from Devra."

A Plague of Angels
By Christian H. Smith

Beyond the cracked sidewalk, and the telephone pole with layers of flyers in a rainbow of colors, and the patch of dry brown grass there stood a ten-foot high concrete block wall, caked with dozens of coats of paint. There was a small shrine at the foot of it, with burnt out candles and dead flowers and a few soggy teddy bears. One word of graffiti filled the wall, red letters on a gold background: Rejoice!

Rainbow, defiant, refused. She saw nothing to rejoice about. Face down in the dead grass, she watched the ants creep perilously close to her wide-open eyes. She doubted she could summon the will to blink them away. Beyond and above the ants, she saw the wall with that single, taunting word. *Rejoice?* Rainbow thought. *Rejoice my ass.*

Ravens perched high in the branches of the lone pine tree in the corner of the lot. Rainbow heard them cawing, calling to one another. She'd learned enough of their language to gather that they were discussing her. Until her fall, Rainbow had flown among them. She'd even fancied herself part of their congress. (*Murder of crows*, she'd read in a book once. *Congress of ravens*.) Now, having fallen, she understood that the ravens had seen her merely an object of curiosity. An aberration. A freak.

Her wings had sprung from her sickness. They were the second stage. In the first stage of the disease, the patient's entire body was covered with red splotches that felt like tiny biting insects crawling all over the skin. The maddening itch crept inside, into the nose and ears and throat and lungs. Many people flayed off swaths of their own flesh, seeking relief. Others resorted to suicide. Rainbow had given serious consideration to both those options in the depth of her suffering.

In the next stage, infected females grew appendages from their shoulder-blades. Long, spread out digits, covered with a thin patagium of membranous flesh. Like a bat's wings. The wings were fully functional, allowing the afflicted to take flight. Only women grew wings, no one knew why. Men skipped this stage entirely and passed directly into the third, terminal stage, which was the same for everyone. Near-total paralysis, along with a delirium that mounted higher and higher until the infected individual finally expired.

The winged stage was accompanied by a euphoric bliss. Cool, blessed relief from the hellish rash, coupled with the ecstatic, soaring freedom of flight. In their joyful flying, the women sang, as birds do. Rainbow had sung old Beatles songs, *Hey Juding* for all the world to hear. For some, this stage only lasted a few hours. Rainbow, luckier than most, had been able to fly and sing for several days. There was no angel song in the air anymore, though. Rainbow wondered if she was the last one.

When the sickness had first started, and the news was full of hysterical doom-crying, Rainbow had hidden alone in her apartment. By the time she was finally forced to venture out, foraging for food, the plague had already ravaged most of the city. In a mostly looted grocery store not far from where she lived, Rainbow made a fatal error borne of compassion. She knelt to give water to a dying man. By the time she made it back home, the red sores had already appeared on her hands. If Rainbow had been one of the last to become infected, perhaps now she was among the last ones left alive.

The entire planet cleansed by a plague of angels.

Attendant to the plague had been an inevitable religious mania. The pestilence was a call for many, like the anonymous graffiti artist, to rejoice. This was the Lord's final judgement of mankind, they said. In His infinite mercy, He had sent us angels to sing us through our suffering. Rainbow wasn't so sure. She'd never been the religious sort. It didn't matter anyway. All that mattered now was the dying. The only question that remained was how best to occupy her mind until death came for her.

She was unable to move, unable to speak, barely able to draw breath, but her senses remained sharp. There was nothing to see but that cursed wall and those encroaching ants, but her hearing could range far and wide. Rainbow listened.

The ravens, bored by her paralysis and uninterested her dying, had flown away. Without their raucous conversation, her world was much quieter. She heard chirping crickets and the distant grousing of frogs. A wet, percussive thud that she gradually realized was the sound of her own pulse. After a long while listening, she heard another sound, not immediately identifiable. Far away but growing closer.

She strained to hear. There was a squeaking sound, constant and repetitive. Squee-squee-squee-squee. Rainbow thought of wheels turning, of unlubricated axles squealing in protest with every rotation. There was also a kind of rattling thud, metallic sounding. At first, she had no idea what it could be, but then the answer came to her.

A wagon. Someone was pulling a wagon. The clanging sound was the wagon rattling as it rolled over the cracks in the sidewalk. Something else, too. A voice. A boy, chanting with the boldness of a sermon or a lecture, but with the rhythm of a commercial jingle.

A little closer and Rainbow made out the words. "Hand-tossed dough," the boy chanted. "Secret sauce and a seven-cheese blend. Your choice of toppings, fresh-baked to order, take home a slice or a pie today." If Rainbow's lips had still worked that way, she would have smiled.

It was the kid she'd seen wheeling a bicycle-driven pizza cart downtown, selling slices to the workers on their lunch breaks. When he came closer still, Rainbow smelled oregano and tomato sauce, and **the warm, yeasty aroma of baked dough**. Her mouth watered and her stomach groaned. For the past two days, she'd eaten only what she could scavenge with the ravens.

The kid had used to work alongside his father, but Rainbow hadn't seen the older man for several weeks before the plague struck. Maybe he'd determined that his son had learned enough of the business to be trusted on his own, despite his condition. The pizza kid had a pleasant, childish face and a stooped, hulking body. Rainbow had never been able to determine if he was a young adult who had retained the mind and face of a child, or a child whose body had aged at an accelerated rate. He barely spoke beyond what was required to take orders and receive payment from his customers. He did, however, make the best pizza in town.

The pizza kid stopped pedaling and came over to where Rainbow was lying on the ground. He picked her up into his strong arms. She saw that he'd hitched a red wagon to the rear of his pizza cart and had placed a sleeping bag inside. He gently laid Rainbow down in this soft nest, smiled at her and said, "Take home a slice or a pie today." Then he climbed onto the bike and towed her away.

The ride was jostling but not uncomfortable. Rainbow was on her back now, looking up at the clear cobalt sky and the tall trees the kid pedaled past. The pine needles, still wet from the morning's rain, glinted like steel pins in the sunlight. Far above, a wheel of buzzards eyed her rescue with the disappointment of a lost meal.

Was it a rescue? For all she knew, the pizza kid could be carrying her away to some dungeon to subject her to cruel tortures for his own sick gratification. Somehow, Rainbow didn't think so. The gentleness with which he'd carried her, and the softness of his voice, reassured her. Besides, whatever he was taking her to had to be better than dying alone in a vacant lot, paralyzed, prey to birds and insects.

They rolled for a long time, long enough for towering grey thunderheads to gather, gently swirling in the western sky like a squirt of ink in a massive glass of water. Finally, they came to an old-growth residential neighborhood, shady and quiet. The kid pulled into the sloping driveway of a small yellow house with an attached two-car garage. Both of the garage doors yawned open.

When the ride ended, she was lifted again. The kid slid her body onto a soft pile of clothing among the boxes in the garage. He pulled an old coat over the top, creating a cave that emanated the sweetness of old ladies who frequently powdered themselves—a light rose motif that played ironically well in the deep recesses of Rainbow's ancestral brain. The pizza kid lifted her head to help her lap water from a hubcap. He broke bits of pepperoni and crust into bite-sized pieces and left them where her tongue could reach them. Much later, she heard him practicing his orations like songs. Like monks chanting in the distance, they were a comfort.

Rainbow slept. She awoke sometime later to crashing thunder. Outside the open garage door, the sky had turned the color of lead. The rain fell in silver curtains, turning the suburban street into a shallow, rushing river. Lightning flashed, leaving an after-image of electric blue fissures imprinted upon her retinas. The breeze, cool and rain-scented, coated her face with a refreshing mist.

Rainbow licked the rain from her lips and, in doing so, realized that she could move her mouth again. At least a little. She remembered the tiny pieces of pizza the kid had torn off for her, still resting on the pile of clothes beside her cheek. With tiny movements of her lips and tongue, she was able to work one of the pieces into her mouth. Chewing and swallowing was an enormous undertaking, taking all of her concentration. It seemed almost too much work for the scant nourishment it provided, but when she finally managed to down one piece, her tongue went questing for another.

She ate her fill of the pizza, cold and chewy and delicious. Afterwards, she was thirsty. Rainbow longed for the cool water from the hubcap, which had tasted of chrome and rust. The hubcap was just out of her reach, eight or ten inches away. She thought that she might be able to reach it, given time, with incremental movements of her head. Even contemplating this Herculean task was exhausting, though. Rainbow soon fell asleep again.

When she awoke this time, night had fallen outside the garage door. The dispersing clouds were fringed with misty golden light, low in the sky. When they finally broke, the moon burst through, full and bright, a coppery orange, impossibly huge. Rainbow felt a surge of excitement, as if the moon's dramatic entrance onto the horizon's stage had been performed for her audience alone. Then she felt a light squeeze on her right hand.

A girl lay beside her on the slope of piled laundry. She had black, shoulder-length hair and a small, round face with big, dark eyes that looked calmly up at Rainbow. The girl could have been a teenager, or she could have been Rainbow's age, which was twenty-five. She wore a thin pink sweater, ragged at the back where her wings had torn through. She was very pale and very pretty. Her small white hand clasped Rainbow with a cool, light touch.

"He can't come back tonight." The girl's voice was heavy, and draggy, like someone fresh from the dentist with a mouth full of Novocain. "Maybe he'll come in the morning, but he never comes at night. His father doesn't know that he's keeping us out here." Her eyes glinted, reflecting amber moonlight. "What's your name?"

Rainbow spoke her name in a voice that was even thicker than the girl's, creaky with disuse. Before her paralysis, she hadn't spoken to anyone for weeks except ravens. The girl laughed at her. "C'mon. Your name's not really Rambo." Rainbow didn't have the strength to correct her. Speaking took as much effort as eating had.

"I'm Veronica," the girl said, in a slow, toneless cadence. "I've been here three days. He found me down by the shore. I was trying to fall into the sea, so that I would drown instead of starving to death. But I didn't make it. I fell onto the sand. The crabs... found me. They were crawling all over me, biting me. Eating me. He had to pick them off before he carried me away."

"I was afraid of what he was going to do to me," Veronica went on. "If he was some kind of pervert, he could have done anything he wanted. I couldn't say or do anything to stop him, but I would still have to *feel* everything. But he just took me here and fed me. He's good, I think. Except the nights are so long when he doesn't come back. I'm glad you're here now."

Rainbow made a sound. "Wuh..." She was trying to ask why the pizza kid kept them here, but her mouth was still too weak to form words. "Are you asking for water?" Veronica said. "Here, I'll help you. I can move one of my arms, a little. I think maybe it'll all come back, eventually. Yesterday, I could barely move at all."

Veronica scooted over towards Rainbow, wriggling along with movements of her shoulder and the weak dragging motions of her left arm. She pulled herself close enough that Rainbow could feel her heart pounding from the effort of even these small motions. A gust of night air blew into the garage, clean and cold, almost chilly now. Rainbow welcomed the warmth of Veronica's body pressed against her own.

Veronica reached the hubcap. She pulled it to Rainbow's cheek and tipped it so she could drink. Rainbow's heart was filled with an intoxicating feeling of love and gratitude. She tried to reach one trembling hand up, to touch Veronica's face, but her arm fell uselessly to her side. Rainbow wept for a long time, her misery and despair draining away with her tears. Veronica held her until she was calm again, and then she had her drink some more.

Veronica drank the rest of the water herself. When it was all gone, she scooted closer to hold Rainbow in her frail arms. Veronica pressed her lips close to Rainbow's ear and told her story, in a whispered voice that grew weaker and quieter until it was little more than a rustling breath. Still, Rainbow understood. Drifting on the edge of sleep, Rainbow saw Veronica's tale play out in vivid images cast by her half-dreaming mind. Like watching a terribly sad movie.

"My Mom and Dad were on vacation down in Florida when it happened. My sister Rachel and my little nieces Emily and Nicki came over to the house to stay with me, to keep me company while they were gone. Then everybody got sick. It was bad when we all had the rash. Those beautiful little girls, crying in pain. There was nothing we could do to help them. But then our wings came in and we all flew together, and it was wonderful. You should have seen those girls fly. They were so happy. Little Nicki was barely old enough to walk, but she could fly higher than any of us. She *soared*. And it made her so happy, she couldn't stop laughing. And singing. We all sang together. But the girls... they fell before we did. That was the worst. They fell and they couldn't move. Rachel said she couldn't watch them suffer, so she... she put them in the water. And I *helped* her. I helped her drown those perfect little girls. That broke Rachel. She couldn't go on after that. She flew up as high as she could go, and then she just dived straight down into the water and never came up. I wanted to do that, too, so I could be with them. But I was afraid. I flew for another whole day after they were gone. When I knew I was going to fall, I tried to make it back to the water. But I was too slow. I fell onto the beach and the crabs came. I thought that was the end. For drowning those girls, and then being too much of a coward to follow them, I deserved to be eaten alive by crabs. But then he came for me and brought me here to you and I can't stop thinking that if only we'd waited. He could have saved all of us. We could all be together now, if only we'd waited."

The two women huddled close for warmth and human comfort. Together, they sank like stones into dark, dreamless waters. Awakening again was like surfacing, rising up to the sunlight that filtered warm and red through their eyelids. They opened their eyes and blinked away the blinding light, smacking their parched lips. The clothes beneath them were damp where they had helplessly voided their bladders during the night, but the warm morning had brought them both a new hopefulness.

Rainbow could lift her head now. Veronica was able to prop herself on one elbow. She smiled at Rainbow and touched her cheek and told her everything was going to be all right. Both of them were startled when the door that led to the house opened.

The pizza kid appeared in the doorway, a steaming cardboard box in his hands. "Hand-tossed dough," he greeted. The kid refilled the hubcap at a sink in the corner of the garage. He held it up while each woman drank in turn. Then he opened the box and tore off pieces of pizza to feed to them. Rainbow and Veronica ate greedily, holding their mouths open like baby birds being fed by their mother.

Once they'd finished their breakfast, he changed their soiled bedding, piling more clean laundry under them. "Thank you so much," Veronica said to him. She was close to weeping with gratitude. "Your choice of toppings," the pizza kid replied with a smile.

Then the door opened again, and the kid's father stepped into the garage. He wore a black mask with a respirator that made his face look like that of a giant insect. His voice emerged with a waspish buzz: "What did I tell you about bringing them here? They're infected. Dirty!"

"Secret sauce," the kid protested. "Seven-cheese blend." "No, son," the father said. Even beneath the droning filter, Rainbow heard more sadness than anger in his voice. "You can't help them. It's the same as with your mother. They can't be saved. It's too late."

Rainbow and Veronica both tried to speak up, to insist that it wasn't too late, that the kid had already saved them. The stern, insectile countenance of the father frightened them both so badly that they couldn't find their voices, though. All that emerged from their throats was inarticulate bleating.

"Take them where you took the others," the father pronounced. He turned his back and retreated once again into the house, closing the door on them forever. The pizza kid looked down on them with regret. "Fresh baked to order," he apologized.

The kid loaded them once again into his wagon. Rainbow first, and then Veronica's slight body piled on top. Even with the awkward tangle of limbs and wings, they were comforted by one another's closeness. The kid pedaled away up the street, leaving the carefully groomed neighborhood behind.

They rode past green fields already beginning to grow wild, and through a shady forest alive with the sounds of birds and beasts. Deer standing beside the road, having grown bold now that the deadly cars and trucks no longer coursed through their domain, watched curiously as the strange vehicle and its stranger cargo wheeled past.

The kid finally carried them to the water's edge, just above where the waves lapped the shore. He lifted them from the wagon and gently laid them down on the warm sand. "Your choice of toppings," he said, and Rainbow understood. They were close enough, and strong enough, to crawl into the water if they wanted to.

The pizza kid left them there. He pedaled away, still singing his song. Rainbow looked at Veronica. "Don't go," she said. "Stay here with me." "I'm sorry," Veronica said. "They're down there waiting for me." She kissed Rainbow farewell and began to crawl towards the ocean.

Rainbow turned her head to watch. Perhaps later she would follow Veronica into the depths, but for now she was filled with a listless contentment. The sun was warm on her skin, the sand soft under her body, and the shushing of the waves had stilled her soul. She watched Veronica reach the waterline and continue forward, into the cool gentle waves.

Then, the strangest thing, two angels rose from the foaming sea on either side of Veronica. One had light skin, and the other dark. Both of them were nude and radiantly beautiful in the sun, their wings proud and aloft. The angels helped Veronica to her knees and then up on wobbly legs. They turned her around and half-carried her back to the shore. Whatever the angels were whispering to Veronica, it made her smile and laugh.

They walked over to where Rainbow lay in the sand and helped her to her feet as well. Rainbow was surprised to find that she had the strength to stand on her own. "Rejoice," said the dark-skinned angel. "He can't come back, but we don't need him anymore. He's already saved us. All we need now is each other."

Veronica and the other two angels fluttered their wings to dry them, beating the ocean water away. The cool mist tasted salty on Rainbow's lips. The rescuing angels flapped their wings and rose from the shore. Rainbow and Veronica followed them into the air, unsteadily at first, but growing more confident as the strength returned to their wings. High in the sky, all four angels clasped hands and tilted towards the lush, verdant world they had inherited.

The Pizza Boy

By Mary Spence

Beyond the cracked sidewalk, and the telephone pole with layers of flyers in a rainbow of colors, and the patch of dry brown grass there stood a ten-foot high concrete block wall, caked with dozens of coats of paint. There was a small shrine at the foot of it, with burnt out candles and dead flowers and a few soggy teddy bears. One word of graffiti filled the wall, red letters on a gold background: Rejoice!

I recognized this location. I knew the familiar stack of telephone pole flyers and the blistered wall that bordered the vacant lot on the north side of La Palapa Cantina. It was on Route 528 near Rio Rancho and I sometimes passed by the place when I traveled down south to an assignment in that area. The scene as I remembered it, however, was nothing like what I now saw on display before me.

Before I could censor myself, I clutched my clipboard to my breast, took two steps back, groaned, and blurted, "What is this crap?" a bit too loudly. It wasn't a very dignified comment for a photography contest judge, not to mention it was quite unladylike of me. I was immediately ashamed of myself. No doubt some ingenue photographer was proud to exhibit the "haunting" imagery depicted by Photo 27. Twenty years ago, as a budding photojournalist, I might have made similar cringe-worthy photo editing choices myself. Of course, those were the days before I gained respect for the simplicity of photos that document reality. Nowadays I cherish clean and honest images (and not retouched ones) whenever I judge this annual Chamber of Commerce Photo Contest at Santa Fe City Hall.

I looked around to see if the other two judges had heard my outburst. I was relieved to find that Marcus and Katrina were absorbed in their inspections of other entries at opposite corners of the gallery. They were both busily scribbling their critique notes. It reminded me that I should be doing the same.

Painful as it was to behold, I forced my gaze to return to study the digitally modified image before me. Because my comments would be shared with the photographer, whose identity remained anonymous throughout the judging process, I honed my observations to be informative and not cruel. I wrote that staging a scene in a studio and using digital reconstruction can weaken the impact of the image. My advice for this photographer would be to capture a real-life scene that he or she spontaneously stumbles upon and, apart from cropping and light adjustment, to leave it as it was shot. To add a definitive positive note, I mentioned that the wide variety of colors "added interest," whatever the hell that was supposed to mean. To satisfy my own curiosity, I made a mental note to later check the photographer's required Statement of Intent which would be available in the next stage of judging. In particular, I wanted to understand why the mysterious word "Rejoice" was included in such otherwise maudlin imagery.

Marcus, Katrina, and I continued to circulate around the gallery in silence to each finish our critiques of all 57 images in the contest. With clipboards in hand, we then retired behind the heavy, oaken doors of the City Council Chamber to discuss our impressions as a group. We took up positions around the conference table and began the deliberations after each of us read the list of our favorite ten entries. From those, we easily chose the top five and then eventually, after more discussion, agreed on the three prize winners. As it turned out, on that day we didn't need to refer to the stack of Statement of Intent forms which define what effect the photographer hoped to achieve. We sometimes use these to break a tie as we decide how successfully he or she accomplished the goal.

"Before we go," I said, "I'm dying to hear the story behind the memorial shrine with the candles and teddy bears." Marcus snickered and offered the opinion that just because an Adobe Photoshop palette can have over 40 tools, we don't have to use every blessed one of them in every damn photo. "Christ," he added, "That hack even thought we wouldn't notice that 'Rejoice' was done with the spray-paint tool."

As Karina weeded through the stack of intent forms, she commented, "It was pretty awful, wasn't it, Ellen? Did you catch the studio lighting on the teddy bears? Wrong shadow angles for that outdoor light source. And the burnt-out candles looked like they were levitating three inches above the ground." She paused to glance at the crumpled intent form in front of her and then said, "Wow."

"Does it say why we should rejoice?" I asked. She rolled her eyes and circled her index finger toward her temple in a "cuckoo" gesture. She handed the paper to me so I could see for myself. The Statement of Intent, handwritten in pencil, filled every portion of the page, both front and back. The writing was miniscule and was barely legible, but I could discern a few phrases like " the pizza boy can't stop," "like the taste of that last popsicle of summer," "lines of patterned perpendiculars of plaid," "Rainbow ran away with the desert wind," and "everything that happens, must happen." I didn't see how any of this scrawl was specific to the intent behind Photo 27 nor could I find any evidence of sanity in the free-flowing stream of consciousness that spilled across the page before me. The Statement of Intent was a manifesto of an obviously disturbed individual. Katrina looked amused by my expression when I returned the form to the folder, shuddered, and pulled out a pocket-sized bottle of hand sanitizer.

***

The judging process ended at about 4 PM and the three of us went our separate ways. Because the Friday afternoon traffic was often heavy in the City Hall neighborhood, I had arranged to meet Mike Giardano by the drop-off zone on Lincoln Avenue where he had left me earlier in the day. I watched for the arrival of his very dusty, ten-year-old, white pick-up. Good friend that I am, I had promised to drive him to the airport for his business trip to Boston. While I waited, I had my first encounter with the pizza boy.

Someone said something that sounded like, "How'd he do?" The song-voice appeared to be emanating from a young man whose age was impossible to tell. My guess would be early twenties even though he had no apparent facial hair. What he did have was a raging case of cystic acne and shoulder-length black hair that looked drenched in grease. He was taller than my 5-foot-8-inches, but he couldn't have weighed more than 120 pounds. He was dressed in jeans and wore a shirt and cap which both were emblazoned with a Venis Pizza shop logo. From one of his long, boney hands he dangled an insulated pizza-delivery bag. He came closer and stood within a few feet of me, staring, and apparently having a whispered conversation with himself. I turned away and tried to ignore the bizarre young man. He circled around to face me again. He seemed to be a mouth breather.

"How did the pizza boy do?" he asked. I couldn't tell if he had a problem with his larynx or if he was talking like a five-year-old girl on purpose. As I desperately searched the traffic in hopes of seeing Mike coming to rescue me, the boy continued. "You are Ellen Tanning, the photography judge." he said. He launched into a verbatim narration of the biography that I display on my web page including when and where I earned my MFA. Part way through, he stopped, scratched at a bloody scab on his arm, and said, "You can tell if the pizza boy won a prize in the contest. He wants to know about the picture he made when Rainbow went away. And if the rejoice will come true. Will you go in the car with the pizza boy to get coffee? Talk to him about everything that has to happen?" With a "your chariot awaits" expression, he pointed toward a rusty green sedan that bore a car-top Venis Pizza sign. It idled in readiness at the curb in the drop-off zone.

"Gee, I'd love to," I lied. "But we're not allowed to talk to the photographers in the contest." Another lie. "And since you're the pizza boy, you must have been the one who took the photo, right? So I can't talk to you any more." I wondered if he would fall for this crazy logic. I felt a visage of pity crossing my face. Obviously he was lucid enough to have a license to drive and to hold a job, yet his social skills left something to be desired. I felt real sympathy for this pathetic young man.

My rescue could not have arrived at a more opportune time. I sprinted to Mike's truck and lunged into the passenger seat with the speed of a frightened gecko fleeing from a hungry rattle snake. From Mike's expression when he saw my mad dash, I knew that he sensed something might be amiss.

"Don't pull away yet," I said, "I want you to kiss me." He gave me a sideways glance, but when he heard me add, "passionately," he didn't ask any questions and he didn't waste any time. In order to grant my request, he parked the truck, slid across the front seat, and took me into his arms. He snared my hair with his hands and covered my lips with his. At first I almost giggled because Mike and I are not in that kind of relationship. Although we had known each other professionally for ten or more years, the only "kisses" we had exchanged were of the friendly "Hello," "Goodbye," and the "Happy Holidays" peck-on-the-cheek ilk. While Mike had been divorced for a few years, I had always lingered under the impression that I would one day be getting married. That is, until my live-in fiance walked out a few weeks earlier.

When we finally paused to breathe—To my surprise, I didn't want to!—Mike asked, "Was that for the benefit of that pizza delivery boy? Was he bothering you?" I was hoping the young man had taken off when he saw me smooching with Mike, but such was not the case. I followed Mike's gaze to see that the pizza boy had instead gone to the trunk of his car, taken out a Canon EOS 6D with a long lens, and the little creep was busily snapping off shots of our activity in the front seat of Mike's truck. I was able to talk Mike out of "beating the shit out of him" so as not to be late for his flight or mess up his business suit.

***

At last, after a hectic afternoon of driving all over central New Mexico for what seemed like an eon, I finally pulled Mike's truck into my driveway and parked it beside my Mini. I wanted nothing more than to begin a relaxing weekend with no assignments until Monday. My only chore tomorrow would be to plant the seeds for my herb garden in the bed under my kitchen window. After that, I planned to spend the rest of the weekend binge-watching film noir on Turner Classic Movies. To celebrate I treated myself to a home-cooked meal of grilled vegetables, barbecued shrimp skewers, Moroccan rice pilaf, and a cold beer. Well, maybe more than one cold beer. I was feeling pretty happy by the time I finally climbed into bed. I slept well.

The following day I took my time with my morning ritual. At 10 AM, I decided that I'd better do my planting before the sun was at its highest. While dragging the garden hose, I carried my tools and seed packets of dill, coriander, basil, and cilantro around to the back of the house. When I got to the garden area, however, I nearly dropped the entire lot when I saw the pair of footprints pressed into the soil directly under my kitchen window. I froze while I decided what, if anything, I should do. I gave up the gardening idea and went back in the house. Suddenly, I felt like someone was watching me and I wanted to hide. For some reason, I couldn't get that creepy pizza boy out of my mind. Was he clever enough to track down my address? Was he crazy enough to be a stalker?

By the middle of the afternoon, I had convinced myself that the footprints had been made months ago when a trash hauling crew removed some old furniture from my storage shed. I told myself that one of them probably left the footprints when he stood there to pee. It was disgusting to think about, but it was better than all the other alternatives. I was in a better mood when I went to my mailbox and found the envelope containing the CD. The only way to find out what was recorded on it was to play it. I plugged it into my laptop and that's exactly what I did. I wish I hadn't.

When the ride ended, she was lifted again. The kid slid her body onto a soft pile of clothing among the boxes in the garage. He pulled an old coat over the top, creating a cave that emanated the sweetness of old ladies who frequently powdered themselves—a light rose motif that played ironically well in the deep recesses of Rainbow's ancestral brain. The pizza kid lifted her head to help her lap water from a hubcap. He broke bits of pepperoni and crust into bite-sized pieces and left them where her tongue could reach them. Much later, she heard him practicing his orations like songs. Like monks chanting in the distance, they were a comfort.

I didn't need to play the CD more than once. The voice was unmistakable. The flowery descriptions and sentimental imagery, the reference to pizza, the obsession with Rainbow, which I now assumed was an adopted animal of some kind, all pointed to the pizza boy. Who else would speak about himself in third person? I racked my brain to figure out what I had done to make him focus his perverse attentions on me.

I debated whether to call the police. Could they do anything if the pizza boy had posed no outright threat? He talked to me on the street and sent me a CD with part of a story he had written. So what? I decided to wait until Thursday when Mike was due to return from Boston. If I was still having a problem perhaps, between the two of us, we might come up with a solution. I crossed my fingers and wished that nothing more would happen in the interim. Unfortunately, that wish was not to come true.

The remainder of Saturday and most of Sunday went well. By 5 PM on Sunday afternoon, I was at last beginning to relax. I told myself I was silly to worry about the antics of a harmless kid who had probably already redirected his interests elsewhere. I thought about whether to fix an Asian-inspired chicken stir-fry or veggie lasagna as the main course for dinner. I decided on the former and took some chicken tenderloins from the freezer and put them in a bowl of warm water in the sink to thaw.

While I waited, I pulled out my calendar and reviewed my assignments for the week. I chuckled because only when a photojournalist works for the Sun-Herald could she get assigned all in one day (Monday) to photograph a political rally in the morning, a local high school basketball championship game in the afternoon, and a food-truck cook-off competition in the early evening. Tuesday schedule was light with only a human-interest story shoot of day-care toddlers on a hot-air balloon ride. After that, who knew?

My musings were interrupted by a knock at the front door. I assumed it was my neighbor Jeanne who sometimes brings me vegetables from the Farmer's Market because she thinks I don't eat "healthy" enough. I had the chain in place because I was still a little apprehensive about a certain unwelcome visitor.

"Who is it?" I asked after I opened the door just a crack. There was no reply so I repeated my question. The only response was the draft of a hot desert wind accompanied by a pungent smell I couldn't quite place. I checked the chain, shut the door, and returned to the kitchen. I felt safe as long as I was inside and he was outside. I had a strong front door and a strong chain lock. I must have been in a state of denial. I still thought that the pizza boy posed no real threat. Foolishly, I clung to the wait-and-see approach.

Soon there was a second knock. I was reminded of classic horror films in which the third knock is always the deadly one. I went again to the front door, opened it a crack, and said, "I'm warning you. If you don't cut this out I'll call the police." I slammed the door.

Then I heard a falsetto voice announce, "No you won't." That was the point where I froze in terror. I couldn't turn around to see who it was. I didn't have to. I knew from the smell of pizza that permeated the front hall of my home and the feel of the corner of a 14-inch cardboard box poking me in the ribs.

***

"The pizza boy thought you'd like a Veggie Delight. It has mushrooms, tomatoes, black olives, peppers, and onions. And he made sure to get extra cheese," he said. We sat at my kitchen table. Somehow he had coaxed me there and I went along with him to prevent him from becoming upset and possibly violent.

I wanted to plan an escape. But how? The pizza boy was more clever than I had originally thought. I realized that he had used my first door opening to slip in a piece of tape across the door latch to prevent it from locking. After I went away, he could then open the door and, using his boney fingers, somehow take off the chain. Once inside, he re-fastened the chain. To get my attention, and nearly scare me to death, he knocked again from the inside so that I would return to the hallway.

I took a slice of pizza. Under normal circumstances it would probably taste delicious, but it tasted like bitter cardboard to me. I ate slowly to buy time while I thought about what to do next. Then I took a second piece and started chatting inanely.

"This is the best pizza I've ever had in my entire life," I said. "The crust is so tender with has just the right amount of crispiness on top." I hoped I didn't sound as phony as I felt. His only response was to stare at the clock on the front of the stove, repeatedly comparing the time with his own watch, while he drummed his fingers on the table top. He seemed to be waiting for something.

"Tell me about Rainbow." As soon as I asked the question, I realized it was a mistake. He sat bold upright in the chair and a scowl covered his face as I continued to probe. "Was Rainbow your cat? Or your dog? Did Rainbow run away?"

"Rat," he answered. I wasn't sure I heard correctly. My ears were suddenly feeling like they were stuffed with pizza dough. At that point, I had finished two very large slices and they were starting to feel very heavy on my stomach. I thought with all the adrenaline in my system I should be feeling more awake. Not so very, very sleepy.

***

The room was dark because it only had one small barred window. It was high over my head which made me think that I was in a basement apartment that was once a garage. I recognized the soft pile of clothing among the boxes that had once been Rainbow's cave.

I wasn't sure how long I had been asleep after the pizza boy had drugged me. Even in my semi-conscious state, I concluded that he would have to have drugged me. I would never have gone there on my own! No wonder the pizza had tasted so bitter.

I realized that my kidnapper was nowhere to be seen. This might have been a good opportunity to escape if my wrist had not been wearing a shackle that was chained to a heavy bolt in the wall. The chain was just long enough to reach the drywall bucket with the toilet seat on top. Although there was not privacy, at least there was toilet paper. (Lucky me!)

I was also physically incapacitated by the nausea and dizziness whenever I tried to sit upright on my cot. For that reason, I remained prone. I soon found myself drifting off to sleep once again. I don't know how long I slept.

I awoke when the pizza boy returned and started speaking to me. It took a while for me to understand the words. I made myself concentrate and eventually I heard, "The pizza boy was going to have a wife, but she went dead." He didn't say how. Probably starvation or dehydration or a reaction to whatever drugs he fed her. "Then the Rainbow ran away with the desert wind. The pizza boy fixed it when he made a picture. The picture will come real and there will be rejoice. The pizza boy can get married again and the Rainbow will come home. And everything that happens, must happen."

I had no idea (and still don't know) why he chose me to be his newest bride. Wrong place at the wrong time, I suppose. I reminded him, "But we can't get married if I go dead like the first bride. It's very hot in here and I can't live long without water."

"You're trying to trick the pizza boy," he said. "But you can't trick the pizza boy." He went to a pantry closet in the kitchenette and brought me a partially filled bottle of water. The cloudy appearance made me suspect that it contained something else to drug me. I only took a tiny sip, just enough to wet my lips, even though I wanted to chug the entire contents of the bottle.

Under those conditions, it was hard to tell when one day ended and another began. Dehydration was taking its toll. I needed to drink just enough water to stay alive until someone might find me. On the other hand, whatever drug the pizza boy was feeding me was making me too dopey and weak to defend myself. I was determined not to let the pizza boy consummate our marriage because I happened to be asleep.

The dreaded day finally arrived. For whatever reason, the pizza boy decided that it was time for our wedding ceremony. He pulled a frilly white dress from the pile on the floor and draped it across me. I made the connection to the sweetness of old ladies who frequently powdered themselves—a light rose motif. Even that cloying fragrance was a welcome relief from the smelly clothes I had been wearing since my day of abduction. The pizza boy used threadbare sofa cushions to prop me up on the cot because I was so weak. Through the ringing in my ears and the fluffiness inside my brain, I faintly heard the sound of "Here Comes the Bride." Or maybe it was a knock at the door.

The knock came again, much louder, this time. Someone shouted "Pizza delivery" and the door crashed in. Mike Giardano took one look in my direction, noticed the state I was in, saw the shackle and chain, and promptly decked the pizza boy. The young man held his hand to his bloody nose and whimpered. He crawled to the corner, clutched his knees, and began to rock back and forth.

Mike towered over him. "Where's the key, you piece of shit?" The pizza boy, with his eyes downcast, dutifully removed the lanyard from around his neck and submissively offered it to Mike. It held a solitary key. Mike snatched it and immediately came to release me.

Mike saw how weak I was. He asked me if I could move and I shook my head from side to side. My mouth was too dry to talk. He washed one of the dirty glasses in the sink and brought me a heavenly glass of cold water. I held back tears and, even though my mouth still felt like it was stuffed with cotton, I squeaked out, "How'd you find me?"

He explained that he got worried when I wasn't at the airport. He took a taxi to my house and saw both cars, found the tape on the front door latch, and smelled the rotten chicken in the sink. My purse, keys, and phone on the counter confirmed that something was seriously wrong. When Mike called the police, it turned out that my boss had already filed a missing person report. Even though I had missed all my assignments for the previous three days, the police weren't too concerned.

Mike said, " But I was! The give-away was the empty Venis pizza box. It scared the shit out of me because I remembered that weird pizza delivery boy and the way he was bothering you. He worked for Venis. I went there and found out from Mr. Venis that the kid stopped showing up for work a few days ago. He gave me his home address. And here I am." He touched my cheek. "Thank God you're alright."

He pulled a business card from his pocket and entered a number into his phone, he said, "Detective Henderson. This is Mike Giardano. I found Ellen Tanning and she's been held against her will." He gave an address that was unfamiliar to me and then added, "Better send an ambulance." Then he glanced at the sniveling mess of the pizza boy in the corner and said, "Better make that two ambulances."

After he hung up, he knelt beside the cot and held me in his arms. He continued to assure me that help was on the way. As far as I was concerned, the best help I could possibly ask for was already there. Rejoice.

How to Fake
Your Own Death
By Emily Sperber

Beyond the cracked sidewalk, and the telephone pole with layers of flyers in a rainbow of colors, and the patch of dry brown grass there stood a ten-foot high concrete block wall, caked with dozens of coats of paint. There was a small shrine at the foot of it, with burnt out candles and dead flowers and a few soggy teddy bears. One word of graffiti filled the wall, red letters on a gold background: Rejoice!

Rainbow hadn't been to the funeral—she hadn't known the man smiling back at her from the picture frames. But she had seen the special on the news of the candlelight vigil. The news so sad, especially nowadays, that she often went to bed sad. She watched anyway and this, despite being a funeral, made her happy. Seeing all of the people, dozens, maybe a hundred, holding candles and honoring this life they loved at one point or was still a stranger to. It didn't matter. She hoped it wasn't the best party he's ever been thrown but it definitely was heavily attended. And she couldn't remember the officer's name, just that he was a Detective and investigating a narcotics case when things had gone south. He had a wife and a son, pictures flashing across the screen, who was in his Little League uniform. Walking past slow enough to take everything in, Rainbow saw that word: Rejoice! With the exclamation point. It seemed counterintuitive, she thought, to publicly vandalize a former officer's shrine albeit in a very heavenly expression. And, although the reason for this shrine was a sad one, as Rainbow walked by it, thinking of all the people with all the flowers and all the stuffed animals and not consider it a time to rejoice.

Rainbow had walked home a different way from work and hadn't seen the progression of the shrine. The news footage showed all of it at the beginning when the notes and teddy bears were still safe from the Seattle rain. But that doesn't last long here. Walking home from the restaurant she served at, Rainbow protected her head underneath her hood. The biodegradable box where she scooped cheese ravioli for dinner, however, was caving in on itself from the raindrops.

After turning into her neighborhood, she climbed the stairs to her mother-in-law apartment. The garage she lived above belonged to the young couple in the next house. They were the kind of people that owned an electric car, weren't married, and had dogs instead of children. But she didn't bother them and they didn't bother her. Sometimes, she did hear the dogs bark and the sound of the car being plugged into the wall. Her apartment was a decent size. A living room, a bar that connected it to the kitchen, a bedroom. The bathroom was styled in all green: the tile, sink, and toilet in that green that was probably old-fashioned even when it was installed. Rainbow arranged her leftovers on a plate and placed it in the microwave. The officer and his shrine were still in her mind. She thought about his funeral, thought that it was well-attended, thought he was well-missed by the sheer amount of things cluttering that corner of the city with the shrine. The microwave dinged and brought her back. Rainbow, blowing on her ravioli, found a movie on cable to watch while she ate. Later, she dabbed at a spot on her uniform so it was clean for the next day. She did the People's crossword and had to look up who Rosebud was in *Gone with the Wind*. But, for some reason, as Rainbow crawled under the covers that night, she couldn't stop thinking about what songs they might've sung at the officer's funeral.

Her parents had a sick sense of humor. Her mother, a hippie, and her father, a cowboy, named their little girl Rainbow. The weather sensation that made people stop their cars to look up and point at the sky, take pictures to show no one. They named her something happy in a last-ditch effort to make themselves happy. And her father, too much of a cowboy to keep still long enough to be a father, and her mother, too much of a hippie to ask him to stay, told each other goodbye. Their love only lasting long enough for one kid, leaving Rainbow a lonely only child.

She was stuck with a name that everyone said was beautiful but was just a reminder to her of how love just can't be enough sometimes. When she was still small enough to hold in her arms, Rainbow's mother would take her outside, hold her so they were cheek-to-cheek, and point at the faint colors of a rainbow after a storm. She would say, "You! It's you!" And that love was enough.

Customers would pity her, a thirty-something waitress evidenced by her only deepening crow's feet, thinking she was a single mother trying to put her kid through school, thus, giving her a bigger tip. She didn't bother correcting their assumptions, sliding the cash into her apron. The other wait staff were high school and college kids who were actually paying their way through school while simultaneously blowing it on alcohol once it was closing time. Rainbow would come back to her apartment smelling like lukewarm Italian food and stupidly thought, if she had someone to share her life with, he would love the scent of her when she walked through the door.

College hadn't been an option for her with no money in her

mother's pockets or her own. And high school was something she groaned her way through. Neighbors kept to themselves. The people at the restaurant couldn't relate to her and her them. Dating sites seemed too much for her. This left her without a Facebook profile, without people wishing her happy birthday and adding her to event groups. People grew up with hobbies but she grew up with her mother, which was almost the same thing. Rainbow did whatever her mom did, helping her with her canning and painting and cooking but not retaining much to carry it to her own adult life. She grew up working because her mother didn't; work was her hobby. Sometimes she went to pet stores and made it seem like she was this close to taking the little puppy home but told the employees that her husband would kill her if she got another one.

It was called pseudocide. Staged; the act of convincing others of your demise without truly being demised. A quick search showed that people actually did it. To skip out on jail time, to collect insurance money, to escape stalkers or abusers. But you only heard about the ones that had failed. The successful ones, the website claimed, were still out there on foreign soil or even walking among us. Rainbow was still thinking about the officer's funeral, so grand and so popular, which made her think about her mother's funeral and then made her think about her own funeral. And it ran around her head like a horse around a track. She doubted she would have a shrine, trying to count on fingers who would even come.

There was a long history of it, a simple Google search showed her, as far back as the eighteenth century where a man with Lord in front of his name faked his own death to see how people would react. The other reasons she read of didn't jump out as desperate: the ones with large sums of money, hidden women, and stupid mistakes. They screamed second chances. Even though these people got themselves into those messes and it was hard to root for them, all Rainbow could hear was the hope of a second chance.

But, with whatever she seemed to click on, people played devil's advocate and posed the question of suicide instead of pseudocide. At first, she considered it for a moment. But, despite having not much to live for, Rainbow still wanted to live. She would have to give up most things but couldn't imagine giving up everything. There was a part of her too that made her spine straighten as she thought she might be doing something instead of running away. And maybe someone else would think it was running away but, at least, she might be getting off her ass and running. Rainbow had everything going for her in terms of pseduocide. She didn't have people that would miss her: her mother gone from ignoring the infection that was eating her body, her father long skipped out on both of them, no husband or boyfriend to tell her not to do it. They would hire another waitress, one maybe getting her degree in something useful like biochemistry or engineering. And while she counted the terrible evidence of her life, Rainbow couldn't help but smile.

There was a dream that she would have over and over again, yet she didn't call it recurring. Rainbow was the only one on the roller coaster and, without the other people to weigh it down, she felt truly weightless. But being weightless always scared her, not being able to understand the appeal of space that astronauts tried to sell. There was nothing to ground her and there was nothing to pull her back. The roller coaster started and she thrashed from within the rubber restraints and against the rubber seat. It made an awful noise on the track like clanging tin cans together and, while this brought to mind the bumper of a car with a Just Married sign, this wasn't a pleasant sound. Like something was breaking every single minute. She never understood the joy other people got from roller coasters after years of having it fling her body around like a rag doll. But she always woke up before she finished the ride. And she took that as a blessing. One morning, Rainbow decided to look up the meaning but didn't like what it said. She then decided, with the rock of the ride still in her bones, whether or not it was indeed a dream or a nightmare.

When Rainbow's mother died, she didn't have the emotional capacity to know how to deal with it. She had only lost her father before, but just from him deciding to leave instead of being taken. And her father had grown up an orphan, being raised by families here and families there, while her mother was raised by parents who notoriously ended with, only heard about in movies or news stories, murder-suicide. Rainbow didn't even have a pet that died, helping her learn how to mourn.

And that meant that Rainbow didn't cry when her mother died from an HIV-related infection, a disease her mother didn't know she had from avoiding doctors and medicines. It was sudden for everybody but she had been suffering from it for years but slowly treating her small symptoms here and there with homemade remedies that only really remedied it for so long. So Rainbow's form of grief involved taking all of the clothes from her mother's house and stuffing them into her own closet that was already too small for her own clothes. Each morning, dressing for the day, she got to smell her mother. It was a mixture of patchouli, chai, and her own body smell. Some of the clothes that she took, however, weren't her mother's. The day she passed, Rainbow's mother was hosting the Asian Women's Coalition for Bettering. She found them from a poster with frayed edges of phone numbers. That session, she was teaching them how to tie-dye. Next week, one would teach the others how to make a soufflé, how to watercolor, how to write poetry. Her mother had been the youngest, learning from the older women who were too busy immigrating to the states, raising a family, and supporting that family to do the things people did to relax. The paramedics came before they were even able to dye. The older women, who still dressed to the nines and sprayed themselves with rosewater, didn't want to bother with their coats still hanging in the hall closet and didn't want to impose by coming back. Now hung in Rainbow's closet, their beige wool coats, with their floral smell, clashed with her mother's shawls.

She hadn't been to work in a couple days. All her time was spent visiting countless articles online, checking out books from the library, and pouring over newspaper ads. You would be surprised by the amount of information there was at your fingertips on faking your own death.

Without waitressing and the constant flow of leftovers as her main source of food, Rainbow was knee-deep in pseudocide research when her stomach grumbled. She dialed the pizza place that put the cheese in the crust that you can pull apart. The doorbell rang in under thirty minutes. The pizza boy, once Rainbow opened the door, smiled showing all his teeth. His black hair was cropped short underneath his visor. He looked like a boy that would, if he didn't already, watch birds in his free time. "That'll be twelve ninety-five." Rainbow patted her pockets, realizing there was only a ten-dollar bill. "Hold on. Come on in," she said, going to her bedroom for her purse. The kid stood just inside her apartment which, because of its size, made him privy to the whole space. "What's all this? Working on a project?" As Rainbow searched for a five, the pizza boy had found her desk littered with the work she had been doing. She straightened from leaning over the bed, the five in her hand, and turned back toward the kid. Rainbow sucked on her teeth. There was a gnawing feeling in her stomach, possibly mixing with hunger, that basically like a eulogy. It's so beautiful. I know the English translation of one of the most famous speeches and I'm working on the Greek right now but it's really hard. My parents didn't decide to get divorced, just kept arguing, so it's come in handy. But, yeah, people don't take too kindly to a kid reciting funeral orations under his breath."

Unbeknownst to either Rainbow or the pizza kid as they spoke, wires were short-circuiting and batteries were overheating below them in the garage. Names of car parts and faults that neither of them would be able to name or remedy. The electric car becoming truly electric. And Rainbow was about to reach out to him, to ask to hear the speech, to ask him his name she realized she still did not know. She was about to do all these things but then the bang of a huge explosion interrupted her. It completely knocked her over and then rung in her ears. The last thing she saw was everything of her's on fire. Her eyes closed and she was knocked out cold. Behind her eyelids, she was on that roller coaster. Up and down, side to side, knocking her body all around. Just when she thought it was about to get worse, the ride seemed to lift her. High into the sky like she was an offering, as if to relieve her from the rattling her bones were doing inside her skin. And then, just like that, she fell to the ground.

When the ride ended, she was lifted again. The kid slid her body onto a soft pile of clothing among the boxes in the garage. He pulled an old coat over the top, creating a cave that emanated the sweetness of old ladies who frequently powdered themselves—a light rose motif that played ironically well in the deep recesses of Rainbow's ancestral brain. The pizza kid lifted her head to help her lap water from a hubcap. He broke bits of pepperoni and crust into bite-sized pieces and left them where her tongue could reach them. Much later, she heard him practicing his orations like songs. Like monks chanting in the distance, they were a comfort.

wanted to tell someone. To divulge her whole plan. To impress someone with all of her research and work. Maybe someone to tell her not to do it. There was another part that knew that was silly. But a devious smile spread across Rainbow's face. "Do you wanna see something cool?"

With the hot, greasy pizza box brushed to the side and growing colder, Rainbow regaled the pizza boy with her plan. At first, he appeared like he had wandered into an over-sharer like you sometimes do delivering pizzas but then he grew fascinated. She went over everything. Pointing out passages in books about how you can use burner phones or cash and still be traced, clicking across tabs on her computer listing what's included in a death kit like a burial plot and death certificate, and showing him the newspaper clippings of contacts that surprisingly enough could help her with all this. Rainbow could tell that he was a nice kid, listening to her with complete enrapture, listening to her at all. But the look on his face kept her mouth moving and it was as if it was completely separate from her head telling her to shut up.

He was nodding his head like a bobblehead. "You know, I totally get it. It's kind of extreme but like the idea of just not being who you are anymore is so appealing sometimes." The pizza boy stopped there. He looked at Rainbow from the side of his eye but then believed he could tell anything to someone who just told him she's faking her own death. "It's the age-old story of kid does something a little different, bully doesn't like it, kid gets the shit kicked out of him," he said, sitting at the desk. She only had one chair so she stood. "I don't know who down the road said it was weird to talk to yourself. When I was younger, I found it was easier to make noise, even if it was talking to myself, then to listen to my parents fight. I needed things to say, to have memorized. In my World History class, we learned about this tradition in Ancient Greece of funeral orations,

"I thought you were dead there for a minute. You could've skipped the fake stuff and cut straight to the real thing." He took a bite of the pizza he had been feeding her, his face cut up, his visor lost to the rubble. Rainbow's body actually felt like it had been on that roller coaster she felt so banged up. As she tried sitting up, the boy told her the car in the garage below them, that they were now in, had exploded. "It was bang, boom, then crash as your place basically fell into the garage. The whole place shook, the garage door flew off, everything was ruined." And it looked like her neighbors weren't home. The street was eerily quiet. She almost laid back down, never getting up again. But her eyes snapped open and she knew she had to act fast.

There was a girl who, from first until sixth grade when she eventually switched schools, terrorized Rainbow. Her name was Allie. She was one of those girls who grew up thinking that this was love, what her parents showed her and what she then showed everyone else. Allie wasn't hugely creative or violent, however, settling for the subtle bullying that she reserved for the playground everyday. To avoid the eyes of teachers, Allie would march up to Rainbow on the swing set, grab the chain link supports, and whisper that she was ugly. Sometimes she was stupid, sometimes she was unlovable, and other times she simply pulled the corners of her eyes to the sides. Allie's family moved at the end of sixth grade, before Rainbow could stand up to her despite not having any plans to do so anyway. It was this that Rainbow thought about when thinking of a new identity. She could no longer be Rainbow, nor did she want to be Rainbow anymore. So she decided in her new life, as an homage, she would be Allie Loveless.

She was running. There were bruises all over her body, scratches up and down her limbs, and something definitely felt broken in her leg but she was running. She was in the wig she bought, a pixie-cut blonde that contrasted her long black hair tucked underneath, her black-rimmed glasses she hadn't worn since elementary school, and the heavy clothes that wouldn't show how torn up she was, or luckily, who she was period.

Allie had changed the plan after her neighbor's plug-in electric car burned up underneath her, a freak accident she may thank her lucky stars for later. Before, she thought she still had some time to get her affairs in order, actually drown in the Pacific like she had planned. But when she landed in the lap of what was left of their energy efficient car, Allie knew she could use it to her advantage.

The pizza boy, who was too busy nursing her and seemingly singing her eulogy despite his own injuries, never told her his name. But they had gotten past names at that point. When she jumped up, as much as her body could allow, he pinky promised her that he wouldn't tell anyone about her plan and she believed, with little she knew about him, that it was binding. The pizza boy didn't take the money for the pizza, mainly because it was almost impossible in the mess of insulation and wood shards. He saluted her as she ran from her crumbled apartment, hearing his sing-song voice fade as she ran farther and farther from him.

Luckily, amongst her research, Allie had packed a bag already. In it was her wig and glasses, a change of clothes, wads of cash stuffed in a money belt, a flashlight, a map of Seattle, a bottle of water, and sleeves of saltine crackers with a jar of peanut butter. She left behind her wallet with her credit cards and driver's license, along with one shoe, so the police could hopefully "identify" her.

That was the plan anyway. The explosion would get called in, the officers would respond, see her apartment totally destroyed, and assume she had gone up in flames. She was hoping that they'd think it was suicide. That she was in the car with a hose from the exhaust pipe running in through a window. But they'd figure out it was an electric car, maybe assuming that because of the lack of exhaust, she had to get creative. They would just never know how creative she actually got.

She tried not to get too excited, her literally running into a new life, but she did smile while she ran. A new life that she would actually live and people would actually celebrate when it came to an end. There would be burning candles and fresh flowers and dry teddy bears. But the backpack, as she ran, hit against her butt and reminded her she wasn't there yet. Her left ankle buckled every time she landed on it. She was never really one for exercise, consistently gaining weight since working at the restaurant. Her lungs were pounding. Allie decided to stop, hands on her knees, catching her breath. She stood back up and realized she didn't know where she was running. Directions were also never her strong suit.

Despite the big overall Asian population in Seattle, she knew that some people weren't expecting a tall Asian woman to take their order at an authentic Italian restaurant. Most didn't pay attention, willing to spout off their orders without looking up from the menu. Some will look her up and down, considering her long black hair, her eyes small from genetics and fatigue, her breasts slightly larger than they would assume, and her black uniform that was the only thing that made her look like everyone else. This, plus her name, made customers interested in her. An older man had asked her where she was from and rolled his eyes when she said she was born here. "But like where is your family from?" Even though it was the truth, when Rainbow said her mother was Vietnamese, she immediately regretted it. "Ah, we got you pretty good back in the day," letting out a hearty laugh that she was sure had punctured many people's feelings in his lifetime. He ordered the Chicken Piccata and she didn't spit in it.

That day, long after the Chicken Piccata man left, Rainbow was still smiling through it, making her eyes look even smaller. All she had to do before her shift was over was deliver the little dish of pistachio ice cream, free with birthdays, to the little girl at the table in the corner. They didn't sing there or, at least, she didn't feel like singing but she set the ice cream down, wished the girl happy birthday, and was about to walk away to rip off her apron and head home. But the little girl, the cards on the table alluding to her being eight, looked up at Rainbow with the biggest eyes. "You look like Mulan," she said, then giving a hee-yah, karate chopping the air. Without waiting for a response, the newly-eight-year-old dug into the ice cream, holding the spoon with her whole fist.

She thought about that now. Walking through the streets of Seattle. Her hair tucked into the small wig, thinking she'd have to cut down her real hair, maybe even shave it, to make it a better fit. Her eyes adjusting to the glasses after only wearing contacts for a couple decades. She thought about the weight she might have to start losing to be even less recognizable. Allie took the little girl's comment as a compliment but, right now, hoped she looked nothing like Mulan.

They lived by the airport, the sound of takeoff the first thing Rainbow remembered hearing. It was a bit ironic as they lived close enough to a place that could take them anywhere in the world but Rainbow and her mother never went anywhere.

Not long after her father left, her mother took them to Alki beach. A little neighborhood of the city that she couldn't believe people actually lived in year round. It was about fifteen miles away but she biked them there, taking well over an hour and a half. Rainbow, only about five, remembered her mother's sobs into the wind and the air pushing her tears into her ears and off her face. She jostled in the back, strapped into the seat, in a position that made her mother look as big as a mountain. But that mountain was crumbling. She always said that going to Alki felt like going on vacation by not going very far. She didn't pack her sunscreen or floppy hat or a book to read. She hopped on her bike and rode. It was where the fresh air was, she'd also say. Rainbow didn't know that much about air, fresh or not, but she breathed it in on that first trip to Alki beach and did feel a freshness in her lungs.

She hopped off the bike, unstrapped Rainbow, and walked the two of them on the sidewalk parallel to the water. Holding her hand, she told Rainbow that Alki was long and not very deep. You walked more around it than in it. It was getting away from the city by still being in the city. Her mother had stopped crying. The sun was setting. Leaving Rainbow outside with the bike, she went inside a bar and got herself a margarita in a plastic cup and Rainbow a cup of margarita mix on ice. On the patio, the two sat there sipping their sugary drinks through their straws.

Her mother went to Alki beach often enough for Rainbow to notice. Only bringing her daughter some of the time. She went there until she stopped and Rainbow started. Like her mother, it was to be her place. Sometimes she still ordered a glass of margarita mix on the rocks, the sickly sweet taste taking her back to the salty ocean and the view of her mother's profile.

When you zoom into a map of the city of Seattle, you'll see Alki Point. Literally a point on the edge of land and water. It will look like the profile of a bird with its beak pointing to the west, away from everything else. That's where they were, that's where she was.

The overhead light in her motel room flickered when she turned it on so Allie kept it off most of the time. She preferred being lit by the thick TV, the one so old that she remembered when it was new growing up. It proved harder to find an apartment than get a job, Allie found. Restaurants that just needed a hostess or server were a lot more open to paying under the table than landlords that wanted bank statements. The disinterested clerk at the desk didn't bat an eye when she pulled cash out of her money belt, sliding over a week's rent.

She took the first job that would hire her. She was bussing tables at a Mexican restaurant, a step backward from where she was when she was "alive," but it promised growth. They said she could bartend after waitressing for a bit. Allie liked the idea of learning the recipes and names of crazy mixed drinks, being that cool bartender that shook the shaker with one hand. She could never see herself doing that before. But she could definitely see her new self doing that. Maybe she needed a tattoo. The new her would be the type of girl to make light conversations with people at the bar without looking at the drinks she was making and have the courage to be poked at with a needle for the sake of art.

Like when she was working in the Italian restaurant, Allie had her mornings to herself, not having to go on until the lunch rush. She became a coffee person. Before this all happened, she had read in one of the many books and articles she poured over for research that one of the hardest parts of faking your own death was not experiencing those little delights you once enjoyed. The little things that made you you. But Allie was surprised to find she was enjoying the new her much more than the old. She did miss watching the news. Her little love/hate relationship of the scope of human nature being the best and worst all within an hour of broadcasting. But she read that poking around in your old life could easily get you caught. Like Patrick McDermott, Olivia Newton-John's on-again/off-again boyfriend of nine years. After they had broken up, he presumably fell overboard while off the coast of Los Angeles and drowned. Private investigators found through IP addresses, however, he was hiding out in Mexico, constantly checking in on a website made for tracing his whereabouts. She wasn't going to screw up like that and it was easy without a computer. But Allie was curious about her neighbors, their car and their garage, but she dared not even pick up a newspaper.

Lorenzo was the kind of guy who could hold two huge trays stacked with sizzling food and not even flinch. It made the muscles in his arms pop from his short sleeves. His favorite music was country, even going out line dancing once a week. In the basement at the small library, there was an old dance hall, his cowboy boot heels clicking on the hardwood, and, on his way out, he'd pick up some foreign films.

Allie, during breaks and after work, would cross the street to the beach. Turning around, she could look right into the glass windows of the restaurant, see who was serving and who was cooking. But she spent that time looking forward. The water had this magic about it that made it always nice to look at. She sat out there by herself for so long. Even getting hit on by guys and some girls, dogs came sniffing. But then Lorenzo sat with her. One day, he was just there and they both looked forward, her left arm warm from his right. She cursed herself for finally making a friend once she was dead.

She is known on a first name, her new first name, basis at the tattoo shop on the street named after a state she's never been to. Her first time in, she wanted to look more confident than she actually was, like she'd done this before and wasn't scared of pain. So, by just scanning the designs on the walls, Allie pointed to one at eye level and said that that's the one she wanted. That's been how all the other ones went too.

You get over the needles repeatedly stabbing your skin pretty quickly. The vibration of her bones rattling around inside reminded her of her roller coaster dream she hadn't had since the explosion. Her head leaned back, she closed her eyes and leaned into it.

Only when they asked her questions did she look up. The metal music that blared over the speakers so loud sometimes they'd have to repeat themselves. She was surprised in the lies she could come up with on the spot. Her parents died in a car accident in California so she was shipped back to China to live with her grandparents. She'd only come back stateside five years ago. They were all so impressed with her English. She pretended she was the chef at the restaurant she worked at as they could smell the food on her. In that room, she was a lesbian going through a dry spell. Her favorite color was green. She didn't know what she was saying until it was already said. It was lucky that all the guys that worked there didn't really care. There were many times where Allie caught herself in her own lies but they didn't look fazed at all. One time, Max was giving her the aftercare spiel and she said she would have to skip doing laps in the pool for a couple weeks even though, during the aftercare spiel for her last tattoo, she said she wouldn't have to worry because she had a fear of water from a bad experience as a kid. Max just kept wrapping her arm.

Allie tried not to hope but she did anyway. She didn't know but she hoped that they figured she died in the fire. She hoped the pizza boy maybe told the police and the firemen, when they showed up, that everything happened so fast—one second she was here, the next she was gone. She hoped they believed that. She hoped they gave her a nice ceremony: nobody would be there but maybe they'd give her a plot next to a tree, a headstone with the word Rejoice! Exclamation point and all. But maybe she was naive thinking they would do anything at all.

What she liked about the shop was that they still read magazines and newspapers, having them lay about for customers. Max tattooed some roses on her thigh which actually brought the scent back of those old Asian women's coats. She wished she could put all of them on at once. Forgetting about it, Allie's eye wandered over the front page of the Seattle Times. A boy, his name was presumably on the other side of the crease, had won a speech contest. Contestants were supposed to recite something from memory and with feeling. The winning boy won with his arresting recitation of a famous Greek-to-English funeral oration and everybody was celebrating him. He had a trophy and everything.

At the precinct, Officers Robinson, Ludcek, and Waterson stood around a table with various items in evidence bags strewn about. "It's like she wanted to be found. I mean, she practically left clues for us to follow like bread crumbs," Officer Robinson said; he was the serious one that would try to deadpan a joke like he saw in cop movies. Her Rainbow driver's license was in one bag, her social security card in another, a brush with black hair in a third. Next to them was printouts of her checkout history at the library and her search history on her computer. Eyewitness testimonies from neighbors that saw her run away from the burning garage. "What with all the research she did, I don't think this was poor execution. Either this was her plan all along—fabricate this game—or she didn't want this toward the end. We'll find," he looked down at some paperwork, "Rainbow. Maybe there'll be a pot of gold at the end of all this."

Officer Waterson laughed at Officer Robinson's jokes. He was the nice one of the group. This meant getting everybody lunch and lying to the mens' wives about working late for them. This also meant that he was on stakeout trying to find this Rainbow character while

Robinson and Ludcek had their feet up.

This was a first for them but they had enlisted advice from others and heard that with these types of cases the target, by now, was either far away in a foreign country or only a few miles from where they started, hiding in plain sight. Waterson crossed his fingers hoping for the latter. He was making his way through all the Seattle neighborhoods when Ludcek called him saying, before she had stopped using her computer, the target had looked up motels in Alki. Waterson turned around and headed for the point. The other guys definitely took advantage of him and he knew that but he liked having friends, never really having any of his own growing up in a big family.

He had been driving all day, the printed out picture from her ID blown up and crumpled from the grip in his hand, and the sun was just about to set. Pulling over, Waterson got out from the car and faced the beach. The glow from the sun warmed him. He decided to sit on the edge of the concrete wall just to watch the sunset then he'd get back to it. The sound of the waves was so relaxing. The wind was just cold enough to be a breeze. A loud crash to the concrete behind him made Waterson whip his head around to see kids jumping and falling from their skateboards. But the look he gave them apparently so serious they hurried off on foot, boards clenched in their hands. Once they moved, Waterson saw the restaurant behind them and then could smell it. The customers at tables by the windows were enjoying overstuffed burritos and sipping large margaritas. He thought he might stop in and get a little dinner. Looking through the windows, he saw a woman up against them, cleaning the glass with a rag and cleaning the tables and booths with the same rag. Her face inches from the glass. She had short hair the color of bubble gum and glasses, tattoos up and down her arms. He looked back at the picture he was, for some reason, still gripping in his hand and looked back up at the woman bussing tables. But the light from the sun bounced off the glass she had just cleaned, hiding her from him. He could see, though, a man who came up behind her and grabbed her waist, then twisted and twirled her. The woman was laughing and smiling, completely unlike the frown the woman in the picture was sporting. But the frown from her concentration before of wiping the windows could be identical. Waterson looked back and forth. Finally, the sun set and she was on to her next table and he had decided to go home for dinner, getting in his cop car and tossing the picture to the passenger seat.

Some Time Had Passed Since The Animation

By Thos. West

Beyond the cracked sidewalk, and the telephone pole with layers of flyers in a rainbow of colors, and the patch of dry brown grass there stood a ten-foot high concrete block wall, caked with dozens of coats of paint. There was a small shrine at the foot of it, with burnt out candles and dead flowers and a few soggy teddy bears. One word of graffiti filled the wall, red letters on a gold background: Rejoice!

The bears, on closer expectation, formed a loose arc around the wall. They were a bit of a gallimaufry: a pair of them Victorian in waistcoats and crinoline; a handful of Beanie Babies and Beanie Baby knockoffs; isolated, a little, at the arc's end, a sodden plush panda, mid-sized. At the semicircle's center, in his worn mohair, any trace of accessories or clothing long gone, stood the Prophet.

We remember not, he began, whence we came, what packaging we wore in that time. Nor know we whither and where we shall pass. We know only that we are here, stuffed with the stuffing—of Life! Bound together with the stitches—of Community!

Among the Beanie Baby contingent stood out one multifarious in her coloration, a riot of pastels bleeding into one another. She was a fastidious bear, too, kept herself away from rain and dirt, and was still bright. A scar of stitching in her back recalled where some of the polyethylene pellets inside her had once been lost to the aggression of a rotund, marmalade-colored family cat. She was the *Garcia* model, introduced in 1993: not that she knew this.

The Prophet had eased into it. Was talking of the coming of the True Bear. Rainbow was not paying attention, her mind was on the past. Before a number of resales, listings online, shippings cross-country in dark boxes crowded with foam popcorn, she remembered being addressed as Rainbow by a child not yet old enough to quite say the word properly. Pictured the child, her coo-ing grandmothers. The child had become an adult human, of course, and sold her on; she wondered what had become of it now.

Sister Urs, came a voice to her side, I fear you are not paying attention to the sermon. This was Albert, one of the two Victorians present, the one in the waistcoat and top hat. He carried a cane; was known, along with his partner, Edward—the one in the rather tatty lace gown—to give himself airs.

Brother Bruin, rejoined another of the Beanies, I will thank you to regard your own cognizance, and not that of our Sister. The three Beanies present at the congregation (a *Cubbie*, a *Valentino*, and a fake *Billionaire #1*; they had not taken names) had automatically formed a protective wall of bear in front of Rainbow. Psht, said Edward, peevish, why does she not answer for herself. The Beanies parted ranks in order that she might do so: and found her gone.

***

Rainbow was following the road. She walked past the new-build close where most of the houses featured an occupation of her sibling Beanies, more and more of them arriving every day; then the grander, slightly older residences of the Victorians. The bears took as their homes garages, family rooms, dens; avoided upstairs, where human husks might still remain.

Behind her was the mangy panda from the service, who went by Panda: such had been his appellation in the days before the Animation, and he had seen no reason to change it. On four paws he dashed from cover to cover, though he might have saved himself the effort, for Rainbow was paying no attention to what lay behind her. They moved towards the edges of the development: they were outside of bear territory now, moving through, in the neutral zone between the robots and the dinosaurs. A sign indicated the freeway, and Rainbow kept going; Panda followed.

***

In a strip mall at the next exit stood what was, as far as one can tell, the last operating Domino's Pizza in North America. Its one remaining employee, a late-adolescent human, had continued to show up for work, albeit he had seen no customers in quite some time now, nor had any of his colleagues reported for duty. Each day he would faithfully man the register for the eight hours of his shift before, while closing up, baking for himself a medium pepperoni. This borrowing he logged, week-by-week, in a double-entry accounting book, increasing in ratio to the wages owed on the other side of the page.

He'd felt eyes on him before. A platoon of GI Joes had run a reconnaissance mission, and while he'd not caught them he had found a pair of miniature dog-tags caught on an air-vent. A Transformer had appeared in a mesh trashcan outside, one day, and remained there for a handful of hours; he'd looked up one day to find it gone. But when an exhausted Rainbow collapsed, muzzle-first, outside the glass door of the store—having been attracted by the light, but lacking the strength or size even to attempt ingress—it was the first time he'd seen movement he would swear to. He pulled the door inwards and lifted her up in one hand, registering, as he did so, a scuttling in black-and-white at the edge of his visual field.

She regarded him from his palm: long hair, shoved under the dome of his uniform cap; a t-shirt in worn polyester, with the Domino's logo; blotchy skin, battling the constant diet of cheese and processed meat. She was the first person he had spoken to in he couldn't remember how long. He told her of the lonely vigil, waiting for custom that never arrived; she told him of the local situation, of the habitations of the robots, the dinosaurs, the action figures—who lived in a circle of abandoned vehicles, down by the river. Of the rumors of what lay beyond their part of the Dilapidate: a shopping mall inhabited by Bratz dolls, a village of Furbies, an entire self-constructed city of Lego. Told him, too, of the Cult of the True Bear.

He took her back, then, on his scooter, concerned she didn't have the strength to make it alone. The congregation had assembled for evening service. The Beanies had immediately gathered around her in a protective huddle. The prophet had been courteous but distant. Edward and Albert had offered him a cup of rainwater from a scratched plastic tea-set which they considered an heirloom. He had declined. When conversation had stilled he'd said, well, my break is about over, I have to be getting back.

The mood shifted with his departure. The Victorians demanded Rainbow account for her actions. The prophet had tried to intervene: said something about a hairless cub, a harbinger of the True Bear. The assembled bears did not buy it, he had not mentioned it before. Brothers Bruin, he said, the cub seems quite harmless—Brother, said Edward, we are at risk. Do you not remember the dark days before the Animation. (Behind him, Albert was dragging Rainbow from her siblings by one paw. The *Billionaire #1* Bear tried to come to her defense; he knocked it down with a blow from his cane.) We remember the years of subjugation, Edward went on, the years of meat and flesh determining what we were to be. We must prevent her from going back to him. (Behind him, Albert lifted Rainbow aloft, dashed her down. The stitches in her back burst open.)

***

The pizza kid had stopped only a block or two away, where his headlamp had illuminated the mangy figure of the panda, menaced by a pack of plastic dinosaurs, six or seven of them, each of them coming up to about shoulder height. They were velociraptors, of 90s manufacture: featherless, paleologically inaccurate. Cast from the same mold, their hides bore identical patterns of wrinkles.

Guys, Panda was saying, we don't need to do this. He shied away as one of them struck out at him with a claw. It had been sharpened, the pizza kid noted; he wondered how they'd managed that. Another of the raptors barreled into the bear from behind, knocking him into a puddle. He whimpered, kept his head down, waited for the blow that would end it.

Which never arrived, of course. The kid revved his engine, put-putted into the melee, and the dinosaurs scattered. Panda twisted up to look at him. *Grande Ourse*, he said, you took your time. Ignoring the hand the pizza kid proffered, he rolled over and wonkily pushed himself to his feet. It took obvious effort; he had no articulation in his limbs. Listen, he said, maybe you wouldn't mind dropping me off down a ways.

So the kid came to return to the scene of the bear meeting just as the altercation was really getting into it. The bears froze, all of them, hedgehogs in headlamps. Panda hopped from the scooter and walked over to Rainbow's supine form. She was moving, a little, spilling out what was inside of her. He cradled her in his arms—insofar as he could, given his anatomical deficiencies—and called to the pizza kid. Listen, he said, maybe you'd better take her with you. I'll stay here, try to talk some sense into these lunatics.

Was Rainbow conscious? Not really. She was fading in and out. Panda offered the armful of her to the kid, who took her in both hands, this time, trying not to spill any more of her. She was conscious only of the sensation of being lifted. He took the scooter off at something not much more than a walking pace. There was silence from the bears behind.

When the ride ended, she was lifted again. The kid slid her body onto a soft pile of clothing among the boxes in the garage. He pulled an old coat over the top, creating a cave that emanated the sweetness of old ladies who frequently powdered themselves—a light rose motif that played ironically well in the deep recesses of Rainbow's ancestral brain. The pizza kid lifted her head to help her lap water from a hubcap. He broke bits of pepperoni and crust into bite-sized pieces and left them where her tongue could reach them. Much later, she heard him practicing his orations like songs. Like monks chanting in the distance, they were a comfort.

The hours of operation for each location are determined by the Company, he read. *If a Team Member decides that he/she will neither show up at their scheduled start time nor call in, the General Manager and/or Supervisor may take disciplinary action against the Team Member up to and including immediate suspension.* He'd had recourse to the Employee Manual on a couple of occasions: every time he would wipe the layer of dust off it with a wet-nap, then dry it with a regular napkin, before replacing it in its home under the customer service desk. When his shift ended, after checking on Rainbow—who mewed quietly up at him from under the coat, trembling—he went home.

The next day he came in early, bearing with him a sewing kit he'd retrieved from a room in his home; a room which, in the normal course of things, he had stopped venturing into. An amateurish overcast stitch held Rainbow together, for now, and she sat up and whispered a few hoarse words of thanks. For his part, stroking her muzzle, he promised he'd do whatever he could to mend her. Fix her up better.

**

So he took himself, that evening, to the bigger retail development, out where the suburb ended, in search of a Toys "R" Us. Out on unfamiliar roads the progress was slower, he had to thread his way around cars he'd had no chance to grow familiar with. He tried not to look in any windows, forced himself to think of other things. He wondered what toys were making these parts their homes.

The Toys "R" Us still stood: at least, the building was still there, the big concrete shoebox of it, and the outline of where the name had been had left its mark. The still-bright paint in the grid of the big front window lent the building a spurious lightness; if he'd had the education he'd have thought of the International Style. He had forgotten that the company had ceased trading a little before the Animation.

He ventured in, anyhow, hoping to find—what? An unawakened bear, in some stockroom, from which he might salvage its innards? He was to be disappointed. The building was dark and nearly empty. On a rack near the entrance there were a handful of product lines, the kind of brand-free stuff even the bailiffs had left behind: skipping ropes, deflated balls, bows and arrows with sucker pads at the end of their shafts.

The building was dark, little of the gloaming-light outside making its way in, and as he went deeper, he wished he'd thought to bring a flash. The aisles faded into darkness as he looked up to the ceiling. He walked into the dark in hope, and then stopped mid-stride, hearing a growl from the next aisle over.

Something was padding along—something heavy but quiet. It stopped a second after he did. He tried to tiptoe backwards; realized the thing on the other side was tracking him. There was a scent in the air, he realized, an animal fetor. He cursed the months or years of pepperoni that had left him alienated from his sense of smell.

Twisting on his heels, he broke into an awkward fore-foot sprint: the thing was moving quicker, too, now, and on all fours. He ran towards the light.

Whence emerged a brown bear, a real one. He wasn't surprised; what else would it be, after all. Things were starting to out-grow their boundaries, out here on the edge of town, trees in their fall raiment crowding out the parking lots, and bears, they were curious animals. He caught himself wondering what it was eating, in here, and another part of his brain headed the thought off at the pass. He had a lot of time to think, it felt like: there was a lot of thinking time between one foot-fall and the next, under the circumstances.

It didn't even go for him. It reared up on its back legs as he sailed past it, and one familiar with the body language of bears might have been able to decipher what hormonal packet it was processing—surprise, confusion, aggression, fear, admixed in some proportion—as it then it folded its legs back and sat down, forepaws in its lap. Its head lazily tracked him round. He half expected it to wave.

***

When he pushed open the door Panda was waiting in the same pose. Kid, it opened, you look like you've seen a ghost. The kid half-collapsed, forehead on the counter, dizzy, hyperventilating, eyes dilated. He had no memory of the drive home. Panda put out a forelimb—fuzzy, rounded, no claws—and gently kneaded a temple. Hey now, Panda said, hey. The kid turned to look at him, and their eyes met: kid's, human, liquid; bear's, no longer glass exactly, something not so cold or reflective, but deeper, somehow, with a warmth underneath.

The story came out of him in gasps. A True Bear! Panda said, how excited the others will be. But I don't think we can be mended, not in the way you intended. I'm not sure if we can be mended at all. He paused, looked away, wiped at the ragged fur of one ear with the end of his limb. But can I see her?

Rainbow was weaker now. She was awake, still, and recognized them both, but not up to speech. Panda climbed up on the crate, laid his head down beside hers. Panda was twice her size, perhaps. He was proportioned like a giant child; she, a kind of miniature adult. Rainbow was sobbing, little sounds catching. Shh, Panda said, shh. Me and the kid, we'll get you fixed right up.

***

The kid went home to get some sleep. Panda had insisted. That night, the bear made the trip back through the endangered, moonlit streets to bear territory. Under a dim streetlamp—there hadn't been any artificial light in a while—he heard a velociraptor snarl from the porch of a house along the way. Ah, the hell with you, Panda cried, and broke into a loping run.

The Prophet was curled up beside the shrine. Panda pawed at him. It's kind of urgent, he said, wake up. Oh, my child, said the Prophet, our congregation is split, what does it matter? (After the confrontation the day before, the Victorians had renounced religion. The Beanies were just hiding out, probably, looking for safety in numbers.) But the human, said Panda, has seen a True Bear.

There followed a silence. There were katydids somewhere nearby, sounding off in the night, and as Panda listened, they were joined by a dry, hiccoughing choke of a sound, repeating itself at irregular intervals. It took him some time to realize that this was the Prophet laughing. Don't you see, said the Prophet, there is no True Bear, he was a bear wholly of my invention. Well, said Panda, I always kinda figured.

The Prophet blinked and looked at him sideways and stopped laughing. What can I do for you, then, he said. And Panda explained the situation: Rainbow lying stricken in the garage in back of the Domino's, their only ally a human of dubious intelligence. The

Prophet considered. There's something I overheard, he said, once upon a time, it might help you.

***

The kid was raising the shutters at the Domino's when the bear showed up again. He looked on as the kid opened up, stationed himself at the register, sobbing all through the process. He was practically dry-heaving with tears. What's up, said the bear. The kid just looked at him. Panda went to the garage to scope out the situation. Rainbow was comatose now; the tie-dye fuzz of her chest rose and fell minutely.

He perched beside the register all that day, explaining what needed to be done. The idea had come from the Prophet: whose owner, scion of a middle-class family, revealed by a DNA test to be 6% Native, had set himself up as a shaman of the Klamath tribe. Not that it had done much for him, in the end. Anyway, the kid said, he couldn't steal from the Company. This struck Panda as funny, though he didn't want to hurt the kid by explaining any of the reasons why. Look, he said, it might be Rainbow's last chance, do you want to live with that on your conscience: which argument won the day, it turned out.

The True Bear was not there when they arrived at the Toys "R" Us. This is good, Panda said, we need the time to set up. He rummaged around in the pizza delivery bags they'd laden themselves down with, which contained a number of two-lb bags of sausage meat and two knives: a chef's knife for the kid, and a paring knife for him. He looked over at the poor handful of goods remaining and said, well, let's see what we can do with this.

They kept vigil all night, hid in the depths of the store, made preparations. They'd filled a kiddie-pool with sausage meat—rancid, of course. Refrigeration had failed a few days into the Animation, and while the walk-in freezer at the Domino's was cavernous and insulated enough to reach only the low forties Fahrenheit even in the summer, it had been certainly long enough for the stuff to expire. The kid had shown some rudimentary animal intelligence in only going for the pepperoni, Panda supposed. He might have been able to make more of himself, in other circumstances. Pity.

As the first intimations of dawn bled wetly into the horizon, the kid piped up. He didn't want to be late for work, he said. Panda shushed him, indicated a shape silhouetted in the window. The True Bear strode in, nuzzled the pond full of sausage.

Okay, okay, said Panda, softly softly catchee monkey. He scaled the racks, a kid's bow-and-arrow set looped around his shoulders. The kid was checking what they'd done with the skipping ropes, knife in hand. The True Bear sniffed the air, but the repast before it was too fragrant to take in much else. It raised its snout, quizzed: and took an arrow to the eye—Panda had broken the sucker pads off, filed them down with the paring knife. It roared, and went rampaging enormously towards the end-of-aisle display where Panda was ensconced. Panda fell, bounced a little, the bear rounded on him where he lay prone.

Hey, hey, called the kid, one hand in the loop of a skipping-rope noose. Pick on someone—though he didn't have time to finish the sentence. The bear came at him. The rope was in a slipknot: he looped it round the bear's neck and was backhanded into the racks. His head bounced off the metal edge of a shelf. Deflated soccer balls rained down around him. Shame we couldn't think of any use for those, you know, said Panda, approaching, cautious.

The kid was sitting on the ground, dazed; the bear kept lunging forward, but the rope was fixed fast to the aisle-wall opposite, and every time it went for him the rope caught it short, and it choked a little more. Hey, kid, kid, stay with us, Panda said, cuffing him lightly with where his own paw would have been. We need you.

The True Bear started to nod out eventually. It wasn't a quick process. Panda scaled it, somehow—the kid was seeing double, watched the toy swim in and out of focus as he made his ascent—and plunged the paring knife into the other eye, leaning in on it with what weight he had. The larger animal subsided. Come on, come on, come on, there's no time, said Panda.

As he took the chef's knife to its stomach, the kid expected a blast of stuffing to well forth. Instead blood and meat. His Domino's uniform was rapidly soaked through with blood as, under Panda's direction, he peeled the skin back from the ribs. Okay, said Panda, take that, and that, and do you know what a gallbladder looks like, by any chance, take that, maybe that, I don't know, play it safe.

***

The kid more or less fell off the scooter as they pulled up outside the pizzeria. He leaned heavily on the door, uncertain what he was doing. On his shoulders was a pizza bag, wet with viscera; it had left a trail of blood and muck behind him. His eyes opened and closed, opened and closed. Inside, said Panda. And turn on that oven quick.

They blasted the parts of the True Bear they had borne with them in a pizza oven, pounded them into a mulch, mixed them with a bottle of Coca-Cola, unchanged by the Animation, lukewarm. The work done, the kid had slumped on the floor. Panda, bearing with him a seething soda-fountain cup of gore, had made his way to the garage.

Rainbow was insensate. He tried to convince her to drink; realized words were of no use; tipped the mess over her. A minute or two passed and she came back, choking, spluttering. The stitching in her back had healed, somehow; her coat shone with a new mint-condition brightness. Even from the contact buzz Panda was looking better, himself, less mangy. She looked up at him in a mute desperation, as if wanting to know the cost.

The two of them made their way, hand in hand, to the restaurant. She leaned on him to start off with: by the time they were there she was supporting herself. The kid was sitting with his back to the oven, somewhere beyond pain. She ran to him; Panda stayed in the doorway. The kid's head lolled, his jaw twitched, he tried to look at her. His eyes were shiny pebbles, his tongue a rasp of fuzz.

SMILE!
By Elizabeth Wilder

Beyond the cracked sidewalk, and the telephone pole with layers of flyers in a rainbow of colors, and the patch of dry brown grass there stood a ten-foot high concrete block wall, caked with dozens of coats of paint. There was a small shrine at the foot of it, with burnt out candles and dead flowers and a few soggy teddy bears. One word of graffiti filled the wall, red letters on a gold background: Rejoice!

Rejoice about what, Nancy wondered. She picked her way down the partially cobbled dirt lane between the wall that separated the Arthur Road Jail from the informal neighborhood of matchstick houses and tiny shops that comprised this slice of Mumbai. Why rejoice, when somebody died? Probably a child, given the teddy bears. Nancy stopped, suddenly stricken. *Oh, I hope it wasn't one of mine!*

Nancy was on her way to the Nutrition Clinic, where she volunteered every week to chart weights, serve snacks, and babysit the toddlers being treated for severe malnutrition by a small NGO. The work made her feel better about living in a two-million-dollar apartment with a staff of three. She tucked her light brown hair behind her ears, and thought about the weirdness of expatriate life. Her friends back home in Mission Hills envisioned an extended foray into the glossy pages of *Travel and Leisure*. To them, India was one fabulous week aboard the Palace on Wheels, or a jetport-equipped yoga retreat where everyone was given matching designer workout gear. Even the most "woke" (Nancy felt quite hip using this new expression) did not understand that *Beyond the Beautiful Forevers* described middle class Indians. Those characters had actual walls!

The shrine-bedecked jail wall reflected the heat of Mumbai's sun. She felt the right side of her neck burning above the collar of her oxford cloth shirt. Her long red skirt swung loosely from her hips. Her first year in India, Nancy learned that it was much cooler to wear long clothing that kept the sun off her skin. Lipstick always; her lips burned and blistered otherwise. Dodging the vegetable sellers who sat in the middle of the narrow lane with little baskets of wilted produce, Nancy tried to walk in the shade of the small huts selling SIM cards, single-use shampoo packets, and used clothing that were crammed across from the wall proclaiming *Rejoice!*

A few alleys further, Nancy caught the stench of the Bombay Municipal Corporation public toilets. Ugh. Six toilets for a thousand people in this slum. That frowning Nationalist woman (the Toilet Guard) was on self-appointed duty again, demanding a bribe from each and every lady who wanted to relieve herself in privacy. The Toilet Guard held long stick in her right hand, a *lathi*, just like the Bombay police carried. She wore a faded maroon and green sari, the colors of Maharashtra State, which had been appropriated for political use by the far right.

Toilet Guard caught Nancy's eye inadvertently. Always polite, Nancy forced herself to wave. "Hello! Good afternoon," she called pleasantly. The woman gave her a responsive glare, as if Nancy were distracting her from important duties, like running a sewage treatment plant, instead of preventing poor women from using the only sanitary facility for miles. *Maybe she works for the pharmacy that sells cheap antibiotics for bladder infections*, Nancy thought as she caught a glimpse of the large green cross, twined with serpents, on a nearby shop stall.

A young man walked out of the toilet. He wore the uniform of a pizza delivery company, one of many foreign franchises trying to tap into the new middle class of India. He spoke briefly to the Toilet Guard, and then walked over to Nancy. "Pizza coupon, madam?" he said, leering up toward Nancy. His hair was well oiled, swept back from his face in a vaguely otter-like way. She accepted the unwanted coupon. "Thank you." She folded and put it in her canvas carryall. He stood in her path. Nancy smiled uncertainly. "See you later," she said with a little wave, and stepped briskly around him. He exchanged a glance with Toilet Guard before nodding smugly in agreement. Nancy was right.

***

"Hello, Nancy," Shruti called from the porch of the Clinic. "No Aisha today?" Shruti pushed her short black hair away from her glowing face and adjusted her pink kurta over her round stomach. Rings of sweat were visible around her armpits. She smiled cheerfully. Nancy was surprised to see the Program Head on site. "It's just me today," Nancy apologized. "Aisha's out of town and I couldn't round up another volunteer. But I can stay late—Tim's travelling so I don't have any commitments." Shruti sighed, hands on hips. "Well, we will do the necessary," she said. "Priya's out sick, so we are very short staffed." She laughed loudly and looked up at Nancy. "A staff of two. But only one of us is short!"

The women smiled and discussed the work plan as they walked past the luxurious private outdoor water tap, up two uneven stairs, through the main hall where more than thirty women with their attendant children squatted on the bare wooden floor below a rusted tin roof. The cacophony of that many people crammed into such a small wooden firetrap of a room—it couldn't be more than fifteen by fifteen feet—assaulted Nancy's ears.

Shruti, who was a trained nurse, unlocked the cabinet at the side of the room and removed the baby-weighing scale and her official records. It took her a minute to find a working pen. Nancy, who was unafraid of rats, went into the big closet to pull out plastic crates of Nutri-Bars. The Nutri-Bars were cooked at home by Nancy's friends (or their maids) according to a strict recipe. The Bars provided needed micronutrients for developing toddler brains. They tasted reasonably good. Nancy set the bars out in stacks of ten on a trestle table she constructed each week out of two wooden sawhorses and a couple of old boards. She set up a hand-washing station on a pair of stools: one pink plastic tub of soapy water, one blue plastic rinse tub of clear water. Only one rag for hand drying. Nancy made a mental note to raid Tim's t-shirt drawer and cut some old jerseys into towels.

Shruti made a small motion with her head toward the waiting families. "I think we can get started. If you could line up the mothers?" Nancy looked at her with raised eyebrows. Line discipline was her biggest gripe in India. She clapped her hands as loudly as she could. Nobody paid attention. She cleared her throat and shouted, "Namaste! *Meera nam* Nancy *hai!* My name is Nancy, and I am going to weigh your children today. Could I please have the first five mothers—how about you here? Line up with your toddlers only." A seething crowd of mothers rose and pressed against Nancy like a dust-coated tsunami. Their children darted around and between the women like minnows evading a school of trout.

"No! *Haan!* Sit down now." Nancy made firm sitting motions with her arms. The women complied. "Okay, you first." She grabbed a woman nearby and pushed her toward the scales and Shruti. The rest she blocked from disturbing the examination, which was carried out in full view of the crowd. For more than three hours, Gatekeeper

Nancy and Nurse Shruti weighed and charted all children between eighteen months and four years of age. There were fifty-three of them. Most already had medical records with the Clinic.

The one new patient was a tiny woman clad in a cheap blue polyester nine-foot sari. Her head was covered with the tail end of the extra-long cloth. In her arms was a wizened child of indeterminate gender or age. "Probably new, probably from Bihar," Shruti murmured, looking upset. "Wow, this is awful." Nancy picked up a folder to prepare a new record. "Hello," she said to the new woman, who stared back uncomprehendingly. "*Meera nam* Nancy *hai*," Nancy tried. No reply. The woman looked painfully aware of her lack of speech, eyes darting from mother to mother, looking for a translator. "Welcome to Mumbai," murmured Shruti sarcastically.

Nancy pointed at herself and smiled in what she hoped was a friendly professional way. "Nancy." She pointed at several children in the group, slowly introducing them one by one. "Dolly. Arun." She pointed back to the new child and raised her eyebrows to indicate a question. The woman muttered something. "*Kya*? What?" "Haridoon." Nancy repeated what she heard. "Harry Dune? *Nam* Harry Dune *hai*?" She smiled as the woman nodded. "Welcome, Harry Dune."

Shruti and Nancy had a quick chat about the new baby—how should they spell his name? Both women were aware that the decision they made on this was permanent. Whatever they wrote down—this child's first formal record of existence—would follow him forever. Is it Har-i-dun? Hari Dune? "Harry O'Doon," suggested Shruti slyly in a mock brogue. "Aye, a fine Irish lad!" "Yikes," said Nancy. She laughed delightedly. "Twenty years from now, if I'm checking into the Oberoi and an Indian Harry O'Doon is behind the desk!" The women settled on a one-word name, Haridoon.

With the weighing-in complete, the women divided the clients into two groups. While Shruti gave a lecture on toddler development, Nancy led the older children in an action song, the "Itsy Bitsy Spider". The spiders were exceptionally lethargic today; too hungry to climb a waterspout. Nancy overheard parts of Shruti's presentation. "If the baby spits out chapatti, it doesn't mean baby isn't hungry. It means he doesn't like chapatti! So try banana." It was so hard for the moms, reflected Nancy, seeing their sad, compliant faces. All they had was chapattis.

Finally, it was feeding time. The older children anticipated the treat they were to receive and eagerly pressed up against Nancy and her sawhorse table, grabbing as many bars as possible. The mothers were only slightly less restrained. Free food was why the women endured lectures on the benefits of bananas. Filthy and exhausted by the unwanted physical contact, Nancy surreptitiously checked her phone. Look at the time! The roads would be jammed with cars, trucks, buses, and bodies. She shuddered to think about the bruising fight that would be her return trip out of the neighborhood, and the two hours it might take to travel the four miles back to the quiet safety of her apartment. Even though it smelled disgusting, she used the tiny pit toilet behind the Clinic. She washed her hands in the dirty water of the pink bin before dumping it out.

"Excellent day," Shruti said as she locked up the scale and record books. "Most everybody has gained. Back next Tuesday?" Nancy nodded. She reached into her canvas bag and pulled out a can of Perrier kept frosty in an orange foam koozie. She held the can to her forehead, enjoying the small relief from the heat in that one spot above her nose. Popping the top, she greedily sucked down a beverage she would never drink in front of the mothers; it cost more than their men earned in a day. Nancy suddenly remembered the shrine. "Hey, Shruti," she said, "What's the story behind the new shrine on the Jail wall? The one that says *Rejoice!*" Shruti shrugged. "Some Muslim ran over a kid there, I heard," she stated flatly. "At least, it was a Muslim that got dragged out of his water truck and beaten in revenge." Nancy squinted at Shruti. "How can you say that so calmly?" Shruti looked up at the rusty tin roof above her head, as if the answer to Nancy's query would be found there, and sighed. Meeting Nancy's gaze, Shruti said, "It's Mumbai."

Nancy texted her driver for a pickup. She shoved her way through a swarm of men—most women were safely home by now—toward the main road. The Toilet Guard had abandoned her pungent post, but Nancy noticed that the pizza boy was still hanging out by the toilets. How odd! He saw her, smiled and waved. Nancy did a little finger wave back. That was when Toilet Guard struck her across the back with the *lathi*. Nancy fell forward, hitting her head on a cobble. "Is this the woman," asked a man's voice, as Nancy felt herself lifted and carried to a small three-wheeled delivery truck. "Yes, that's Rainbow," replied the pizza boy. Nancy tried to kick him. He sat on her legs. The noisy engine, compounded by the traffic horns, muted all further words.

***

When the ride ended, she was lifted again. The kid slid her body onto a soft pile of clothing among the boxes in the garage. He pulled an old coat over the top, creating a cave that emanated the sweetness of old ladies who frequently powdered themselves—a light rose motif that played ironically well in the deep recesses of Rainbow's ancestral brain. The pizza kid lifted her head to help her lap water from a hubcap. He broke bits of pepperoni and crust into bite-sized pieces and left them where her tongue could reach them. Much later, she heard him practicing his orations like songs. Like monks chanting in the distance, they were a comfort.

Nancy rolled over on the pile of clothing. The scent of mold disturbed her nose. She sneezed violently, twice, which helped clear her head. The soothing chanting that had lulled her now irritated her. "*Har Hindu ki yahi puka,*" the boy's song, translated into "every Hindu has the same demands." Breaking free from the icy fear that had frozen her behind the boxes, Nancy thought, *I have some demands, too!*

Her clothing was intact; she hadn't been raped. Praise Jesus. The untouched pizza bits next to her had already attracted a nauseating variety of insects. Suddenly itchy all over, and spurred by the thought that the clothing pile was probably infested with fleas, Nancy sat up. Her aching disoriented head popped up over the top of the cage of dirty boxes. She was in a small, tin sided warehouse. Her canvas bag, with her phone, money, and water was gone.

Nancy cleared her scratchy throat. "Hello? Excuse me," she called over to the pizza boy. She made an effort to sound sweet and calm, the same way she did when she was weighing frightened toddlers. "Could you please come over here?" The kid stopped mid-chant, and made frantic shushing motions. He held his finger to his lips as he tiptoed over. He glanced over his shoulder to make sure nobody could see him.

"My name is Nancy and I volunteer at the Nutrition Clinic," Nancy whispered, rising to her knees on the pile of fabric, as far from the food scraps as possible. "Can you please tell me where I am? Please, why am I here?" Her hands were clasped together in a tight knot, nails digging into the freckled backs of her hands, as if hurting herself would cause the anxiety to abate from her voice. *Please, please, please,* Nancy randomly thought. Tim said she was too polite to the locals, that they only respected strength or arrogance. Well-mannered Nancy added, "Please tell me your name." *And please don't kill me.*

"Ram," said the pizza boy. "My name is Ram." He looked

delighted that she had asked. He stood just a little taller, ran his hand over his shiny oiled hair, and adjusted his uniform shirt so that she could see the embroidered company logo on the left chest pocket. He was proud to deliver pizza for an international fast food chain.

"Ram, you speak such good English," Nancy said, as if she were conversing with a passport control officer and not an assistant thug. "What's going on? Who's in charge?" Ram stared at her the same way he might take notice of a passing mouse. Nancy's manners began to fray as her pulse raced. "I think there's been a mistake. I'm a volunteer in the Clinic!" Ram shook his head in that meaningless (to Americans) sideways manner called the head bobble. The dam of Nancy's self-control burst. Her words gushed loudly as she repeated her questions. "What's going on? Who's in charge?" More bobbling. Nancy screamed, "Do you want money?"

"Shut up! We know who you are, and we know what you do," Ram yelled. "We don't need you or your filthy money! We don't want Pakis in our neighborhood. Even English ones like you." Nancy was completely bewildered. "I'm not English and I'm not Pakistani." Ram towered over the parapet of boxes, his fists clenched. "Liar! You're Muslim. India is for Hindus. Our leader says so," declared Ram.

They think I'm Aisha, Nancy realized, which would be funny if the situation weren't so serious. Aisha was a half-Pakistani British citizen with olive skin, waist length black hair and a fascinating nose. Mistaking Nancy for Aisha was like mistaking Amy Adams for Angelina Jolie, because they both had blue eyes.

Nancy hid an inappropriate hysteria-induced giggle behind a fake cough. She wondered what Tim would do. After a moment, she stood up on the unsteady hill of clothing so that she towered over Ram. With the most arrogant expression she could muster, Nancy felt inside her shirt for the small gold cross she wore. "Is this

Muslim," she demanded, thrusting the necklace in his face.

***

"How did this happen!" shouted a deep voice from beyond the corrugated tin walls of Nancy's prison. Several voices, female and male, interrupted each other with angry replies. The mix of Hindi and Marathi was confusing. Nancy cringed and wondered if they were going to kill her. She'd thought about dying, of course, but she'd envisioned something normal, like cancer, or being run over by a Mumbai taxi. Murdered by right-wing politicians had never crossed her Republican mind.

Now seated on a cracked tan plastic stool, Nancy sipped water from a brand new bottle. She'd tested the seal herself. Her legs itched frantically from a jungle's worth of insect bites. Ram explained in excruciating detail every step of planning "Operation Rainbow"—the surveillance, the stalking, the procurement of gasoline for the getaway trishaw—all to kidnap a wealthy Muslim to trade for some Nationalist bomb-makers who awaited trial in the Arthur Road Jail.

"Madam, it really is your fault for wearing the red skirt," he claimed. "That Muslim woman normally wears many colors." Nancy nodded as if this made perfect sense, just like she nodded at banquets when an important customer of Tim's described his most recent round of golf. ("And then there's quite a tricky dogleg left on fourteen…") She fought the urge to slap some sense into Ram. Her face hurt from smiling so long.

She saved her energy for the meeting she anticipated with the Boss. She made little active listening "mm-mms" as Ram described to her all the ways that Muslims had never invented a thing, never helped Mother India, and how they should "just go home." (*Wherever that was*, Nancy thought. *It's been hundreds of years.*) Her perch on the stool was getting slick with her sweat.

"The Muslims take credit for the Taj Mahal," Ram complained.

"Hindus built houses on pillars long before the Mughals invaded." Nancy squinted at him disapprovingly. "You know, I've noticed that people all over the world elevate their huts in flood plains," she pointed out. Ram completely missed the irony. "No! They just copy us."

Nancy started to work long division problems in her head to reduce Ram's long list of grievances to background noise. Put down the eight, carry the three. She jumped when the door was thrown open, clanging against the metal wall. Shruti and the Toilet Guard strode in. Judging from the fearful way Ram backed up to the wall and squatted down, the man behind them, the short one in the clean white shirt, expensive jeans, and aviator sunglasses, was the Boss.

***

"This is not what I paid for." Shruti sounded like she was haggling at the electronics market over a defective toaster. "Have I ever been even one day late? No!" The Toilet Guard nodded vigorously in agreement. "Always on time. Always," she said. "Truly Boss, she is punctual."

"What are you talking about," Nancy asked Shruti. Shruti glared at Nancy as if she were a slightly defective bump on a log. "I pay the slum committee every week so that we can operate the Clinic there." Nancy immediately thought of *The Sopranos*. "Are you saying that you bribe these people to allow you to run a nutrition program for their children," Nancy demanded. She jumped to her feet, hands on hips. A mental picture of wizened little Haridoon sprang to mind. "I think that's the worst thing I've ever heard!"

Shruti looked upward and sighed as if she were explaining the hierarchy of a bee colony and not that of a terror-friendly political organization. "Nancy. I don't expect you to approve how Mumbai works. You must accept that, without payment, nothing happens here."

Nancy shook her head, no. "I don't accept that. I don't accept the idea that I'm out there, guilting my friends into giving money so that you can pay bribes to him!" She shook her finger angrily at the Boss. "How can you literally take food out of the mouths of starving children?" she demanded. Whirling to Toilet Guard, she pointed straight at her and said, "And you! Charging to use what's supposed to be a free bathroom?" Toilet Guard's lower lip trembled as her eyes welled up. "It's my job," she said.

Nancy felt the weight of the Boss' silent inspection of her from head to foot. She met his eyes defiantly; her mouth was a straight slash across her face. The next to talk would be the loser in this negotiation. In the absence of words, Nancy could hear the murmur of passing slum dwellers, the crunch of plastic containers being crushed for recycling. She scrunched her toes into her sandals; anything to distract herself from making nice Midwestern conversation. The seconds stretched into what felt like days. Was it really just yesterday that she'd hopped out of her chauffeured white Toyota and strolled past *Rejoice?*

Finally, Boss reached into his pocket and removed Nancy's phone. "A mistake has been made," he said. He handed the phone to Nancy. "Show me a photo of your friend." Wordlessly, Nancy pecked away at her phone like the pigeons that flocked in every park in Mumbai. She saw Tim's unanswered text—U OK TONIGHT—and bit her lip in concentration. She scanned through photographs until she found one of Aisha and herself presenting a large mock check to the Nutrition Clinic, courtesy of the International Women's Club. "Here you go," she said tightly. "Here we are giving one lakh rupees to feed starving kids." She handed the phone over. Boss examined the photo, compared it to the woman standing in front of him.

Toilet Guard broke the silence. "You see, Boss, they look alike.

Anybody would mix them up!" She chattered on, comparing the long skirts, the ridiculous height, the blue eyes, and the light skin. It was a mistake that anybody could have made. Boss looked from the photo to Nancy, back and forth.

Toilet Guard switched to Marathi. She and Boss jabbered back and forth for several excruciating minutes. From Shruti's expression, Nancy understood that her almost-enemy was soon to be the victim. Toilet Guard started crying as she pleaded with Boss. For her job? For her life? Nancy raised her hand to cut off the flow of tearful words. Gesturing to Boss to come closer, she snatched the phone from his hand. Rage made Nancy stronger. "Know what? You and me need to talk. Privately."

***

Shruti kept a bruising grip on Nancy's arm as she guided her around the dizzying twists and corners of the slum. The night was nearly over, and a grayish light penetrated the *chawl*. A light breeze stirred the air. Nancy almost dropped her canvas tote when she stumbled over a sleeping mutt, which whined and moved out of her path.

"When are you going to tell me what happened," Shruti asked. Nancy stopped walking. She smirked and folded her arms. "I explained that it was in his interest to forget this entire adventure." Shruti bobbled her head, puzzled. "I don't understand."

This struck Nancy as extremely funny. "It's Mumbai!" she giggled, to Shuti's astonishment. Nancy laughed so hard tears ran down her cheeks. "You always say I can't understand," she gasped. "And now you don't!" Shruti tapped her foot in annoyance. "Okay, okay, I'll tell you. When he gave me the phone, I took a few photos of Ranvir—did you know the Boss's name was Ranvir? and texted them to Tim with an SOS." Shruti's eyes were the size of *thali* platters. Lightly, with the intonation of a sorority rush chair turning down an heiress, Nancy said, "I *shared* with Ranvir that my husband thought it was *so nice* to have a photo of the man I spent the night with. One with such a distinctive smile." Nancy laughed again.

"He will be angry, very angry! He will probably burn down the Clinic," Shruti said resignedly. "I should go get the scales as soon as I deliver you to your driver." Nancy shook her head. "No, he won't," she said. "And he won't hurt the Toilet Guard either. Part of the deal." Nancy started walking again. It felt good to be outdoors. In another few minutes, the sun would rise. It was her favorite time of day.

Nancy's driver was waiting at the first paved road in her white minivan. It was strange that he looked the same as yesterday. His short-sleeved shirt was unwrinkled, his grey trousers and brown sandals neat and clean. As always, he jumped out of his seat, and opened the door closest to Mrs. Nancy. He reached his large hand down to her, and helped her step up from the sidewalk. "Allow me, madam."

Shruti leaned in the door. "Very good. Will we see you at the clinic on Tuesday?" Just like nothing ever happened, Nancy marveled. She thought about the long hot shower, and the fruit plate prepared by her cook that awaited her. She'd send a maid to fetch some calamine lotion, or whatever the Indian equivalent was, for her itchy welts. By the time she woke up from her air-conditioned nap, Tim would be back. Nancy envisioned their upcoming six-point discussion: no, you can't go there again; the babies need food; it's not safe; thirty eight percent of all Indian children are stunted; I want you safe; I'll bring both maids.

Nancy nodded confidently at Shruti. "Yes. I don't want the Boss to forget we have a deal!" Shruti looked like she might cry. "I will light a candle at the shrine," she said. "Candles are nice," agreed Nancy, "but I'll email you the photos."

ABOUT THE AUTHORS

E. Michael Brehm has been a part-time writer for years, but this is his first published work. He is currently writing Book Two of a fantasy series about the qualities of good government. When not writing, he teaches Social Studies in central Wisconsin.

India Choquette grew up on a small farm in Vermont. She attended Barnard College and Prague Film School. She currently lives in New York City with her partner. She has been published in *TulipTree Review*. More of her work is available at ww.indiachoquette.com.

Curtis Clarke (1989 -) has a Bachelor of Fine Arts (Drama) from Queensland University of Technology. He has spent the last few years working in the film industry in North America. His writing has appeared in *Idiom 26*, and in 2009 he received a High Recommendation in the State Library of Queensland 'Young Writers Award'.

J Stuart Croskell teaches Drama to kids with special needs. His published short stories include 'Dave Danver's Final Foray into All Things Woo Woo' (Shallow Creek - Storgy Books) and 'Pastor Goodman's Five-Spot Onanist' (Mystery Library - Tell-Tale Press). He is currently trying to write a novel about a haunted house.

Originally from Florida, **Elsa Cruz** has since made her home in Anchorage, New York City, Miami, and anywhere she finds a cozy, vibrant corner of the world. She currently lives in São Paulo, Brazil with her husband. In addition to fiction, she enjoys writing about spirituality, art, culture, food & drink, and traveling.

Michelle Denham is Korean American and lives and writes in the desert. She has a Ph.D. in English Literature, and her fiction has appeared in *Daily Science Fiction*, *Flash Fiction Online*, and *A Future Fire*.

Phil Dyer is a scientist and SF writer in Liverpool, England. His work has recently appeared in *Diabolical Plots* and *Liminality Magazine*. He retweets animal gifs at @ez_ozel

Carnegie Euclid grew up in Northeast Ohio with ten siblings, innumerable farm animals, and a pet raccoon named Fester. He earned his MFA in Creative Writing from Ashland University. A resident of Hudson, Ohio and Folly Beach, SC, his prose often channels the infinite sadness he experiences as a Cleveland sports fan.

M.J. Fahy writes and illustrates for children, from inside a home-built writing shed. She lives on the south coast of England with her husband, two adult children, two dogs, and a cat. *Pack* is her first published story for older readers.

Jilly Funnell is a writer, musician and performance poet currently living in a small market town in Hampshire, England.

Ella Rachel Kerr lives, writes and surfs in the Pacific Northwest. Her first novel, *Sugar and Dust* was published last year and provides social commentary of the plight of child brides all over the world through a story of loss and adventure. Ella was nominated by *Sky Island Journal* for the Pushcart Literary Prize, and has been published in *Elephant Journal* and *Sivana East*. You can read more of her work at ellakerr.com.

Alex Lee is an author from Nashville, TN, who primarily writes literary and speculative fiction. He's a winner in the 2019 Porter Fleming Literary Competition, and when not writing he enjoys painting and throwing darts in the local taverns—occasionally at dartboards.

After practicing medicine in the badlands of Palo Alto, **Arthur Liu** returned to his hometown of Oakland, California, where he and his wife now reside. He is working on his first novel.

Becca Loevy is a freelance writer and dancer based out of Colorado Springs. Her writing is deeply influenced by travels through Asia and Europe, her career as a movement artisan, and her relationship to meditation and the elements. Her most recent publication was for *Relax Melodies*, a phone application for audio bedtime stories to help with sleep and anxiety. Loevy owns and manages innerchildtravel.com, a blog based on her physical and spiritual journeys.

Desirae Matherly is the nonfiction editor for *The Tusculum Review* and the Chair of English & Fine Arts at Tusculum University. In *Echo's Fugue*, Matherly explores Bach's *Art of Fugue* through eighteen essays on music, myth, and games. Her essays appear in *Assay*, *Hotel Amerika*, and *Fourth Genre*. Desirae earned a Ph.D. in nonfiction from Ohio University and is a former Harper Fellow at The University of Chicago.

Jeffrey Montanye is a newcomer to the writing community, creating three novels and several short stories in the past two years. He is an IT specialist and teaches adult education self-enrichment classes in the evening. Jeff loves photography and spends his free time hiking and biking the Hudson Valley where he lives.

Aaron Muller is a twenty-something author and poet based in Kingston, NY, where he lives with his husband and cat. He is the winner of two May 2019 SUNY New Paltz Tomaselli Awards in both fiction and nonfiction for his short story "The Lighthouse" and his personal essay "The Slow Burn." He is currently working on a novel.

Tyler Nelson's first literary foray — a space epic about Mario and Luigi — was published out of his notebook at the age of eight. After taking a twelve-year hiatus from writing, he decided to jump back in, and since he has enjoyed working with local writing groups and finding new challenges. His two years of living in Russia has given him fluency in the language, and a love for foreign literature and culture. He currently lives in central Utah, where he attends university and loses frequently at Uno to his wife.

Kate Osment was born in 1999 in Plymouth, UK, and spent as much of her childhood as she could in public libraries. Since being accepted to read German at St. Anne's College, Oxford, she has moved on to bigger and better libraries. You can read more of her work at https://blog.reedsy.com/creative-writing-prompts/author/kate-osment/ .

Emily Polk lives and writes on a small island east of San Francisco, and she teaches writing at Stanford University. Her writing and radio documentaries have appeared in *Creative Nonfiction*, *National Geographic Traveler*, the *Boston Globe*, *NPR*, *National Radio Project*, *AlterNet*, *Central America Weekly*, and *Whole Earth Magazine*, among others. Her first book, *Communicating Global to Local Resiliency: A Case Study of the Transition Movement*, was published in 2015. For more please go to empolk.com.

Henry Silvia is published member of the Florida Writers' Association and the Brandon Writers' Group and is currently focused on completion of his first novel.

Christian H. Smith lives in the dark, corn-fed heart of the Midwest. He is the author of the 'Bloody Bakersfield' trilogy (*The Black Monkey*, *Bloody Bloody Bakersfield*, and *New Salem*) available from Permuted Press. Visit him on Facebook or at christianhsmith.com.
xxx
Mary Spence grew up in Baltimore, Maryland and still lives nearby. She is a retired NICU nurse who now divides her time between creative writing, photography, and illustration. She is a 2018 graduate of University of Baltimore with an MFA degree in Creative Writing and Publishing Arts.

Emily Sperber graduated from Willamette University with a Creative Writing degree in 2018 and has been writing in Bellingham,

Washington since then. She works at a library where she did check out books about faking your own death so, if you need to get away, let her know. Her work has also been published in Blacklist Journal and Rattle.

Thos. West was born in England and educated at Oxford and Keele. The winner of the 2018 Machigonne Fiction contest, his work has been published in *The New Guard* and Emrys. He works in Seoul as a teacher and editor.

Elizabeth Wilder is a former banker and ESL teacher who recently moved back to the U.S. after ten years of expatriate life (Saudi Arabia, India, Malaysia).

CPSIA information can be obtained
at www.ICGtesting.com
Printed in the USA
LVHW092019120220
646732LV00001B/42